Environmental Justice and the Rights of Ecological Refugees

Environmental Justice and the Rights of Ecological Refugees

Laura Westra

earthscan
publishing for a sustainable future
London • Sterling, VA

K3230.R45 W47 2009
013411 2267585
Westra, Laura.

Environmental justice
and the rights of
    2009.

2009 11 27

First published by Earthscan in the UK and USA in 2009

Copyright © Laura Westra, 2009

All rights reserved

ISBN: 978-1-84407-797-7

Typeset by JS Typesetting Ltd, Porthcawl, Mid Glamorgan
Cover design by Andrew Corbett

For a full list of publications please contact:

Earthscan
Dunstan House
14a St Cross St
London, EC1N 8XA, UK
Tel: +44 (0)20 7841 1930
Fax: +44 (0)20 7242 1474
Email: earthinfo@earthscan.co.uk
Web: **www.earthscan.co.uk**

22883 Quicksilver Drive, Sterling, VA 20166-2012, USA

Earthscan publishes in association with the International Institute for Environment and Development

A catalogue record for this book is available from the British Library

Library of Congress Cataloging-in-Publication Data

Westra, Laura.
  Environmental justice and the rights of ecological refugees / Laura Westra.
       p. cm.
  Includes bibliographical references and index.
  ISBN 978-1-84407-797-7 (hardback)
  1. Environmental refugees–Legal status, laws, etc. 2. Refugees–Legal status, laws, etc.
3. Environmental justice. 4. Human rights. I. Title.
  K3230.R45W47 2009
  341.4'86–dc22
                            2008054647

At Earthscan we strive to minimize our environmental impacts and carbon footprint through reducing waste, recycling and offsetting our CO_2 emissions, including those created through publication of this book. For more details of our environmental policy, see www.earthscan.co.uk. This book was printed in the UK by TJ International, an ISO 14001 accredited company. The paper used is FSC certified and the inks used are vegetable based.

For Peter Westra

*and for the boys at the Japanese Jongenskamp Baros 6,
Tjimahi, Indonesia (1944–1945) – especially for Jan, Jaap,
Joop and Lloyd, and all the boys in Cabin 37A*

Contents

Foreword by Ved P. Nanda	xi
Acknowledgements	xiii
Prologue	xv

PART I – PRESENT REFUGEE LAW: POLITICAL AND LEGAL ISSUES AND PROBLEMS

1	**The Question of Environmental Refugees**	3
	Introduction – The Recognition of Environmental Refugees	3
	The Question of Environmental Refugees	6
	A Question of Definition?	11
	The Legal Status of Internally Displaced Persons	12
	Persecution and the Problem of Intent	14
	Indigenous and Non-Indigenous: Any Solutions?	20
2	**International Assistance and the Refugee Convention's Five Grounds of Persecution**	27
	Introduction to the Five Grounds for Refugee Status to Establish Persecution	27
	Persecution or Lack of Protection?	29
	The Role of Racial Background in Refugee and IDP Issues	32
	Nationality	34
	Religion and Particular Social Groups	36
	Political Opinions	38
	Further Considerations on the Rule of Law and the New Global Politics: The Appeal of Limoges	39
3	**State Protection and State Responsibility to Ecological Refugees**	47
	Introduction	47
	The Responsibility of States	48
	The Present Crisis: How to Re-conceive Refugee Law?	54
	Forced Relocation and the ATCA Litigation 'Third Wave'	65
	International Law and Domestic Law	68

PART II – ECOLOGICAL REFUGEES AND REFUGEE LAW: THE INTERFACE

4 The Five Grounds Revisited: Who Are the Vulnerable?   79
Introduction: Environmental Migrants – Cause and Impacts   79
Race and Ethnic Background: The Implications   82
The Foundations of Basic Human Rights   86
Religious Beliefs: Holy Sites for Indigenous and Local Communities   90
State Protection or State Complicity?   94

5 Ecological Refugees: Protection and Rights in International Law   105
State Protection – Refugees and the Right to Health and Normal Function   105
Ecological Refugees: The Emergent Realities   108
Ecological and Economic Oppression as Crimes against Humanity   112
Ecological Refugees and Indigenous Refugees: Similarities and Differences   117

PART III – THE WAY FORWARD: EXISTING LEGAL INSTRUMENTS AND NEW PROVISIONS

6 International Law beyond the Convention on the Status of Refugees   135
Introduction: Genocide or Crimes against Humanity?   135
The Need to Re-conceptualize the Rule of Law   139
Climate Change and Public Health: New Categories of International Law   141
Environmental Problems and Health Impacts: A Missing Link   149
Ecological Refugees and Ecological Rights in International Law:
    Lacunae and Under-Inclusions   152
The Water Conflict in the Middle East and the Question of
    Palestinian Refugees   155

7 Towards a Comprehensive Approach to Protecting Refugees and the Internally Displaced   175
Understanding the Issues: The Aetiology of Crimes against Humanity   175
State, Corporate and International Responsibility Before and After the
    Fact: A Review   176
Environmentally Displaced Persons: A Convention for their Protection   180
A Convention Modelled on the Convention against Torture?   186
Towards a Comprehensive Approach: Ecological Integrity for
    Global Governance   195
Global Governance for Ecological Integrity   201

Appendix 1   **Convention Relating to the Status of Refugees (1951)**   215
Appendix 2   **Other Relevant Instruments**   225
  Universal Declaration of Human Rights (1948)   225
  Protocol Relating to the Status of Refugees (1967)   228
  United Nations Declaration on Territorial Asylum (1967)   230
  United Nations Convention against Torture and Other Cruel,
  Inhuman or Degrading Treatment or Punishment (1984)   231

Constitution of the International Organization for Migration (1987)	239
United Nations Convention on the Rights of the Child (1989)	244
Declaration of States Parties to the 1951 Convention and/or Its 1967 Protocol Relating to the Status of Refugees (2001)	256
Appendix 3 Draft Convention on the International Status of Environmentally-Displaced Persons	**259**
List of acronyms and abbreviations	*269*
List of cases	*271*
List of documents	*275*
Bibliography	*279*
Index	*293*

Foreword

After so many years I am still haunted by the sight of Vietnamese refugees in rickety boats on the rough seas, seeking safe harbour and preyed upon by pirates, and the images of frightened asylum seekers confined in a compound with barbed wire around it in Hong Kong. In a similar vein there are other such poignant pictures that have indeed touched humanity. We recall Haitians desperately trying to reach Florida, their boats turned back by the United States Coast Guard. A Norwegian freighter that had responded to the distress call from a sinking Indonesian ferry carrying Afghan asylum seekers was kept away from reaching the Australian shore by that country's navy. Australia then not only refused even medical assistance for sick people on board, but gave the small Pacific island of Nauru $10 million to accept the asylum seekers. And the world is now witnessing refugees and internally displaced persons from Darfur suffering unspeakable indignities in camps in Chad and Darfur.

It is well known how vulnerable refugees and asylum seekers are. It is widely understood, as well, that the available international instruments – the 1951 Convention on the Status of Refugees and the 1972 Protocol on the Status of Refugees – are sadly inadequate to meet their needs and provide them protection. The Convention definition of a refugee, crafted after World War II to address specific situations of that time, is reminiscent of that bygone era.

The UN High Commissioner for Refugees has extended the Convention's definition to include among 'persons of concern' for his Office not only Convention refugees but also civilians who have returned home and still need help, civilians uprooted by violence but displaced within their own countries, asylum seekers, and stateless persons. However, this definition does not include 'environmental refugees', and although the UN Secretary-General's Representative on Internally Displaced Persons, Francis M. Deng, included in his definition of such persons those forced or obligated to leave their homes or places of habitual residence because of natural or man-made disasters, this definition has not received any authoritative recognition.

This in-depth study by Professor Laura Westra focuses on ecological refugees and their rights, which the Refugee Convention's strict and limited definition does not recognize. Under that definition, refugees must be outside their country of origin; they must be unwilling or unable to avail themselves of the protection of their country or return there because of a well-founded fear of persecution; and the feared persecution must be based on reasons of race, religion, nationality, membership of a particular social group, or political opinion.

Critics quibble about the definition of 'environmental refugees', calling the term confusing and legally meaningless. Westra opens her book with El-Hinnawi's definition, used in a United Nations Environment Programme publication in 1987. Noted ecologist Norman Myers of Oxford calls 'environmental refugees' – a new phenomenon on the global arena – and offers a working definition: people forced to leave their country of origin, whether temporarily or permanently, because of 'drought, soil erosion, desertification, deforestation, and other environmental problems, together with associated problems of population pressures and profound poverty.'

The estimated number of such persons is mind-boggling: perhaps 50 million at present and – when global warming is added to the natural disasters or those triggered by people, as causes of environmental disruption – an estimated 200 million people might become victims within the next four decades. Small island chains such as Tuvalu, Vanuatu and the Maldives are especially vulnerable as victims of rising sea levels caused by climate change or global warming. Vanuatu moved a small community inland in 2005 to escape flooding. Tuvalu has entered into an agreement with New Zealand to move its entire population if necessary. The President of the Republic of Maldives is exploring the possibility of relocating its population, as well.

Building on her prior prodigious scholarship, Westra remains faithful in this study to her passions – environmental justice and the protection of indigenous peoples' rights – as she responds to the challenge of ecological refugees by seeking recognition of the environmental aspects of human health and pressing for a framework convention for global health. In addition to appending a Draft Convention on the International Status of Environmentally-Displaced Persons written by several persons at the University of Limoges, she calls for the acceptance and international codification of the interface between human and environmental rights and recommends the use of *jus cogens* norms.

It would be foolhardy to ignore Professor Westra's plea that we pay special attention to the impacts of globalization, global warming, and water shortages, which are responsible for the displacement of millions.

Ved P. Nanda
John Evans Professor, University of Denver
Thompson G. Marsh Professor of Law
and Director, International Legal Studies,
University of Denver Sturm College of Law

Acknowledgements

After the publication of my two most recent studies in environmental justice – *Environmental Justice and the Rights of Unborn and Future Generations* (Earthscan, 2006) and *Environmental Justice and the Rights of Indigenous Peoples* (Earthscan, 2007) – I realized that the final consequence of climate change and other ecological problems on inhabited areas in all regions of the world was indeed harm to individuals, communities and other collectives.

These areas are rendered increasingly uninhabitable and unproductive, as water becomes scarce or is overwhelmingly present through catastrophic events that eliminate whole towns and villages. Also, the relentless advance of neoliberal globalization brings additional harms even to areas that might otherwise have avoided them. Corporate activities bring the hazards of extractive and mining industries right to the most remote communities in the global South.

The result is the displacement of hundreds of thousands of persons, asylum seekers, who do not fit the international legal instruments ostensibly designed for the protection of all refugees. They might be considered internally displaced persons (IDPs) instead, but even then, instruments designed in the 1950s and 1960s are totally inadequate to provide relief for the environmental problems of our age.

Hence I returned to school once again to better understand refugee law, and I am grateful to Amina Sherazee, whose course on the topic gave me the final push to research the question of environmental refugees. I also owe thanks to Agnes Michelot, whose work on the topic introduced me to the writings of a group at the Université de Limoges, who had been working on the issue for some time, and who contributed to the seminal work in the December 2006 issue of their journal, *Revue Européenne de Droit de l'Environnement* at the Centre de Recherches Interdisciplinaires en Droit de l'Environnement de l'Aménagement et de l'Urbanisme (CRIDEAU). Her work and that of her colleagues showed me how to proceed on this difficult and under-researched issue. In fact, that group, under the direction of Michel Prieur, has now produced a proposed Convention on Environmentally-Displaced Persons, which appears as Appendix 3 in this volume.

I am also grateful to the encouragement and inspirational work of Ved Nanda, Thomas Anghie and Wolfgang Sachs, whose words encouraged me to persevere in this research. Special thanks are owed to those who encouraged and supported the completion of this book, despite initial difficulties, especially Ron Engel, Colin Soskolne, Prudence Taylor, Tullio Scovazzi and Richard Westra.

At Earthscan, thanks to commissioning editor Michael Fell and production co-ordinator Hamish Ironside – particularly to the latter, not only for the editing and the research assistance but also for the advice and encouragement.

Finally, thanks are due to Diane Rooke at Osgoode Law School Library, and to Luc Quenneville of the University of Windsor, for his invaluable technical support.

Prologue

One cannot watch televised news or open a newspaper today without becoming aware of the hordes of displaced, dispossessed people in all continents of the globe. They are climate refugees, as they are forced to abandon all their possessions and flee for their lives in the aftermath of hurricanes, tsunamis, earthquakes and other grave disturbances. They are environmental refugees, as the lack of resources and the basic necessities of life forces them to leave their normal places of habitation, as desertification, glacial melts, and increasing environmental pollution of land and water render survival with dignity, and basic health support, nearly impossible. Finally, they are the poor and the most vulnerable: they are the victims of economic oppression, of aggression and ethnic conflict that are, themselves, often based on resource depletion and the desire of powerful states, and of powerful lobbies and groups within states, to colonize and to conquer, especially in regions that may still be rich in oil, minerals or other commodities.

They are, for the most part, the victims of the relentless march of globalization and of capitalism, where the most powerful are intent upon securing for themselves as much as is still available of the depleted and impoverished Earth. These states and non-state actors continue on their unsustainable path, protected by regulatory regimes, such as that of the World Trade Organization (WTO), that emphasize the primacy of economics over the human rights to health and a liveable environment.

The question raised in this work is a simple one: there are a plethora of laws and regulatory regimes that support the status quo, permitting, and in fact encouraging, most of the activities that cause migrations and foster the continuing increases in the number of dispossessed asylum seekers. In addition, there are instruments and legal regimes that do not give primacy to the human costs of growth and so-called 'development' activities. But what, if any, are the legal instruments and regulatory regimes that may be used to halt the ongoing crimes against humanity, and that might speak in defence of refugees and other forced migrants?

This quest appears to be a particularly appropriate one in 2008, on the 60th anniversary of the Declaration of Human Rights. It is also, I believe, appropriate that this work be undertaken not only by any of those affected, who are living now the results of various disasters and environmental attacks, but also by an older person such as myself: a child when my father was beaten up and imprisoned when, as a journalist, he spoke up against Fascism, and when my gifted pianist uncle, seeking treatment for depression in a sanatorium in our native Trieste (Italy), was taken away by Nazi SS with all other patients in that institution, and eventually gassed at Auschwitz. Finally, when I was a young woman, I also met and married the Dutch survivor of a Japanese Children's

Camp in Indonesia (and this book is dedicated to him and the other 'boys' of that camp, who still meet to remember in Holland once a year).

Of course, these were not environmental issues, but they were the issues foundational to the design and preparation of the 1951 Convention on Refugees, and that document is the starting point of this work. The personal experience, limited though it was, means that it is impossible for me to restrain the visceral response to the scenes that now confront us: camps with starving refugees in sub-Saharan Africa, endless lines of refugees of tsunamis in Thailand, hurricanes in Louisiana, earthquakes in China, or the 'open-air prisons' of Palestinian and Lebanese refugees in the Middle East.

Most, if not all, of these ongoing human rights disasters have an environmental or resource-based origin, or at least climate and environmental conditions aggravate the problems faced by these individuals and groups, and are recognized as contributing factors to their eventual flight. Today the plight of ecological refugees[1] and the victims of ethnic- or resource-based conflicts, both before their flight and in the inhumane conditions present in refugee camps, resonates strongly in the very souls of those who lived in times when powerful, amoral policies were unchecked and unrestrained against defenceless people.

Hence, after defending a doctoral thesis on the existence of 'eco-crimes' (Westra, 2004, *Ecoviolence and the Law*), and seeking to expose their application first against the most powerless individuals – those of unborn and future generations (Westra, 2006) – and the most vulnerable groups and communities (Westra, 2007), it seemed right to finish this series of extended 'case studies' by examining what El Hinnawi (1985) terms 'the end of the line'; that is, the final result of eco-crimes, or perhaps crimes against humanity (as I will argue), in their final consequences, not only in the long lines of hopeless, starving refugees, but also in the various shanty towns or other unsafe and unsanitary areas around some cities, where internally displaced persons (IDPs) eke out a meagre existence.

I hope to defend these somewhat radical contentions in the following chapters, starting with a discussion of the 1951 Convention on Refugee Status.

The first chapter starts by documenting the large (and constantly increasing) numbers of refugees and migrants today, as well as introducing the environmental conditions that combined with poverty and vulnerability for most of these people to originate the flight. When we turn to the major convention intended to establish the status of refugees (dating, without emendations, from 1951), the definitions it provides are obviously insufficient to deal with a problem of this magnitude and one which, to all intents and purposes, did not even exist at the time. In 1951 both climate change and the proliferation of hazardous chemicals and harmful industrial operations were not the grave issues they are today.

Hence the 'convention refugee' of that time has little in common with the huge migrations of today. Today's migrants have more in common, for the most part, with another category established in international law, that of IDPs, but unfortunately there is no specific instrument today designed to protect these persons or deal with the difficulties of their situation.

Notwithstanding the original assessment in Chapter 1 of the inability of the Convention on the Status of Refugees (CSR) to address the plight of ecological refugees, the second chapter analyses the five grounds that support the well-founded fear of persecution that characterizes the 'status refugee', in the hope that some of these categories might be understood to reach beyond the obvious issues they were intended to address. The first question raised is whether a state's lack of protection may be termed a form of persecution, especially in cases where a state is complicit with the 'development' agenda of hazardous industries, in ways that would never be permitted in or around richer neighbourhoods, or near citizens belonging to the racial majority of that country. It is then possible to question the issue of race and ethnicity, as well as other grounds, in order to assess whether it might be possible to extend these categories to protect ecological refugees.

Chapter 3 returns to the general responsibility of states to protect their citizens, even in the absence of a specific international convention directing them to do so. When the treatment of migrants is set out in detail, it is clear that their difficulties multiply, rather than being eased, as they escape an untenable situation at home, hoping for hospitality and assistance on their arrival. The case law indicates that those applying for asylum, even under the aegis of the CSR, are most often (illegally) detained, even for considerable periods.

In Chapter 4 we review some of the jurisprudence involving some of the communities in the developing world seeking redress for the activities of corporate actors that render their homes and territories uninhabitable, hence creating the very conditions that generate the initial flight. Three 'waves' of US litigations are reviewed, as are the extreme difficulties encountered by the people seeking redress. Following on, Chapter 5 raises the question of who the most vulnerable people are, and whether it might be possible to view the original victimization that forced them to move under the heading of one of the 'five grounds', thus whether it might qualify their situation as one of convention refugees. The fact that environmental degradation is never considered serious enough to rise to the level of international law, no matter how grave its effects, is certainly one of the major obstacles standing in the path of these migrants. Climate change is an anthropogenic phenomenon, so it cannot simply be considered 'an act of nature', whether it manifests itself as a tsunami, a tidal wave or a glacial melt. Thus the question of international protection under various possible conventions needs to be examined. Given the large number of ecological refugees who belong to specific ethnic or racial groups, it is appropriate as well to raise the question of genocide, although the *dolus specialis* is most often absent.

Chapter 6 reprises this theme, as it raises the question of not only genocide, but also crimes against humanity, as a possible appropriate category to describe the plight of eco-refugees. A special case is that of Arctic peoples, and we analyse the situation of the Canadian Territory of Nunavut, where inhabitants face glacial melts that are destroying not only their territories but also their way of life. As we review various treaties and declarations that are designed to ensure the right to the basic necessities of life, we also discuss the problem of Palestinian refugees (or internally displaced persons, depending on one's understanding of the situation), as their deprivation of water and other necessities appears to be a glaring breach of their rights as human beings.

Finally, Chapter 7 discusses several of the proposals advanced by various legal scholars who note the fact that the only existing convention is neither applicable to ecological refugees nor helpful in their plight. An extension of the present CSR is proposed, as well as a new convention based on the Convention against Torture and other possibilities.

I propose that perhaps the most helpful proposal is the establishment of a Framework Convention on Public Health, with a strong emphasis on the role of the World Health Organization (WHO) in the protection of basic human rights. In addition, a consideration of the need to restore ecological integrity in regulatory regimes and policies would prevent much of the degradations that cause migrations. If designed with that aim in mind, both domestic and international instruments would protect human rights and human health through ensuring safe environmental conditions, rather than giving primacy to economic considerations.

NOTE

1 The term 'ecological refugees' that I use throughout this book is intended to encompass the more familiar term 'environmental refugees', as established by Professor Norman Myers (among others); it is also related to the more recently popularized term 'climate refugees'. However, as will be seen, I use the term 'ecological refugees' deliberately to include some categories of displaced persons – such as those fleeing industrial and chemical hazards – that might not be considered purely 'environmental' or 'climate-related'.

PART ONE

Present Refugee Law:
Political and Legal Issues and Problems

CHAPTER 1

The Question of Environmental Refugees

1. INTRODUCTION – THE RECOGNITION OF ENVIRONMENTAL REFUGEES

Of thirty ways to escape danger, running away is best. (Old Chinese Proverb)

With these words, Essam El Hinnawi starts his 1985 monograph on the topic of environmental refugees. His starting point is the 1972 Stockholm Conference,[1] and he includes in his discussion the concept of 'ecodevelopment' coined in the resulting document. Like this concept, which has in recent times morphed into the watered-down notion of 'sustainable development', the definition of refugee is not totally fixed, according to El Hinnawi. As he writes:

> *Environmental refugees are defined as those people who have been forced to leave their traditional habitat, temporarily or permanently, because of a marked environmental disruption (natural or triggered by people) that jeopardizes their existence and/or seriously affected the quality of their life.*[2]

By adding 'in a broad sense, all displaced people can be described as environmental refugees', El Hinnawi places environmental refugees in a category that he views as primary or foundational, rather than simply viewing them as 'displaced peoples'. They are not accepted as legitimate refuge seekers, according to the 1951 Convention on Refugees (CSR), but rather as internally displaced persons (IPDs), not qualified to claim refugee status.

His argument is both correct and appropriate. In turn, he defines 'environmental disruption' as:

> *any physical, chemical and/or biological changes in the ecosystem (or the resource base) that render it temporarily or permanently unsuitable to support human life.*[3]

This is the aspect of the issues confronting environmental refugees that is at the heart of this work: when the resource base, the integrity of the lands where a community resides, is destroyed, indeed it can no longer support human life. That has been the argument proposed by my work since 1994.[4] If ecological integrity is central to human health and survival, as well as to the normal functioning of ecosystems, then its absence represents an attack on both health and survival, as well as on ecosystem function.

We are all affected in various measure, as I have argued, but the poor and those who live on the land are indeed the most vulnerable. Whether the flight that ensues is temporary or permanent, for most of these refugees it is indeed the dangerous circumstances in which they find themselves that defines their status, even when the circumstances are the result of conflicts or other non-environmental situations. Their numbers are often great, and their relocation poses immense problems even in their country of origin. Large migrations, an increasingly common situation today, may well do great damage to the area to which they relocate.[5]

The magnitude of the problem cannot be overstated. A Christian Aid report predicts that 'given current trends, 1 billion people will be forced from their homes between now and 2050',[6] and they add:

> *Stranded within their countries and largely ignored by the media, they are the world's forgotten people. The numbered include:*
>
> - *50 million people displaced by conflict and extreme human rights abuse. This assumes a rate of displacement of roughly 1 million people a year, which is conservative;*
> - *50 million people displaced by natural disasters. Again this conservatively assumes that around 1 million people will be displaced this way every year;*
> - *645 million people displaced by development projects such as dams and mines (at the current rate of 15 million a year);*
> - *250 million people permanently displaced by climate change-related phenomena, such as floods, droughts, famines and hurricanes;*
> - *5 million people will flee their own countries and will be accepted as refugees.*[7]

Already in 1994, the Almeria Statement on Desertification and Migration estimated that 'the number of migrants in the world, already at very high levels, nonetheless continues to increase by about 3 million each year'.[8] Norman Myers alerted the world to this emerging crisis as long ago as 1993,[9] and in 2005 he revised his estimate,[10] suggesting up to 200 million as a possible refugee number.[11]

However, Sir Nicholas Stern viewed that figure as 'conservative' and Myers has since once again revised his estimate.[12] The daunting numbers of ecological refugees, that is the IDPs that comprise climate and other environmental refugees, as well as those displaced by economic oppression and toxic exposures engendered by 'development' and other industrial projects, are grave enough to warrant a thorough re-examination and discussion of present international law.

The main problem with these large migrations lies in the definition of a refugee, with its strict limits, according to the Convention Relating to the Status of Refugees (adopted 28 July 1951; into force 22 April 1954):

> *Article 1: Definition of the term 'refugee'*
> *A ...*
> *(1) ...*
> *(2) As a result of events occurring before 1 January 1951 and owing to well-founded fear of being persecuted for reasons of race, religion, nationality, membership of a particular social group or political opinion, is outside the country of his nationality*

and is unable or, owing to such fear, is unwilling to avail himself of the protection of that country; or who, not having a nationality and being outside the country of his former habitual residence as a result of such events, is unable or, owing to such fear, is unwilling to return to it.

The well-founded fear that is the basis of any refugee's claim appears to be a single individual's sentiment, although, as we shall argue below, it may be viewed from several perspectives, even to apply to whole affected groups, the Jewish people of Nazi Germany being precisely such a group. Thus the original intent of this document is directed at the plight of single individuals, rather than large migrating groups. But, as El Hinnawi argues, environmental disasters – whether wholly natural (such as earthquakes, droughts and tropical cyclones); partly natural, that is such that human activities play a significant role in their severity (such as floods, tsunamis and hurricanes of particular strength); or even those where human activities play a major role, such as melting ice and permafrost in the Artic, raising sea levels elsewhere – are such that invariably large numbers are affected.

All of these disasters affect disproportionately the poorest people in the world, as they have no infrastructure or social services to protect them or to mitigate the environmental disasters' effects.[13] In addition, land degradation and desertification also render various regions in the South uninhabitable, as does deforestation, as these phenomena generate a mass exodus from the affected region.[14] Hence it is easy to understand why other countries and their governments, beyond the areas where the disasters occur, are not eager to open their doors, but content themselves with sending aid, at best. This 'aid' is often inappropriate, insufficient and hard to distribute to those most at risk.[15]

Often environmental refugees simply attempt to migrate to a different area in their own country, perhaps to the cities. But these are both unprepared and unwilling to receive them and to support their many needs:

> **The End of the Line**
> *When environmental refugees migrate to urban areas, they expect a 'rosy' quality of life. But soon they find themselves in slums and squatter settlements. In such areas they are usually deprived of access to the basic facilities of drinking water and waste disposal. They are frequently forced to use open water for washing, cleaning and the disposal of waste in unhygienic ways; to break open municipal water mains; to use public places such as open ground to relieve themselves; and to live in makeshift shelters surrounded by accumulating domestic waste.*[16]

Equally unacceptable are the so-called 'environmental disasters' such as Bhopal, Seveso, Three-Mile Island or Chernobyl.[17] The industrial operations we take for granted everywhere in developed countries and the developing world result in increasingly visible public health hazards that are not limited to the occasional spill, malfunction or other 'accident'. In contrast, they render the conditions of life around their location hazardous for all, but impossible for those who live a traditional lifestyle on the land, as is the case particularly for isolated communities and indigenous peoples everywhere.[18]

Hence in this work we will consider the impact of these realities, exacerbated by globalization and climate change, as well as the proliferation of industrial chemicals.

In this regard we will consider the CSR and other regulatory regimes regarding IDPs, as well as other international instruments regarding human rights and humanitarian law. Our goal will be to discover whether it is possible to find a legal avenue to mitigate the suffering of these millions of people, starting with the special plight of aboriginal peoples.

2. THE QUESTION OF ENVIRONMENTAL REFUGEES

One cannot delve into the morass of legal instruments, both international and domestic, that affect local communities and indigenous peoples, or the plethora of cases that pit aboriginal groups against corporate developers, without noting that there are several areas of law that simply do not engage the reality of the present situation. The reasons for that lack of engagement are several, including:

1. the introduction of dozens of new chemicals into several areas of industrial production, from agricultural pesticides to cleansers, pharmaceuticals and house building products;
2. the development of hazardous systems of mining and extraction, as well as hunting and fishing devices, that exhaust natural systems;
3. the lack of information and education relating to scientific research, endemic to both legislators and judges, information that would clarify the interface between the environment and public health;
4. the aggressive emphasis on growth through capitalist structures inherent in globalization;
5. the constant, ongoing depreciation of 'the sacred' and of traditional values and knowledge, replaced by technical knowledge, homogenized rather than specific to places and peoples;
6. the effect of the dividing 'borders' between disciplines and the increasing territoriality of 'experts' in various fields;
7. the prevalence of well-paid 'junk-science' supported by big business (for example big tobacco, big oil and big pharma), with nearly unlimited funds to support public opinion campaigns and offering misleading 'expertise' in legal cases;
8. the unexamined persistence of the concept of legal personhood, with all its applicable 'rights', comparable to the rights of natural persons;
9. the lack of an exhaustive definition of 'aggression' in the Statute of the International Criminal Court; economic aggression needs to be added to the understanding of aggression as synonymous with armed conflicts; and
10. the extension of the notion of responsibility to the comparable reach of our power, as – for instance – Agnes Michelot states, citing Hans Jonas: 'l'extension globale de notre puissance entraîne de nouvelles formes de responsibilité'.[19]

These ten modern aspects of the reality of the interface between indigenous communities' survival and the law, and supporting references and discussions of the specific details, will be taken up in Chapter 2. They are not claimed to be the only major problems giving rise to deep injustices to which displaced peoples are exposed, but they are clearly present and representative, I believe, of the major obstacles they encounter in their quest for justice and respect.

The result of this multitude of obstacles is that most of the international instruments that affect the way refugees and displaced persons are treated in law at this time do not include the latest scientific knowledge, and – in general – they do not really consider their position today, in a multidisciplinary context. Rather the main focus is the interpretation of those documents in the light of the drafters' intent when they were enacted.

For instance, in Canada, the Royal Proclamation about the Rights of Indians expresses his Majesty's goodwill and respect for the *sui generis* nature of the relationship of those communities with their lands. But in 1793, he could not be expected to anticipate that even to demarcate and assign lands to 'Indian' groups did not guarantee the quality of those lands, only, at best, their quantity. Hence even strict adherence to the Proclamation could not possibly ensure their ongoing rights to hunt and fish, according to their traditional lifestyle, unless buffer zones were also declared around indigenous lands to ensure the conditions of both the lands and the animals within them. In addition, the emergence of climate change and of hazardous industrial operations upstream and around those areas could not be anticipated.

Thus even treaties and declarations intended to protect local and indigenous peoples may fall quite short of the mark a century or more after their enactment, or even several decades after it. Another example of international instruments falling short of their stated aim is the Convention on Genocide. After the Second World War, the Convention was adopted by most states, and scholars such as Raphael Lemkin (1944) attempted to define genocide exhaustively, as one of the major international crimes, imposing an *erga omnes* obligation and including both 'biological' and 'cultural' genocide. But the recent jurisprudence of the International Court of Justice has not supported Lemkin's thorough definition and has concentrated instead only on the most obvious aspects of the crime.[20]

These are just two examples of regimes that, although technically intended to support and defend local communities and lifestyle, or at least human rights, cannot do the job they were intended to do because of changed external conditions, such that they render the original requirements incomplete or even obsolete.

There is also a second aspect of insufficiency regarding laws that may govern the interaction with IDPs: laws that govern the protection of refugees. When developments such as climate change or the arrival of mining and other extractive activities occur close to their communities, local peoples may be forced to leave their territories behind. Most often, they are forced to leave because of their living conditions, without being able to avail themselves of effective state protection. Not unlike refugees who require the protection of their country or, failing that, the protection of international law, indigenous and local peoples do not enjoy the protection of these instruments, despite their inability to safely inhabit their traditional territories in many cases.

Hence what is required is a critical assessment of, first, all instruments specifically related to the rights of IDPs/refugees, in order to determine whether any *lacunae* are present in their interpretation of the conditions required to implement those rights and second, other legal instruments, which must be canvassed to ascertain whether some of their provisions, presently exclusive of peoples in local communities, might need to be expanded to include protection for those groups in their stated intent.

Even a cursory review of the instruments and case law involving local communities and aboriginal groups shows clearly the limitations and deficiencies present in the laws intended for their protection.[21] In addition, international instruments designed for the protection of human rights, despite the occasional reference to indigenous peoples, also seem to be gravely deficient when they are viewed from this perspective.

Many scholars have studied specifically the problems of protecting indigenous rights through a review of the cases and the instruments designed for that goal. This work proposes to look critically at various instruments in human rights and humanitarian law, in order to focus on the present *lacunae* that affect indigenous peoples, local communities and ecological refugees in general, particularly taking as a starting point the CSR.[22] The reason why that instrument is singled out is the fact that, to my knowledge, there have been no specific studies that consider its importance in relation to ecological refugees and indigenous peoples, nor does the CSR specifically address such issues. Moreover, the grounds of discrimination as identified in that document bring into play all the major human rights instruments, and address major international obligations, of an *erga omnes* nature.

From this perspective, it is quite different from other international human rights instruments, such as the 1948 UN Declaration of Human Rights, the two 1966 Covenants (ICCPR and ICESCR), ILO Convention No. 169 (1989) and other important documents,[23] as the CSR does not even address the problem directly.

Nevertheless, in its 53rd session,[24] the UN General Assembly met pursuant to the 'High-Level Dialogue on International Migration and Development',[25] as it evaluated existing mechanisms on this topic: the September 2006 event was the first to focus exclusively on 'the relationship between international migration and development'.[26] Although no new binding instruments emerge from this document, the very fact that large forced migrations are now recognized is extremely important and worth reviewing. It is even more important to re-examine the 1998 Guiding Principles on Internal Displacement.[27]

2a. International migration and development and the Guiding Principles on Internal Displacement

> *The UNDP, in collaboration with the IOM, UNICEF and the World Bank, is preparing a handbook on integrating migration into national development strategies. On behalf of the European Commission with other United Nations agencies and the IOM, the UNDP is managing a programme on knowledge-sharing related to migration and development.*[28]

The potentially hopeful presence of the International Organization for Migration (IOM) and the Global Forum devoted to the same issue lose their relevance when one considers the main focus of these documents: 'development' or, essentially, trade:

> *The IOM seeks to engage expatriate communities as partners for development, including through the transfer of knowledge and skills.*[29]

Clearly, the drafters do not have in mind the starving millions of IDPs and refugees in sub-Saharan Africa, their deep poverty and the burden of disease; nor do they consider that today's large migrations are, for the most part, the result of trade and 'development', both pursued without any concern for sustainability[30] or the connection between environment and human rights to health.[31]

The basic difference between 'migration' and 'forced migrations' is instead clearly recognized in the work of the Refugee Studies Centre at the University of Oxford, together with UNEP, as well-researched and analysed in the latest issue of *Forced Migrations Review*.[32] As Achim Steiner, the UN Under-Secretary General and Executive Director of UNEP, notes:

> *Human migration, forced or otherwise, will undoubtedly be one of the most significant consequences of environmental degradation and climate change in decades to come.*[33]

Steiner acknowledges that 'unsustainable human development', together with sea-level rise and the 'loss of coastal wetlands', contributes significantly to the millions who will be fleeing by 2080. Rather than focusing on trade advantages, the challenges to human security policies are grave, and 'environmental migrants' are recognized now as a separate category, whose numbers have not yet been acknowledged in law but are constantly increasing because of 'longer-term environmental degradation', which aggravates the situation created by the impact of sudden disasters:

> *Environmental migrants are understood to be those individuals, communities and societies who choose, or are forced, to migrate as a result of damaging environmental and climatic factors.*[34]

Climate change impacts will follow three separate avenues:

1. *The effects of warming and drying will significantly disturb ecosystem services;*
2. *The increasing presence of catastrophic weather events, such as flooding, will generate mass displacement; and*
3. *Sea-level rise will permanently destroy the traditionally territories of millions.*[35]

The ongoing development of all these concurrent events demands 'proactive intervention';[36] it also requires the organization and institutionalization of several areas of research, with a view to promoting readiness for mitigation and assistance.[37] These organizations do not have binding force to impose the conclusions they might reach about the necessity of aid and assistance for migrants, let alone the power to be truly 'proactive', in the sense of being able to proscribe the hazardous and negligent human activities that produce 'overwhelming negative' impacts on peoples and environments and which, in turn, generate mass environmental and climate migrations.

To sum up, the primary responsibility for IDPs rests with their territorial state, because of the principles of sovereignty and non-intervention. However, as Goodwin-Gill and McAdam note:

> *The governing principles of sovereignty and non-intervention stand potentially in opposition to other governing principles of international organization, including the*

commitment to human rights and to international cooperation in the resolution of humanitarian problems.[38]

The major problem is that 'neither the UNHCR [United Nations High Commissioner for Refugees] nor any other UN agency has any legal authority 'to protect persons within their own country'.[39] Hence the protection of IDPs, although a 'broad consensus' exists in principle on the need to protect,[40] remains unsolved, at least at the international level. The question on the ground remains almost exclusively regional and political, although for certain specific circumstances the internally displaced may be considered in international law, given the ongoing failures of states to provide protection:

In each case, however, there is a clear gap between what may be called functional responsibilities and expectations, on the one hand, and the legal obligations of States on the other hand.[41]

The presence of such 'gaps' does not appear to be purely an oversight, as states have consistently avoided the drafting of a new, binding convention that might solidify and render mandatory the rights of IDPs in relation to their state of origin. Since 1990, however, the legal concept of 'complementary protection' has had a history dating back to the League of Nations,[42] as the formal 'refugee' definition was found to be increasingly incomplete. Complementary protection was intended as a legal term to be distinguished from the protection 'granted solely on humanitarian grounds', based on humanitarian and human rights law.[43] However, neither human rights nor humanitarian law apply to all who may need protection: for instance, the norms of humanitarian law are applicable only during an armed conflict, and other forms of 'low-intensity conflict' do not qualify.[44] Human rights law also needs the clarification of its principles, and how they might apply to eco-refugees, as the protection of life is certainly present within it, as are 'free movement and access to international assistance' and 'the right not to be arbitrarily displaced'.[45]

In addition, the right not to be arbitrarily displaced is not explicitly formulated in any human rights instrument except ILO Convention No. 169, but that document refers exclusively to indigenous and tribal peoples. The Universal Declaration of Human Rights includes implicitly applicable language, and the Human Rights Committee in 1999 stated that:

the freedom to choose one's residence[46] *includes protection against all forms of forced internal displacement.*[47]

The only instrument that defines specifically the rights of IDPs and states' and others' obligations is the Guiding Principles mentioned above, but these do not represent a binding obligation, and most of the other international instruments from which the protection of IDPs might be inferred include both 'ratification gaps' and 'consensus gaps';[48] hence we can conclude that, at this time, no binding instrument exists for the protection of all IDPs, although perhaps indigenous peoples may fare slightly better.

Nevertheless, the problem of IDP protection remains a highly significant one, not only because of the presence of climate change and the pressures of globalization that ensure ever-increasing numbers of migrants who are presently unprotected, but also because the problem it represents reflects the culmination of the modern tension between sovereignty and human rights problems.[49] For this reason, primarily, the 1951 CSR is not only a flawed instrument as such: as we shall see below, it cannot properly protect even all its own defined 'clients', and it is also less than useful to accommodate the growing new phenomenon of IDPs. And this is true even though most of the categories of 'persecution' on which it is founded would lend themselves well to a possible extension to IDPs, at least in principle.

At any rate, solutions for both categories of affected persons, refugees and IDPs, would benefit more from the immediate adoption of preventative measures to protect them 'at source', in other words long before the circumstances of their existence deteriorate to the point at which flight is the only option for survival.

Hence, given the lack of specific binding instruments addressing the problems of climate and eco-refugees (as IDPs, or as asylum seekers in other countries), it might be best to start with a brief overview of what are the existing binding legal instruments, if any, that prescribe the appropriate treatment of refugees, although, clearly, at present this category of affected persons does not include environmental displacement. There is only one official convention, the CSR of 1951, and the protocol of 1967 that allows the Convention's purview to be extended to the victims of situations and events prior to the 1951 starting point.

3. A QUESTION OF DEFINITION?

The first problem that must be faced in order to assess the CSR is the strongly limiting definition of 'refugees', which leaves little room for debate or expansion:

> *Article 1 – Definition of the term refugee*
> *A. For the purposes of the present Convention, the term 'refugee' shall apply to a person who:*
>
> *1 ...*
> *2 As a result of events occurring before January 1951 and owing to a well-founded fear of being persecuted for reasons of race, religion, nationality, membership of a particular social group or political opinion is outside the country of his nationality and is unable or, owing to such fear, unwilling to avail himself of the protection of that country; or who, not having a nationality and being outside the country of his former habitual residence as a result of such events is unable or, owing to such fear, unwilling to return to it.*

Several problems emerge at the outset. First, although for refugees it is acceptable to envision a 'flight to safety' of sorts, the definition omits the consideration of:

> *Flight from oppression, from a threat to life or liberty, flight from persecutions; flight from deprivations, from grinding poverty; flight from war or civil strife; flight from natural disasters, earthquakes, floods, drought or famine.*[50]

In addition, Goodwin-Gill acknowledges the presence of an inherent contradiction in the definition of a refugee, even beyond the list of omissions he cites:

> *On the one hand, [the UNHCR Statute] affirms that the work of the Office shall relate, as a rule, to groups and categories of refugees. On the other hand, it proposes a definition which is essentially individualistic, seeming to require a case-by-case examination of subjective and objective elements.*[51]

But today's humanitarian situation, as well as that of environmental disasters of various kinds, including climate change, hurricanes and tsunamis and other widespread effects of environmental degradation, affects large groups at a time, even whole regions (for example the Arctic and island and coastal states). In addition, if we consider the definition in the light of the specific plight of indigenous communities, another inherent contradiction, one of even graver import, emerges.

The ideal situation for refugees in general regarding the CSR, is, first, the possibility to include their 'flight to safety', that is, the ability to avoid the pressing dangerous or otherwise unliveable situation that threatens them, and second, the result of their flight ought to lead them to a safer haven, to another location, where the imminent threat is neutralized. This may be a solution that is ideal for most groups, as it ensures the group's safety in another region, or in another country, when one is available. But the problem that remains from their standpoint is that indigenous peoples have a *sui generis* relationship with their territories, one that includes their history, tradition, and cultural and religious practices and beliefs: this relation is not necessarily transferable to another country or region.

The result of this particular situation is such that even the 'ideal' result sought by refugees – that is, relocation – is far from ideal in these specific circumstances; while individuals of an indigenous community may feel and be safer elsewhere, the move effectively results in the elimination of the community as a 'people'; that is, the effect of such a move results in cultural genocide. Nevertheless, this problem remains purely conceptual at this time, as the indigenous groups that would be affected are not covered under the aegis of the CSR. At best, they are considered 'internally displaced persons' (IDPs).[52] Assistance to these 'displaced persons' was to be 'undertaken within the framework of [UNHCR's] Good Offices function', and 'on a purely humanitarian basis'.[53] For another view of this issue, see Roy Todd's 'Between the land and the city',[94] although the possibility of keeping some of the cultural ceremonies and activities alive in an urban setting yields, at best, a limited cultural expression as the traditional stewardship of the land is no longer possible.

4. THE LEGAL STATUS OF INTERNALLY DISPLACED PERSONS

> *Persons who have been forced to flee their homes suddenly or unexpectedly in large numbers as a result of armed conflict, internal strife, systematic violations of human rights, or natural or man-made disasters, and who are within the territory of their own country.*[55]

This definition comes a lot closer to the situation faced by indigenous communities and indicates an entirely different group from that of true 'legal' refugees according to the CSR. The definition also follows several years of 'resolutions' suggesting multiple approaches to 'displaced persons'.[56] IDPs were, initially, primarily the result of civil wars within countries.

This is the main instance of a case where the general rules of international law (including sovereignty and non-intervention) are clearly insufficient. Civil conflict does not ensure *all* citizens equal protection, and its presence guarantees a volatile situation that is not conductive to providing state protection to all, or even a situation where it is easy to obtain the documents necessary for legal travel outside the country. The precarious situation of IDPs has been known for some time; since the late 1940s, the simple provision of legal aid to displaced persons by the UN has been viewed as totally inadequate by several countries (including India and Pakistan), when those requiring assistance were in need of basic aid, such as food, water and medicine.[57] The UNHCR has included both aid and rehabilitation in its resolution at least since 1972.[58] Later UN resolutions did refer to 'displaced persons', without specifying whether they were internal or external to their country of origin. By 1992, a UN Commission on Human Rights appointed a representative (Francis Deng) who, in 1994, stated his goal as:

> *the development of a doctrine of protection specifically tailored to the needs of the internally displaced.*[59]

Eventually the proposed 'new approach' and the totality of legal norms relating to it were published in a field handbook in 1996.[60]

Once again, the primary responsibility for these displaced persons remains with the states, in fact the UNHCR's Committee Conclusion No. 75 (1994) distinguishes between 'humanitarian intervention and the provision of humanitarian assistance'.[61] In other cases, the international community may provide help only 'in consultation and coordination with the concerned State',[62] but in the case of indigenous groups, for the most part, the circumstances that turn them into environmental refugees (to use the commonly used expression, rather than the technically appropriate legal one) are the effects of activities permitted, and in fact most often promoted, by the state at issue, such as advantageous deals with corporate entities (see points 1, 2, 7 and 8 under '2. The Question of Environmental Refugees' above).

Even when this is not the case, the environmental degradation that depletes the ecosystems and wildlife of their territories is – once again – part and parcel of the operation of Western economies, hence it is both legal and supported by the states involved, and by legitimate organizations such as the World Bank Group (WBG) and the International Monetary Fund (IMF).[63] In fact, 'persecution and state complicity' are viewed together in some of the case law regarding refugee claimants in Canada. See for instance La Forest J in *Canada Attorney General versus Ward*:[64]

> *I propose to approach the issues by the parties in the following order:*
>
> A. *Persecution and State Complicity*
> (a) *Is the element of State complicity either through direct persecution, collusion with the persecuting agents, or wilful blindness to the actions of the persecuting agents, a*

requisite element in establishing a refugee claimant's 'unwillingness' to avail him- or herself of the protection of his or her country of nationality?
(b) Is a claimant considered 'unable' to avail him- or herself of the protection of the State only in those circumstances where he or she is physically unable to seek out this protection?

Wilful blindness describes well the general attitude of both governments of affluent Western countries and that of the governing bodies of most developing countries, who view the economic benefits arising from the presence of various extractive and mining industries as the only criterion worthy of note when reaching decisions regarding those corporate activities, even when these take place close to the territories of indigenous communities.

According to a recent Declaration of the European Parliament,[65] the main concern in law ought to be that of responsibility. The present focus on state 'security' and that on humanitarian law should take second place to that primary concern: that of responsibility to the human beings involved.[66]

To return once again to the question of IDPs, the threat or the persecution for these people can be circumscribed to a specific area in their country, thus permitting in-country migrations in certain cases. Nevertheless, if we consider indigenous peoples in this context, those seeking refugee status must be able to demonstrate that, even in another region of their country, the 'relevant criterion is the availability in fact of protection in another region, and the chance of maintaining some sort of social and economic existence'.[67]

For indigenous peoples, the social and economic aspects of their existence are either seriously compromised or eliminated, especially in the case of traditional communities, once they are forced to flee their territories. Hence the unavoidable conclusion is that even if the definition of 'refugee' is not applicable to them, the label of IDP does not fit them any better. Because of these and other difficulties, it is easy to appreciate why many scholars today are attempting to establish yet another category, that of 'environmental refugee' or 'ecological refugee', in order to add something more specifically useful to the sparse arsenal of human rights instruments that might be applicable.

5. PERSECUTION AND THE PROBLEM OF INTENT

So far we have been speaking primarily of obstacles, but there is one major aspect of the CSR that may give one hope for its possible use in defence of environmental refugees. Most of the international instruments that deal with grave human rights issues focus primarily on those who impose harms. A certain state of mind, *mens rea*, is required to prove that the harms imposed originate from actors who are committing a crime, such as genocide, perhaps, or torture. For instance, Schabas is most specific abut the need to prove a specific intent (*dolus specialis*) before that crime (genocide) can be proven before an international tribunal.[68]

In contrast, I have argued that the elements of knowledge, and the careful organizational or corporate planning that often result in disastrous environmental conditions for local populations and indigenous communities, merit the appellation of genocide, although, technically, the concept does not fit precisely according to the jurisprudence that is available on the topic.[69] Nevertheless, in attempting to 'transfer' civil liability cases, for which the final question remains – at best – 'how much', to criminal law procedures, where the problem of *mens rea* looms large, there is also a different probative aspect, that is, the need for evidence/proof 'beyond a reasonable doubt', rather than 'the balance of probabilities'. Hence, the CSR's intent requirement is already clearly a lesser one.

The Convention under consideration, however, uses a standard that is more than the civil one, yet less than the one demanded by criminal cases.[70] The easier ground required to establish refugee status arises from the fact that, according to Article 2 of the CSR, the main mental state at issue is that of the refuge seeker, not the mental state of those who persecute. Persecution is judged according to the UN *Handbook*, and the 'grounds', as defined by Article 2 of the Convention, are both subjective and objective, but they focus on the beliefs and the conditions of the one seeking refuge. According to the Convention, the intentions of the persecutors need not be examined in depth (as they would be in a tribunal dealing with the charge of genocide), a point often neglected in the scholarly literature on the topic, as we shall see. Essentially, the 'subjective' aspect applies only to the person seeking refuge. The objective aspect is judged mainly on factual grounds, which include not only whatever knowledge the refuge seeker can provide, but also the 'facts' (or factual grounds) are extended to the conditions present in the seeker's original country of residence.

Even though the focus remains firmly on the asylum seeker, as far as the mental element is concerned, Hathaway, for instance, states that:

> *the best evidence that an individual faces a serious chance of persecution is usually the treatment afforded similarly situated persons in the country of origin.*[71]

Hence, not only a specific 'singling out' of an individual for persecution, but also 'generalized oppression' may indeed give rise to refugee status, although the presence of oppression in a country may complicate matters for an individual asylum seeker.[72]

In contrast, Pratte J. A. in *Musial versus Minister of Employment and Immigration*[73] reasons that 'the mental element which is decisive for the existence of persecution is that of the government, not the refugee'. I am not entirely convinced by this position, because the conditions prevailing in the country of origin, as part of the factual assessment of the well-foundedness of the fear of persecution, do not require a study of the mental element of either the government of that country or of those that government might be supporting. All that is required is the factual element, not an analysis of the motivation of agents who contribute to the factual situation, and the latter is not required, to my knowledge, by any immigration court considering the case of an asylum seeker.

For instance, most often corporate actors have no particular hate or dislike for any ethnic group. The aim is simply to complete their plans as expeditiously as possible, avoiding controversy and delays, however caused, in order to ensure maximum profitability as a result.

But although a specific will to harm is not always present in activities that are recognized to produce racist results, the CSR is based upon the nexus between persecution and the specific cognizable ground that may give rise to persecution. Hathaway emphasizes the 'nexus to civil or political status', as he states:

> *Refugee law requires that there be a nexus between who the claimant is or what she believes and the risk of serious harm in her home state.*[74]

The persecution, no doubt, is intended, but no specific proof of intent is required for the assessment of refugee status, nor is the *mens rea*, or the mental element of the crime of persecution, whatever its ground, ever needed to be proven before a claim of asylum may be approved in any country. The case law does not require any enquiries into the motivation of persecution; on the contrary, it requires only factual, objective understanding of the circumstances of the persecuted asylum seeker, not any proof of the specific intent of the persecutor.

In the section cited above, Hathaway explains the extent of the subjective aspects of the persecution:

> *Due to variations in the psychological make-up of individuals in the circumstances of each case, interpretations of what amounts to the persecution are bound to vary. And it is possible that a particular form of mistreatment will constitute persecution when applied to one applicant, but not when applied to another.*

This paragraph re-emphasizes the subjectivity of the 'well-founded fear' element, while the focus remains on the refugee, the applicant, not on the mental state of the persecutor.

Another major difficulty with locating a specific focus of intent is the problem of those living in an oppressive state that puts them at risk in a general sense. Hathaway's analysis of this issue supports my argument. He says that many 'may nonetheless succeed on a claim to refugee status, if some element of differential intent *or* impact based on civil or political status is demonstrated'.[75] The 'or' in this sentence clearly indicates that to demonstrate a different impact is equivalent to showing a different intent, even in such a difficult situation as that of 'generalized oppression', which, as such, is insufficient to ensure refugee status.

In his discussion of this topic, Gagliardi says that 'persecution need not, and frequently does not, have any articulable motivational basis'.[76] He argues that the need for cognizable grounds may exclude persecuted individuals from achieving asylum today, just as it would have done when the CSR was originally conceived. He cites a case involving an individual from Haiti,[77] where persecution, in the context of widespread government oppression, includes indiscriminate arrests, torture and disappearances involving large numbers, but without a specific focus on any identifiable segment of the population.

No specific intent could be discerned, hence none of the five grounds appear necessary to trigger persecution. Gagliardi also argues that the five cognizable grounds would not have protected even all the victims of Nazism, despite the fact that the CSR was ostensibly written to protect the Jewish victims of the Nazi regime who needed to find asylum. He argues that 'Jews fleeing the Holocaust would easily have qualified under the religion category',[78] and so would have Gypsies, as a separate racial group. However the 'social group category' would not have been sufficient to protect 'the disabled, the mentally ill, the mentally deficient, the terminally ill and the homosexuals'.[79]

In addition, McHugh (*Chan versus Minister for Immigration and Ethnic Affairs*, 1989, 169 CLR 379, H.C.A., at 34) states:

Courts, writers and the UNHCR Handbook agree, however, that a 'well-founded fear' requires an objective examination of the facts to determine whether the fear is justified. But are the facts which are to be examined confined to those which formed the basis of the applicant's fear? In Sivakumaran, the House of Lords, correctly in my view, held that the objective facts to be considered are not confined to those that induced the applicant's fear. The contrary conclusion would mean that a person could have a 'well-founded fear' of persecution even though everyone else was aware of the facts which destroyed the basis of her fear.

Here both the primacy of the subjective belief of the applicant and the secondary position of even factual confirmations of that fear are reiterated. The case law often speaks of various possible interpretations of well-foundedness, such as persecution as 'a reasonable possibility', a 'real chance', a 'reasonable chance', 'substantial grounds for thinking' or a 'serious possibility'.[80]

Another important issue hinges on the position of a government (or those a government allows to operate within its borders). This issue is whether majorities can be excluded from state protection just as minorities often are:

Since refugee law is concerned with the absence of protection rather than with minority status per se, the members of a country's ethnic majority may be protected as racially defined refugees if they are disenfranchised in terms of respect for core human rights.[81]

In sum, the nexus between persecution and the five grounds enumerated in the CSR is primarily the subjective fear of the refugee, coupled with the factual grounds that will convince a court that the fear is indeed 'well-founded'. The fear itself remains primary, and the 'objective' conditions that give rise to that fear do not include the state of mind and the specific intent of the persecutor. The latter is not part of the burden of proof the applicant for asylum must meet.

The ascertainable, factual conditions are important: the United States Committee for Refugees[82] offers a comprehensive 'functional' definition:

A person was considered to be a refugee if his forced movement, whether within his own country or to asylum elsewhere, means that he is deprived of a minimally decent life.[83]

In that document, persecution is not defined, as it is not in the CSR. Fragomen adds:

The phraseology 'well-founded fear of persecution' raises the extremely difficult question of what constitutes persecution. The determination is usually quite stringent. The de facto refugee responds in his own manner to the circumstances in his environment. The interpretation of this phrase, with the emphasis on the objective factors, eliminates many who subjectively have reacted by fleeing.[84]

It is worthy of note that even here, where the emphasis is on the difficulties of establishing refugee status, there is no mention of any special intent to be sought or proven in the country from which the flight originated.

At any rate, the stringent conditions present in the CSR, and enforced by various courts to establish refugee status, are quite different from the requirements of instruments intended to establish racist discrimination, for instance, where the question of intent plays little or no part. Because 'race' is one of the major grounds of persecution, it will be useful to see how environmental racism is viewed in the literature and in the courts.

5a. Environmental racism

> *On 12 December 1991, Lawrence Summers, [then] chief economist of the World Bank, argued in a memo to colleagues that toxic pollution should be located in poor countries ... where human health is impaired, it should be in the poorest countries, he argued. The measurement of the costs of health-impairing pollution depends on the foregone earnings from increased morbidity and mortality. From this point of view, a given amount of health-impairing pollution should be done in the country with the lowest cost, which will be the country with the lowest wages.*[85]

The acknowledged leader of the scholarly movement towards environmental justice in North America is Robert Bullard. His seminal paper, 'Decision making',[86] describes the five 'theoretical perspectives' required to eliminate the scourge of environmental racism and restore environmental justice. He writes:

> *To end unequal environmental protection, governments should adopt five principles of environmental justice: guaranteeing the right to environmental protection, preventing harm before it occurs, shifting the burden of proof to the polluters, obviating proof of intent to discriminate and redressing existing inequities.*[87]

It will be useful to refer to all five principles in this work. For now, the focus is on the fourth, 'obviating proof of intent', as intent represents a major stumbling block in the case of other treaties such as the Convention of Genocide. It is important to note that, in contrast, recent legal literature does not fully appreciate either the historical roots of the quest for environmental justice or the robustness of that discipline today.

After the major research work by the United Church and other religious groups in 1987,[88] there has been steadily mounting evidence of environmental racism, particularly in the scholarly literature on the topic in the US.[89] Most of the abundant literature on the topic couples the problem with public health issues.

Eventually, former US President Bill Clinton's Executive Order on Environmental Justice (No. 12898) was signed on 11 February 1994, and the history of the US Environmental Protection Agency (EPA), leading up to that watershed decision, can be found in the paper co-authored by Clarice Gaylord, first holder of the EPA Environmental Justice Position.[90] Prior to the Executive Order, the Working Group reporting to the EPA researching the conditions of 'people of colour', including Indigenous Peoples, as Gaylord and Bell reported that:

> *American Indians are a unique ethnic group with a special relationship to the Federal Government and have distinct environmental problems. Tribes generally lack infra-*

structure, institutions, trained personnel and resources necessary to protect their members.[91]

It is therefore inaccurate to simply view environmental racism as a 'nascent social science concept', as Aurelie Lopez did in 2007, citing a 1998 article.[92] Lopez argued that:

In order to establish persecution, a person has to demonstrate both the persecution impact and persecutory intent in the part of the governmental entity. The nature of the intent required is more than volition or awareness of the consequences.[93]

Nevertheless, 'persecutory intent' is not part of the probatory burden of refuge seekers, according to the CSR. Even if the *Handbook* contains such a language, the fact remains that, unlike the Convention, the *Handbook* is not binding law. Of course, racial discrimination may not rise to the level of persecution in all cases, although when it is part of a systemic pattern, it should be viewed as more than a random incident of discrimination. Essentially, even the US EPA does not require proof of discriminatory intent in order to trigger an equal response, whether the harmed community is predominantly white or African American.

The case of Browning Ferris Industries (BFI) in Titusville, Alabama, clearly supports this contention.[94] In 1990 BFI decided to site a 'garbage transfer and recyclery' in Titusville, Alabama, a predominantly black neighbourhood, across from an elementary school. But not only did BFI employ several underhand manoeuvres to achieve their goal with a minimum of fuss, without disclosing their real aim until after corrupt city officials had rubber-stamped the permits for their plans (as an example, they claimed they were building an extension to a potato chip factory), but they already had a large number of EPA violations on their record. 'A pattern seemed to be present, since 26 of 28 BFI garbage operations were located in black neighbourhoods'.[95] The African American neighbourhood, ably represented by David Sullivan and Wm. Horn, were involved in a costly and protracted fight, but they eventually won. The Supreme Court of Alabama reversed its earlier ruling, and granted over US$5.5 million to the plaintiffs and their advocates, without the need to prove discriminatory intent on the part of BFI.

In fact, this author was asked by the attorney for the plaintiffs to set out in point form why a decision in their favour would support 'the common benefit', in order to rebut an earlier court finding to the effect that the 'benefit' would only concern 'a few black people'. It is interesting to note that my argument, successfully used in the final hearings of the Alabama Supreme Court, did not even address the question of intent:

1. The public interest in general is under attack when powerful interests and even public officials, sworn to uphold the laws, ignore or seek to circumvent laws designed to be equally binding on all.
2. When justice is not sought and respected in a society, and those in power do not speak out against violations and do not try to redress the inequities that ensue, then all citizens lose.
3. The major public good lies in the defence of public safety and the prevention of harm (in the physical sense), that is, the protection of public health. But both BFI's antecedents, its previous practices and present goals, raised grave doubts about the

> *safety of its enterprise and its commitment to corporate responsibility in general. A further aspect of this problem is the presence of at least two major difficulties with environmental rules and regulations: (a) the question of the burden of proof and (b) the incommensurability of industry risks (that is, economic harms) and public risks (physical/health harms).*
>
> 4 *Harms not only physical. When freedom of information, free consent, due process and equal protection are all under attack, we are all losers.*[96]

In conclusion, the CSR itself only requires a full examination of the mental state of the refuge seeker, not that of the agents of persecution, whether governmental or corporate. The appeal of environmental racism, or to environmental justice, stands, as it may well disclose racial discrimination, one of the five grounds of persecution according to the CSR, even if it does not prove persecution on its own. The repeated, systematic targeting of areas where indigenous and local communities lead traditional lives, to 'develop' various extractive and mining operations without, for the most part, securing free, informed consent from the inhabitants,[97] appears to have clear persecutory results, even if the persecutory intent cannot be proven.

6. INDIGENOUS AND NON-INDIGENOUS: ANY SOLUTIONS?

The previous sections of this chapter have raised far more questions than they have provided answers. What has emerged from our discussion can be summed briefly, as it will provide the basis for the research and the arguments of the chapters that follow.

The first important point arises from the date and the composition of the CSR. It is clearly a document designed to deal with issues far removed from those to which we are attempting to apply it. Large human migrations did not appear to be one of its concerns, nor did the issues of industrial development, climate change, environmental disasters or any of the grave issues of our times.

Because of this non-inclusiveness, the most vulnerable persons today are removed from its protection a priori. This is the second point we need to consider. The most vulnerable persons share various characteristics, first and foremost poverty, but also gender and age, because women, children and the preborn are particularly at risk, and this is not only true of exposures in developing countries, although this is where it happens for the most part.[98]

In addition, persons living in developing countries' aboriginal communities are among the poorest of the poor,[99] and they share the appellation of most vulnerable with other IDPs. The third point is the *sui generis* relationship between traditional aboriginal communities and the lands they inhabit, a relationship that is totally unlike that of any other group. This unique relationship makes their situation equally unique and, from this perspective, much more difficult than that of all other environmental refugees, in ways that touch upon all 'five grounds of persecution' (see Chapter 2).

Whatever solution might be sought for the mass migrations of people connected either with environmental disasters, most often arising from an aetiology that includes human agency, or directly resulting from human activities, their situation is far more complicated and grave than the already difficult problems of other communities. The fourth point emerged in the discussion of the second one: the vulnerability of environmental refugees is based, for the most part, on public health issues,[100] without considering for a moment the unique case of aboriginal peoples. The problem is that the interface between environmental issues and health is not well represented in today's international or domestic law instruments.

This reality affects all the jurisprudence that deals with cases that involve environmental harms. Hence the lack of usefulness and cogency of the present legal infrastructure is a major obstacle to the quest for environmental justice, and an immediate correction of this state of affairs is urgently needed. In fact, this point colours at least one of the solutions that are present in the scholarly literature at this time as possible solutions to the lack of protection of environmental refugees. We will discuss those proposed solutions in a later chapter, but it might be helpful to briefly mention a few of the possibilities at this time.

Dana Zartner Falstrom proposes a new convention, designed along the lines of the Convention against Torture.[101] Others, in contrast, prefer attempting to reinterpret the requirements of the present Convention on Refugees,[102] or to match the crime of ecocide to the crime of genocide, thus declaring the 'killing of the Earth's systems' a criminal activity.[103] A position similar to this one was the one proposed by this author, long before any consideration of refugee issues, in *Ecoviolence and the Law: Supranational Normative Foundation of Ecocrime*,[104] simply as a general approach to environmental harms. On a different tack, Michelle Leighton Schwartz proposes an approach based on a consideration of 'environmental abuse'.[105]

Finally, this author has also argued for the need to have an authoritative voice, such as the WHO (that is also an organ of the UN that has the right to make law) pronounce itself as clearly on the connection between the environment and human health and survival as it regularly does on emerging and re-emerging infections and vector-borne diseases.[106] Lawrence Gostin goes even further, as he proposes a new convention to ensure the legal status of public health. He does not address his proposal directly to the question of environmental refugees, but, as we noted, the two issues are closely connected (see Chapter 7).

All these proposals will be discussed and evaluated in the final chapter of this work. However, none of the possible solutions proposed in the scholarly literature differentiate between the different groups of environmental refugees or attempt to deal separately with the grave problems that affect aboriginal peoples on this issue, over and above the problems facing all other IDPs. We will also address this question in the final discussion.

Hathaway sees the decisive factor in the plight of refugees in their inability to influence their own governments. Absent that ability, he argues, the root cause of refugee persecution is the fact they are essentially disenfranchised:

> Early refugees were not merely suffering persons, but were moreover persons whose position was fundamentally at odds with the power structure of their own state. It was the lack of a meaningful stake in the governance of their own society which distinguished them from others, and which gave legitimacy to their desire to seek protection abroad.[107]

It is this 'fundamental marginalization'[108] that Hathaway sees as the major factor in their situation. Yet even if this argument is accepted, it applies in a different way to indigenous peoples: they often do possess a measure of self-governance in their own societies, yet this internal 'power' does not help to protect them from 'outside' persecution, most often not only permitted, but also supported by their country's government. In some sense, this reality applies to most people in varying degrees. But those who live in close communion with the land are the ones most deeply affected.

NOTES

1 Stockholm Declaration of the United Nations Conference for the Human Environment, 16 June 1972, ILM 11 141; El Hinnawi, E. (1985) *Environmental Refugees*, United Nations Environment Programme (UNEP), Nairobi, Kenya.
2 El Hinnawi, ibid , p4.
3 Ibid.
4 Westra, L. (1997) 'Terrorism at Oka', in A. Wellington, A. Greenbaum and W. Cragg (eds) *Canadian Issues in Environmental Ethics*, Broadview Press, Peterborough, ON; Westra, L. (1998) *Living in Integrity*, Rowman Littlefield, Lanham, MD; Pimentel, D., Westra, L. and Noss, R. F. (2000) *Ecological Integrity: Integrating Environment, Conservation and Health*, Island Press, Washington, DC; Soskolne, C. L. (ed) (2007) *Sustaining Life on Earth*, Lexington Books, Lanham, MD; Westra, L. (2006) *Environmental Justice and the Rights of Unborn and Future Generations*, Earthscan, London; Westra, L. (2007) *Environmental Justice and the Rights of Indigenous Peoples*, Earthscan, London.
5 El Hinnawi, op cit Note 1, p5.
6 Christian Aid (2007) 'Human tide: The real migration crisis', May.
7 Ibid, p6.
8 International Symposium on Desertification and Migration (1994) 'The Almeria Statement', International Symposium on Desertification and Migration, Almeria, Spain, 9–11 February.
9 Myers, N. (1993) 'Environmental refugees in a globally warmed world', *Bioscience*, vol 43, p752.
10 McAdam, J. (2007) 'Climate change refugees and international law', NSW Bar Association, 24 October, p1.
11 Myers, N. (2005) 'Environmental refugees: An emergent security issue', 13th Economic Forum, Prague, 23–27 May.
12 Stern, Sir Nicholas (2007) *The Economics of Climate Change: The Stern Review*, Cambridge University Press, Cambridge, UK.
13 El Hinnawi, op cit Note 1, pp6–20; Pogge, T. (2008) 'Aligned: Global justice and ecology', in L. Westra, K. Bosselmann and R. Westra (eds) *Reconciling Human Existence with Ecological Integrity*, Earthscan, London, pp147–158.
14 Goodland, R. (2008) 'The World Bank's financing of climate change damages integrity', in L. Westra, K. Bosselmann and R. Westra (eds) *Reconciling Human Existence with Ecological Integrity*, Earthscan, London, UK, pp219–244.
15 El Hinnawi, op cit Note 1, pp23–30.
16 Ibid, p31.
17 Westra (2006), op cit Note 4, Chapter 8; El Hinnawi, op cit Note 1, pp35–36.
18 Westra (2007), op cit Note 4, Chapters 1 and 2.
19 Michelot, A. (2006) 'Enjeux de la reconnaissance du statut de réfugié écologique pour la construction d'une nouvelle responsabilité internationale', *Revue Française de Droit de l'Environnement*, 4 December, p428.

20 Schabas, W. (2006) *The UN Criminal International Tribunals*, Cambridge University Press, Cambridge, UK.
21 Westra (2007), op cit Note 4; Imai, S. (2001) 'Treaty rights and Crown obligations: In search of accountability', *Queen's Law Journal*, vol 27, no 1, p49; Huff, A. I. (1999) 'Resource development and human rights: A look at the case of the Lubicon Cree Indian Nation of Canada', *Colorado Journal of International Environmental Law Policy*, vol 1, no 120, pp161–174.
22 Convention on the Status of Refugees (1951), 189 UNTS 150, into force 22 April 1954.
23 United Nations Declaration of Human Rights, GA Res. 217A (III), UNGA a/810, 10 December 1948; International Covenant on Civil and Political Rights (ICCPR), GA Res. 2000, UN GAOR, 21st Session, Supplement No. 16, UN Doc. A/6316 (1966); International Covenant of Economic, Social, and Cultural Rights, UN Doc. A/6316; ILO Convention No. 169, 1989, 28 ILM 138.
24 UNGA A/63/265.
25 UNGA Resolution 61/208, New York, 14–15 September 2006.
26 UNGA 62/270.
27 E/CN.4/1998/53/Add.2, 11 February 1998; see Appendix 2.
28 UNGA, 11 August 2008, A/63/265, p11.
29 Ibid, p13.
30 Soskolne, C. L. (2008) 'Eco-epidemiology: On the need to measure health effects from global change', in L. Westra, K. Bosselmann and R. Westra (eds) *Reconciling Ecological Existence with Ecological Integrity*, Earthscan, London, UK, pp109–123
31 Gostin, L. O. (2008) 'Meeting basic survival needs of the world's least healthy people: Toward a framework convention on global health', *Georgetown Law Journal*, vol 96, no 2, January, pp331–392.
32 Couldrey, M. and Herson, M. (eds) (2008) *Forced Migration Review*, University of Oxford, Issue 31, October.
33 Ibid, p4.
34 Morton, A., Bancour, P. and Laczko, F. (2008) 'Human security police challenge', in Couldrey and Herson, op cit Note 32, p5.
35 Ibid, p6.
36 Ibid.
37 The Climate Change Environment and Migration Alliance (CCEMA) was established in April 2008 in Munich by the United Nations University (UNU), the IOM, UNEP and the Munich Re Foundation (MRF) with the goal of ensuring both preparedness and collaboration.
38 Goodwin-Gill, G. S. and McAdam, J. (2007) *The Refugee in International Law* (third edition), Oxford University Press, Oxford, UK, p33.
39 Ibid, p34; see also UNGA Res. 60/168 'Protection and Assistance to Internally Displaced Persons', 16 Dec. 2005 (adopted without a vote).
40 Goodwin-Gill and McAdam, op cit Note 38, p48.
41 Ibid, p47.
42 Marrus, M. R. (2002) *The Unwanted: European Refugees from the First World War Through the Cold War* (second edition), Temple University Press, Philadelphia, PA
43 Goodwin-Gill and McAdam, op cit Note 38, p286; see also Executive Committee, Standing Committee, 18th Meeting, 'Complementary forms of protection: Their nature and relationship to the international refugee protection regime', UN Doc. EC/50/SC/CRP.18, 9 June 2000, especially paragraphs 4 and 5.
44 Phuong, C. (2004) *The International Protection of Internally Displaced Persons*, Cambridge University Press, Cambridge, UK, pp48–49.
45 Ibid, p51; see also Stavropoulos, M. (1994) 'The right not to be displaced', *American University Journal of International Law and Policy*, vol 9, p689.
46 Article 12(1) of the ICCPR.

47 Human Rights Committee (1999) 'Freedom of movement', Article 12, CCPR/C/21/Rev.1/Add.9, CCPR General Comment 27, 2 November; see also discussion in Phuong, op cit Note 44, p51.
48 Phuong, op cit Note 44, pp49–50.
49 Anghie, T. (2006) *Imperialism, Sovereignty and International Law*, Cambridge University Press, Cambridge, UK; more specifically, see Dacyl, J. (1996) 'Sovereignty versus human rights: From past discourses to contemporary dilemmas', *Journal of Refugee Studies*, vol 9, p136.
50 Goodwin-Gill, G. S. (1996) *The Refugee in International Law* (second edition), Clarendon Press, Oxford, UK, p3.
51 Ibid, p8.
52 ECOSOC Resolution 1655 (LII), June 1972, eventually UNGA Resolution 3271 (XXIX), 18 December 1974; see also Resolution 3454 (XXX), 9 December 1975.
53 Goodwin-Gill, op cit Note 50, p12, note 47.
54 Todd, R. (2000/2001) 'Between the land and the city: Aboriginal agency, culture and governance in urban areas', *London Journal of Canadian Studies*, vol 16, pp48–66.
55 UN Doc. E/CN.41/1995/50.
56 UNGA Resolution 3454 (XXX), 9 December 1975; UNGA Resolution 43/116, 8 December 1988.
57 Goodwin-Gill and McAdam, op cit Note 38, p482.
58 Ibid; see also ECOSOC Resolution 1705 (LIII), 27 July 1972, referring to Sudan and 'the assistance required for voluntary repatriation, rehabilitation and resettlement of the refugees returning from abroad, as well as persons displaced within the country'.
59 Goodwin-Gill and McAdam, op cit Note 38, p43; see also UN Document E/CN.4/1994/44, paragraph 28; UN Document E/CN.4/1995/50.
60 UNHCR (1966) *International Legal Standards Applicable to the Protection of Internally Displaced Persons: A Reference Manual for UNHCR Staff*, UNHCR, Geneva.
61 Goodwin-Gill, op cit Note 50, p267.
62 Ibid.
63 Westra, L. (2007), op cit Note 4, Chapter 4.
64 *Canada Attorney General versus Ward* (1993) 2 S.C.R. 689, paragraph 17.
65 Declaration of the European Parliament, DC/523 175 FR.doc., PE342.103 Or.Fr., February 2004.
66 Michelot, op cit Note 19, p429; see also Chemillier Gendreau, M. (1995) *Humanité et Souveraineté – Essai sur la Function du Droit International*, Editions de la Decouverte, Paris, p368.
67 Goodwin-Gill, op cit Note 50, Chapter 2, 5.2.2; see also *Rasaratnam versus Canada* (Minister of Employment and Immigration) (1992) IFC 706.
68 Schabas, W. (2000) *On Genocide in International Law*, Kluwer Publishing, The Hague; see also Schabas (2006), op cit Note 20.
69 Westra, L. (2007), op cit Note 4, Chapter 7.
70 Lecture by A. Sherazee, Osgoode Hall Law School, 1 October 2007.
71 Hathaway, J. (1991) *The Law of Refugee Status*, Butterworth's, Toronto, p97.
72 *Reg. versus Secretary of State for the Home Department, ex parte Adan* (1998) House of Lords decision No. 15 (H.L.); per Lord Loyd of Berwick, paragraph 34.
73 *Musial versus Minister of Employment and Immigration* (1982), I.F.C 290, p550.
74 Hathaway, op cit Note 4, 137.
75 Ibid, p140 (emphasis added).
76 Gagliardi, D. P. (1987/1988) 'The inadequacy of cognizable grounds of persecution as a criterion for awarding refugee status', *Stanford Journal of International Law*, vol 24, pp259–273.

77   *Coriolan versus INS*, 559 F 2d 993 (5th Cir. 1977); see also 'Comment, *Coriolan v. Immigration and Naturalization Service*: A closer look at immigration law and the political refugee', *Syracuse Journal of International and Comparative Law*, vol 6, 133 (1978).
78   Gagliardi, op cit Note 8, p275.
79   Ibid; however, recent case law in Canada and elsewhere has considered sexual orientation as an acceptable possible ground as belonging to a social group, for instance in Refugee Appeal No. 131/93, GJ, dated 30 August 1995 (NZRSSA), where the applicant's homosexuality was judged to be objectively valid ground for a fear of persecution in Iran.
80   *Immigration and Naturalization Service versus Stevic*, 467 US407, p453; see also footnote 24 of that case.
81   Hathaway, op cit Note 71, p143.
82   World Refugee Report 2 (1969) at paragraph 3.
83   Fragomen, A. T. Jr (1970/1971) 'The refugee: A problem of definition', *Case Western Journal of International Law*, vol 3, pp45–56.
84   Ibid, p48.
85   Westra, L. and Lawson, B. (2001) 'Introduction', in *Faces of Environmental Racism* (second edition), Rowman Littlefield, Lanham, MD, pxviii.
86   Bullard, R. (2001) 'Decision making', in Westra and Lawson, ibid.
87   Ibid, p9.
88   United Church of Christ Commission for Racial Justice (1987) 'Toxic wastes and race in the United States: A national study of the racial and socioeconomic characteristics of communities with hazardous waste sites', United Church of Christ, New York.
89   Bullard, R. (1990) *Dumping in Dixie: Race, Class and Environmental Quality*, Westview Press, Boulder, CO; Lavelle, M., Coyle, M. and MacLachlan, C. (1992) 'Unequal protection', *National Law Journal*, 21 September, pp1–2; Austin, R. and Schill, M. (1991) 'Black, brown, poor, and poisoned: Minority grassroot environmentalism and the quest for eco-justice', *Kansas Journal of Law and Public Policy*, vol 1, pp69–82.
90   Gaylord, C. E. and Bell, E. (2001) 'Environmental justice: A national priority', in Westra and Lawson, op cit Note 85.
91   Ibid, p32.
92   Purrington, R. and Wynne, M. (1998) 'Environmental racism: Is a nascent social science concept a sound basis for legal relief?', *Houston Law Journal*, vol 35, March/April, p34.
93   Lopez, A. (2007) 'The protection of environmentally-displaced persons in international law', *Environmental Law*, Spring, pp365–380.
94   Jefferson County Circuit Court House No. CV-93-6975, Supreme Court case 1931248; Alabama Court of Civil Appeals, AV 93000104, WmF. *Horn et al versus City of Birmingham et al*, Jefferson Circuit Court CV-93-50132, 14 October 1994.
95   'True or false', a handout by the Total Awareness Group, Titusville Neighbourhood Association; this leaflet was handed to the author during her visit; see Westra, L. (2001) 'The faces of environmental racism', in L. Westra and B. Lawson (eds) *Faces of Environmental Racism* (second edition), p113.
96   Westra, L. (2001), ibid, p127.
97   Westra, L. (2007), op cit Note 4, Chapter 5.
98   Gostin, L. (2008), op cit Note 31.
99   Ibid.
100 Ibid.
101 Zartner Falstrom, D. (2000) 'Stemming the flow of environmental displacement: Creating a convention to protect persons and preserve the environment', *Colorado Journal of International Policy*, vol 2.
102 See, for instance, Lopez, A. (2007), op cit Note 93, p365.

103 Berat, L. (1993) 'Defending the right to a healthy environment: Toward a crime of genocide in international law', *Boston University International Law Journal*, vol 11, p327.
104 Westra, L. (2004) *Ecoviolence and the Law*, Transnational Publishers Inc., Ardsley, NY.
105 Leighton Schwartz, M. (1993) 'International legal protection for victims of environmental abuse', *Yale Journal of International Law*, vol 18, p355.
106 Westra, L. (2007), op cit Note 4, Chapter 10.
107 Hathaway, op cit Note 71, p136.
108 Ibid, p135.

CHAPTER 2

International Assistance and the Refugee Convention's Five Grounds of Persecution

1. INTRODUCTION TO THE FIVE GROUNDS FOR REFUGEE STATUS TO ESTABLISH PERSECUTION

Economic reasons or motivations alone will not entitle a person to refugee status, but a government's 'economic measures' may well be the cloak for action calculated to destroy the economic livelihood of specific groups; in such cases a fear of persecution can be well founded.[1]

The concept of persecution, basic to the established 'five grounds' required to support refugee status (i.e. race, religion, nationality, social group, political opinion), is both complex and unclear. It appears to be intended exclusively to establish status in individual cases, and it is problematic in the case of large migrations due to various causes, including environmental disasters and unliveable conditions in certain regions, due to both natural and man-made causes.[2] Does each member of an affected group have to meet the criteria required for well-foundedness? And does the fact that the unliveable conditions are not such that they 'single out' one or another individual represent a serious obstacle?

These questions and related ones are discussed in detail by James Crawford and Patricia Hyndman. Writing of a case before the Australian Federal Court,[3] they explain the Court's decision thus:

> It is held that singling out, or 'individualization', is not required by the convention, but that the decision-maker has not applied an incorrect test on the facts of the case.[4]

The fear of persecution refers to a subjective, individual emotion or sentiment, but, as Crawford and Hyndman add, that 'that fear is individual does not mean that the persecution itself needs to be'.[5] Moreover, the fear may be 'well-founded' even if the government of the country where the refuge seeker was persecuted (or fears being) was simply 'unable to provide protection against the persecutory acts of others', and that is most often a general, not an individual, situation.[6]

In an example from an Australian case,[7] a dissenting judge, Judge Burchett, makes this point in unequivocal terms: speaking of 'strong compassionate or humanitarian grounds':

> *does not require an applicant to suffer uniquely. There may be strong compassionate or humanitarian grounds for the grant of an entry permit to an applicant who happens to be able to apply, because already outside his country, though thousands of his compatriots are desperately situated but cannot even apply. The plight of German Jews in 1938 provides a ready illustration.*[8]

Often courts and tribunals apply too restrictive a test to this aspect of persecution, and this may result in less recognition for refugees, and less granting of refugee status. Of course, a decline in the number of refugees that follows the application of more rigorous tests to their cases would be purely definitional, hence not a true advancement of human rights and the rule of law.[9]

In contrast, the numbers of refugees are on the increase, especially from so-called 'natural disasters'.[10]

Perhaps the lack of definitional clarity that leaves uncertain the status of whole groups and communities contributes to the exclusion of persons fleeing from ecological disasters; each one may indeed share with others in his community a well-founded fear, but this individual sentiment is both shared and validated by equal or similar feelings on the part of fellow sufferers. The most vulnerable among these are those residing in developing countries, and within those, as well as elsewhere in the developed world, indigenous peoples:

> *De nouveaux indicateurs*[11] *montrent une très fort corrélation entre le niveau de développement d'un pays, et les taux de mortalité associé aux catastrophes naturelles. On estime aujourd'hui que plus d'un être humain sur deux habite dans une zone ou la probabilité de l'occurrence d'une ou plusieurs catastrophes naturelles est elevée.*[12]

But it would be an error to conclude that large groups of refugees only occur after ecological disasters; the number of refugees fleeing from 'ethnic cleansing', genocidal attempts or other conflict situations are also on the increase, especially, though not exclusively, in developing countries. Hence the importance of understanding the damaging aspects of an unclear or incomplete definition that does not clearly embrace the needs of groups, beyond the single individual.

The Convention on Refugees' (CSR's) own year of formulation, following World War II, clearly indicates that the plight of Jewish people fleeing from Nazi Germany could not have been far from the drafters' mind at the time.[13] But even allowing that ecological refugees are most properly defined as 'internally displaced persons' (IDPs) does not eliminate the necessity to clarify the issue of group persecution:

> *Where individual or collective measures of enforcement are employed, such as coercion by denial of employment or education, restriction on language and culture, denial of access to food supplies, expropriation of property without compensation, and forcible or involuntary relocation, then fear of persecution in the above sense may exist; mere membership of the affected group can be sufficient.*[14]

2. PERSECUTION OR LACK OF PROTECTION?

Persecution results where the measures in question harm those interests [protected interests] and the integrity and inherent dignity of the human being to a degree considered unacceptable under prevailing international standards.[15]

For the most part, ecological disasters and – in general – environmental conditions that might render a territory unsafe and unliveable are not the direct result of deliberate persecution by governments. Nevertheless, if they happen within governed territories, it is clear that the local or central government, or both, has allowed the activities that produced the hazardous results. In developing countries, it is often the case that the bureaucracy is complicit with the harm imposers, as corporate interests ensure that local governments receive economic benefits from their industrial operations as well as, at times, additional support for their own interests in clearing an area of unwanted populations.[16] There may also be special inducements for governments to agree to permit industrial operations when their own plans coincide with those of the industrial operation proposed.[17]

Domestic laws are intended to protect the life and basic rights of all citizens, including minorities, and that is, as indeed it should be, the main function of elected governments.[18]

When governments make 'deals' that advance their interest and those of their elites together with those of multinational corporations (MNCs) or other foreign interests, they are failing in their most basic obligation, and they are ultimately complicit in the harms that ensue.[19] The 1951 Convention is less than clear on this issue as well. The 1969 OAU Convention and, especially, the Cartagena Declaration,[20] define refugees more liberally than the CSR as:

> ... *every person who, owing to external aggression, occupation, foreign domination, or events seriously disturbing the public order in either part or the whole of his country of origin or nationality, is compelled to seek refuge in another country.*

This more liberal definition helps with the problem discussed in the previous section, as well as the present one. 'Aggression', 'occupation' and 'foreign domination' are not such that they can target a single individual, as they affect the whole community or region. Further, both 'occupation' and 'foreign domination' may also apply to economically motivated 'domination' of an area, and unwarranted intrusion into the affairs of non-consenting communities.[21]

Thus, from the perspective of lack of protection, the language of the Cartagena Declaration is equally helpful. Aside from the responsibility for the life and basic rights of individuals, governments are equally responsible for the protection of local communities from 'external aggression' and exploitation, no matter what particular shape such aggression might take.

Although states are not responsible for all possible human rights violations within their borders, often it is only the most fundamental rights that are considered for refugees, not any and all rights.[22] In addition, state power is not absolute, hence most of the difficulties affecting refugees are based on corporate activities that a state must recognize or stand accused of persecution, based on one of the five grounds. In fact, while seeking the reasons why some communities are so affected, many will disclose that the grounds of persecution are present.

The most important issue from our point of view at this time is whether state protection is present for IDPs, when humanitarian international law is not yet required to intervene, at least in principle:

> *From an international law perspective, primary responsibility for the protection and assistance of internationally displaced persons rests with the territorial state, in virtue of its sovereignty and the principles of non-intervention.*[23]

However, for IDPs, it is the lack of state protection, far more than persecution, that is the main issue. Pentassuglia explains the 'extralegal justifications of group protection', from the individualistic liberal political theory point of view:

- *individual (mainly civil and political) rights set limits on action of others (individuals and the state);*
- *the state serves as guarantor of such rights; and*
- *both the above combine to create a climate of individual choice.*[24]

Hence, even in a neoliberal context, state protection is an integral component of human rights. For IDPs, in the wake of environmentally hazardous circumstances, it is not 'individualists', but 'communitarians',[25] that is, those who put community and group interests over those of an individual, who should prevail.

State protection is a catch-all expression that incorporates several separate strands: there is (1) the direct physical protection exemplified by the presence of police forces for internal, domestic protection and armies for its transborder counterpart; then there is (2) the indirect protection that ought to be employed when certain groups and organizations victimize more vulnerable communities, as in all cases of non-consented industrial development in the territories of indigenous peoples and other local groups.

The latter also has at least two main aspects: (a) the industrial/economic interests' direct activities that are harmful to these communities are neither forbidden outright nor curbed in each instance; and (b), on more general grounds, the state's legal infrastructure is not capable or willing to legislate the restraints necessary to curb abuses. Where the second form of state protection is missing, both (a) and (b) apply, and the situation is akin to that which often faces school officials. It is the problem of bullying, which is not an illegal activity, but is very harmful to those who are vulnerable, as it violates the rights of the bullied children, and is increasingly being recognized as a dangerous phenomenon that must be curbed.[26] In other words, like bullying, these harmful activities are not clearly defined as illegal, but they should be recognized as harmful as well.

Although patently different from activities that physically abuse vulnerable communities, some elements of 'bullying' help to cast light on the difficulties inherent in the situations we are considering. First, it is the presence of nuances: bullying in schools ranges from name-calling or picking on and ridiculing a weaker child all the way to outright threats and even beatings. Bullying also combines inflicting physical and mental or emotional harms and manifests a form of discrimination against certain individuals or even groups.

Similarly, industrial activities are – for the most part – legal, even welcome in developing countries, as they bring economic benefits, especially to governing officials. Industrial activities are equally nuanced: they may range from mildly disturbing to ecosystems and local communities to hazardous to natural processes, wildlife and normal human development.[27] Again, like school authorities, the bureaucracies of developing countries or even Western democracies may be torn between the freedom of speech and choice of individuals and the limits required by the imposition of harms, through the exercise of those freedoms, especially by legal persons.

In the final analysis, the protection of children's health, both mental and physical, must take precedence over the choices and freedoms of other individuals. However, governing bodies seldom take such a stance in favour of vulnerable individuals and groups. In addition, the two situations share further common ground, upon which possible solutions might be based: they are such that after-the-fact solutions are less than optimal. Like emotional harms inflicted upon children, harms imposed on vulnerable populations should not be left to be resolved after the fact, and neither should be considered compensable liabilities. What is needed in both cases is the presence of regulations that do not allow either form of abuse *before* it happens.

For instance, certain chemical exposures from which IDPs are forced to flee impose reproductive harms,[28] developmental harms, and even intellectual and emotional harms.[29] The analogy here proposed, however, breaks down on the issue of individual versus collective rights. Although bullying targets the most vulnerable among children, the targets are always individuals, not groups, even if certain shared characteristics might help to view bullied children as a 'group'.

In fact, the existence of communal rights for IDPs is an additional burden in the quest for legal protection from states and international law, especially when these are persons from aboriginal communities. In the case of refugees and minorities in general, some consider collective rights to be a threat to the 'integrity' of states.[30] In contrast, the requirements of communitarian or group rights fit better with the international law regimes than they do with domestic instruments. For instance, in discussion of Article 27 of the ICCPR, UN Special Rapporteur Capotorti says:

> *It is inconceivable that the individuals forming a group may be entitled to treatment, based on advantages to be ensured to each member of the group. At the same time, this approach has significant repercussions on the status of the group as the formal holders of the rights described in it, but rather stresses the need for a collective exercise of such rights. Therefore it seems justified to conclude that a correct construction of this norm must be based on the idea of its double-effect protection of the group and its individual members.*[31]

Hence we can perhaps also speak of the 'collective exercise of individual rights' for IDPs, as we can for other ethnic or religious minorities, at least when the IDPs are a group of indigenous peoples. The divisions between those who view individual rights as paramount and those who view communitarian rights as most important have been argued in the scholarly literature for a long time.

Will Kymlicka's distinction between 'individualists' and 'collectivists'[32] is very helpful. It eliminates, at the outset, what he terms 'internal restrictions' from 'external protection',[33] thus assisting with the clarification of what he terms the 'ambiguity' of collective rights.[34] The main concern of this work is with 'external protection', as internal dissentions, or forms of internal governance that may not be entirely democratic or fully egalitarian, are beyond the scope of this discussion.

Hence, from the standpoint of 'external protection', in the next section we will start the examination of the grounds required to establish the presence of persecution for refuge-seekers, and also to examine these grounds in order to decide whether they might also be appropriate to IDPs.

3. THE ROLE OF RACIAL BACKGROUND IN REFUGEE AND IDP ISSUES

The first form of disenfranchisement within the scope of refugee law is that based on race. While the drafters of the Convention did not specifically define the term, the historical context makes clear that the intent was to include those Jewish victims of Nazism who had been persecuted because of their ethnicity, whether or not they actively practised their religion.[35]

Racial and ethnic backgrounds are most often the basis for persecution of large groups.[36] Recent history has a number of examples, such as those of Rwanda or Darfur. Indigenous groups are – almost by definition – distinct communities, identifiable as visible minorities and belonging to separate ethnic groups, not to be confused with the majority of a country's citizens. And herein lies the most difficult aspect of treating refugees and IDPs as groups possessing, for the most part, similar problems and similar goals for the solutions for those problems.

For instance, if we consider the problem of apartheid in South Africa or of racial discrimination in the US,[37] we notice that in these cases the persons involved were suffering because they were treated in a substantially different way than other citizens, who were white. Their aim was to regain equality with the other, dominant, racial majority. Parity was (and is) sought in housing, schooling, healthcare and, very often, environmental exposures. Bill Clinton's Executive Order of 11 February 1994[38] is a case in point: the same prompt assistance to communities of colour that the US Environmental Protection Agency used to provide to white communities. So equality is the aim of racial minorities, vis-à-vis a different racial majority.

But, as mentioned briefly in Chapter 1, the case of indigenous peoples is completely different: protection in their case cannot mean simple equality, as that would also imply assimilation; if successful that approach eventually eliminates them as a people. Hence the difficult problem that arises: how to ask for international protection on the basis of racial discrimination on the one hand, yet to demand special treatment, consonant with the group's *sui generis* status, on the other.

The recent Inuit Petition presented to the US Supreme Court, and spearheaded by Sheila Watt-Cloutier, is a case in point.[39] The Inuit of the Circumpolar Conference, ably represented by several lawyers, including James Anaya, argued that they had been unfairly targeted because of their ethnicity and the unique relationship to their territories, as the latter increasingly succumbed to global warming.

The Inuit are by no means the only population affected by climate change. But although the citizens of coastal cities, sub-Saharan Africa, island states and other affected locations may find the conditions of their lives becoming brutally harsh, not all of them are in the position of losing entirely their existence *as peoples* if they could be helped to relocate, the way the Inuit are. Their existence can be supported and re-established elsewhere in most cases. The different status of indigenous peoples can be seen in other regions and continents, for example the Pygmies of Congo, the former inhabitants of Chagos in the Indian Ocean and most other aboriginal communities.[40]

The Inuits are now presenting once again their plight to the European Court of Human Rights, requesting redress under CERD.[41] Their argument is not that the conditions of their lives are becoming increasingly intolerable and that therefore they seek refuge elsewhere, to seek a better life; rather they are essentially saying that those who impose the intolerable conditions must cease and desist, that those activities are in breach of major human rights instruments, and that hence the perpetrators should be punished and ought to be forced to offer compensation and mitigation for the present circumstances of the circumpolar peoples.

This is probably the best approach to the problem of all IDPs (and environmental refugees), but it is absolutely necessary for indigenous peoples. The whole Earth is presently affected by both climate change and various industrial toxic exposures. Even if it were feasible, moving populations from one site to another would be presently difficult, and probably impossible in the future. Analogously, populations moving westward at the time of the arrival of the first Europeans in North and South America eventually had no place to which to migrate, no territory left to conquer and colonize.

Hence, the threats presented by climate change and toxic industrial exposures have rendered most of the Earth hazardous to all life, including humans. Mitigation is possible only in wealthy nations, and that will simply postpone the inevitable, ongoing ecological collapse. But for indigenous peoples, living on and off the land and water, the present hazardous conditions, imposed by so-called 'development', represent a form of biological genocide.[42] Also, perhaps they could be termed conditions of persecution, imposed because of the vulnerability for these peoples, based on their ethnicity, which precludes equal access to the centres of power. We will return to this problem in the next chapter.

For now we need to focus on the role of 'race' once again. On the one hand, indigenous groups may join with other refugee groups pleading well-founded fear of persecution on the grounds of race. On the other, they must demand special treatment, special protection precisely on the bases of their race and ethnicity, which render their situation unlike that of any other group of refugees or IDPs. The key concept in their case is that of the environment and their relationship to it.

That relationship is more direct and more necessary than that of other groups, as well as providing the basis for their uniqueness, their special ethnicity and their 'cultural integrity'. Theirs is not simply a valuable historical situation of academic interest to some scholars. It represents the basis of a respectful interaction with the Earth that most modern citizens of other communities can no longer sustain.[43]

That said, it is clear that indigenous peoples represent far more than a tradition in our past history. They also indicate and instantiate in their traditional cultures the principles upon which the future of humanity must be based. To disrespect, let alone persecute, those who proudly live that specific ethnicity and culture is not only to impose irreparable harm on aboriginal communities, but also to ignore, at our own grave risk, the lessons we should learn to help us protect and ensure our future.[44]

The original drafters of the Convention and of the United Nations High Commissioner for Refugees (UNHCR) certainly did not have indigenous peoples in mind, as Hathaway clearly indicates.[45] He cites their recommended definition as follows:

> *Race, in the present connexion, has to be understood in its widest sense to include all kinds of ethnic groups that are referred to as 'races' in common usage. Frequently it will entail membership of a specific social group of common descent forming a minority within a larger population.*[46]

He goes on to write that:

> *this UNHCR-derived interpretation has been explicitly adopted into Canadian law in a series of decisions, commencing with Boleslaw Dylow, as well as immigration policy guidelines. The relevant case law has equated race with ethnic background,*[47] *'heritage'*[48] *and 'distinct minority' status.*[49]

Some of the language of the Immigration Appeal Board decisions are particularly appropriate for Canadian First Nations (FNs), as well as for other aboriginal communities. The same can be said about the next two 'grounds' under discussion: nationality and religion.

4. NATIONALITY

> *International law does not require threatened individuals to exhaust all options within their own country first, before seeking asylum; that is, it does not consider asylum to be the last resort. The concept of internal flight or relocation alternatively should therefore not be invoked in a manner that would undermine important human rights tenets.*[50]

This issue sharply divides other environmental refugees from those needing to leave an aboriginal community, most clearly in Canada. The context for indigenous peoples in Canada is that they are presently living as First Nations or territories: they are therefore in Canada, but their self-government, limited though it is, and their appellation as 'First Nations', separates them from other Canadian citizens. They are *in* Canada, but in some sense they are not *of* Canada, if they are presently living the traditional lifestyle in the territories they have historically occupied. They are, however, still Canadian, so that the government of Canada owes them, minimally, the protection that is owed all other citizens of the country.

However, as the Canadian government also recognizes their *sui generis* relationship with their land, it must also owe them more than that, precisely because of that relationship, which is explicitly recognized in both provincial and federal legal instruments.[51] To be sure, it can also be said that the states owes *all* its citizens protection from environmental conditions that are hazardous to their health. The abundant scientific research that is available from public health bodies such as the World Health Organization (WHO) and epidemiologists indicates clearly the many aspects of environmental harms to which we are all exposed.[52] The extent of the scientific findings today indicate the extent of the duty to protect both directly and indirectly from such harms: it is the state that has the obligation to regulate and restrain the sources of these harms, that is the industrial activities that are pursued by domestic and multinational corporations. These activities give primacy to the economic results that benefit corporate persons. Especially in the developing world, but also in Western developed countries, the environmental and health effects are viewed as 'collateral',[53] not as intended imposition of harm.

The reality of most aspects of globalized trade is that it is hazardous to the citizens of all countries in the world. Recent studies regarding the effects of farmed animals and all sorts of processed foods in the exponential growth of cancers (especially prostate, breast and colon cancer)[54] are a definitive step forward, as not only obesity, but the sort of diets on which affluent Western people live are increasingly indicted in the exponential spread of these diseases as well as heart disease. However, even these studies tend to place the onus on individual choices, while they neglect the presence of chemical additives such as growth hormones, antibiotics, preservative agents and colorants in all processed food, including factory-farmed animals and farm-raised fish. Against these insidious product additives, even the wealthy have little recourse, except those who can afford organically grown food and are most likely vegetarians or following the Mediterranean diet promoted by the WHO.

Wealth, however, makes a difference in other environmental exposures. It erects a temporary barrier between the harmful activity and the physical presence of citizens. Poverty eliminates the possibility of defending oneself from exposures by finding a different occupation or perhaps seeking a different location for oneself and one's family. Poverty effectively closes all these avenues.[55] Hence, for instance, 'equal treatment' is largely non-existent, as 'brown fields', that is areas already used for other hazardous enterprises,[56] continue to offer corporations the 'best' economic alternative to site their operations.

There are two major considerations that make even 'equal treatment' insufficient in the case of indigenous peoples. One is the fact that poverty, in their case, conspires with the economic approach that directs corporate industrial activities, just as it does for people of colour in developed countries. The second consideration applies to aboriginal peoples in developing countries, where most of the sought-after resources are still found. That is where the oil, gold, diamonds, silver and other commodities are; therefore, even if the area represents a sacred traditional landscape, or is close to the boundaries of a traditional community who depend on the clean water, healthy wildlife and functioning ecosystems in the area for their survival, corporate interests still move in to enforce their brand of 'development'.

A case in point might be that of the Mayan community at Sipakapa in Guatemala and the Glamis Gold Corporation.[57] The community, comprising agricultural families of Mayan descent, lives on the land and practises sheep farming in the high and dry regions of the *altiplano*. Water is always an issue for both crop irrigation and family use. Hence when Glamis Gold sought their 'consent' for their development plans, the overwhelming majority of the area's inhabitants responded by asking what the 'development' was expected to do for them. However, their 'no' was not heeded, as the central government dealt directly with the corporation, simply ignoring the fact that such unconsented development was contrary to their own constitution, as well as to the tenets of international law.

While the case was debated in the courts, the unconsented operations continued, and the community had to face fields polluted by leaching cyanide ponds and not enough water for either family use or irrigation.[58] The question here is 'nationality' in the sense that, while they are part of Guatemala, just as First Nations and Nunavut or Northwest Territories are parts of Canada, their local decision making should have been, for the most part, in their own hands.

Hence to interfere with that process is indeed to attack an aboriginal community that, in some sense at least, is a 'nation', a partially self-governing entity which is indeed attacked as such, as wealthy Guatemalans in their cities are not treated in the same way, any more than are Canadian residents of Toronto, Vancouver or smaller Canadian cities. Self-governance per se does not create a separate nation, but it indicates even more clearly the aboriginal peoples' *sui generis* relationship to their lands.

Indigenous communities have borders; in fact their territories' demarcation has often been the result of hard-fought battles in the courts. Whatever these borders eventually are, they certainly are not flexible, that is, no indigenous group may ask for another, safer territory, beyond its own community's borders. Unlike even the poorest people affected by environmental disasters, their culture, their traditions, their way of life, hence their national identity, are not portable.

One may recall Katrina's effect of the African American poor in New Orleans. Whatever their commitment to their area of residence, had they received the appropriate facilitations their plight could have been eased by an effective relocation plan and the reconstruction of the properties they had lost. African Americans are an ethnic group within a national population, but they are not a separate community with at least a partial form of self-governance and a traditional history connected to one place and one place only.

The same *sui generis* relationship to the land will also form the basis of the aboriginal peoples' position regarding both 'religion' and 'social group'; hence these two issues will be discussed together in the next section.

5. RELIGION AND PARTICULAR SOCIAL GROUPS

At first, considerations of religion and social grouping appear to be truly remote from the issues affecting large groups of refugees, forced to migrate because of grave environmental problems, whether man-made or natural.[59] Religion in general should be an intensely personal, internal experience. In addition, it may generally be practised anywhere: Christians persecuted in the Roman Empire went underground in the catacombs that are still visible today, as one of Rome's many great archaeological sites. Hence, for the most part, both beliefs and practices are not site-specific, with the exception of holy places that should be visited at specific times for many of the great religions, such as Mecca for Islam or the Vatican for Roman Catholicism.

In contrast, both the concept of the sacred, most religious practices and the Earth itself at a particular location are fundamental to the religious beliefs and observances of indigenous communities. Like their 'nationhood' and their local self-governance, their religion is not portable, or transferable to another area. In fact, many cases in international law include specific references to aboriginal religious beliefs, as they are tied to the significance of specific places. This is true of the jurisprudence in both Canada and the US under the Alien Torts Claims Act (ATCA).

For instance, the Oka case in Canada, which eventually culminated in a blockade and armed confrontation with the Mohawks in Quebec, and brought in the provincial army to 'resolve' the situation, started with the Mohawks' outrage at the local decision to build a golf course over an old burial place of their community.[60] Another similar case involved an aboriginal burial place and the French government,[61] and this cultural/religious harm was part of the plaintiffs' detailed narrative about the harm they suffered. This case hinged on the harms to their 'cultural integrity', which is one of the grounds upon which indigenous peoples' rights are based. The cultural integrity of aboriginal groups is protected in both international and domestic law,[62] and it is also included in the mandates of the International Covenant on Economic, Social and Cultural Rights (ICESCR).

Their cultural integrity, in turn, is based upon their specific social group or community's traditions. These are place-based, so that the cultural integrity of indigenous peoples cannot exist without its foundation in the ecological integrity of their lands.[63] Hence their forced flight from these areas represents an attack on their religion, their ethnicity and their group affiliations, but also on their existence as a people. This point applies best in a discussion of IDPs, or environmental refugees, because the definition found in the CSR does not include them.

The same argument becomes substantially weaker, however, when we appeal to the Genocide Convention instead, because of the 'intent' aspect of that instrument, as William Schabas, for instance, argues.[64] In contrast, for the CSR, it is the well-foundedness of the fear facing the migrants that bases their claims, as argued above.

The well-founded fear itself is based on two factors: (1) the subjective, mental state of the refuge seeker and (2) the objective conditions in his former country of residence that have prompted his flight, which of course include the general intent to persecute on the part of governments.

The fear of total elimination as a people, losing one's traditions, holy sites and socially cohesive community, is a real one. When indigenous peoples find themselves in a changed landscape, whether because of global warming in the Arctic or desertification and famine conditions in the global South, or even in territories that have become unsafe and unhealthy, then it seems that the conditions required by the CSR's definition have been met. Yet even if this is the case, and if, contrary to common practice, IDPs and environmental refugees in general are but a subspecies of asylum seekers, as El Hinnawi has argued,[65] the expected remedy cannot be applied to mass migrations of people. Even if – *per absurdum* – it could be applied, it would be counterproductive in the case of aboriginal peoples of all continents.

Nevertheless, as we consider the status of millions of people, who may not be deliberately targeted, but who are suffering under all the aspects mentioned above, because of negligence on the part of corporate actors and complicit governments,[66] or 'collateralism',[67] or 'wilful blindness',[68] it is imperative that some just solutions be found, and we will return to that topic below. For now, there is one final reason for persecution to be discussed, that is 'political opinion'.

6. POLITICAL OPINIONS

Are there any particular 'political opinions' that contribute to the hazards to which indigenous peoples are exposed? Even in the case of this 'reason', indigenous peoples present an entirely different situation from that of other environmental refugees. Thus the first point to note is that the latter, as such, are not characterized by any specific political opinions that may run counter to the expectations and beliefs of their country of origin, let alone those who contribute to the ecological problems they encounter.

The situation is different, however, when we consider aboriginal communities. Whatever their country of origin, for the most part they share the beliefs that the land they inhabit, and whatever lived on it or is produced therein, does not belong to each of them singly, but is held in common. In Canada and elsewhere, legal instruments confirm this anomaly.[69] Actually, this position represents more than a political opinion: it is a deeply held traditional belief, part of indigenous peoples' worldview. Each tribe and community is understood to be part of the territory they inhabit; yet they do not own it, but are part of the natural rhythms that nature exhibits in different regions, according to different seasons.

In some sense, therefore, rather than a political opinion, this worldview represents one element of their religious beliefs, as discussed in the previous section. But there is an aspect of this approach that has important and far-reaching political implications, unwanted and unaccepted by both the host country and the multinational economic interests that stand behind the 'development' to which the hazardous conditions are owed. Corporate development is based on capitalism, which in turn relies on the principle of private ownership.[70] For this reason, the initial aspect of seeking to develop an area where aboriginal peoples dwell, on the part of various industrial interests, starts often with an attempt to influence this aspect of their self-governance. A demarcated border around a community is far harder to ignore (and to breach) than a number of individually owned and held houses and plots of land.[71]

Hence the deepest beliefs of indigenous peoples tend to run counter to the tenets of capitalism, 'development' and even globalization. As such, they are not viewed favourably and, most often, they are not respected. These beliefs cannot be classified as 'political opinions', as they are more fundamental and unchanging than that. They must be treated, instead, as the instantiation of a worldview that is *lived*; hence it is far more than an 'opinion' that might be changed by various marketing tools and campaigns of persuasion.

7. FURTHER CONSIDERATIONS ON THE RULE OF LAW AND THE NEW GLOBAL POLITICS: THE APPEAL OF LIMOGES

The first question that has to be addressed when one thinks about issues of justice that transcend the normative boundaries of state, is whether one is looking for principles of international or global justice. Whereas the former view takes political communities organized into states to be the main agents of justice, the latter takes persons, regardless of their political membership, as the primary focus of justice.[72]

The year 2008 was the 60th anniversary of the United Nations General Assembly's Universal Declaration of Human Rights (UDHR). It also saw the culmination and recognition of the grave harms perpetrated upon the Earth, harms that include the environment, and all the life that depends upon it. The recognition of the ongoing disintegrity and degradation is at a peak.[73]

Starting with Al Gore's Nobel Prize for his work on global warming, and the scientific work of the IPCC on the same topic, the recognition of global change and all its implications has now arrived in many sectors.

But the results of global harms, that is the migration of peoples, fleeing from unliveable environmental conditions in all continents of the Earth, is not often discussed or even acknowledged. Given that the CSR deals primarily with individual rights, and given the proliferation of these rights in contrast with the lack of collective rights instruments (several Western nations did not sign the United Nations Declaration on the Rights of Indigenous Peoples[74], the opponents being the US, Canada, Australia and New Zealand), and no new formulation of the Convention on the Status of Refugees appears to be in the works at this time. Yet the 60th anniversary of the UDHR is a milestone that might be appropriately celebrated by a revision of the CSR, as it dates from 1951, with particular emphasis on the question of IDPs, given the accumulation of evidence regarding ecological refugees.

It is primarily a question of justice, and not only of international justice; that is, it is not only the problem of the fair treatment of questions between states; rather, it is a matter of *global*, transnational justice. We are living, as Pogge argues, in a 'skewed global order that aggravates international inequalities and makes it exceedingly hard for the weaker and poorer societies to secure a proportional share of global economic growth'.[75]

Aside from the unsustainability of 'economic growth', no matter who may be enjoying it,[76] given the finitude of the Earth's systems, we are facing conditions of 'multiple dominations',[77] as the treatment of asylum seekers after the flight, as well as that of local communities that will eventually become ecological migrants or refugees, are causally related to the dominant economic powers that destroy their safety and life conditions.

We can therefore say with Forst that 'the question of power is the first question of justice', not only in general, as he argues, but also in the specific circumstances we are discussing. The basis of this claim is that the present situation of injustice is not limited to the practices of the institutions of specific states, whose interdependence is not characterized by social cooperation, let alone adherence to high moral principles. Non-state actors such as international institutions and multinational corporations are even less likely to be constrained by principles of justice of any kind, despite their status as transnational entities. Forst considers these multiple problems and adds that:

> *there is a global ecological context of institutions, from the United Nations to the International Monetary Fund (IMF), as well as the non-governmental institutions (Greenpeace and Amnesty International for example), of migrations within and across continents; and there is, of course, an ever growing global context of cultural production, consumption and communication.*[78]

That said, and in the additional context of forced displacements, we do not face conditions of reciprocity and collaboration among different actors, rather:

> *what emerges is a complex system of one-sided and largely coerced cooperation and dependency, rather than interdependence.*[79]

This system is characterized by domination, both internal (as states may be dominated by less than legitimate governments, or elites of various kinds) as well as external, as only a few benefit from the present market-oriented globalization, and these few do not include a nation's poor.[80]

True global justice is cosmopolitan.[81] The Universal Declaration of Human Rights (1948) proclaims the universal applicability of human rights, but is largely silent about the universal obligations to ensure and secure these rights. For instance, Article 1 ascribes rights to all human beings, and according to Article 2 'no distinction shall be made on the basis of the political, jurisdictional or international status of the country or territory to which a person belongs'.

In this case, 'everyone' surely includes all the inhabitants of communities that are the victims of so-called 'development', engendered – to paraphrase O'Neill – by various 'agents of injustice', rather than agents of justice as discussed in her work. From our point of view, Article 14 is particularly relevant:

Article 14
1   Everyone has the right to seek and enjoy in other countries asylum from persecution.
2   This right may not be invoked in the case of prosecutions genuinely arising from non-political crimes or from acts contrary to the purposes and principles of the United Nations.

Hence countries, in general, have the obligation to admit all refugees and guarantee their rights: that role should apply to both the country of origin of ecological refugees, and the country where they end their flight, if they cross a border. Forst and O'Neill address the morality of the current global situation and its complex injustices, as does Thomas Pogge. However, the legal framework within which the injustices and the human rights breaches occur are not considered explicitly in their work.

Recently, some legal scholars have addressed the international law components of these complex systems:

> *There needs to be a move beyond these existing international law models because, in light of contemporary changes in law and politics, the theoretical structures cannot adequately account for present foreign policy making. A better understanding of the present international legal system's role in contemporary global politics is urgently needed.*[82]

The new 'humanity's law' or humanitarianism is, in fact, the legal regime that is most often used for IDPs, as we saw, because they do not presently qualify for the protection available under the CSR, as they do not have refugee status. Humanitarianism has dramatically expanded the reach of the law, because of its 'merger with international human rights law'.[83] This recent change in the global rule of law promises a new discourse, and a wider reach for criminal justice in the protection of human rights (see Chapter 6 below for a discussion of humanitarian law for the protection of IDPs).

Perhaps the 60th anniversary of the Universal Declaration of Human Rights might lead to the application of the law of war to the problem of ecological refugees, and we might see its extension to:

> *... situations of internal political conflict. Contemporary humanitarian law reaches well beyond the parameters of international armed conflict to regulate persecution internal to states as evidenced in the new treaties, charters and ad hoc tribunals.*[84]

The 'regulation of persecution', as an aspect of an ongoing change and perhaps a new global law, may well provide the starting point for the recognition that the CSR is in dire need of revision and expansion, as the environmental and health hazards that are increasingly causative of large migrations today cannot be ignored by an international community committed to the protection of human rights.

Perhaps a fruitful starting point for a review of the CSR may be found in the 'Appeal of Limoges':[85] The Appeal starts by restating the '*problematique*' of the age:

> (a) *The environmental situation is alarming, given the increasing ecological degradation;*
> (b) *The cases of degradation include desertification, epidemics, climate change, deforestation, soil erosion, armed conflicts and other risks, both natural and technological;*
> (c) *These causes involve the displacement of populations, which should appropriately be termed the displacement of ecological refugees;*
> (d) *Present international law regarding refugees does not include any instrument that envisions the conditions of ecological refugees, and that might be invoked in their favour;*
> (e) *These ecological refugees may be present within their country, or they may be forced to flee their borders;*
> (f) *But the number of refugees is increasing in proportion to the actually increasing rhythm of degradation;*
> (g) *The participants in the Limoges meeting appeal to their countries, to regional and international organizations, and to all citizens to reflect upon these facts and to support and attempt to develop and implement the following propositions:*

They are invited to:

1 Acknowledge the situation of ecological refugees;
2 Accept and proclaim an international statute of ecological refugees that will permit the protection of this separate category of refugees;
3 Act to prevent the different causes that lead to the creation of ecological refugees (catastrophes, poor management and planning regarding natural resources, armed conflicts and so on):
   - through a stronger application of presently existing regulatory regimes, national, regional and international, in order to fight against attacks on the natural environment, or on safety and public health in all its manifestations;
   - through the elaboration of new texts in order to achieve the same objectives, and through reinforcing mechanisms for the application of present regimes;
4 To respond to urgent situations of all kinds, in order to assist ecological refugees:
   - to enact financial and institutional dispositions for that assistance;
   - to rehabilitate habitats that have been destroyed;
   - to define and create an international Agency [of 'green helmets'], to be represented in each region of the world;
5 To elaborate long-term policies intended to protect ecological refugees:
   - through the creation of an international fund to aid ecological refugees, or through the redeployment of existing funds;
   - to assign specific responsibilities to one or several of the institutions of the United Nations, especially by widening the responsibility of the High Commissioner for Refugees;
   - to study the opportunity to elaborate a specific Convention for the Protection of Ecological Refugees or a specific international treaty. (Loosely translated from the French by the author)

In the following chapters, we will appeal to most of the issues singled out in this document, in order to elaborate on the various points raised, and to research present jurisprudence that might be applicable.

NOTES

1 Palley, C. (1978) *Constitutional Law and Minorities*, Report no 36, Minority Rights Group, London.
2 Goodwin-Gill, G. S. (1996) *The Refugee in International Law* (second edition), Clarendon Press, Oxford, UK, p76.
3 *Gunaleela versus Minister for Immigration and Ethnic Affairs* (1978) 74, ALR 263.
4 Crawford, J. and Hyndman, P. (1989) 'Three heresies in the application of the refugee convention', *International Journal of Refugee Law*, vol 1, no 2, pp155–160.
5 Ibid.
6 Ibid; UNHCR (1979) *Handbook on Procedures and Criteria for Determining Refugee Status*, UNHCR, Geneva, paragraph 65.
7 *Simmathamby versus Minister for Immigration and Ethnic Affairs* (1986), 66 ALR 502 506.

8   Crawford and Hyndman, op cit Note 4.
9   Ibid, p167.
10 Myers, N. (1993) 'Environmental refugees in a globally warmed world', *Bioscience*, vol 43, pp752–761; Cournil, C. and Mazzega, P. (2006) 'Catastrophes écologiques et flux migratoires: comment protéger les "réfugiés écologiques"?', *Revue Européenne de Droit de l'Environnement*, no 4, December, p417.
11 UNDP (2004) *Reducing Disaster Risk: A Challenge for Development*, Bureau for Crisis Prevention and Recovery, United Nations Development Programme, New York.
12 Cournil and Mazzega, op cit Note 10, pp418–419.
13 Hathaway, J. (1991) *The Law of Refugee Status*, Butterworth's, Toronto.
14 Goodwin-Gill (1996), op cit Note 2, p77; also note that 'the 1990 US Asylum Regulations explicitly dispense with the "singling out" or "targeting" requirement, if the affected applicant can show a pattern or practice', 8CFR§ 208.13 (b)(2)(1); §208.16 (3)(i)(ii).
15 Goodwin-Gill, op cit Note 2, p77.
16 See Talisman case, Westra, L. (2007) *Environmental Justice and the Rights of Indigenous Peoples*, Earthscan, London, Chapter 6.
17 Rosencranz, A. and Campbell, R. (1999) 'Foreign environmental and human rights suits against US corporations in US courts', *Stanford Environmental Law Journal*, vol 18.
18 Gostin, L. O. (2008) 'Meeting basic survival needs of the world's least healthy people: Toward a framework convention on global health', *Georgetown Law Journal*, vol 96, no 2, January, pp331–392.
19 Westra, L. (2004) *Ecoviolence and the Law*, Transnational Publishers Inc., Ardsley, NY.
20 Convention Governing the Specific Aspects of Refugee Problems in Africa, Organization of African Unity (OAU) (1969) 10 September, Addis Ababa; Cartagena Declaration, UNGA, 30 November 1973; Res 3068 (XXVIII), into force 18 July 1976.
21 Westra, L. (2007), op cit Note 16, Chapter 6.
22 Goodwin-Gill, op cit Note 2, p79.
23 Ibid, p264.
24 Pentassuglia, G. (2002) *Minorities in International Law*, Council of Europe Publishing, Koelblin-Fortuna, Druck, Germany, p46.
25 Ibid, p47.
26 Dyson, R. (2000) *Mind Abuse in an Information Age*, Black Rose Press, Montreal, Canada.
27 For a discussion of the public health harms endemic to chemical and industrial exposures, see Westra, L. (2007), op cit Note 16, Chapter 8.
28 WHO (2002) 'Summary', in *World Report on Violence and Health*, WHO, Geneva.
29 Grandjean, P. and Landrigan, P. (2006) 'Developmental neurotoxicity of industrial chemicals', *The Lancet*, November; see also Westra, L. (2007), op cit Note 16, Chapter 8.
30 Pentassuglia (2002), op cit Note 24, p47.
31 Capotorti, F. (1979) 'Study on the rights of persons belonging to ethnic religions and linguistic minorities', UN Doc. E/CN.4 Sub.2/384/Rev/I, 1979, 353–354; see also Pentassuglia (2002), op cit Note 24, pp48–49.
32 Kymlicka, W. (1995) *Multicultural Citizenship*, Oxford University Press, Oxford, UK, p47.
33 Ibid, p45.
34 Ibid.
35 Hathaway, op cit Note 13, p141.
36 Goodwin-Gill (1996), op cit Note 2, p43; Grahl-Madsen, A. (1966) *The Status of Refugees in International Law: Volume 1*, A. W. Sijthoff, Leyden, pp217–218.
37 Bullard, R. (2001) 'Decision making', in Westra and Lawson (eds) *Faces of Environmental Racism* (second edition), Rowman Littlefield, Lanham, MD.
38 Executive Order 12898, 'Federal actions to address environmental justice in minority populations and low-income populations', Federal Registers No. 32.

39 7 December 2005, see www.earthjustice.org/library/legal_docs/petition-to-the-inter-american-commission-on-human-rights-on-behalf-of-the-inuit-circumpolar-conference.pdf.
40 Westra, L. (2006) *Environmental Justice and the Rights of Unborn and Future Generations*, Earthscan, London, Chapter 6; see also Chapter 3 of this volume.
41 International Convention on the Elimination of all Forms of Racial Discrimination (1965), Article 14(1), 660 UNTS 195, 230 5 ILM 350.
42 Lemkin, R. (1944) *Axis Rule in Occupied Europe*, Carnegie Endowment for International Peace, Washington, DC.
43 Westra, L. (2006), op cit Note 40, Chapter 9; see also the Earth Charter for a soft law expression of that approach.
44 Westra, L. (2006 and 2007), op cit Notes 40 and 16.
45 Hathaway, op cit Note 13.
46 UNHCR (1979), op cit Note 6.
47 Pierre Katanku Tshiabut Tshibola, Immigration Appeal Board Decision M84-1074, 30 May 1985.
48 Ganganee Janet Permanand, Immigration Appeal Board Decision T87-10167, 10 August 1967.
49 Boleslaw Dylow, Immigration Appeal Board Decision V87-6040X, 7 July 1987; Hathaway, op cit Note 13, p142.
50 UNHCR (2003) 'Guidelines on international protection: Internal flight or relocation alternative within the context of Articles 1A(2) of the 1951 Convention and/or 1967 Protocol relating to the status of refugees', HCR/GIP/03/04, UNHCR, 23 July, No. 4.
51 Westra, L. (2006), op cit Note 40, Chapter 6.
52 Grandjean and Landrigan, op cit Note 29; Soskolne, C. L. (ed) (2007) *Sustaining Life on Earth*, Lexington Books, Lanham, MD.
53 Leader, S. (2004) 'Collateralism', in R. Brownsword (ed) *Global Governance and the Quest for Justice* (Volume IV), Hart Publishing, Oxford, UK.
54 Grandjean and Landrigan, op cit Note 29.
55 Pogge, T. (2008) 'Aligned: Global justice and ecology', in L. Westra, K. Bosselmann and R. Westra (eds) *Reconciling Human Existence with Ecological Integrity*, Earthscan, London, pp147–158.
56 Gaylord, C. and Bell, E. (2001) 'Environmental justice: A national priority', in L. Westra and B. Lawson (eds) *Faces of Environmental Racism*, Rowman Littlefield, Lanham, MD.
57 Caracol Production, Guatemala (2005) 'Sipakapa no se vende', www.sipakapanosevende.org.
58 See also Westra, L. (2007), op cit Note 16, Chapter 6.
59 El Hinnawi, E. (1985) *Environmental Refugees*, United Nations Environment Programme (UNEP), Nairobi, Kenya; see also Chapter 1 of this volume.
60 Westra, L. (1997) 'Terrorism at Oka', in A. Wellington, A. Greenbaum and W. Cragg (eds) *Canadian Issues in Environmental Ethics*, Broadview Press, Peterborough, Ontario, Canada.
61 *Hopu and Besent versus France*, UN GAOR, 52nd Session, Supplement No. 4, O.N. Doc. A/52/40 (1997).
62 Westra, L. (2007), op cit Note 16, Chapter 1; see also Anaya, S. J. (2004) *Indigenous Peoples in International Law*, 2nd edition, Oxford University Press, Oxford, UK.
63 Westra, L. (2007), op cit Note 16, Chapter 1.
64 Schabas, W. (2000) *On Genocide in International Law*, Kluwer Publishing, The Hague; see also Westra, L. (2007), op cit Note 16, Chapter 7 for a contrasting argument.
65 El Hinnawi, op cit Note 59.
66 Edgerton, H. W. (1927) 'Negligence, inadvertence and indifference', *Harvard Law Review*, vol 39, p849.
67 Leader, op cit Note 53.

68 Westra, L. (2004), op cit Note 19.
69 Westra, L., Miller, P., Karr, J. R., Rees, W. and Ulanowitz, R. E. (2000) 'Ecological integrity and the aims of the Global Integrity Project', in D. Pimentel, L. Westra and R. F. Noss (eds) *Ecological Integrity: Integrating Environment, Conservation and Health*, Island Press, Washington, DC.
70 Westra, R. (2008) 'Socio-material communication in eco-sustainable societies', in L. Westra, K. Bosselmann and R. Westra (eds) *Reconciling Ecological Existence with Ecological Integrity*, Earthscan, London, UK, pp303–318.
71 Borrows, J. (1997/1998) 'Frozen rights in Canada: Constitutional interpretation and the trickster', *American Indian Law Review*, vol 22, pp37–64.
72 Forst, R. (2001) 'Towards a critical theory of transnational justice', in T. W. Pogge (ed) *Global Justice*, Blackwell Publishers, Oxford, UK, pp169–179.
73 World Science Forum, UNESCO, Budapest, 7–10 November 2007; anecdotally, in 2005 the World Science Forum, also organized by UNESCO, in Budapest from 10–12 November, concentrated primarily on talks about funding required by scientists to continue their research and on proposing some vaguely worded responsibility of science to society. This author presented on environmental 'responsibility', primarily to unborn and future generations, at a special, marginalized session that included some references to the Earth Charter as well. The conference in 2007 focused on 'investing in knowledge, investing in the future', and the issue of future generations in relation to climate change, the increasing ecological footprint of Western nations and over-consumption, from the standpoint of systems science, was central.
74 UN Declaration on the Rights of Indigenous Peoples, GA Res. 61/295 on 13 September 2007.
75 Pogge, T. (2001) 'Priorities of global justice', *Metaphilosophy*, vol 32, p17.
76 Wackernagel, M. and Rees, W. E. (1996), *Our Ecological Footprint*, New Society Publishers, Gabriola Island, Canada.
77 Forst, op cit Note 72, p176.
78 Ibid; see also Held, D., McGrew, A., Goldblatt, D. and Perraton, J. (1999) *Global Transformations: Politics, Economics and Culture*, Polity Press, Oxford, UK.
79 Forst, op cit Note 72.
80 Ibid, p175.
81 O'Neill, O. (2001) 'Agents of justice', in T. Pogge (ed) *Global Justice*, Blackwell Publishers, Oxford, UK, p188.
82 Teitel, R. (2002) 'Humanity's law: Rule of law for the new global politics', *Cornell International Law Journal*, vol 35, pp355–356.
83 Ibid, p359.
84 Ibid, pp360–361.
85 Appel de Limoges sue les Réfugiés Écologiques (et Environnementaux), adopted in Limoges, France, 23 June 2005, compiled by the Scientific Committee of the Faculty of Law and Economic Sciences of the University of Limoges and the Directors of CRIDEAU/CNRS/INRA and the OMIJ.

CHAPTER 3

State Protection and State Responsibility to Ecological Refugees

1. INTRODUCTION

The alien was to be protected, not because he was a member of one's family, clan or religious community, but because he was a human being. In the alien, therefore, man discovered the idea of humanity.[1]

In this chapter we will review the responsibility of states to apply what is, ultimately, an international legal instrument in the domestic setting, as well as the responsibility to monitor corporate and institutional behaviour, to ensure that local environmental conditions are kept at a safe level so that hazardous situations requiring the flight of affected people will not arise.

The United Nations High Commissioner for Refugees (UNHCR) prescribes certain procedures to be followed regarding all applicants for asylum in all countries. But the governments of most countries find themselves in an invidious position as their obligation to apply the Convention on Refugees (CSR) to refugees at their borders often conflicts with the strong opinion of their constituents regarding these admissions:[2]

In the context of Western host societies, in particular, a discourse separating 'deserving' refugees from those deemed to be 'undeserving' or 'false' governs and restricts the acceptance of refugees.[3]

In fact the general public tends to react either with mistrust for those seen to be abusing the system, or with strong feelings of rejection, especially in the cases of weaker domestic economies or situations of high unemployment, where all asylum seekers are viewed as usurpers or unfair 'contenders' for the Western countries' 'real' citizens in their quest for jobs.

In addition, however, the CSR as a specific international human rights instrument has no mechanism that it can employ in order to ensure compliance from states since it relies entirely on the latter's goodwill.[4] Hence, in this chapter, we will consider, first, how best to trigger state responsibility against the background of present reality, before discussing what other instruments could be called upon to establish the gravity of states' obligation to comply. At the same time, the insufficiency of the CSR's purview, starting from its dated definition of refugee, will also be re-examined in the light of today's global change.[5]

2. THE RESPONSIBILITY OF STATES

Whatever the intentions of the drafters, the nature, scope and geopolitical setting of refugee protection today simply differ too fundamentally from the reality of 1951 for the Convention's rights regime to be taken seriously as the baseline of the international response to involuntary migration.[6]

The very need for international intervention in refugee issues depends on the actions of the state involved. There is the state from which the person or group is fleeing, and the responsibility they may bear for allowing, or not mitigating, the conditions that make life unliveable for individuals and groups, in various ways. Then there is the state to which the individuals or groups first arrive on the way to their desired destination. Finally there is the state they are attempting to reach.

Even at their final destination, refugees may be detained, put in special camps or held in various jail-like receiving areas:

Most disturbingly, asylum seekers can be detained for failing to arrive with the necessary travel documents, and can remain in detention for the entire length of the asylum process. And while many states have established special holding centres for asylum seekers and irregular migrants, in other countries they are detained in regular jails, alongside common criminals.[7]

Hathaway and Neve's lengthy study of the realities of the refugees' situation clearly demonstrates the urgent need for reform.[8]

There are at least two major initial problems with the refugee situation today: the first is procedural – that is, connected with the way in which they are treated when they attempt to enter a country; the second is substantive – that is, it refers to the treatment refugees receive once they are admitted.

2a. *Non-refoulement*, interception and other difficulties encountered by asylum seekers

The Executive Committee ... (b) expressed the opinion that in view of the hardships which it involves, detention should normally be avoided. If necessary, detention may be resorted to only on grounds prescribed by law to verify identity; to determine the elements on which the claim to refugee status or asylum is based; to deal with cases where refugees or asylum seekers have destroyed their travel and/or identity documents or have used fraudulent documents in order to mislead the authorities of the state in which they intend to claim asylum; or to protect national security or public order.[9]

This detailed and explicit declaration of the UNHCR Committee attempts to address the various practices that enable the gatekeepers of many states to detain, restrain or even return asylum seekers to their country of origin in direct conflict with the requirements of the CSR. The worst problems are faced by large groups of migrants as their collective rights are seldom respected.

According to natural justice, as well as the CSR itself, they should have the right to be heard (including the right to oral hearing, to call evidence, to counsel, and to make submissions); they should also have the right to a fair and impartial tribunal (this includes the right to notice, to full disclosure, and to a non-biased assessment of their situation).[10] Of course, the situation is aggravated by the presence of large migrations, due to conflicts, but primarily to man-made and natural disasters.

The refugee crisis to which Hathaway refers is primarily based on numbers: there are, increasingly, large numbers of asylum seekers, as noted in Chapter 1;[11] most often their flight is from developing countries to the developed states in the North. The Northern states have a correspondingly decreasing interest in admitting large numbers of impoverished and untrained refugees:

> *As the interest convergence between refugees and developed countries has disappeared, Northern states have sought to avoid the arrival of refugees by adopting policies of external deterrence.*[12]

At the time of the drafting of the CSR, most of the refugees seeking asylum after World War II were Europeans, so that their assimilation was not in question in North America. In contrast, today's refugees are 'different', both racially and socially, and not all desire to be assimilated, or would be easily assimilated, should they desire it.[13]

It is worth emphasizing: if the refugees/asylum seekers were part of an indigenous group from any continent, then the whole question would be moot since 'assimilation' in their case, as previously argued, would compound the crime(s) already committed against them in forcing them to leave their territories by adding the crime of cultural genocide.[14]

The first problem that faces *all* asylum seekers, without distinction, is the way in which they are 'greeted' upon their arrival at the borders of their country of choice. Their first experience of the new country is, for the most part, not one of welcome, but a harrowing experience of interrogation and detention, even if they are not held back from the country's borders. States want to retain fully their sovereignty over their territories, and this includes strict border controls, so that the first reaction to large influxes of refugees is rejection.[15]

Perhaps the rejection is neither explicit at the start, nor eventually irrevocable; but the sort of reception that is offered speaks volumes regarding their resistance to invited 'guests'. These feelings and the practices that ensue are observed by the International Organ for Migration:

> *Many States which have the ability to do so, find intercepting migrants before they reach their territories, is one of the most effective measures to enforce their domestic migration laws and policies.*[16]

In fact, many states try their best to ensure that migrants never reach their borders in the first place.[17] Hence, interception represents the first of three steps intended to reduce the flux of migrations. In other words, even before refuge seekers arrive at their state of choice, every effort is made by states to prevent them from approaching their borders. The UNHCR Executive Committee has defined interception as 'active intervention' by states to impede migrants, as follows:

... one of the measures employed by States to:

(i) prevent embarkation of persons on an international journey;
(ii) prevent further onward international travel by persons who have commenced their journey; or
(iii) assert control of vessels where there are reasonable grounds to believe the vessel is transporting persons contrary to international or national maritime law; where in relations to the above, the person or persons do not have the required documentation or valid permission to enter.[18]

One of the most egregious examples of the preventive interception is the *Tampa* case.[19] The *Tampa* was a Norwegian freighter that answered the distress call of a sinking Indonesian ferry. Most of the 430 passengers were Afghans who wanted to seek asylum in Australia and to be taken to Christmas Island. The government of Australia, however, refused responsibility, and responded that either Indonesia or Norway should take responsibility for the refugees; in fact, Australia even refused the requested medical help for the affected individuals in the group.

Finally, on 1 September, Australia announced its 'solution' to the problem, which was becoming increasingly acute as the *Tampa* was not equipped for the number of people whom it was then forced to carry, and even its crew was at risk. Australia paid US$10 million in aid, in exchange for Nauru's agreement (Nauru was an island in the Pacific) to accept the asylum seekers, while their claims would be processed with the support of the UNHCR. The authors conclude their narrative by adding: 'Australia's Pacific solution was born.'[20]

Essentially, like Australia, most countries would rather not have to face large numbers of refugees at their borders, and thus be bound by the appropriate articles of the convention. Various dilatory tactics are used to practise interception before the actual borders are reached. Some countries require a visa for non-nationals intending to enter their borders: Canada is such a country. In 2001, Canada introduced visa requirements for the citizens of Hungary and Zimbabwe. Visas are not easy to obtain and represent an impossible requirement for a person who is persecuted in her home country, and, hence, cannot risk asking her government's officials for a visa.

Other interception practices are the imposition of sanctions to carriers which attempt to carry refugees who are improperly documented.[21] This is another manoeuvre often practised in order to avoid 'asylum overload'.[22] The practice of 'maritime interception', or 'interdiction', is often based on the same rationale. The US intercepts vessels coming from the Caribbean, Australia and those originating from Indonesia; other countries such as Greece, Italy, Malaysia, Spain and Turkey practise interception both on their contiguous waters and on the high seas. Often interceptions are carried out disguised as 'anti-smuggling' or 'anti-trafficking' operations.

It is often hard to separate intended interceptions from well-intentioned 'rescues at sea' which are required by international law. The US leads the world in interception: according to Brouwer and Kumin, from 1982 to 2002, 185,801 people were intercepted at sea.[23] In addition, these migrants are not viewed as asylum seekers, no matter their country of origin or the location of their interception – that is, this judgement follows even if the interception took place in US waters. Australia has concluded an agreement with Papua-New Guinea, similar to the one with Nauru, but with a significant difference:

unlike the Nauru situation, in Papua-New Guinea only Australian authorities would process the migrants.

The practice of interception at sea represents a denial of the rights of refugees: the right to seek asylum and the right to *non-refoulement*. Denial of these rights, in effect, often continues even after refugees manage to reach the borders of their country of choice.

2b. Denial of refugee rights: Detention and other initial measures

> *Other States viewed detention as prima facie a violation of rights; detention for the purpose of deterrence, it was said, went beyond the spirit of the convention, and entry in search of asylum should not be considered an illegal act.*[24]

Arriving at a country's borders, for the purpose of seeking asylum is not an illegal act; yet those who do arrive are viewed – to say the least – as a threat to a State's sovereignty, hence several countries, such as The Netherlands, thought that even detention at will would be appropriate for peoples who travelled without the required documents.[25]

As always, in the case of immigrants, it is primarily mass migrations that raise the red flag in the minds of border officials; but even single individuals may create enough uncertainties in the mind of a board examiner in Canada, for instance, to lead him to view detention as a desirable alternative. According to Canadian regulations regarding refugees, Part 14, 'Detention and Release', lists the factors to be considered:

> *244. For the purposes of Division 6 of Part 1 of the Act, the factors set out in this Part shall be taken into consideration when assessing whether a person:*
>
> (a) is unlikely to appear for examination, an admissibility hearing, removal from Canada, or at a proceeding that could lead to making of a removal order by the Minister, under subsection 44(2) of the Act;
> (b) is a danger to the public; or
> (c) is a foreign national whose identity has not been established.

At the outset, the questioning of refugees is, if not hostile, certainly not welcoming. For those who flee a government who may not be willing or able to cooperate with them, securing the appropriate documents requested by the host country's officials may well be an impossible task. Hence, the UNHCR itself[26] explained the need for very serious grounds before detention could be viewed as legal and acceptable.

In the case of *Sahin versus Canada*,[27] a Turkish citizen was detained in 1993, upon arrival, and remained in detention to 1994, because he was not in possession of a valid passport or visa (as required by subsection 9(1) of the Immigration Act, and subsection 14(1) of the Immigration Regulations). The applicant argued that his refusal to return to his country of origin was not enough to warrant prolonged detention.

In fact, the right not to return is well established in international law, and this fact supports the applicant's position. Goodwin-Gill argues that:

> *The evidence relating to the meaning and scope of* non-refoulement *in its treaty sense also amply supports the conclusion that today the principle forms part of general international law. There is substantial, if not conclusive authority that the principle is binding on all States, independently of specific assent.*[28]

Yet, there was a strong possibility that the applicant would have been forced to return to Turkey as long as his status as a convention refugee was not established. In contrast, an applicant found to be a convention refugee is entitled to the protection of section 7 of the Canadian Charter:[29]

> *Section 7 Charter considerations are relevant to the exercise of discretion by an adjudication under section 103 of the Immigration Act which confers on him a necessary but enormous power over individuals... Fundamentally, justice requires that a fair balance be struck between the interests of the person who claims his liberty has been limited and the protection of society.*[30]

Yet, despite the recognition of the gravity of the decision to detain, Rothstein continues, by adding:

> *In many cases, the most satisfactory course of action will be to detain the individual to expedite the immigration proceedings.*

In this case, Counsel for the Applicant objected to the treatment the latter had received on the basis of two major challenges to the Canadian Charter of Rights and Freedoms:[31]

> *7. Everyone has the right to life, liberty and security of the person and the right not to be deprived thereof except in accordance with the principles of fundamental justice.*
>
> *12. Everyone has the right not to be subjected to any cruel and unusual treatment or punishment.*

The prolonged detention of an applicant under section 103 of the Immigration Act,[32] although that act makes no express reference to the charter, seems to contravene section 7 as it is patently unfair to detain someone primarily because an adjudicator is not sure that he will make himself available for possible return to a country to which international law explicitly forbids his return.

A similar problem was encountered by the High Court of Australia.[33] In this case the appellant, of Palestinian origins, was currently stateless and entered Australia without a visa. The immigration detention provided by the Migration Act 'is not detention for an offence';[34] but prolonged detention and 'deprivation of freedom will after a time or in some circumstances become punitive'.[35] The problem is that a non-citizen, who has entered the country unlawfully, now depends upon securing another country that might be willing to harbour him.

Apparently there is an obvious conflict between the principle of *non-refoulement*[36] and the right to, in some sense, force admission into a country unwilling to accept a migrant. The principle applies to all states, even to those that have not ratified the CSR, although:

> ... *a significant element of contingency attaches to the obligation, particularly in the case of a mass influx that may constitute a threat to the security of the receiving state.*[37]

In the case of the mass exodus of refugees after an ecological disaster, justification of the fear that impels the flight is not in question, although its foundation in 'persecution' is a problem and it clearly remains an objectively observable condition as well as a subjective opinion: this renders the situation quite different from that of individual asylum seekers. In contrast, however, the sheer number of migrants may well represent a possible harm to the country to which admission is sought:

> *Whenever temporary refuge is sought, the existence of danger caused by civil disorder, domestic conflicts or human rights violations generates a valid presumption of humanitarian need. This has important consequences for the process of determining the entitlement to protection of individuals or specific groups. In particular, the presumption should shift the burden of proof from the claimant to the state.*[38]

The level of obligation of states is not fully specified in any international instrument. The need for protection and assistance is undeniable: *something* must be done to provide aid. What is needed, indisputably, is a 'meaningful response to the humanitarian needs of victims of serious disruptions of the public order'.[39] Hathaway proposes four categories of refugees:

1 'refugees defined by the Convention and Protocol' – such refugees are entitled to *non-refoulement* and to all the rights set out in the convention;
2 'refugees who are protected by regional agreements', who may also be protected against return and enjoy other specific rights;
3 'refugees who fear harm as a result of serious disturbances of the public order' – these refugees may be entitled to special consideration because of man-made harms to which they have been exposed;
4 'all persons who are involuntary migrants as a result of natural or man-made causes' may claim UNHCR assistance for resettlement and legal protection, but they are not automatically covered by international law.[40]

Although Chapters 1 and 2 of this book have attempted to lay out the legal situation of convention refugees and the main problems that they encounter (and this has been the main topic of the scholarly work of James Hathaway and Guy Goodwin-Gill), the main focuses of this volume are the legal status and living conditions of the refugees categorized under points 3 and 4 in the above list. These are the individuals whose conditions already are, and are increasingly becoming, intolerable because of climate change and other man-made assaults, but who are not explicitly and clearly protected under international law.

3. THE PRESENT CRISIS: HOW TO RE-CONCEIVE REFUGEE LAW?

Zaire admitted huge numbers of Rwandan refugees following the genocide and ensuing civil war that left perhaps 1 million Tutsi and thousands of moderate Hutu dead in 1995. There was, however, considerable local hostility and resentment directed at the refugee population, which was blamed for environmental degradation and increased insecurity in the area.[41]

Although the fourth category of refugees listed above fits well the new category of ecological refugees, ecological problems may well apply in two separate senses. Migrants who are the victims of floods, famines or melts are fleeing from ecological disasters; but even if admitted in large numbers to a new country, they may well bring new ecological problems to their new land. A similar problem was faced by the crew of the *Tampa*, as we saw: by accepting the responsibility for refugees, the *Tampa*'s own Norwegian crew was put at risk.

In general, the refugee crisis is yet another aspect of the interface between human rights and globalization. Once major powers have organized and entrenched various 'free' trade deals, such as the North American Free Trade Agreement (NAFTA), and have sanctioned the superior power of the World Trade Organization (WTO), together with its ability to enforce its decisions (and for the most part these activities proceed, ensuring the supremacy of trade over human rights),[42] then the difficulties facing refugees have multiplied.

Immigrants' rights fall under the category of human rights, in general, and at this time all human rights appear to be under attack even in Western democracy, with a long history of respect for civil liberties. For instance, it is almost useless for the advocates of asylum seekers to involve international human rights law, as it may well 'do more harm than good'.[43] Speaking of the present policies of the US, in general, David Cole says:

> *Claiming that this is a new kind of war, the administration has sought to employ the extraordinary powers of war while evading international law limits on those powers, refusing until suffering defeat in the Supreme Court to provide Guantanamo detainees with any sort of hearings to assess their status,*[44] *and maintaining secret Justice Department and Pentagon memos that the international law prohibition on the torture cannot constrain the president in wartime.*[45]

When most non-citizens are viewed with suspicion and treated, for the most part, as possibly dangerous, it is clear that the position of migrants from developing countries cannot be viewed in a friendly light, but have to 'prove' themselves to be harmless in some way. They are seen as 'them' in an 'us–them' dichotomy that so often dominates public discourse and consciousness in time of war.[46]

This approach is the reality in a real war, but, at least, in the US at present, otherwise law-abiding citizens have been convinced by high-placed government officials that most 'aliens' represent an immediate threat, rather than representing the same humanity they themselves share.

In addition to the feelings engendered by erroneous information, and the 'us–them' mentality just referred to, the procedures regarding the implementation of international legal instruments can be, and often are, manipulated in ways that are deleterious to migrants. International legal instruments must be incorporated within domestic constitutions and charters in order to ensure that they are binding in specific states (see, for instance, the *Baker* case for Canada).[47] If they are not part of domestic legal regimes, they remain hard to use in any of the cases:

> *There is a dearth of lawyers trained to employ international human rights arguments, and judges are unaccustomed to hearing such arguments, much less to taking them seriously.*[48]

Hence, this is a particularly grave moment for migrants and asylum seekers: on the one hand, globalization and climate change render the living conditions of many increasingly intolerable. On the other, the present geopolitical situation tends to have affected peoples viewed as suspect and undesirable, almost taken to be 'guilty' until such time as they can prove themselves to be harmless.

In the United States, the Alien Tort Statute[49] was initially intended for the redress of certain specific human rights violations that were recognized as such at the time: 'injuries against ambassadors, denial of safe conduct, and piracy'.[50] Today other torts may fall under the purview of the act; but there is no discernible 'development of international human rights claims in Alien Tort Statute lawsuits'.[51] This remains true despite the fact that the law of nations is acknowledged to be part of federal common law.

At any rate, much of recent ATCA jurisprudence deals with cases involving corporate activities, primarily those of extractive industries, whose operations affect indigenous peoples and other local communities. These cases are particularly interesting from the point of view of this work because although the merits of the cases and the respective narratives of the victims clearly indicate the harms resulting from the interface between hazardous activities and the health and socio-cultural life of those affected, international and domestic instruments are insufficient to offer redress. It is worth noting that although much of the corporate activity supported by the World Bank conflicts with the requirements of sound ecological judgement in the light of global warming, the indigenous communities who appeal to the World Bank's investigative panels for redress tend to do a lot better in that forum than they would with a lawsuit under the Alien Torts Claims Act (ATCA).[52]

In fact, the precarious position of migrants in the present global political situation is clearly reflected in the recent US jurisprudence under the ATCA: while the Supreme Court affirmed that 'international law is part of our law' in the recent *Sosa* case,[53] there is little or no clear application of that principle in the case law. Some argue that ATCA jurisprudence has gone through 'three waves' of litigation.[54]

It will be useful to review briefly some aspects of the first two waves, and the related cases. Julian Ku suggest that 'the first wave' consisted of 'lawsuits ... generally brought against foreign government officials, acting under the colour of foreign law': some examples of this first period included the seminal case of *Filartiga versus Pena Irala*.[55] During this period – that is, between 1980 and 1991 – 31 lawsuits were filed.[56]

The 'second wave' brought a dramatic increase in the number of cases (79 cases before 2000), and the cases targeted US and foreign corporations as they 'aided and abetted' foreign governments in their violations of international human rights law.[57] We will review some of these cases in order to pinpoint their general approach to the human rights of individuals in developing countries, before turning to the most relevant period from our point of view – that is, the 'third wave'.

3a. Living conditions in local and indigenous communities: Corporate responsibility under ATS: *Doe versus Unocal Corporation*[58]

The case dates back to 1992, when Unocal Corporation 'acquired a 28 per cent interest in a gas pipeline project (Project) in Myanmar, formerly known as Burma'.[59] One of the main questions in the case is whether the Project actually hired the Myanmar military (Military) to facilitate their operations, as some of Unocal's own employees suggested. The plaintiffs, villagers from the area where the Project was taking place, alleged that they had been forced 'to serve as labourers on the Project', with threats of violence, and that, in order to protect the Project's security, the Military:

> ... *subjected them to acts of murder, rape and torture. One plaintiff testified that, after her husband was shot for attempting to escape the forced labour programme, she and her baby were thrown into a fire resulting in injuries to the woman and death of her baby.*[60]

Two groups of villagers brought action for human rights violations against Unocal and the Project (under the Alien Torts Claims Act).[61] The treatment to which the villagers had been subjected was termed by the Ninth Circuit, the 'modern variant of slavery', and Unocal's role, a form of aiding and abetting, to say the least. Unocal's earlier response that the plaintiffs were barred from bringing this action by the 'act of state doctrine' was not accepted by the Ninth Circuit.[62]

Although this case is not directly related to environmental harms, it is – in many ways – similar to the *Saro-Wiwa* case in that the nefarious alliance between corporate crime and egregious human rights violations are clearly present, and so is the corporate support for the role of the military to ensure citizens' compliance through rape, murder, torture and terror. Scholarly writings on this case are divided on whether the concept of slavery should have been introduced by the Ninth Circuit, as forced labour is also proscribed in both national and international law. Tawny Aine Bridgeford argues that the Ninth Circuit was practising judicial activism in this case. Andrew Ridenour instead argues that the use of 'slavery' is entirely apt in this case.

Ridenour's concern is that municipal law should not be considered to determine when acts are brought before the courts under ATCA 'as section 1350 of the Judiciary Act of 1789 (the Alien Torts Claims Act) ... permits federal district courts to hear claims by aliens for torts committed "in violation of the law of nations"'. When we consider the import of ATCA's history, it is evident that an act intended to deal with matters of liability must deal exclusively with criminal matters instead: 'Crimes such as genocide, slavery, summary executions, and torture have been universally held by courts as violations of contemporary *jus cogens* and, thus, subject to liability under ATCA.' In essence, violations so defined, according to *Barcelona Traction*, must be of norms that are 'universal, specific and obligatory';[63] hence, they must be of a character *beyond* even the general concerns of customary international law. For the most part, international treaties are enacted for the interests of their signatories,[64] and derogation from their mandates does not entail penalties other than economic or procedural, although customary law evolves over time 'to include offences that the international community universally prohibits'.[65]

Ridenour remarks on the odd coupling of criminal and tort law in ATCA. He says: 'While these violations are criminal in nature, international law allows states to fashion remedies under universal jurisdiction, which the United States has done in a civil form through ATCA.'[66] Ridenour's important article was written in 2001, and in 2002 the International Criminal Court of Rome came into force. Eventually, perhaps, ruling under ATCA will form the basis for additional criminal prosecutions best suited to these crimes of universal jurisdiction, which, like genocide, piracy, the slave trade and war crimes, extend beyond the scope of state action.

The main point for our argument is that although 'no court [had] found a corporation liable for a violation of *jus cogens* under ATCA',[67] until this case, a test for conspiracy (under US 1983 law) is that 'both public and private actors share a common, unconstitutional goal' and, hence, fit the Principles of Nuremberg as well.[68] This is the incalculable importance of this case, not only to show a clear example of corporate liability, but also to establish the foundations for a possible eventual criminal prosecution, based on *jus cogens*, for the violations of which corporations were found liable.

3b. Extractive industries and environmental and health harms: *Jota versus Texaco*[69]

> *Citizens of Peru and Ecuador brought class action suits alleging that defendant oil company polluted rain forests and rivers in their countries, causing environmental damage and personal injury.*[70]

This case is typical of this kind of jurisprudence and it has a long previous history that led to this unsuccessful appeal.[71] Texaco's oil operation in Ecuador was initiated in 1964, when Texaco Petroleum Company (TexPet) began oil explorations and drilling in the Oriente region of eastern Ecuador.[72] A petroleum concession was initiated in 1965 for a 'consortium' whereby TexPet was part owner with Gulf Oil Corporation and, in 1974, then Republic of Ecuador (PetroEcuador) joined in with a 25 per cent ownership. Eventually, Gulf Oil relinquished its shares to TexPet and the latter operated a trans-Ecuadorian oil pipeline and continued to operate the consortium's drilling activities until 1992. At that time, PetroEcuador took over that aspect of the operation, and finally, in 1999, TexPet left the consortium entirely in PetroEcuador's hands.[73]

The plaintiffs brought a suit against Texaco in 1993, as the latter's activities had 'polluted the rain forests and rivers' in both Ecuador and Peru, and those polluting and harmful activities were 'designed, controlled, conceived and directed ... through its operation in the United States'.[74]

> *The indigenous peoples sought to recover damages, citing ... negligence, public and private nuisance, strict liability, medical monitoring, trespass, civil conspiracy and violations of the Alien Tort Claims Act, 28 USC § 1350 ('ATCA').*[75]

These requests were appropriate redress for contaminated water and environment, for the restoration of hunting and fishing grounds, and for both medical and environmental monitoring funds; and the establishment of standards for future Texaco operations as well as 'an injunction restraining Texaco from entering into activities that risk environmental or human injuries'[76] all appeared reasonable and appropriate.

These details are vital to a full understanding of the specifics of the case as well as an appreciation of these proceedings, in general. Note that *substantive* claims based on indisputable scientific evidence, and the extensive research that supports this sort of claim (in relation to extractive industries' operations), can be found in the work of the World Health Organization (WHO) and in that of many epidemiologists, public health and cancer specialists, among others.[77]

But the US courts' responses are, once again, typical of the courts' analyses in this sort of claim: they do not answer any of the claims made with counter-claims, and they do not even attempt to dispute the factual issues as set out by the plaintiffs. But the logic of their responses is flawed. *Forum non conveniens*, for instance, is based on the 'fact' that too many witnesses should be brought in to testify, speaking various languages and dialects. But the injuries and diseases that the plaintiffs name are well-known consequences of chemical and toxic exposure, not some obscure symptom that needs to be personally verified by someone who 'saw' the development of the disease, an almost impossible feat for illnesses such as cancers. Not only are certain diseases well documented as following upon certain exposures, but their treatment is equally well known, and no member of an indigenous community can be better informed about both illness and treatment than scientists and practitioners at local universities and hospitals, or the WHO itself. In fact, the corporation could not say that *their* operation did not and could not result in the harmful consequences that the claimants outlined. When the extractive operations are pursued in the usual way, one can and should expect the resulting harm, both ecological and biological.

The certainty of this expectation renders the resulting injuries more than unexpected 'collateral' harm: it adds the knowledge of the relation between the cause (extractive operations) and the harm itself. I have argued that it is this aspect of 'eco-crime' that ensures the presence of a significant mental element, and, hence, facilitates or should facilitate the transition from environmental regulatory breaches to 'eco-crime'.[78] When this knowledge is ignored with regard to indigenous peoples and groups, because it is clearly more than an unexpected externality, the ensuing effects of extractive practices are very close to genocide or attacks against the human person.

This aspect of the ATCA jurisprudence, together with the details of the responses offered by Texaco and the court's assessment of those responses, sheds a different and much clearer light on these proceedings.

These were some of the major issues discussed instead of the material/factual complaints themselves:

1. Texaco's motion to dismiss on grounds of *forum non conveniens*, accepted by Judge Rakoff;

2 Texaco's motion to dismiss because of 'international comity';
3 Texaco's motion to dismiss because the Republic of Ecuador was not joined and neither was PetroEcuador; Judge Rakoff believed both would be 'indispensable partners' in order for the court to assess the relief sought (and because the Foreign Sovereign Immunities Act, 28 U.S.C. & 1603(b) and 1604, 'prevented the assertion of jurisdiction on either');
4 class disputes and common damages would require 'large amounts of testimony with interpreters, perhaps often in local dialects, (which) would make effective adjudication in New York problematic at best';[79]
5 these cases have 'everything to do with Ecuador and nothing to do with the US';[80]
6 'environmental torts are unlikely to be found to violate the law of nations';[81]
7 'the US has no special public interest in hosting an international law action against a US entity that can be adequately pursued in the place where the violations occurred'.[82]

As a result, the reasons for the suit were not even addressed, only the reasons why a US court should not be involved. Nor are such arguments separate and, thus, sufficient to rebut the listed harms by the plaintiffs. In the following paragraphs I will discuss some of the points on the above list in more detail (referring to them by number).

First, point 6 is factually incorrect, and this error is the main reason for this book, and for much of my previous work, as well as that of the scientists whom I cite:[83] 'environmental torts' are not simply that. For the most part, 'environmental torts' entail gross breaches of human rights to life, to health, to normal function and to 'family life'. These rights and their violations are routinely addressed by international courts and the European Court of Human Rights; hence, they do, indeed, 'violate the law of nations'.[84] To simply provide a wrong description of the situation, without providing adequate support for the validity of that interpretation, is insufficient to prove one of the major claims of this US court (point 4).

Another counter-example to the approach taken by the US court on the same question (point 4) might be the international jurisprudence regarding nuclear tests.[85] In this case, the courts decided on the issue *without* requiring individual witnesses either from the area in question, or from any other area that might have been affected by nuclear weapons (say, Hiroshima or Nagasaki survivors) in order to demonstrate the harm that would result from exposure to radioactivity. The effects of nuclear weapons were judged to be given – that is, universally accepted harms would ensue; hence, the court judged there was an *erga omnes* obligation to resist from those tests because of the possibility of inflicting harm on both New Zealand and Australian citizens.

While the harms that result from exposure to the practices of extractive and mining industries are perhaps less catastrophic and immediate that those produced by a mushroom cloud, the long-term effects of exposure to carcinogens and other toxic substances that are part of those practices parallel those resulting from radiation exposure and today are equally well researched. That said, it is worth repeating: neither the court nor Texaco itself attempted to refute the plaintiffs' claims, and, as noted, the procedural answers that were used instead are based on mistaken facts and misunderstandings.

Similarly, neither 'comity' (point 2) nor the fact that the relief sought should have been shared by Ecuador (point 3) are really applicable, when the gravity of the harms perpetrated are fully understood: bilateral obligations are superseded by *erga omnes* obligations instead. Nor are the claims that these cases 'have everything to do with Ecuador' (point 5) and that there is no 'public interest' (point 7) for the US in these cases acceptable responses. The 'collateralism' inherent in business as usual (BAU) practices, I have argued, is as harmful to human rights as any other attack on human life, including the better-known 'disasters', such as Bhopal, Seveso and the like. In all of these cases, the countries of origin of the hazardous operation did not succeed in avoiding their responsibility by saying that the citizens of India, or Italy, should bear the burden of redressing the harms that had occurred.[86]

In sum, even the appeal to procedural matters in order to avoid the consideration of real reasons advanced in the plaintiffs' claims should fail since the factual material (hence, scientifically provable) elements of the crimes committed by Texaco are implicitly denied by the court's assessment of the case. Nevertheless, the *forum non conveniens* doctrine is the first step to overcome; this is the first question asked on 'whether a court having jurisdiction may decline to exercise it'.[87] The question is closely tied to whether local remedies have been exhausted; but it is often employed as a way of escaping the *responsibility* to provide a forum against multinational corporations (MNCs):

> *One important reason forum non conveniens doctrine is so susceptible to being employed to remove human rights-related suits against MNCs from Northern courts is the ease with which judges in home states of MNCs persist in thinking in highly parochial terms about whether the home state has an interest in being the venue for global justice against its national MNCs.*[88]

3c. Forced relocation, war crimes and genocide: *Bancoult versus McNamara*[89]

> *The plaintiffs in this case are persons indigenous to Chagos, their survivors or direct descendants ... they bring this action against the United States and various current and former officials of state and the Department of Defence ('the individual defendants') for forced relocation, torture, racial discrimination, cruel, inhuman and degrading treatment, genocide, intentional infliction of emotional distress, negligence and trespass.*

Although the Chagos Archipelago comprises 52 islands administered by the UK government but leased to the US, the US was responsible under the British Indian Ocean Territory (BIOT) Agreement. During the late 1960s and early 1970s, the whole Chagos population was moved to Mauritius and Seychelles in order to allow a US military facility to settle in their space. The original inhabitants were not allowed to return, and were offered no compensation to help ease their transition into a new environment and the loss of their homes.

Those who had not left had to suffer from being forced on 'overcrowded ships for Peros Banhos and Salonen, from whence they eventually were taken to Mauritius and Seychelles'.[90] The US Congress went ahead with the construction of a military base on Diego Garcia Island despite hearings where multiple human rights violations were detailed, from the lack of relocation assistance, to harsh removal conditions that cause injuries to the survivors, including miscarriages, and eventual living conditions that include poverty, unemployment and other deprivations.[91]

Before the judgement proper could be decided, the 'individual defendants' all claimed that they had been obeying superior order, based on 'the statutory immunity granted to the federal officers under the Federal Employee Liability Reform and Tort Compensation Act'.[92]

Yet, the gravity of the effects of the forced removal bring to mind the language of the Nuremberg Principles – hence, the international law's denial of such claims of immunity. In Canada, organization crime is addressed in Bill C-45, now part of the Canadian Criminal Code as an Amendment to Section 22.1:

> *The main changes effected to the Criminal Code are as follows: S 1.(1) extends the definition of 'everyone', 'person' and 'owner' to include 'an organization'. In turn, 'organization' means, (2) (a) a public body, body corporate, society, company, firm, partnership, trade union or municipality, or (b) an association of persons that:*
>
> *1 is created for a common purpose;*
> *2 has an operational structure; and*
> *3 holds itself out to the public as an association of persons.*

Here and in the amendments to Section 22.1, Bill C-45 ensures that a wide array of actors within an organization may be viewed as responsible for an offence, 'whether by act or omission' (Section 22.1 (ii)); it also ensures that if the prosecution is required 'to prove fault – other than negligence' (Section 22.2), then senior officers or representatives may manifest the requisite 'mental state' also by '(c) knowing that a representative of the organization is or is about to be a party to the offence, or does not take all reasonable measures to stop them from being a party to the offence'. The bill also adds a section (217.1) to define 'the legal duty to take reasonable steps to prevent bodily harm' on the part of anyone who is in the position to direct and order how work is to be done.

In addition, several sections deal with making or causing to be made false statements with respect to the financial conditions of the organization (Section 362 (1) (c)) or, in general, committing fraud or causing it to be committed. For the sake of the present purposes, I will limit my observation and my discussion to the aspects of Bill C-45 that are directly relevant to this book and to eco-crime rather than white collar crime, in general.

The expanded definition of organizations is of cardinal importance in cases where the authority, other responsible senior party or those directed by the senior individuals 'depart markedly from the standard of care' (5.22.1) in ways that could reasonably be expected and who may be found to be provincial or federal officials. There is no case law yet to determine whether this interpretation might eventually be part of the positive developments arising out of Bill C-45; and, of course, 'depart markedly' from the standard of care does not define the 'standard of care' itself or what, precisely, a 'marked' departure from a non-specified form of behaviour might be. In fact it may be the case that the standard of 'due diligence' (also largely undefined) that has been the expected test is not different from the standard included or implied by the changed wording of Bill C-45.

Another important point worthy of attention is that after Section 718.2, the act now provides Section 718.21 on 'organizations' and the 'factors regarding the offence' that must be taken in consideration in sentencing. Some of the most interesting of these factors, in relation to our main concern, are:

(a) *any advantage realized by the organization as a result of the offence;*
(b) *the degree of planning involved in carrying out the offence, and the duration and complexity of the offence;*

...

(g) *whether the organization was, or any of its representatives were, convicted of a similar offence or sanctioned by a regulatory body for similar conduct;*

...

(j) *any measures that the organization has taken to reduce the likelihood of it committing a subsequent offence.*

Briefly, the first factor cited shows that economic advantage renders the offence graver; the second parallels the premeditation aspect as it renders a homicide committed by an individual a murder instead; planning may also include 'conspiring', something that has become a crime in itself according to the Nuremberg Charter. Previous crimes are now admissible at sentencing: (g) recognizes that an organization does not require the same constitutional (charter) protections as does the individual offender, at least implicitly. The commitment not to repeat the crime (j) also allows a degree of official intervention that is not possible with individual persons.

Even if the individual defendants are eliminated from the action (justly or unjustly), that leaves the US as the sole defendant. However, all of those who perpetrated knowingly the actions involving the Chagos indigenous population violated the tenets of international law:

> *Pursuant to the Alien Tort Claims Act, 28 U.S.C. & 1350 ('ATCA'), the district courts shall have original jurisdiction of any civil action by an alien for a tort only committed in violation of the law of nations or Treaty of the United States.*[93]

Other issues used to rebut the plaintiff's claims were the fact that 'they had failed to exhaust their administrative remedies' despite the fact that they were not allowed to return to their home base, now a US military base (in Chagos) or in the other islands, where the UK itself was not likely to offer an impartial forum after entering into an agreement with the US, which led to the very actions in question.

Another issue was 'the judicial expertise' of the court, as it was required to pass judgement on US policy:

> *Neither our federal law nor customary international law provide standards by which the court can measure and balance the foreign policy considerations at play in this case, such as the containment of the Soviet Union in the Indian Ocean 30 years ago, and today the support of military operation in the Middle East. The court concludes that it is ill equipped to review the conduct of the military operation challenged in this case because they implicate foreign policy and national security concerns.*[94]

Essentially, if the US government political branches made a decision 30 years earlier, the court was not prepared to second guess that decision today.[95] Of course, even if the court was not prepared to question either the decision of the US government at the time those decisions were made, or the reasons for those decisions, the *way in which* those decisions were carried out appears to remain untouched by this argument. Even if a country's political or other decision cannot be judged under ATCA:

> *Article 2(3) of the Torture Convention explicitly states that 'An order from a superior official or public authority may not be invoked as a justification for torture'.*[96]

Torture is forbidden by *jus cogens* norms, and so is genocide, so that appealing to this article appears to be appropriate, and we will address this question below.

This point is also made clearly in the *Filartiga versus Pena Irala* case.[97] In that case, the US Supreme Court recognized that the law of nations:

> *... may be ascertained by consulting the work of jurists writing professedly on public law; or by the general usage and practice of nations; or by the judicial decisions recognizing and enforcing the law.*[98]

Nevertheless, it must be acknowledged:

> *Unlike the criminal remedy, there is no treaty that clearly obliges or even authorizes courts to take jurisdiction over civil actions respecting torture committed abroad with the exception of the US; there is no domestic legislation in any other country that expressly grants courts jurisdiction with respect to these matters.*[99]

Because ATCA permits individual citizens to sue for torture and other such injuries, without the far more complicated requirements of initiating a criminal action for an International Court of Justice or International Criminal Court, this avenue appears to remain the preferred one by claimants in various venues:

> *While it is premised on the principle that victims of torture must be compensated, its true role in many cases is admittedly symbolic: the third country tort remedy provides recognition for, and emotional vindication of, the victims of torture and places moral and political pressure on rights abusing governments.*[100]

3d. The end of the story: *R (on the application of Bancoult) versus Secretary of State for Foreign and Commonwealth Affairs*[101]

> *On 3 November 2000 the Divisional Court (Laws LJ and Gibbs J) gave judgement in favour of Mr Bancoult.*[102] *They decided that a power to legislate for the 'peace, order and good government' of the territory did not include a power to expel all the inhabitants.*

Beyond the ATCA trials, Bancoult and other Chagossians also attempted to find justice from the other superpower involved in their case: the UK government. Lord Hoffman describes the original lifestyle of the inhabitants of Chagos, working for the 'Company' (Chagos Agalegal Company Ltd), tending coconut trees and producing copra, working their gardens, and keeping chickens and pigs to add to the provisions that the Company provided for its workers. Yet, despite their lack of education and their simple lifestyles, they had 'a rich community life, the Roman Catholic religion and their own dialect, derived from the French'.[103]

For this case, their main points of contention were based on the history of their interaction with the UK government:

1. The British Indian Ocean Territories Order[104] had made the Chagos Archipelago a separate colony. The order also appointed a commissioner of BIOT, with the power to 'make laws for the peace, order and good government of the territory'; hence, the inhabitants retained British citizenship.[105]
2. In 1966, Her Majesty's Government corresponded with the government of the US: the result was to grant a lease of at least 50 years to the latter to establish a base on Diego Garcia, and to occupy other islands as required. In 1967, the UK government bought out the Company, which was only allowed to run the coconut plantations until July 1971 when the US required vacant possession. This prompted the commissioner to make the Immigration Ordinance 1971 (section 4(1)) providing that only a special permit would allow the former inhabitants to re-enter the territory.
3. From 1968 to 1971, the UK government removed the whole population, primarily to Mauritius and the Seychelles, without the use of force, but stating that the company was ceasing its operations and no more supplies would be available to them.[106]
4. The whole operation established a 'callous disregard for their interests', and the members of the community were left to fend for themselves in the slums of 'Port Louis'. The ordinance denying them the right to return had been prompted by US concerns about 'non-aligned countries' objecting to the construction of a military base in the Indian Ocean.[107] During more recent times, other objections could be raised about the alleged renditions flying into that base or taking place, with concomitant torture episodes, in ships anchored just beyond Chagos. The miserable conditions of the Chagossians in Mauritius, and their poverty and unemployment prompted negotiations between Mauritius and the UK, eventually culminating (in 1977) in payments ('depleted by inflation') to 595 Chagossian families. The Chagossians sought legal advice, and with the support of Michael Vencatessen, issued a writ in the High Court in London on behalf of all Chagossians, and eventually a trust fund of UK £4 million was set up in Mauritius in exchange for abandoning all claims, and this was signed by most Chagossians.
5. After the judgement (Divisional Court, Laws L. J. and Gibbs J.) in favour of Mr Bancoult on 3 November 2000 effectively quashed Section 4(1) of the Immigration Ordinance as *ultra vires*, Foreign Secretary Robin Cook announced a feasibility study to attempt to resettle the Chagossians in their former territory. He concluded his press release by saying:

> *This government has not defended what was done or said 30 years ago. As Lord Justice Laws recognized, we made no attempt to conceal the gravity of what happened. I am pleased that he has commended the wholly admirable conduct in disclosing material to the court, and praised the openness of today's foreign office.* (para 17)

The points that remained in contention were the Chagossians' right to return and the very legality of the official Constitution Order and the Immigration Order, as well as their 'irrationality', as:

> *The orders were not made in the interest of the Chagossians, but in the interest of the United Kingdom and the United States.* (para 28)

Furthermore, the authority to remove persons of British citizenship from their chosen residence, without, at any time, any compensation was also questioned. Lord Hoffman and the other Lords recognized the impact of the law made for a colony, citing Blackstone:[108]

> *But no power on earth except the authority of Parliament can send any subject of England out of the land against his will; no, not even a criminal.*

The Crown, therefore, and its appointed commissioner, has no authority to transport anyone against their will (para 44) through what constituted, essentially, threats of starvation to them and their families. But even the acknowledged wrong that had been done at the time did not result in a favourable judgement at this time: the main problem was the costs and logistics of total resettlement, although the Chagossians were now permitted to return for a time, to visit family graves and the like.

Were the Chagossians ecological refugees? Perhaps not, or they were only in the sense that their migration was, indeed, forced like many others by lack of resources and economic pressures from outside, although the main causative factors at the time were clearly political. Their case is worth studying in detail because of the different treatment they received at the hand of US, first, and the UK courts, second. The former appealed to procedural flaws in the case. The UK court instead tackled the factual elements of the case head on and admitted its own fault in regard to the series of events outlined above.

In addition, it is important to note the forces of neocolonialism seeking power, (rather than natural resources at this time): those who initiated and authorized the Chagossians' displacement manifested the callous disregard for the rights of local and indigenous communities that is, generally speaking, typical of forced migrations.

4. FORCED RELOCATION AND THE ATCA LITIGATION 'THIRD WAVE'

> *It would take some explaining to say now that federal courts must avert their gaze entirely from any international norm intended to protect individuals.*[109]

Justice Souter, however, also expected such international norms to be 'accepted by the civilized world';[110] hence, one might interpret his words as endorsing non-derogable obligations *erga omnes* despite their lack of specificity, as required instead by the US court.[111] Yet, a lower court *had*, indeed, found that Alvarez-Machain's claim of arbitrary detention constituted a violation of customary international norms.[112]

The forced relocation, lack of information and consent, and the arbitrariness of the decisions reached in the case described in the previous section[113] surely should reach the level of customary international law (CIL) that ATCA litigation requires. Nevertheless, as we saw, the resulting judgement did not favour displaced persons (see section 3c).

Although none of the cases described deals with refugee issues, the CSR is but one of many international legal instruments that are ignored or bypassed on various technicalities in the pursuit of a 'higher good', such as the so-called 'war on terror' or, more generally, the primacy of the interests of the US. The next case discussed opens the door in some small measure to the possibility of supporting international human rights law in a US court. Although this does not deal with refugees either, it is an important case because the main issue is that of unlawful detention.

4a. *Rasul versus Bush*: The implications[114]

The related cases of *Rasul* and *Al Odah* arose because, from 2002 onwards, 'more than 600 persons who had been captured abroad during hostilities between the United States and the Taliban regime in Afghanistan' were detained at Guantanamo Bay.[115] These cases are particularly relevant, I believe, because they raise the difficult question of detention and of its legality, in detail. In addition, the cases conclude with a majority decision of the US Supreme Court that, indeed, the cases should be retried as the Federal District Court was held to have a jurisdiction[116] to review the legality of the 'executive detention' of foreign nationals. Hence, these cases might provide a useful precedent for asylum seekers as the latter are not detained in a way that might be related to a war situation.

The plaintiffs included 2 citizens of Australia and 12 citizens of Kuwait, and neither of these countries was at war with the US, nor are they now. The plaintiffs' claims were as follows:

- They denied 'having engaged in or plotted acts of aggression against the US'.
- They alleged that they were 'held in federal custody in violation of the laws of the US'.
- They stated that 'they had been imprisoned without being charged with any wrongdoing'.
- They alleged that they had been denied access to counsel, or courts, or other tribunals.

So far, the decision reached was simply that 'the District Court had jurisdiction, under 28 UCSC § 2241, to review the legality of the plaintiffs' detention'.[117] Kennedy J. concurred, as he stated that:

(1) Federal courts had jurisdiction to consider challenges to the legality of the detention of foreign nationals held at the Guantanamo base, in light of (a) the base's status as a US territory in every practical respect and as a territory far removed from any hostilities; and (b) the indefinite pre-trial detention of the detainees; and (2) although

there were circumstances in which the base maintained the power and responsibility for the protection of persons from unlawful detention even when military affairs were implicated, there was a realm of political authority over military affairs where the judicial power could not enter.[118]

Thus it was not total support for the plaintiffs' position; but it was a favourable opinion, at least procedurally, after their defeat at the hands of the lower courts. Nevertheless, this decision should be considered in the context of the US's general approach to international law.

4b. The US executive branch and domestic and international law

It is sadly academic to ask whether human rights law should trump US domestic law. That is because, on the few occasions when the US government has ratified a human rights treaty, it has done so in a way designed to preclude the treaty from having any domestic effect.[119]

It would be easy to be led by optimism, and to consider that the final resolution of *Rasul versus Bush* is the precursor of a new era in which the affirmation of human rights prevails. Yet, it would be wrong to overestimate the value of this decision. Also, it is not wrong to concentrate on the US because other powerful countries such as Canada and Australia often follow the lead of the US in their approach to international obligations. In contrast, European Union (EU) countries often march to a different drummer. The recent 2007 Bali meeting on climate change, is a case in point.[120]

Even if the US government ratifies an international treaty with human rights implications, the lawyers of the Justice Department are expected to look very carefully at the document in order to ensure that it could not extend human rights protection beyond the standards present in their domestic law instruments. Should that not be the case, and should the international document propose additional human rights considerations, 'a reservation, declaration or understanding is drafted to negate the additional rights protection'.[121]

A particularly ugly example of this practice is the efforts of US representatives, regarding one of the most important human rights conventions: the Convention on the Rights of the Child.[122] The US representatives made every effort to change Article 38 regarding child soldiers. The US wanted to be able to continue recruiting children under 18 years of age. Eventually, the article lowered the age of prohibition of recruitment to age 15, at which time children are permitted to fight. In addition, the US is today the only Western power to permit life sentences for convicted juveniles.[123] Finally, even with this change, the US did not ratify the convention: it is one of only two countries to abstain (the other is Somalia).[124]

5. INTERNATIONAL LAW AND DOMESTIC LAW

The Convention against Torture provides that no exceptional circumstances whatsoever, whether a state of war, or a threat of war, international political instability or any other public emergency, may be invoked as a justification for torture.[125]

The question that arises is a twofold one: first, what exactly constitutes 'cruel, inhuman or degrading treatment' in the case of detainees, in general. Second, how 'elastic' have those concepts become against the background of the present geopolitical situation and the US power to influence other countries.

One of the countries where the US exerts the strongest influence is its immediate neighbour to the north, Canada. Canada has had a long history of strength and even leadership in the field of human rights; but lately the grounds of that stellar record have been eroded:

There is a sense that Canada is moving away from its total commitment to multi-nationalism, and is now, I think, advancing other forms of either national or regional alliances... Canada has to work very hard to maintain what invariably has been the perception internationally that it's a consensus builder and it's a valid interlocutor to all.[126]

The international non-governmental organization (NGO) Amnesty International is particularly concerned with Canada's recent record toward indigenous peoples and the protection of refugees: it has renewed its longstanding request that Canada should amend its laws to comply with its obligation under Article 3 of the United Nations Convention against Torture, as both in 2006 and in 2007 Canada deported asylum seekers to countries where they were at serious risk of being tortured.[127] In addition, Canada's response to the more than 4 million Iraqis currently displaced and 2 million who are refugees in adjacent countries under conditions that violate their human rights should be far stronger than it is.

As well, section 117 of the Immigration and Refugee Protection Act allows persons such as Janet Hinshaw-Thomas, the director of the US-based PRIME-Ecumenical Commitment to Refugees, to be charged with aiding and abetting the entry into Canada of individuals without proper passports and visas, although the charges were eventually withdrawn. Hence, section 117 should be reformed. Finally, although the 2001 Immigration and Refugee Protection Act established a new Refugee Appeal Division (RAD), the provision has not yet been implemented.

This series of hesitations and uncertainties in the face of mounting human rights violations, especially regarding detainees, appears particularly ominous in the wake of Canada's lack of outspoken condemnation of current US practices regarding detainees, as the 'legal conscience of the [US] Executive Branch', in the context of Abu-Ghraib,

... treated the torture prohibition as if it were a tax code, and as if the main function of the lawyer was not to ensure that the letter and the spirit of the law be honoured, but to find loopholes in the code.[128]

Some of these 'loopholes' included the opinion of the Office of Legal Counsel (OLC), which stated that it was all right to threaten a detainee with death, but not with 'imminent death'; 'to administer personality-altering drugs as long as they did not penetrate to the core of an individual's ability to perceive the world around him'; and that the infliction of mental harm was all right, provided that it was not 'prolonged' and that physical pain was acceptable, provided that it was not severe enough to signify 'organ failure'.[129]

There is no attempt made here to claim that this sort of torture was present or even contemplated in the case of detained asylum seekers in Canada, Australia or elsewhere. But the relaxing of standards in the US were, indeed, followed by 'renditions' elsewhere, without a general outcry from any of the major Western powers.

In fact, after *Sosa*, the 'third wave' of ATCA lawsuits already challenge some of the 'key elements' of the US government's strategy for detaining and interrogating suspected terrorists.[130] Once these practices have been exposed, it is not only claims of 'terrorism' that spur states to ignore the dictates of international law and natural justice, starting with the presumed legitimacy of 'pre-emptive strikes'.[131]

Thus, many other grave human rights issues are in jeopardy because of a specifically 'nationalist jurisprudence' approach on the part of US courts.[132] The opinion of such justices as Scalia or Clarence Thomas view the law beyond the US Constitution as 'irrelevant or, worse yet, an impermissible imposition on the exercise of American Sovereignty'.[133]

Unlike 'nationalist jurisprudence', 'transnationalist jurisprudence', or the approach taken by such justices as Breyer, Ginsburg, Stevens, Souter and Chief Justice Marshall, as well as many others, includes one of the leaders of this camp, Justice Harry Blackmun.[134] What precisely is 'transnational jurisprudence'? Koh explains:

> *Unlike nationalist jurisprudence, which rejects foreign and international precedents and looks for guidance primarily to national territory, political institutions and executive power, the transnational jurisprudence assumes America's political and economic interdependence with other nations operating within the legal system. Nor, significantly, do these justices distinguish sharply between the relevance of foreign and international law, recognizing that one prominent feature of a globalizing world is the emergence of a transnational law, particularly in the area of human rights, that merges the national and the international.*[135]

Essentially, then, it is vital that the US courts go beyond the promotion of narrow American interests and aims, to support and promote the 'mutual interests of all nations in a smoothly functioning international legal regime'.[136] The US position of power imposes a grave responsibility to abide by international law and all the principles of natural justice, upon which the country's judicial system is based, not only because of the immediate effects of its own decisions, but because of the import of all its policies on other Western democracies.

5a. Indefinite detention and US plenary power in *Zadvydas versus Davis*[137]

> *Zadvydas will thus remain a fixture in the legal landscape. Like Plyler v. Doe it will be seen as an important monument to human rights, immigrants' rights and constitutionalism; but without a substantial change in the court's membership, it will have little generative power. As if the sun were directly overhead, it will shine brightly but cause almost no shadow.*[138]

At issue is the question of indefinite detention, particularly in the aftermath of the enactment of the US Patriot Act.[139] In fact, in this act, the then attorney general 'appears to authorize indefinite detention without either administrative or judicial process'.[140]

'Detaining plenary power' is present in the US at this time, although, technically, it does not exist in Canada or other countries discussed so far. But aliens seeking asylum at both Canadian and Australian borders are, for the most part, detained immediately, and may be so held for an indefinite period of time. As in the passage cited at the start of this section, substantive changes in political will are necessary for all Western powers before serious consideration of human rights can moderate or, better, eliminate present policies.

Aleinikoff advocates the need to increase 'constitutional sensitivity' to current lawmaking and jurisprudence:[141]

> *The draconian 1996 legislation violated deep norms of due process, proportionality and fairness. Rather because the court's reading cannot be understood as faithful to legislative intent, its opinion should be read as a constitutional holding.*[142]

The previous discussion of the interface between international human rights law and domestic constitutions (at least in the example of the US) noted that the goal of the former is to introduce higher standards into the present constitutional legislature. Like the presence of *erga omnes* obligations, it puts states and non-state actors on notice about the standards that must be followed and the non-derogable obligations that these norms imply. *Zadvydas* is here described as a 'landmark decision' because, in that case, the court:

> *... has moved beyond invoking a 'phantom' constitutional norm to justify an interpretation of a statute that accords for notions of fundamental fairness.*[143]

Essentially, aliens entering the US should benefit from the general constitutional rights from which US citizens benefit, including 'the right to be free from arbitrary detention'.[144] Even the presence of 'dangerousness', absent the proof that crimes have been committed, is insufficient to permit indefinite detention of immigrants or other aliens. The court cited *United States versus Salerno*,[145] which included substantial procedure protections for detainees. It is instructive to consider Justice Marshall's dissenting opinion from that case:

*This case brings before the court for the first time a statute in which Congress declares that a person innocent of any crime may be jailed indefinitely, pending the trial of allegations which are legally presumed to be untrue, if the government shows to the satisfaction of a judge that the accused is likely to commit crimes, unrelated to the pending charges, at any time in the future. Such statutes, consistent with the usages of tyranny and the excesses of what bitter experience teaches us to call the police state, have long been thought incompatible with the fundamental human rights protected by our constitution. Today a majority of this court hold otherwise. Its decision disregards basic principles of justice established centuries ago and **enshrined beyond the reach of government interference** in the Bill of Rights.*[146]

Emphasizing the fact that there are norms that are 'beyond the reach of government interference' points to the presence of norms of natural justice, *jus cogens* norms and the principles that may derive from them that are part of the origins of international law,[147] which inspired most constitutions of civilized countries today. These must be followed whether or not they are 'enshrined' in the constitutions of specific countries.

This is the most important message to be taken from this case and, in general, from the discussion of the recent treatment of aliens, whether migrants, asylum seekers or others, in the context of recent circumstances and of the present US administration. Although the other countries discussed thus far (i.e. Canada and Australia) have not experienced an immediate attack by a specific alien organization, such as has befallen the US in 2001, the unfortunate 'race to the bottom' of normativity and justice that has happened in the US has unduly influenced other Western countries in their attitude to aliens, in general, including asylum seekers of various national and ethnic backgrounds. It has also helped to 'normalize' in the eyes of other non-US governments the other unacceptable practices that have followed in the US, from the legitimization of 'first strikes', no longer apparently considered illegal aggression in an unjust war, or the barbarous (and equally illegal) practices of 'interrogations' and 'renditions' of detainees.

NOTES

1 Cole, D. (2006) 'The idea of humanity: Human rights and immigrants' rights', *Columbia Human Rights Law Review*, vol 37, p627.
2 Rousseau, C., Crepeau, F., Faxen, P. and Houle, F. (2002) 'The complexity of determining refugeehood: A multidisciplinary analysis of the decision-making process of the Canadian Immigration and Refugee Board', *Journal of Refugee Studies*, vol 15, no 1, pp1–28.
3 Ibid, p8.
4 Hathaway, J. (2005) *The Rights of Refugees under International Law*, Cambridge University Press, Cambridge, UK, pp991–1002.
5 Ibid.
6 Ibid, p992.
7 UNHCR (2006) *The State of the World's Refugees 2006: Human Displacement in the New Millennium*, Oxford University Press, Oxford, UK, p43.

8   Hathaway, J. and Neve, A. (1997) 'Making refugee law relevant again: A proposal for collectivized and situation-oriented protection', *Harvard Human Rights Journal*, vol 10, no 115, spring.
9   UNHCR Executive Committee Conclusion No. 44 (XXXVII), 13 October 1986.
10 Rocco Galati, in lecture, Osgoode Hall Law School, 20 November 2007.
11 Hathaway, J. (1996) 'Can international refugee law be made relevant again?' US Committee for Refugees, *World Refugee Survey*, vol 14.
12 Ibid, pp 49–120; Bell, D. (1980) 'Brown v. Board of Education and interest convergence dilemma', *Harvard Law Review*, vol 93, p518.
13 Hathaway (1996), op cit Note 11.
14 Westra, L. (2007) *Environmental Justice and the Rights of Indigenous Peoples*, Earthscan, London, Chapter 7.
15 Brouwer, A. and Kumin, J. (2003) ' Interception and asylum: When migration control and human rights collide', *Refuge*, vol 21, no 4, December, pp6–24.
16 UNHCR (2001) 'Refugee protection and migration control: Perspectives from the UNHCR and IOM', UN Doc. EC/GC/01/11, United Nations High Commissioner for Refugees, 31 May, p14.
17 Brouwer and Kumin, op cit Note 15, p6.
18 UNHCR Executive Committee, Conclusion No. 97 (LIV) 2003.
19 USCR (2002) *World Refugee Survey 2002*, US Committee for Refugees, Washington, DC.
20 Ibid.
21 European Council, Schengen Directive, 28 June 2001 (June 28 Council Directive 2001/51/EC Supplementing the Provision of Article 26 of the Convention Implementing the Schengen Directive (of 2001 L 187/46)).
22 Brouwer and Kumin, op cit Note 15, p11.
23 Ibid.
24 Hathaway, J. (1991) *The Law of Refugee Status*, Butterworths, Toronto, Canada, p249.
25 Ibid, p250.
26 UNHCR, 13 October 1986, No. 44 (XXXVII).
27 *Sahin versus Canada Minister of Citizenship and Immigration* [1995] 1 F.C.214.
28 Goodwin-Gill, G. S. (1996) *The Refugee in International Law* (second edition), Clarendon Press, Oxford, UK, p167.
29 Ibid.
30 *Sahin versus Canada*, op cit Note 27.
31 Immigration Act (fourth supplement), R.S.C. (1985), s 7 and 12.
32 Ibid, s 103.
33 *Al-Kateb versus Goodwin* [2004] HCA 37, 6 August 2004.
34 Ibid, paragraph 247.
35 Ibid.
36 Article 33 of the CSR.
37 Goodwin-Gill, op cit Note 28, p169.
38 Goodwin-Gill, G. S. (1986) '*Non-refoulement* and the new asylum seekers', *Virginia Journal of International Law*, vol 26, pp897–918.
39 Hathaway (1991), op cit Note 24.
40 Ibid, section 1.5, 'An expanded refugee concept in customary international law?'.
41 Hathaway and Neve, op cit Note 8, pp115–125.
42 Westra, L. (2004) *Ecoviolence and the Law*, Transnational Publishers Inc., Ardsley, NY.
43 Cole, op cit Note 1, p631.
44 *Rasul versus Bush*, 542 U.S. 466 (2004).
45 Danner, M. (2004) *Torture and Truth: America, Abu Ghraib, and the War on Terror*, New York Review Books, New York, p115; Cole, op cit Note 1.

46 Danner, ibid.
47 *Baker versus Canada* (M.C.I.) [1999] 2 S.C.R. 817(S.C.C.).
48 Cole, op cit Note 1, p632.
49 Alien Torts Claims Act, 28 USC 1350, 1798.
50 Sosa, 542 U.S. at 725.
51 Cole, op cit Note 1, p633.
52 Westra, L. (2007), op cit Note 14, pp103–124; see also Goodland, R. and Counsell, S. (2008) 'How the World Bank could lead the world in alleviating climate change', in L. Westra, K. Bosselman and R. Westra (eds) *Reconciling Human Existence with Ecological Integrity*, Earthscan, London, Chapter 13.
53 Petition by National Association of Manufacturers, *Sosa versus Alvarez-Machain*, 124 S. ct.2739 (2004).
54 Ku, J. (2005) 'The third wave: The Alien Tort Statute and the war on terrorism', *Emory International Law Review*, vol 19, p105.
55 *Filartiga versus Pena Irala*, 630 F.2d 876 (2d Cir. 1980); *Kadic versus Karadzic*, (1996) 74 F.3d 153 (2d Cir. 1998).
56 Ku, op cit Note 54, p108; see also note 15.
57 Ibid.
58 *Doe versus Unocal Corporation*, 2002 W.L. 3d 63976 (9 Cir. 2003).
59 Harrington, C. (2002) 'Doe v. Unocal Corp. (2002 WL 31063976(9th Cir.2002))', *Tulane Environmental Law Journal*, vol 16, p247
60 Ibid, p248.
61 ATCA, 28 U.S.C.S. 1350 (2002), the Ninth Circuit reversed the original verdict; *Doe/Roe versus Unocal Corp.*, 110 F. Supp. 2d 1294,1306 (C.D. Cal. 2000).
62 Harrington, op cit Note 59, p249.
63 *Filartiga versus Pena Irala*, 630 F.2d 876, 881 (2d Cir.1980).
64 Bridgeford, T. A. (2003) 'Imputing human rights violations on multinational corporations: The Ninth Circuit strikes again in judicial activism', *American University International Law Review*, vol 18, no 4, p1022.
65 Ibid.
66 Ridenour, A. (2001) 'Apples and oranges: Why courts should use international standards to determine liability for violations of the law of nations under the Alien Tort Claims Act', *Tulane Journal of International and Comparative Law*, vol 9, Spring, p589.
67 Ibid, p590.
68 See Chapter 1; Ramasastry, A. (2002) 'Corporate complicity from Nuremberg to Rangoon: An examination of forced labor cases and their impact on the liability of multinational corporations', *Berkeley Journal of International Law*, vol 20, no 1, pp100–104.
69 *Jota versus Texaco Inc.* 157 F 3d 153 (2d Cir 1998).
70 *Maria Aguinda and others including the Federation of the Yagua People of the Lower Amazon and Lower Napo versus Texaco, Inc.*, 303 F 3d 470; 2002 US App. LEXIScl6540; 157 Oil and Gas Rep. 333, 16 August 2002, Decided.
71 *Aguinda versus Texaco, Inc.*, 1945 F. Supp.625 (5 D.N.Y. 1996); *Aguinda versus Texaco, Inc.*, 142 F. Supp.2d 534 (S.D.N.Y. 2001); *Jota versus Texaco, Inc.*, 157 F 3d 153 (2d Cir.1998).
72 Ibid.
73 Ibid, p472.
74 Ibid, p473.
75 Ibid.
76 Ibid, p474.
77 See, for instance, Epstein, S. (1978) *The Politics of Cancer*, Sierra Club Books, San Francisco, CA; Soskolne, C. and Bertollini, R. (1999) *Global Ecological Integrity and 'Sustainable Development': Cornerstones of Public Health*, discussion document based on an international workshop at the

World Health Organization European Centre for Environment and Health, Rome Division, Rome, Italy, 3–4 December 1998, www.euro.who.int/document/gch/ecorep5.pdf; WHO (2002) 'Summary', in *World Report on Violence and Health*, World Health Organization, Geneva; Licari, L., Nemer, L. and Tamburlini, G. (eds) (2005) *Children's Health and the Environment*, World Health Organization Regional Office for Europe, Copenhagen, Denmark; also Westra, L. (2006) *Environmental Justice and the Rights of Unborn and Future Generations*, Earthscan, London.

78 Westra, L. (2004) op cit Note 42, Chapter 7.
79 Ibid, p674.
80 Ibid, p475.
81 Ibid, pp552–553.
82 Ibid.
83 Westra, L. (2004 and 2006) op cit Notes 78 and 77.
84 *Guerra versus Italy* (116/1996/735/932), 19 Feb. 1998; *Lopez-Ostra versus Spain* (1995) 20 HER 277m (1994) ECHR 16798/90.
85 *Nuclear Test Case, Australia versus France, New Zealand versus France* (1974) I.C.J. Rep. 253.
86 Westra, L. (2006) op cit Note 77, Chapter 7.
87 Scott, C. (2002) *Torture as Tort*, Hart Publishing, Oxford, UK, 'Introduction', p9.
88 Baxi, U. (2002) 'Geographies of injustice: Human rights at the altar of convenience', in Scott, op cit Note 87, Chapter 7.
89 *Bancoult versus McNamara*, 217 FRD 280, 2003.
90 Ibid, pp22–23.
91 Ibid, pp31–33.
92 Federal Employees Liability Reform and Tort compensation Act of 1988, Fub.L. No. 100-694, 102 Stat.4563 (1988) (codified at 28 U.S.C. & 2671-2680).
93 Ibid, p24.
94 Ibid, paragraph 42.
95 Ibid, paragraph 47.
96 Steiner, H. J. and Alston, P. (2000) *International Human Rights in Context* (second edition), Oxford University Press, Oxford, UK, p1072.
97 *Filartiga versus Pena Irala*, US Court of Appeals, 2d ct, 1980 630 F 2d 876.
98 *United States versus Smith*, 18 U.S., 153, 160-161, 5 L. Ed. 57 (1920).
99 Terry, J. (2002) 'Taking Filartiga on the road', in Scott, op cit Note 87, p110.
100 Ibid, p133.
101 2008 UKHL 61: an appeal from [2007] EWCA Civ. 498.
102 *R (Bancoult) versus Secretary of State for Foreign and Commonwealth Affairs* [2007] QB 1067 (Bancoult 1).
103 Ibid, paragraph 5.
104 British Indian Ocean Territories Order 1865 SI No. 1920.
105 Ibid, paragraph 6.
106 *Chagos Islanders versus Attorney General* (2003) EWCH 2222 (QB), (2003) All ER (D) 166.
107 Ibid, paragraph 10.
108 Blackstone, W. (1765–1769) *Commentaries on the Laws of England*, vol 1, Clarendon Press, Oxford.
109 Justice Souter, writing for the Court, *Sosa versus Alvarez-Machain*, 124 S. Ct. 2739, pp2764–2765.
110 Ibid.
111 Ku (2005), op cit Note 54, p117.
112 *Alvarez-Machain versus United States*, 331 F.3d 604, 620 (9th Cir.2003).
113 *Bancoult versus McNamara*.

114 *Shafiq Rasul et al Petitioners versus George W. Bush, President of the United States et al, Fawzi Khalid Abdullah Fahad Al Odah et al, Petitioners versus United States et al* (No. 03-334), (No. 03-343) 542 U.S. 466; 124 S. Ct. 2686, 28 June 2004, Decided.
115 Ibid, Summary, p548.
116 Under federal *habeas corpus* provisions (28 USCS §2241).
117 *Rasul v. Bush*, op cit Note 114, opinion by Stevens J., O'Connor, Souter, Ginsburg and Breyer JJ.
118 Ibid.
119 Roth, K. (2000) 'The charade of US ratification of international human rights treaties', *Chicago Journal of International Law*, vol 1, no 2, Fall, pp347–354.
120 United Nations Climate Change Conference in Bali, COP 13, CMP3, SB 27, AWG 4, December 2007.
121 Ibid, p347.
122 United Nations Convention on the Rights of the Child (UNCROC) 20 November 1989, GA 44/25.
123 Convention on the Rights of the Child, Art. 37(a), 20 November 1989, 1577 U.N.T.S. 44 55; see also Nilsen, E. S. (2007) 'Decency, dignity and desert: Restoring ideals of humane punishment to constitutional discourse,' *University of California, Davis Law Review*, vol 41, p111.
124 Roth (2000), op cit Note 119, p350; see also Westra, L. (2006) op cit Note 77, pp83–95.
125 UN Convention on Torture and Other Cruel, Inhuman or Degrading Treatment or Punishment, Art. 2, S. Treaty Doc. No. 100-20, @20, 1465 U.N.T.S 85, 114 (entered into force 26 June 1987).
126 Louise Arbour, UN High Commissioner for Human Rights, speaking in Ottawa, 22 October 2007.
127 Amnesty International (2007) 'Canada and the international protection of human rights: An erosion of leadership? An update to Amnesty International's human rights agenda for Canada', Amnesty International, Canada, p17, available at www.fafia-afai.org/files/HumanRightsAgenda2007.pdf; on 2 July 2006, Bachan Singh Sogi was deported to India, on 22 October 2007, Said Jaziri was deported to Tunisia.
128 Cole (2006), op cit Note 1, p636; see also Memorandum from J. S. Bybee to Alberto Gonzales regarding Standards of Conduct for Interrogation under 18 U.S.C. §§2340–2340A, August 2002 (links to full text and other relevant documents, and summary of salient points, available at http://en.wikipedia.org/wiki/Bybee_memo).
129 Cole (2006), op cit Note 1, p636; see also Bybee Memorandum, ibid; on the question of torture see also Luban, D. (2007) 'The torture lawyers of Washington', in *Legal Ethics and Human Dignity*, Cambridge University Press, Cambridge, UK; Luban, D. (2006) 'Liberalism, torture, and the ticking bomb', in K. J. Greenberg (ed) *The Torture Debate in America*, Cambridge University Press, Cambridge, UK, pp55–68.
130 Ku (2005), op cit Note 54, pp126–127.
131 Semple, K. (2007) 'US falters in terror case against 7 in Miami', *The New York Times*, 14 December; where 'seven indigent men were charged with plotting to blow up the Sears Tower in Chicago as part of an Islamic Jihad', despite the fact that their discussions took place in an abandoned warehouse, and that there was no evidence of arms or bombs, nor of any funds to secure these in the future.
132 Koh, H. H. (2004) 'Agora: The United States Constitution and international law: International law as part of our law', *American Journal of International Law*, vol 98, no 1, pp43–56.
133 Ibid, p52; see for instance *Foster versus Florida*, 537 U.S. 990(2002).
134 Koh, op cit Note 132, pp52–53; see also Koh, H. H. (1991) 'Transnational public law litigation', *Yale Law Journal*, vol 100, pp2362–2363; Blackmun, H. A. (1994) 'The Supreme Court and the law of nations', *Yale Law Journal*, vol 104, p39.

135 Ibid, p53.
136 Stephen Breyer, keynote address, 2003, 97 ASIL PROC. 265; see also Sandra Day O'Connor, Keynote Address, 2002, 96 ASIL PROC. 348.
137 *Zadvydas versus Davis*, 121 S.Ct. 2491 (2001).
138 Aleinikoff, A. T. (2002) 'Detaining plenary power: The meaning and impact of *Zadvydas v. Davis*', *Georgetown Immigration Law Journal*, vol 16, pp365, 386.
139 US Patriot Act of 2001, Pub.L.No. 107-56, 115 Stat.272; as well as the Continued Detention of Aliens Subject to Final Orders of Removal, 66 Fed.Reg. 56, 967, 56, 967-82 (15 November 2001).
140 Aleinikoff (2002), op cit Note 138, p366.
141 Ibid, p360, referring to the 1996 Illegal Immigration Reform and Immigrant Responsibility Act, INA §241(a)(6), 8 U.S.C. §1231(a)(6) (2000).
142 Ibid.
143 Ibid.
144 Ibid, p371.
145 *United States versus Salerno*, 481 U.S. 739 (1987).
146 Salerno, 481 U.S. @755-56; Marshall J. dissenting; emphasis added.
147 Lauterpacht, H. (1950) *International Law and Human Rights*, Steven and Sons Publishers, London.

PART TWO

Ecological Refugees and Refugee Law: The Interface

CHAPTER 4

The Five Grounds Revisited: Who Are the Vulnerable?

Humanitarian law and human rights law consider environmental degradation from an anthropocentric point of view, addressing the adverse effects of environmental degradation on human beings. While migration to escape an environment temporarily or permanently disrupted is a critical aspect of the issue, the current international legal regime disregards the correlation between environmental degradation and human migration.[1]

1. INTRODUCTION: ENVIRONMENTAL MIGRANTS – CAUSE AND IMPACTS

In the first three chapters of this work, we examined the regulatory regime that governs the status of refugees. Flights from their homelands are motivated by a number of events today: environmental disasters, whether direct, such as a tsunami or volcanic explosion, or indirect, such as severe fires or ice melts due to climate change; conflicts which may also be ecologically caused, such as those motivated by scarce resources or water issues; or, finally, migrations due to ethnic or religious differences, or to being victimized by development activities of various extractive industries. Given that almost all large movements of people arise from one or another of the causes mentioned or by a combination of several, it is hard to see why the significance of ecological harms to large migrations has not been officially recognized.

The individual asylum seekers who are persecuted for minority/ethnic reasons, however, are not the main topic of this work. As well, they are not the main targets of fear, rejection and dislike by the affluent countries that ought to render assistance.

Paradoxically, the gravest 'threat' perceived is posed by the migrants who escape conditions that are not easily rectified, who flee in large numbers and who, in addition, because of their very number, pose not only a social and, perhaps, a cultural threat to the existing dominant social groups: the (potential) host country, is ecologically threatened as well. Hence, these asylum seekers are perceived as posing a double threat: first, a threat simply because they are 'aliens' – thus, because of their different racial, social, religious presence; but also, second, because of their humanity, which ensures that their needs are our needs. Hence, they will compete with other citizens, not only for livelihoods, but also for resources.

We cannot expect that the burgeoning population of countries already burdened by population growth and immigration problems, both of which may pose a stress to their security, will welcome further stresses:[2]

> Immigration into the United States, both documented and undocumented, has grown steadily over the past two decades and now exceeds one million persons per year. In a time of shrinking government budgets, stagnant or declining real wages, and job instability, immigration again has become a politically charged issue.[3]

Nor is the US the only country facing an 'immigration crisis' at this time.[4] Statistics show that, for instance, natural catastrophes in the regions of Asia and North Pacific from 1972 to 2000 have affected millions of people:[5]

Impacts of natural disasters in Asia-Pacific regions, 1972–2000

	Number of people killed (millions)	Number of people affected (millions)	Cost of damage (US$ millions)
South Asia	761	2,164,034	60,881
Southeast Asia	73	284,074	33,570
Northwest Pacific and East Asia	606	1,447,643	317,174
Central Asia	3	4895	986
Australia and New Zealand	1	15,761	21,900
South Pacific	4	4061	33,139
Total	1447	3,920,467	437,649

Source: United Nations Environment Programme (translated from the French)

Note that the already overwhelming number of people who are 'affected' ('touchée' in the original French table) by the catastrophes listed above – that is, who are in dire need of immediate humanitarian assistance as well as possible refuge – do not include the much larger number of people affected in Indonesia, Thailand and surrounding areas as a result of the Indian Ocean tsunami in December 2004 (nor the Indonesian floods of 2007).[6]

Thus both natural and anthropogenic disasters, industrial 'accidents',[7] and environmental and ecological damage caused by armed conflicts are increasing exponentially. In addition, the United Nations Development Programme (UNDP) indicates the strong correlation between the level of development of a country and the level of mortality following disasters. Finally, there are various regions, including the ones named in the table above, where the possibility of the occurrence of natural disasters is high.[8] The reality of these current disasters and of the increasing risks is not adequately considered in either international or domestic legal regimes.

Hence, I propose reconsidering the 'five grounds' on which the recognition of persecution (hence of refugee status) is based in the light of global threats in order to ascertain whether any other international legal instrument related to those issues may assist in protecting refugees in the current crisis. We will return to the related public health problems and other issues below. For now, we need to respond first to a basic objection to the argument here presented.

Some argue that the definition of environmental refugees that is available today is both 'ambiguous and inconsistent'.[9] As well, there are those who view 'poverty', 'population growth' and 'resource scarcity'[10] as so inextricably interwoven with environmental issues that 'removing environmental processes from social, economic and political processes in which they are embedded is virtually impossible'.[11] But if we dilute the realties that give rise to the phenomenon of environmental refugees, we may well confuse them with other social, economic and institutional processes which, instead, are themselves root causes of the environmental changes that are, in turn, directly causative of large migrations today.

It is the same 'root causes', institutional, social and economic, that give rise to the other concomitant problems that render environmental issues such that they result in whole areas and regions that become unliveable for too many, who are then forced to migrate.

To contrast social/economic problems to environmental ones is to commit a major error, which leads to the further mistake of assuming that, after all, environmental degradation may be a 'gradual process' – hence, if this aspect is the most significant, then we might want to critique immigration estimates, thus denying the magnitude of the problem:

> None of the estimates of migration associated with global warming gives any consideration to adaptation mechanisms.[12]

Hence, 'adaptation' is proposed by minimizing the impact of climate change as well as that of the other issues listed above as causing forced migrations and environmental refugees. But most such circumstances are not amenable to 'adaptation': island states and coastal cities after hurricanes and tsunamis, Arctic regions after glacial melts, and areas of desertification are no more liveable than are areas where chemical and other industrial discharges have taken place, and they will remain unliveable for very long periods.

A simple consideration of the New Orleans area affected by Hurricane Katrina, several years after the fact, will demonstrate the truth of this contention, even when the disaster happens in a developed, industrial country such as the US. Unfortunately, the reason why these errors remain unconvincing to large segments of the population, and especially to their leaders, remains tied to the interests and the nationalist, even racist feelings that often support those interests, especially when they are expressed in economic terms.

1a. A short aside on the economics of immigration

In all countries, those who belong to visible minorities appear particularly unwelcome and disturbing to a country's citizens, whether they are Albanians or Gypsies in Italy; Kurds in Germany, or Hispanics in the US: on the one hand, they are not easily assimilated; on the other, they may take away citizens' jobs, or lower wages through their greater availability, and even 'drain the resources of social welfare programmes'.[13] Although working age immigrants do not use the services of welfare agencies as much as local citizens (hence, by working and paying taxes, they do not deplete the welfare system), the situation is quite different in the case of refugees. The latter, like the elderly, require immediate assistance as they may enter the host country too late to contribute positively to the economy, or to earn a pension.[14]

An important question may well be whether current legal systems are capable of protecting refugees in a way that also permits them to contribute positively to the local economy. Detaining them, aside from the human rights violations that it involves, also provides an insurmountable barrier to the possibility of integrating asylum seekers into the economy, if not into their new social milieu.

However, it is worth keeping in mind, 'integration' itself may present a greater danger to refugees than it does to the society of the host country, when they are part of a specific indigenous local community, with a particular ethnic and cultural background.

2. RACE AND ETHNIC BACKGROUND: THE IMPLICATIONS

> ... *no federal or state court that has addressed the question during the past fifty years has held that the charter's human rights clauses are self-executing; indeed many courts have held specifically that they are not.*[15]

The development of human rights law originates from the United Nations, which, like the 1951 convention, was originally formed precisely to oppose the atrocities and gross human rights violations that came to light at the end of World War II:

> *The development of the law of international human rights wrought a significant change in international law making the individual a subject, as opposed to an irrelevant object of international law for the first time.*[16]

All legal instruments originating from and sanctioned by the UN share this character, and most have the character of obligations *erga omnes* upon both state and non-state actors, as well as individuals. In fact, such documents were designed with the express purpose of elevating the standards of all national legal regimes beyond their usual support for self-interested goals, often pursued with minimal regard for the right of individuals.

Once again, we must consider the insufficiency of treaties, which may or may not be signed, ratified or, finally, properly incorporated into domestic legal instruments, so that they can be appealed to in the appropriate cases. In contrast, the presence of *erga omnes* obligations, based upon *jus cogens* norms, at least in principle, may not be shrugged off as inappropriate or irrelevant to a country's constitution or other basic rights instrument.

The dictum of the Barcelona Traction and Light and Power Co[17] cites four examples of these non-derogable obligations, grounded in basic human rights: the first is the 'outlawing of acts of aggression'; the second is 'the outlawing of genocide'; the third is 'the protection from slavery'; and the fourth one is 'protection from racial discrimination'.[18]

We will return to the other examples below; for now the most relevant of the examples is the protection against racial discrimination, elements of which are present in all constitutions today. This instrument embodies an absolute principle, as Judge Tanaka, for instance, indicated:

> *States which do not recognize this principle [i.e. the protection of human rights] or even deny its existence are nevertheless subject to its rule.*[19]

Few, if any, states today would be prepared to claim that they officially 'deny the existence' of human rights in general, or that they support racial discrimination as such. Nevertheless, the treatment of refugees, including especially large groups of ecological refugees, indicates the presence of this sort of discrimination in two separate but related forms.

The first is the obvious result of 'we–them' policies, aimed at denying access to the procedural or social/economic rights of these individuals, as we have noted in Chapters 2 and 3, as these groups belong, for the most part, to different ethnic and racial backgrounds from those of the receiving country. The second represents an even more insidious form of discrimination: the presence – in fact, the very existence – of ecological migrants is ignored. They are the faceless alien; not only do they have no voice in policy-/decision-making – that is, in the decisions that render them essentially homeless – but they are also not 'present' when policies and legal regimes are created that could at least offer them some protection 'after the fact'.

2a. Environmental change and large human migrations: The interface

> *... environmental disasters are traditionally classified into three categories:*
>
> 1 *long-term environmental degradation, including global warming, deforestation, land erosion, salinity, waterlogging and desertification;*
> 2 *sudden natural environmental disruptions, including earthquakes, droughts, floods, hurricanes, monsoons, tidal waves, tornadoes and volcanic eruptions;*
> 3 *accidents, including both industrial and chemical disasters.*[20]

Examples may be multiplied, as they are highlighted almost daily in the media, as they continue to occur. The most obvious and, perhaps, the most publicized is the effect of global warming on Arctic ice – hence on the Arctic peoples whose traditional lifestyle depends on it.[21] The discriminatory negligence (if not knowledge as intent) is clearly in evidence as the result of global warming can be seen, first and foremost, on the people who, as Sheila Watt-Cloutier put it, 'have the right to be cold' (October 2006, COP9, Montreal).

The racial/ethnic aspect of this form of discrimination emerges most specifically here, as these peoples are Inuit, indigenous Arctic peoples, whose lifestyle is entirely dependent upon the specific territory they occupy, and its normal environmental conditions. I have argued that, in this case, those responsible are not only guilty of grave human rights violations, as a violent form of environmental racism; but because recent environmental conditions lead to the elimination of these traditional peoples as such, they are also guilty of a form of genocide.[22]

At the opposite end of the spectrum is the African Sahel and desertification in this region due to global warming as the area 'surpassed thresholds of irreversible depletion, and was no longer able to retain adequate moisture and rainwater'.[23] The Sahel is said to have originated some of 'the largest numbers of environmental refugees in proportion to its total population'.[24]

Another consequence of global warming that creates large numbers of refugees is the problem of rising sea levels.[25] In addition, one third of the world's current population lives within 60km of a coastline today and, given current population increases, the number of present and potential migrants will become truly staggering.[26] Arthur Westing has documented displaced persons in 1990. Using UN data, the total he found was 41.5 million persons, including officially recognized refugees (16.7 million), unrecognized, cross-border refugees (3.5 million) and unrecognized internal refugees (21.3 million).[27]

It cannot be doubted that after another ten years of unchecked global warming and unrestrained industrial activities, these statistics will have risen to an increasingly unmanageable number. Already in 1985, Mustafa Tolba, executive director of the United Nations Environment Programme (UNEP), said:

> ... *these people are the millions fleeing from the droughts of Northern Africa, the victims of Bhopal, and the thousands made homeless by the Mexican earthquake. They are environmental refugees.*[28]

Yet, notwithstanding the well-established links between environmental causes and human migrations as effects, the 'solution' of reducing, mitigating or eliminating the practices that cause environmental degradation with its expected results, Western countries still continue to view the refugees that emerge from these ongoing disasters as 'threats', rather than as victims of the environmental violence these states perpetrate:

> *It is not anti-human or antisocial to say that too many people can be problem... People pollute, and too many people living in an area can degrade that area irrevocably. Immigration at higher levels exacerbates our resource and environmental problems. It will leave a poorer, more crowded, more divided country for our children.*[29]

It appears illogical to acknowledge the role of pollution and other environmental problems as causative of human misery related to resource depletion and environmental degradation, but, at the same time, to ignore the causative role of Western industrial activities and so-called 'free trade' agreements, whether conducted on location (i.e. as a direct, immediate threat to local and indigenous populations in the developing world) or indirect, through the activities that have been recognized as causative of climate change far from the borders of the affluent countries from which they originate.

It is more than a case of negligence in the assertion of various 'rights' of states and non-state actors; it is, I maintain, a case of 'wilful blindness' in the commission of crimes that show the understanding and acceptance of certain consequences to one's actions, while refusing to face the final results that will, inevitably, ensue.[30]

It is not the case that hordes of migrants wilfully descend on innocent industrial Western countries, ready to impose hardships on the legitimate citizens of those states. On the contrary, the ongoing practices of Western industrialized nations is to extend their 'eco-footprint' in any way that serves their interests, without undue concern for the resulting environmental/human consequences.[31]

The results that follow are the appropriation of biological resources and the imposition of grave conditions of scarcity. In addition, exporting industrial practices in this manner also results in exporting hazardous operations, dangerous wastes and, in general, hazardous exposures for the local population who are totally vulnerable, as they most often lack even the flimsy protection of Western public health/environmental regulations.[32]

The careless extension of Western ecological footprint dominates present global institutions and legal regimes. Hence, even to insist, as many scholars do, that the economic need to migrate does not make a refugee, appears to be a superficial and basically flawed position. The International Covenant on Civil and Political Rights, Article I(2), states:

> *All peoples may, for their own ends, freely dispose of their natural wealth and resources without prejudice to any obligation arising out of international economic co-operation, based upon the principle of mutual benefit and international law.* **In no case may a people be deprived of its own means of subsistence.** [emphasis added]

Hence, it is clear that all activities, whether by states or non-state actors, that result in environmental degradation leading to the elimination of a people's 'means of subsistence', commit a breach of the civil rights of these people, especially when the affected community is a traditional one, living on the land. It is then, almost by definition, a poor one, one that cannot provide for its needs by importing water and food from abroad, or from other parts of its country.

Because the clause of the International Covenant on Civil and Political Rights (ICCPR) is particularly significant in the case of impoverished communities, especially but not exclusively indigenous ones, deprivation represents a form of racial discrimination. Hence, when the elimination of the 'means of subsistence' forces the inhabitants to migrate, the non-recognition of their plight, and the lack of acceptance on the part of the very Western countries that contributed directly or indirectly to their deprivation, is also an unacceptable form of racism.

Specific circumstances, as we saw, could not possibly provide a justification for the use of torture on detainees or others, even in extreme situations in war. I believe that the same non-derogability argument can be applied to persons of a different race from the majority of citizens of an affluent country. This argument is based on the fourth example of *erga omnes* obligations in the Barcelona Light and Traction case, discussed in the previous section.

If the action of state officials regarding asylum seekers at their borders were viewed in this light, it would be far harder to claim the treatment of such refugees to be a legitimate form of self-protection, or, better yet, a 'moral right' to a position intended to safeguard domestic distributive justice. Mathias Risse argues in favour of coercive restrictions on immigration:

> ... all the justification states need to prohibit arbitrary and uncontrolled immigration ... is that they are doing something morally defensible, even morally praiseworthy, that in general cannot be maintained if there is no access to regulation. What states do that deserves such protection is to provide for their members by maintaining a morally defensible legal framework and social system.[33]

If my argument against this position is acceptable, then it is hard to see how a 'morally defensible legal framework' can coexist with outright discrimination, in direct conflict with national and international law, especially in the context with the economic fact briefly touched upon above. This argument pits domestic distributive justice against its cosmopolitan, international counterpart. As we are now discussing basic principles of law (*jus cogens* norms), and morality, it might be worthwhile to review briefly the legal grounds of human rights.

3. THE FOUNDATIONS OF BASIC HUMAN RIGHTS

> ... the UNHCR's mandate imposes no requirement to ensure the physical welfare or even the survival of refugees. The UNHCR undertakes to provide assistance only in response to explicit request of national governments.[34]

The first question that arises, is how can this be the case when all of the UN legal instruments that comprise the foundation of human rights are based on the common humanity of all. The Universal Declaration of Human Rights[35] and the International Covenant on Economic, Social and Cultural Rights[36] express this belief in the preambular sections of each document, which state that:

> ... recognition of the inherent dignity and of the equal and inalienable rights of all members of the human family is the foundation of freedom, justice and peace in the world...

Hence, none of these instruments addresses specific ethnic or national groups in order to proclaim their rights, as enforceable against others. The United Nations speaks for and about the organized community of nations – hence, for all peoples of the world. In fact, the Universal Declaration declares the rights to freedom from discrimination, freedom of religion, freedom of association and freedom of expression (see Articles 2, 18, 19 and 20); hence, it is foundational to support the five grounds enumerated in the Convention on Social Refugees (CSR) as the acceptable basis for a well-founded fear of persecution.

These rights are not here proposed for states or for specific nationalities, nor do they include the right to exclude anyone from the protection of the covenants and the declaration itself. Natural justice as well as international law demand that certain norms be considered such that no derogation is possible from them, either through a treaty or through an article of municipal law.[37] *Jus cogens* norms have been acknowledged since the first decades of the 20th century, and Ragazzi lists several foundational texts from the late 1920s to the 1930s.[38] Essentially, the drafts of the Vienna Convention on the Law of Treaties codified what eventually became Article 53 in the final version of the document: Special Rapporteurs Sir Hersch Lauterpacht, Sir Gerald Fitzmaurice and Sir Humphrey Waldoc refined the definition, which was later used by the International Court of Justice. Nevertheless, the precise content of *jus cogens* remains uncertain to this day. Article 53 of the Vienna Convention states:

> Treaties conflicting with a peremptory norm of general international law (jus cogens). *A treaty is void if, at the time of its conclusion, it conflicts with a peremptory norm of general international law. For the purposes of the present Convention, a peremptory norm of general international law is a norm accepted and recognized by the international community of States as a whole as a norm from which no derogation is permitted and which can be modified only by a subsequent norm of general international law having the same character.*[40]

Article 64 reiterates the same interpretation. But the most important point to keep in mind is that when the United Nations was founded, positivism reigned and, as some argued: 'The terrible experiences of the two world wars'[41] influenced the UN to seek some non-derogable principles around which to design a true law of all nations, but also of all peoples.

Hence, it became increasingly clear that an international body had to emphasize that certain rules had an absolute character (i.e. that the rules that protected the human person, and ensured the maintenance of peace through justice, had to be understood to have a character separate and different from other rules). The status of these norms, therefore, and the obligation they impose, must be acknowledged before we can attempt to reread them in a way that might fit the present problems of refugees and asylum seekers.

In 1993, the Vienna World Conference adopted a phrase that ought to govern our understanding of human rights, notwithstanding the existence of 'higher' norms, as discussed: 'all rights are indivisible and interdependent and interrelated'.[42] The fact that they are interrelated and interconnected, however, does not mean that there is no hierarchy among them, as Article 53 is clear on that point.

Sir Hersch Lauterpacht explains the relation between international law and human rights following the United Nations Declaration of Human Rights in 1948:

> *What have been the reasons which have prompted the changes in the matter of subjects of international law, with regard to both international rights and to international duties? These causes have been numerous and manifold. They have included, with reference to the recognition of the individual as a subject of international rights, the acknowledgment of the worth of human personality as the ultimate unit of all law; the realization of the dangers besetting international peace as the result of the denial of fundamental human rights; and the increased attention to those already substantial developments in international law in which, notwithstanding the traditional dogma, the individual is in fact treated as a subject of international rights.*[43]

This change of emphasis and inclusiveness move international law away from the formal recognition of state jurisdiction and sovereignty, and that of their diplomatic representatives and their property, to a re-conceptualizing of the subjects of international law in relation to the state.[44] In addition, Lauterpacht argues convincingly that 'the law of nature and the natural rights of man' cannot simply be used as an alternative to changes in the law, but that their power lies in viewing both as foundational to the 'ultimate validity' of the law itself, and as 'a standard of its approximation to justice'. He concludes:

> *Even after human rights and freedoms have become part of the fundamental law of mankind, the ideas of natural law and natural rights which underlie them will constitute that higher law which must forever remain the ultimate standard of fitness of all positive law whether national or international.*[45]

Hence, those who attempt to limit international law to its positivist parameters, and who argue against 'making a distinction between fundamental human rights and other human rights', diminish significantly the value and power of international law. Still, if they can state that the fundamental or basic human rights 'are rights whose validity is not dependent on their acceptance by the subjects of law, but which are at the foundation of the international community', this still defends a special status, without acknowledging the basis for it.[46]

Yet, to view 'elementary' or 'fundamental' rights in this manner is to deprive them of the very standards by which their status and their validity can be judged. It is far better to follow Lauterpacht,[47] Fitzmaurice[48] and Theodore Meron,[49] as well as, more recently, Ragazzi and others,[50] in recognizing the existence of an absolute standard whereby norms may be judged to be *jus cogens* – hence giving rise to obligations *erga omnes*. The gravity of the situation of refugees is increased, and their ability to defend their fundamental rights is significantly reduced if we simply resort to a positivist acknowledgement of the legal instruments and practices of states, as we have seen.

In fact, the prohibition of racial discrimination, one of the recognized grounds of persecution, has close ties with the prohibition of genocide, 'a crime against the moral law ... and the spirit and aims of the United Nations'.[51]

3a. Racial discrimination and genocide, revisited: *Kupreskic et al*

> *The* mens rea *requirement for persecution is higher than for ordinary crimes against humanity although lower than for genocide. In this context the Trial Chamber wishes to stress that persecution as a crime against humanity is an offence belonging to the same genus as genocide...*
>
> *Thus it can be said that from the viewpoint of* mens rea, *genocide is an extreme and most inhuman form of persecution. To put it differently, when persecution escalates to the extreme form of willful and deliberate acts designed to destroy a group or part of a group, it can be held that such persecution amounts to genocide.*[52]

We need to fully understand the reach and ambit of persecution, including a state's reactions to the victims of persecution, by fully appreciating the import to the *mens rea* requirement in genocide, especially by looking at other related cases. For instance, in the *Case Concerning the Application of the Convention on the Prevention and Punishment of the Crime of Genocide*,[53] we retrace the steps of that landmark judgement, citing Kupreskic et al, who clearly view genocide as an 'extreme and most inhuman form of persecution'. Although the concept of genocide is often used in the legal literature to classify the consequences of the treatment imposed, for instance, on indigenous groups by corporate activities supported by local governments, that is not the technical meaning of the concept of genocide.[54]

In fact, even in the Kupreskic case, the court emphasizes that the standard of proof which must be met includes not only 'the *actus reus* of genocide', but also the 'specific intent (*dolus specialis*)'.[55] Neither the treatment of various persecuted populations, or that of religious or indigenous communities may rise to this level, as the deliberate, wholesale killing of group members is not often present in either case.

In contrast, the Convention against Genocide, Article II(b), 'causing serious bodily or mental harm to members of the protected group', is far more appropriate, both before the fact, as a cause for seeking refuge, as well as after the fact, as the reality of the treatment meted out to asylum seekers:

> *The ICTY [International Criminal Tribunal for the former Yugoslavia] in its Judgment of 31 July 2003, in the Stakic case, recognized that: 'causing serious bodily and mental harm' in subparagraph (b) [of Article 4(2) of the Statute of the ICTY] is understood to mean*, inter alia, *acts of torture, inhumane and degrading treatment, sexual violence including rape, interrogation combined with beating, threats of death, and harm that damages health or causes disfigurement or injury. The harm inflicted need not be irremediable.*[56]

Aside from the conditions of persecution that require the flight of asylum seekers, the treatment of large groups of migrants does, indeed, include 'inhumane and degrading treatment' in detention, as well as 'harm that damages health'. Regarding Article II(b), the court concluded the atrocities perpetrated 'in particular in detention camps', may 'amount to war crimes and crimes against humanity', although the *dolus specialis* to elevate these crimes to genocide, appears to be lacking.

The same is true when we consider Article II(c), 'Deliberately inflicting on the group conditions of life calculated to bring about its physical destruction in whole or in part'. One particular aspect of these crimes is listed by the court as 'deportation and expulsion' (paras 330–334) and 'forced population displacements', once again stating that these are crimes against humanity, but that they do not rise to the level of genocide, absent the proven determination to eliminate a group 'in whole or in part' (para 334).

Nevertheless, Kupreskic et al appear to break new ground as they examine the 'more delicate question' of 'complicity in genocide' (para 418), after acknowledging that giving orders or instructions to commit criminal acts is 'considered as the mark of complicity in commission of that act'. Even if one must exclude the presence of genocide, complicity needs to be considered (para 419). Complicity is not present in the law of international responsibility; but Article 16 of the International Law Commission (ILC) articles on state responsibility ('Aid or assistance in the commission of an internationally wrongful act') states:

> *The court sees no reason to make any distinction of substance between 'complicity in genocide' ... and the 'aid or assistance' of a state in the commission of a wrongful act by another state.* (para 42)

In conclusion, although the court did not find that Serbia committed the crime of genocide, or that it was complicit in genocide, it did find that 'Serbia has violated its obligations under the Convention on the Prevention and Punishment of the Crime of Genocide' and decided 'that Serbia shall immediately take effective steps to ensure full compliance with its obligation under the convention ... to punish acts of genocide'.

This decision is a very important one and it is useful as we reconsider state responsibility for the situation of large groups of environmentally affected migrants, both before and after they flee unliveable conditions in their homelands. Other aspects of this judgement may also be useful as we turn to the next ground of persecution – that is, the issue of 'religious beliefs'.

4. RELIGIOUS BELIEFS: HOLY SITES FOR INDIGENOUS AND LOCAL COMMUNITIES

> *Sacred areas are probably the oldest forms of habitat protection on the planet and still form a large and mainly unrecognized network of sanctuaries around the world. A proportion of these sites (probably a large proportion) are also highly successful at conserving natural ecology and biodiversity.*[57]

My life's work has been dedicated to research and study regarding ecological integrity and its centrality in the sustainability of natural systems and of the human enterprise in all its aspects.[58] In my first work, I proposed 'the principle of integrity'. Essentially, I argued that, as life is the most basic value and our biological integrity is representative of both life and health, of which ecological integrity, or the integrity of our 'habitat', is an absolute requirement to support it, the words of Aldo Leopold were, indeed, foundational to the understanding of morally correct action:

> *... that conduct is right which tends to preserve the ecological stability, integrity and beauty of the biotic community, and wrong when it tends otherwise.*[59]

Following this well-known maxim, I then proposed the following:

1. The first moral principle is that nothing can be moral that is in conflict with the physical realities of our existence, or that cannot be seen to fit with the natural laws of our environment.
2. Act so that your action will fit (first and minimally) within universal natural laws.
3. Act so that you manifest respect and understanding acceptance of all natural processes and laws, although self-defence is acceptable.

It is not necessary to review all the argument supporting the principle or those that may be brought against it at this time. But it is important to note that the seminal work that informed all my future research was primarily based on science, so that the scientific value of integrity, as basic to our own life and that of all life on Earth, represented my starting point.[60] Later, still based upon these principles and that early research, I also argued for its significance in the moral life of individuals as well as public policy.[61]

I did not, however, attempt to defend ecological integrity from the standpoint of its value to the human connection to the divine. Hence, I want to explore that connection now because, after researching the interface between indigenous peoples and ecological integrity,[62] I realized the justice of the claims made in the WWF/ARC *Beyond Belief* report from which the quotation at the head of this section is taken, about the links between faiths in the world and protected areas:

> *These links come in two major forms:*
>
> 1 *Sacred places – both sacred natural sites and built environments existing in natural or semi-natural areas. These can contribute very directly to global conservation efforts because they are often themselves well conserved through traditions that sometime stretch back for thousands of years.*
> 2 *Influence of faiths – through their philosophy, actions and influences, faiths can have a major impact on the way their followers view the protection of nature.*[63]

The foundational importance of integrity is connected to these links, as I have argued, that ecological integrity is basic to the 'cultural integrity' aspect of local and indigenous land-based traditional communities,[64] and that the latter is, with the right to 'self-determination', one of the two aspects of the rights of aboriginal peoples protected by international law. Essentially, even ensuring that a certain *quantity* of land belongs to a traditional community is insufficient to guarantee the exercise of their traditional rights (e.g. the right to hunt, fish or pursue other traditional activities), unless the *quality* of their land is equally protected.[65] Hence the preservation of ecological integrity is absolutely necessary for their survival as peoples.

It is also equally necessary for certain proportions and specific percentages of natural areas to be protected in order to protect our own health and the normal functioning of ecosystems, which produce the 'natural services'[66] we need:[67]

> *The wider role of protected areas is now being examined with respect, for example, to the provision of secure supplies of crops, fish and other materials, recreational and cultural opportunities, protection for vulnerable human communities, health, knowledge and stabilization against climate change.*[68]

To my basic, but twofold, argument for the protection and survival of life on Earth and, specifically, of certain land-based peoples, but also of humanity as a whole, we can now add considerations arising from the role that sacred places play in the conservation of protected areas, in the two senses outlined by the *Beyond Belief* report quoted above.

4a. Holy sites, protected areas and the religious persecution of refugees

> *Respect for Creation stems from respect for human life and dignity. It is on the basis of our recognition that the world is created by God that we can discern an objective moral order within which to articulate a code of environmental ethics. In this perspective, Christian and all other believers have a specific role to play in proclaiming moral values and in educating people in ecological awareness, which is none other than responsibility towards self, toward others, towards creation.*[69]

All religions deal with nature as an issue in vastly different ways: the two major religions (Christianity and Islam) may be seen to reject 'sacred natural sites' as a form of idolatry, or as fostering the importance of a material place over a 'more ethereal concept of the divine'.[70] But, aside from these possibly contrasting approaches by the major world religions, there are altogether 11 'mainstream faiths', according to Dudley et al,[71] most of which acknowledge the importance and the spiritual value of natural sites and/or certain species, and the connection between specific areas and religious significance. Nevertheless, the significance of these connections is greatest among the aboriginal communities in the world.

First Nations and other hunting societies invest a great deal of religious significance in the hunt, and special rituals are developed in this regard because of 'the sacred nature of the hunt'.[72] Even today:

> *The hunting of the bowhead whale (Balaena mysticetus) by the Inuit of Alaska is surrounded by complex beliefs and, at least until quite recently, by taboo, magic formulae and the use of amulets.*[73]

In addition, as late as 1978, 'a political leader for ... Inuit independence' characterized the 'taking and sharing of the whale ... [as] the Arctic celebration of the mysteries of life'.[74] And this is precisely the point to be made by a survey of the importance of *preserved* natural holy sites and species: they are central to the religious beliefs and practices of the local and indigenous communities everywhere in the world.

Of course, not all religions relate to nature in the same way. In fact, the first step necessary to understand the relation between conservation of protected areas and world religions is to separate those that at best teach a diffuse respect for nature (such as Christianity, Judaism, Islam, Buddhism, Daoism and Jainism) and the few who actually base their practices on specific sites. For instance, one of the most important precepts of Jainism is:

> *One who neglects or disregards the existence of earth, air, fire, water and vegetation, disregards his own existence which is entwined with them.*[75]

Christianity teaches that 'humanity may not destroy God's creations without the risk of destroying itself'. In the Bible, the book of Ecclesiastes states in Chapter 3, verse 19: 'For the fate of the sons of man and the fate of the beasts is the same; as one dies, so dies the other. They all have the same breath, and man has no advantage over the beasts; for all is vanity.'[76]

From the standpoint of conservation and the respect for the integrity of creation, these random citations as well as many others are important and valuable ones, and they can also be found in Islam, Buddhism, Judaism and many other faiths. In contrast, for instance, Hinduism in most of its schools of thought reveres 'Mother Earth'. In fact, India has a long history of forest protection, as most Indian temples have a sacred tree, dedicated to the gods of Shiva or Vishnu,[77] while in modern times, in the Chipko movement, 'women have protected forests from destruction by surrounding trees with their bodies'.[78]

But it is the more isolated land-based communities who belong to the second group far more clearly, in the sense that their religious beliefs and their traditional practices are based on a specific place and locations, so that, unlike Christianity, Buddhism or even Hinduism, their religion cannot be practised anywhere, aside from their traditional lands. When Christians were persecuted in Ancient Rome, and fed to wild animals as a public spectacle, they could (and did) go underground to continue the practices of their religion in the catacombs.

The situation is entirely different when we consider that there are hundreds of sacred places today within areas that are already designated as protected areas.[79] When we consider aboriginal communities and their traditional areas, there are two major points we must acknowledge:

1 The territories that embody special religious and spiritual significance for these peoples are *not* transferable, nor are their traditional forms of worship.
2 Most of these traditional communities are, in fact, *not* within protected areas and are constantly under attack:

> *Today, many sacred groves are at risk, from multiple factors including breakdown in cultural values, pressure on land and local people from farming and other forms of development and pressure from the outside including poaching, legal and illegal logging, mining and pollution.*[80]

These areas and these groups are the focus of our main concern at this time. When these holy sites are polluted or even destroyed, the local inhabitants lose their moral and legal right to practise their religious beliefs as they choose. When the conditions of life in the area become unbearable or hazardous, either because of natural disasters (especially when these are rendered more grave because of climate change) or because of industrial encroachment in their (formerly) protected areas, their local inhabitants may be forced to flee.

This situation should attract the attention and the protecting power of the United Nations. Essentially, their flight is motivated by conditions affecting their area and their holy sites as the disintegrity of that land precludes the practice of religious beliefs in the traditional ways. This represents a breach of human rights, even of *jus cogens* norms, as noted above; and, I believe, it renders the migrants thus forced to abandon not only their traditional lands, but also their traditional lifestyle and religious practices, very similar to asylum seekers who, according to the convention, are persecuted for religious reasons.

5. STATE PROTECTION OR STATE COMPLICITY?

> *Since refugees are forced directly or indirectly out of their homes in their homelands, they are deprived of full and effective enjoyment of all articles of the Universal Declaration of Human Rights that presuppose a person's ability to live in the place chosen as their home. Accordingly the state that turns a person into a refugee, commits an internationally wrongful act which creates an obligation to make good the wrong done.*
> (Cairo Declaration of Principles of International Law on Compensation to Refugees, ILA, 1992)[81]

This declaration is not legally binding; but it may be persuasive, despite its imprecision. Does the state 'turn a person into a refugee' only by the acts it commits? Or would it be possible to consider acts of omission as equally causative? And must the act or omission be a single one – that is, one committed only by the state from which 'created' refugees are forced to flee? Or would it be possible to consider multiple state (or non-state) actors being complicit in either the act or the omission? A common example of *direct* activities and omissions affecting a specific community may be that of a state either permitting/encouraging a corporate non-state actor to initiate an operation that will cause severe stress to a locality and to its inhabitants, or simply omitting to forbid such activities, which will eventually cause the flight.

Indirect activities/omissions may be seen when states, for instance, pursue economic policies that will render whole areas unliveable, thus causing the flight of large numbers of migrants; or when they omit to sign on to regulatory instruments related to climate change; or, finally, if they will sign on to so-called 'free' trade deals that will significantly affect large numbers of their poorest citizens.

In addition, there is another basic question: although the consideration of the economic needs of migrants is vital, in many cases, especially in the case of traditional indigenous communities, losses such as the ones related to holy sites can never be compensated for. Nevertheless, aside from difficulties of interpretation, and the insufficient clarity of this document, its very existence points to what Chaloka Beyani terms 'an innovative and challenging prospect' in his seminal article on the topic. He is referring to the resort (and return) to 'state responsibility as a means of preventing and resolving the problem of the forced displacement of populations'.[82]

The most salient point is that 'prevention' is, indeed, the only practicable solution for the future, and I will return to the point in the final chapter of this work. Although my perspective will be based on ecology and public health, primarily the perspective proposed here is an extremely sound one. Many of the legal problems arising, as we will see from Beyani's article, have arisen because of changes in the main legal instruments related to his argument, after he wrote it. To my mind, the gravest difficulty is the text of the 2000 revision of the 1996 Draft Articles on State Responsibility (International Law Commission). Originally, Article 19(I) stated:

> *An act of a state which constitutes a breach of an international obligation, is an internationally wrongful act, regardless of the subject matter of the obligation breached.*

In addition, Article 19(3) distinguished between civil and criminal acts of state. At any rate, Higgins, who analyses state responsibility, rather than liability, states that 'the only requirement is causality', which entails that 'responsibility is based on result, not fault'.[83] Special Rapporteur James Crawford explains:

> *In particular, article [1] stated that every internationally wrongful act of a State entails its responsibility, and article [3] identified two and two only elements of an internationally wrongful act, (a) conduct attributable to a State which (b) is inconsistent with its international obligations. There was no **distinct or separate requirement of fault or wrongful intent for an internationally wrongful act to be held to exist**.*[84]

Hence, even in the latest iteration of the ILC, international law does not require intent for the commission of a 'crime' (although this language is no longer part of the ILC), and Higgins's point stands. Thus, the common argument of corporate or institutional wrongdoers, adducing lack of intent as exonerating or at least mitigating their responsibility, cannot be defended as even the due diligence defence is not allowed internationally.

In contrast, the problem of defining a state or institutional wrongdoing as crime (hence, different in kind from other delicts), is no longer as clearly stated as when Article 19 of the ILC (1996) was in existence. Crawford admits that regimes appropriate to corporate crime could apply to state crime, but he views the absence of:

1 precise definition;
2 adequate investigative procedures;
3 due process;
4 appropriate sanctions; and
5 'some method by which the state can, as it were, come clean, expunge the record'

as providing definitive arguments against the use of the concept of crime in regard to the state[85] – thus the necessity of focusing on state liability for now, without losing sight of the desirability to appeal to more serious charges in the future.

One wonders whether the same five elements could not be raised in regard to the accepted crimes of genocide and crimes against humanity, all of which cannot truly be perpetrated without a state's acceptance or participation, and which cannot simply be described as 'a pejorative way of describing serious breaches of certain norms', as he thinks other possible state crimes might more appropriately be termed.[86] We note that if genocide and the like are still considered crimes, why are environmental offences (previously an example of crimes in Article 19) left out, despite the immense damages to human life and habitat these cause? Crawford's analysis states that Article 19 had been viewed as 'divisive' and that states could not agree on the language most appropriate to express Article 19 in a better way.

It is wrong that these self-interested objections aiming not at better expression of commonly held values but at the protection of self-interest on the part of powerful countries were viewed as more significant than the solid arguments provided by a majority of publicists who wrote to defend the principles behind Article 19, whatever the flaws of its presentation. It would seem that absent the problem of intent, the consequences following environmentally hazardous activities should align these activities with other crimes against humanity, particularly in the case of refugees.

The claim that there is no specific intent to produce that result in an identifiable person, as Crawford pointed out, cannot be sufficient to absolve the causative agent(s) of any wrongdoing. Nor is it sufficient to claim that the activities giving rise to the described consequences were legal at the time they occurred, and might even be legal today. In fact, Article 3 of the International Law Commission[87] is short and to the point on this issue: '*Prevention.* States shall take all appropriate measures to prevent, or to minimize the risk of, significant transboundary harm.' Special Rapporteur Srenivasa Rao (8 May 1998) states:

> *The objective of prevention of transboundary damages arising from hazardous activities had been emphasized in principle 2 of the Rio Declaration ... and confirmed by ICJ in its advisory opinion on the Legality of the Threat or Use of Nuclear Weapons, as forming part of the corpus of international law.*[88]

Rao adds that the European Commission had drawn up various schemes to prevent transboundary damages, and that its work emphasized that, because of scientific developments, there was an 'enhanced ability to trace the chains of causation – that is to say, the physical links between the cause (the activity) and the effect (the harm)' – hence, that prevention was indeed the key.[89]

Mr Barboza, another special rapporteur, also indicated that 'the duty of prevention should continue to be treated as an obligation of conduct and not one of result'.[90] On this topic, Alain Pellet added that 'the statement that only (*seulement*, in the French version) significant harm or damages was required to be prevented by states was most inappropriate'.[91]

Pellet's point especially supports the claim here advanced that visible, or otherwise detectable, grave harms are only part of the kind of harms that ought to be proscribed. Even an otherwise moderate hazard may become part of a cumulative or synergistic scenario that eventually transforms it into a severe harm.

It is also useful to consider this document's efforts at defining due diligence. For instance at (6), in the commentary following Article 3 (Prevention):

> *(6) The obligation of states to take preventive or minimization measures is one of due diligence, requiring States to take certain unilateral measures to prevent, or to minimize a risk of significant transboundary harm. The obligation imposed by this article is not an obligation of result. It is the conduct of a state that will determine whether the State has complied under the present articles.*

Note that this commentary may conflate prevention with minimization: two quite disparate concepts. Are we to prevent harm or simply to accept that it will occur, and attempt to minimize it?

In fact, because the notions of responsibility and fault are closely related in international law, the whole regulatory infrastructure should be questioned. Gehring and Jactenfuchs say:

> *However, highly complex industrial activities create risks which can be minimized but not completely eliminated. The concept of state responsibility does not foresee any duty to compensate for damage due to activities which are not prohibited by international law. Furthermore, according to traditional international law, established legal wrongfulness of any activity having caused transboundary harm entails the obligation to cease its operation.*[92]

It appears logical that, if a similar factual harm is produced by a legal activity, a similar obligation to cease should prevail. But, at the present time, no prohibition is codified in international law to stop 'lawful' hazardous activities and, for the most part, states have a strong interest in continuing and even promoting many of these activities. In addition, even:

> *… establishing too close a link between fault and the obligation to compensate for damage frequently does not result in an internationally accepted ban of a particular dangerous activity, but rather in a refusal by the source state to compensate, since any acceptance of the duty to compensate would imply acknowledgement of a violation of international law and thus endanger the future operation of the activity in question.*[93]

Article 53 of the Vienna Convention on the Law of Treaties,[94] as cited above (page 87), spells out explicitly the existence of norms that cannot be 'forgotten' or simply ignored through other treaties or agreements arranged for the economic advantage of certain states. It bears repeating:

> *A treaty is void if, at the time of its conclusion, it conflicts with a peremptory norm of general international law. For the purposes of the present Convention, a peremptory norm of general international law is a norm accepted and recognized by the international community of States as a whole as a norm from which no derogation is permitted and which can be modified only by a subsequent norm of general international law having the same character.*[95]

This article sets the stage: on the basis of Article 53, given the clarification of what is an international crime according to the description of examples of *jus cogens* norms in the former Article 19 of the International Law Commission (1996); although this article is strongly positivistic, thus not entirely helpful from our point of view.

The character of *jus cogens* norms is precisely that of providing the strongest possible citadel in defence of humanity; their role is to rise above the economic and power interests of various states that could band together (and often do), for purposes that conflict with the respect due to all humans.

Hence, *jus cogens* norms are uniquely apt to provide and defend substantive global justice beyond the purely procedural emphasis present in many other legal instruments. Bassiouni says: 'The term *jus cogens* means "the compelling law" and as such a *jus cogens* norm holds the highest hierarchical position among all other norms and principles.'[96]

I believe that the Article 19 of the 1996 ILC draft here cited, despite its demise in the 2000 draft of that document, remains an important landmark document, at least through the discussions of that article by leading publicists, such as those cited in the collection of articles on *International Crimes of State*, edited by Weiler, Cassese and Spinedi (1989). Hence, I believe that doing away with the language of Article 19, especially with the distinction it proposes between crimes and delicts, does not succeed in eliminating either the realities Article 19 intended to address, or the difficulties posed by them, and the learned debates on all these issues. In fact, Chapter III (ILC, 2000) 'Serious breaches of essential obligations to the international community,' reintroduces the difference in kind between certain sorts of breaches of international obligations and others (described in Article 19) by the 'back door', so to speak, as we see in the language of Articles 41 and 42:

Article 41 – Applications of this Chapter

1. *This chapter applies to the international responsibility arising from an internationally wrongful act that constitutes a serious breach by a state of an obligation owed to the international community as a whole and essential for the protection of its fundamental interests.*
2. *A breach of such an obligation is serious if it involves a gross or systematic failure by the responsible state to fulfil the obligation, risking substantial harm to the fundamental interests protected thereby.*

Article 42 [51, 53] – Consequences of serious breaches of obligations to the international community as a whole

1. *A serious breach within the meaning of Article 41 may involve, for the responsible State, damages reflecting the gravity of the breach.*
2. *It entails, for all other states, the following obligations:*
    (a) *Not to recognize as lawful the situation created by the breach;*
    (b) *Not to render aid or assistance to the responsible State in maintaining the situation so created;*
    (c) *To cooperate as far as possible to bring the breach to an end.*
3. *This article is without prejudice to the consequences referred to in Chapter II and to such further consequences that a breach to which this chapter applies may entail under international law.*

The language of either article can be interpreted to say, more vaguely and imprecisely, perhaps, and in the context of consequences, rather than through the description of examples, what the former Article 19 said more explicitly and clearly, although Rapporteur Crawford may disagree with this assessment. Chapter II, in turn, describes the 'Forms of reparation' for 'internationally wrongful acts' and names 'restitution, compensation, and satisfaction' (Article 35) as constituting, singly or 'in combination', 'full reparation'. But when we turn to the articles listed above, the language used is different in kind, not degree, between 'breaches of an international obligation', and 'serious breaches of essential obligations to the international community as a whole and essential for the protection of its fundamental interests' (Article 41). Article 42 adds that the 'damages' assessed should reflect 'the gravity of the breach'.

I find it hard to accept that the different language addresses simply differences of degree, on a continuum. It does not seem to be the case that one sort of language refers to, say, economic damages under US$1 million; the other, economic damages over that limit. The international community as a whole can only be affected in a way that makes it reasonable and appropriate for them to react as a whole. It is unlikely that a scenario can be found that shows economic damages to support such an even-handed, global response. The difference we are trying to pinpoint may be one between 'subjectively injured' and 'objectively injured' states.[97]

Like aggression or genocide, both of which represent the most widely accepted, least controversial forms of these sorts of injuries affecting the international community, I argue that grave environmental pollution should, indeed, be treated as a crime, whether or not the term 'crime' is present in the language of any international law instrument. This is true, *a fortiori*, when it results in mass flows of refugees.

The 2000 iteration of the International Law Commission has eliminated the language, but retained some of the approaches and the distinctions in Articles 41 and 42 (above). That is why placing all these internationally wrongful acts in the same category, the one that contravenes *jus cogens* norms, makes good sense: the effects of widespread environmental pollution, climate change, nuclear threats, food and water scarcity or contamination share the characteristics of doing injury to the most basic human rights in all states, and evoking widespread global condemnation. When these internationally wrongful acts cause the forced migration of populations, these ought to be viewed in the same light.

Alain Pellet notes that not only is there a difference of degree between what can be termed a delict and what must be termed a crime; but there may also be a difference in kind between some illicit acts and others: 'Malgré une thèse souvant soutenue, il n'y a pas la une simple difference de degré entre ces deux categories de faits internationalement illicites, mais, bel et bien, une difference de nature.'[98] Pellet explains further that it is more than the society of states that is affected, it is a question of affecting humanity as such. And this is more than a theoretical argument, it is necessary to recognize the difference between an act of genocide and a 'banal' violation of a commercial treaty's clause, a dispute between two states. It is the former, not the latter, that primarily has 'humanity' as its target.

5a. State responsibility for migrations and *jus cogens* norms

> *In the Corfu Channel case (merits), the International Court of Justice remarked with truism that according to international practice a State on whose territory an act contrary to international law has occurred, may be called upon to give an explanation and that such a State cannot evade such a request by limiting itself to the reply that it is ignorant of the circumstances of the act and its authors.*[99]

This affects the question of the responsibility of states regarding refugees in at least two ways. The first issue is that the state where the damages occur, in most cases, has at least 'the means of the knowledge of harm, and the opportunity to act'.[100] States just act in the light of the principle *sic utere tuo ut alienum non laedas*, whether it is a case of internal persecution of groups of their own citizens, or, and this becomes the second issue, when the conditions that are engendered by a state or tolerated and abetted by it, cause conditions such that mass migrations may follow. These refugees, then, may well 'impose economic, social and other burdens upon the host countries',[101] in addition to the harms imposed on the refugees themselves.

In relation to their own citizens, of course, the state obligation is absolute, as only a deprivation of their nationality may justify a state's unconcern with the protection of all its citizens.[102] For both issues, the resulting harms fit under the categories listed under *jus cogens*, norms – hence, they transcend even convention obligations:

> ... *every state must be held responsible for the performance of its international obligations under the rules of international law, whether such rules derive from custom, treaty, or other source of international law.*[103]

This implies that any act or decision deriving from the domestic legal instruments of states could have grave repercussions not only for the state's own citizens, but also on other states:

> *Even if the state whose conduct results in the flooding of other states with refugee populations be not guilty of an actual breach of law, there can be little doubt that states suffering in consequence would be justified in resorting to measures of retorsion.*[104]

Of course, a state's treatment of its own citizens must also comply with the principles of justice, basic to the concept of obligations *erga omnes*, based upon *jus cogens* norms. These obligations share two basic elements:

1 the element of solidarity, as all states are understood to have an interest in the observance of these norms, and the protection of these obligations; and
2 the foundational 'element of universality', as the obligations are equally binding on all states and non-derogable.[105]

It is undeniable that the conditions of life encountered by the members of communities who are forced to flee to become ecological refugees include all the major violations of human rights law, from the right to life, to the prohibition against cruel, inhuman and degrading treatment, as well as systemic patterns of racial discrimination.[106] Internal displacement of populations is only legal if it initiates with the clear consent of the population involved, otherwise that, in itself is an illegal act.[107]

In sum, rather than viewing internally displaced persons (IDPs) and, in general, ecological refugees as populations who do not quite fit the terms of the 1951 CSR in one way or another, we need to recognize their plight as, indeed, 'superior' to that of regular convention refugees in the sense that the *jus cogens* norms that are not observed from the beginning of the actions or omissions that cause the condition (in turn causing their flight, all the way to the time when they are 'received' by another state and, most often, incarcerated) are non-derogable, whether or not the states involved have signed a convention dealing with their problem.

Another important aspect of state responsibility – that is, their obligations regarding public health issues – will be discussed in the next chapter.

NOTES

1 Lopez, A. (2007) 'The protection of environmentally-displaced persons in international law', *Environmental Law*, vol 37, pp365–367.
2 Passel, J. S. and Fix, M. (1994) 'US immigration in a global context: Past, present and future', *Indiana Journal of Global Legal Studies*, vol 12.
3 Meehan, P. (1997), 'Combating restrictions on immigrant access to public benefits: A human rights perspective', *Georgetown Immigration Law Journal*, vol 11, p389.
4 Ibid, p390.
5 Gouget, J-J. (2006) 'Réfugiés écologiques: Un débat controversé', *Revue Européenne de Droit de l'Environnement*, CRIDEAU, Pulim, Limoges.
6 The Indian Ocean tsunami/earthquake event of December 2004 resulted in 184,168 confirmed dead and an estimated 1.7 million people displaced, according to http://en.wikipedia.org/wiki/2004_Indian_Ocean_earthquake.
7 See Westra, L. (2006) *Environmental Justice and the Rights of Unborn and Future Generations*, Earthscan, London, pp181–183.
8 Cournil, C. and Mazzega, P. (2006) 'Catastrophes écologiques et flux migratoires: Comment proteger les "réfugiés écologiques"?', *Revue de Droit de L'Environnement*, December, p417.
9 Lonergan, S. (1998) 'The role of environmental degradation in population displacement', *Environmental Change and Security Project Report 5*, spring.
10 Ibid.
11 Ibid.
12 Ibid.
13 Meehan (1997), op cit Note 3, p393; see also Simon, J. (1989) *The Economic Consequences of Immigration*, Blackwell, Oxford, where the author argues that immigrants are economically beneficial to host countries.
14 Passel and Fix (1994), op cit Note 2.
15 Lillich, R. and Hannum, H. (1995) *International Human Rights: Problems of Law, Policy and Practice*, Little Brown, Boston, MA, p121.
16 Meehan (1997), op cit Note 3, pp399–400; see also Sohn, L. B. (1982) 'The new international law: Protection of the rights of individuals rather than states', *American University Law Review*, vol 32, no 1, p9.
17 *Barcelona Traction, Light and Power Co. Ltd.*, Second Phase, ICJ Reports, 1970.
18 Charter of the United Nations, Articles 1(3), 13(1), (b), 55(c), 56, 59 and 76(c); see also the Committee on the Elimination of Racial Discrimination (CERD), adopted 18 August 1997, UN Doc. CERD/C/51/misc.13/Rev.4 (1997).
19 ICJ Report, 1966, p298.
20 Lopez (2007), op cit Note 1, p369; see also Lonergan (1998), op cit Note 9; McCue, G. S. (1993) 'Environmental refugees: Applying international environmental law to involuntary migration', *Georgetown International Environmental Law Review*, vol 6, p151.
21 Westra, L. (2007) *Environmental Justice and the Rights of Indigenous Peoples*, Earthscan, London, Chapter 8.
22 Ibid.
23 Lopez (2007), op cit Note 1, p370; see also Myers, N. (1995) *Environmental Exodus: An Emergent Crisis in the Global Arena*, Climate Institute, Washington, DC.
24 Cooper, J. (1998) 'Environmental refugees: Meeting the requirements of the refugee definition', *New York University Environmental Law Journal*, vol 6, p480.
25 Gillespie, A. (2004) 'Small island states in the face of climate change: The end of the line in international environmental responsibility', *University of California at Los Angeles, Journal of Environmental Law and Policy*, vol 22, pp107–129.
26 Cooper (1998), op cit Note 24, p509.

27 Lonergan (1998), op cit Note 9, p1, citing Westing, A. H. (1992) 'Environmental refugees: A growing category of displaced persons', *Environmental Conservation*, vol 19, no 3, pp201–207.
28 UNDP (1994) *Human Development Report*, United Nations Development Programme, Oxford University Press, New York.
29 Lamm, R. and Imhoff, G. (1985) *The Immigration Time Bomb: The Fragmenting of America*, E. P. Dutton, New York.
30 Westra, L. (2004) *Ecoviolence and the Law*, Transnational Publishers Inc., Ardsley, NY, Chapter 4; see also *Pappajohn versus the Queen* (1980) 2 S.C.R. 120, a case concerned with the difference between consensual sexual activity and rape, and the failure of accepting the consequences of the lack of consent.
31 Rees, W. E. (2006) 'Ecological footprints and bio-capacity: Essential elements in sustainability assessment', Chapter 9 in J. Dewulf and H. Van Langenhove (eds) *Renewables-Based Technology: Sustainability Assessment*, John Wiley and Sons, Chichester, UK, pp143–158.
32 Soskolne, C. (2004) 'On the even greater need for precaution under global change', *International Journal of Occupational Medicine and Environmental Health*, vol 17, no 1, pp69–76.
33 Risse, M. (2005) 'What we owe to the global poor', *Ethics*, vol 9, p81.
34 Cooper (1998), op cit Note 24, pp480–481.
35 Universal Declaration of Human Rights, G.A. Res. 217A (III), UN Doc. A/810(1948).
36 International Covenant on Economic, Social and Cultural Rights, G.A. Res. 2200A(XXI), UN GAOR, 21st Sess. Supp. No. 16, UN Doc. A/6316 (1966).
37 Ragazzi, M. (1997) *The Concept of Obligations* Erga Omnes, Clarendon Press, Oxford, UK, pp43–59.
38 Ibid, p44, especially no 3; see for instance von Verdross, A. (1937) 'Forbidden treaties in international law', *American Journal of International Law*, vol 31, pp571–577; von Verdross, A. (1966) '*Jus dispositivum* and *jus cogens* in international law', *American Journal of International Law*, vol 60, pp55–63.
39 Ragazzi (1997), op cit Note 37, p48.
40 Vienna Convention on the Law of Treaties (1969) 1155 UNTS 337, in force 1980.
41 Maresca's intervention, U.N.C.L.T.Off.Rec., First Session, Vienna 26 March–24 May 1968, 'Summary records of the plenary meetings and of the committee of the whole, p311, paragraph 42.
42 Steiner, H. J., and Alston, P. (2000) *International Human Rights in Context* (second edition), Oxford University Press, Oxford, UK, p268.
43 Lauterpacht, H. (1950) *International Law and Human Rights*, Steven and Sons, London.
44 Ibid.
45 Ibid.
46 Van Boven, T. (1982) 'Distinguishing criteria of human rights', in K. Vasak and P. Alston (eds) *The International Dimensions of Human Rights* (Volume I), Greenwood Press, Westport, CT, p43.
47 Lauterpacht, H. (1933) *The Function of Law in the International Community*, Clarendon Press, Oxford, UK.
48 Fitzmaurice, G. G. (1950) 'The law and procedure of the International Court of Justice: General principles and substantive law', *The British Yearbook of International Law*, vol 27, p1.
49 Meron, T. (1989) *Human Rights and Humanitarian Norms as Customary Law*, Oxford University Press, Oxford, UK.
50 Ragazzi (1997), op cit Note 37; see also Salomon, M. (2007) *Global Responsibility for Human Rights*, Oxford University Press, Oxford, UK; and Tomuschat, C. and Thouvenin, J-M. (eds) (2006) *The Fundamental Rules of International Legal Order: Jus Cogens and Obligations Erga Omnes*, Martinus Nijhoff, Leiden, The Netherlands.
51 Ragazzi, M. (1999) 'International obligations *erga omnes*: Their moral foundations and criteria of identification in light of two Japanese contributions', in G. S. Goodwin-Gill and

S. Talmon (eds) *The Reality of International Law: Essays in Honour of Ian Brownlie*, Clarendon Press, Oxford, UK, pp455–477.
52 *Kupreskic et al*, IT-95-16-T, Judgment, 14 January 2000, paragraph 636.
53 ITJ, General List No. 91, 26 February 2007.
54 Schabas, W. (2000) *On Genocide in International Law*, Kluwer Publishing, The Hague; Schabas, W. (2006), *The UN International Criminal Tribunals*, Cambridge University Press, Cambridge, UK.
55 *Kupreskic et al* (2000), op cit Note 52, paragraph 219; see also Krajinsnik, Trial Chamber Judgment, 27 September 2006, paragraphs 867–869.
56 International Tribunal in the Former Yugoslavia (ICTY) IT-97-24-Trial Chamber Judgment, 31 July 2003, paragraph 516.
57 Dudley, N., Higgins-Zogib, L. and Mansourian, S. (2005) *Beyond Belief: Linking Faiths and Protected Areas to Support Biodiversity Conservation*, a research report by World Wide Fund for Nature (WWF), Gland, Switzerland, with Alliance of Religions and Conservation (ARC), Manchester, UK, available for download from www.forestrynepal.org/publications/reports/267.
58 Westra, L. (1994) *An Environmental Proposal for Ethics: The Principle of Integrity*, Rowman Littlefield, Lanham, MD; Westra, L. (1998) *Living in Integrity*, Rowman Littlefield, Lanham, MD; Pimentel, D., Westra, L. and Noss, R. F. (2000) *Ecological Integrity: Integrating Environment, Conservation and Health*, Island Press, Washington, DC; Miller, P. and Westra, L. (eds) (2002) *Just Ecological Integrity: The Ethics of Maintaining Planetary Life*, Rowman and Littlefield, Lanham, MD; Westra, L. (2004) *Ecoviolence and the Law*, Transnational Publishers Inc., Ardsley, NY; Westra, L. (2006) *Environmental Justice and the Rights of Unborn and Future Generations*, Earthscan, London; Westra, L. (2007) *Environmental Justice and the Rights of Indigenous Peoples*, Earthscan, London; Westra, L., Bosselmann, K. and Westra, R. (eds) (2008) *Reconciling Ecological Existence with Ecological Integrity*, Earthscan, London.
59 Leopold, A. (1949) *A Sand County Almanac and Sketches Here and There*, Oxford University Press, NY.
60 Westra, L. (2008)'Introduction', in Westra, L., Bosselmann and Westra, R., op cit Note 58.
61 Westra, L. (1998), op cit Note 58.
62 Westra, L. (2007), op cit Note 58.
63 Dudley et al, op cit Note 57, p5.
64 Westra, L. (2007), op cit Note 58, pp30–32.
65 Ibid, pp133–134.
66 Daily, G. (1997) *Nature's Services: Societal Dependence on Natural Ecosystems*, Island Press, Washington, DC.
67 Noss, R. (1992) 'The Wildlands Project: Land conservation strategy', *Wild Earth Special Issue*; Noss, R. and Cooperrider, A. (1994) *Saving Nature's Legacy*, Island Press, Washington, DC; Pimentel, Westra and Noss (2000), op cit Note 58.
68 Dudley et al, op cit Note 57.
69 Pope John-Paul II and Patriarch Bartholomew I of Constantinople, 10 June 2000, Rome-Venice, text issued by the Vatican Press Office.
70 Dudley et al, op cit Note 57, p23.
71 Ibid, p8. The 11 so-called mainstream faiths are, in alphabetical order: Bahá'i, Buddhism, Christianity, Hinduism, Islam, Jainism, Judaism, Shinto, Sikhism, Taoism and Zoroastrianism.
72 Ibid, p14.
73 Lantis, M. (1938) 'The Alaskan whale hunt and its affinities', *American Anthropologist*, vol 40, pp438–464.
74 Dudley et al, op cit Note 57, p14.
75 Ibid, p26.
76 Ibid, p24.
77 Ibid, p25.

78 Weber, T. (1988) *Hugging the Trees: The Story of the Chipko Movement*, Viking, London; for other nature-related issues, see also Shiva, V. (2002) *Water Wars: Privatization, Pollution and Profit*, Pluto Press, London.
79 Dudley et al, op cit Note 57, pp40ff.
80 Convention on Biological Diversity, 2003, briefing note from the Executive Secretary for the Ad Hoc, Open-Ended Intersessional Working Group on Article 8(j) and Related Provisions of the CBD.
81 Text in Lee, L. (1993) 'The Cairo Declaration of Principles of International Law on Compensation to Refugees', *American Journal of International Law*, vol 87, pp157–159.
82 Beyani, C. (1995) 'State responsibility for the prevention and resolution of forced population displacement in international law', *International Journal of Refugee Law*, Special Issue, Oxford University Press, pp130–147.
83 Higgins, R. (1994) *Problems and Process: International Law and How We Use It*, Clarendon Press, Oxford, p161.
84 Crawford, J. (2002) *The International Law Commission's Articles on State Responsibility*, Cambridge University Press, Cambridge, UK, p12 (emphasis added).
85 Ibid.
86 Ibid.
87 1988 ILC Rep. Ch. 4, at www.un.org/law/ilc/reports/1998/chp4.html.
88 International Law Commission (1998) *Yearbook of the International Law Commission*, volume 1, International Law Commission, New York, p61, available for download at http://untreaty.un.org/ilc/publications/yearbooks/1998.htm.
89 Ibid, paragraph 25.
90 Ibid, paragraph 29.
91 Ibid, at 63 paragraph 41.
92 Gehring, T. and Jachtenfuchs, M. (1993) 'Liability for transboundary environmental damage towards a general liability regime?', *European Journal of International Law*, vol 4, no 1.
93 Ibid.
94 Op cit Note 40.
95 Ibid.
96 Bassiouni, C. M. (1996) *Crimes Against Humanity in International Criminal Law*, Martinus Nijhoff Publishers, Dordrecht, The Netherlands, p67.
97 Dupuy, P-M. (1989) 'The institutionalization of international crimes of state', in J. H. Weiler, A. Cassese and M. Spinedi (eds) *International Crimes of State*, Walter de Gruuyter, Berlin, p180.
98 Pellet, A. (1997) 'Vive le crime! Remarques sur les degrés de l'illicite en droit international', in *International Law on the Eve of the 21st Century*, United Nations, New York, p291.
99 Beyani (1995), op cit Note 82, p132.
100 Goodwin-Gill, G. (1983) *The Refugee in International Law*, Oxford University Press, Oxford, UK, p228; see also *Trail Smelter Arbitration, US versus Canada*, 1931–1941 3 R.I.A.A. 1905.
101 Lee, L. (1986) 'The right to compensation: Refugees and the countries of asylum', *American Journal of International Law*, vol 80, pp532–567.
102 Westra, L. (2006), op cit Note 58, pp7–9.
103 Beyani (1995), op cit Note 82, p132.
104 Jennings, R. (1938) 'Some international law aspects of the refugee question', *Year Book of International Law*, vol 20, p110.
105 Ragazzi (1999), op cit Note 51.
106 Beyani (1995), op cit Note 82, p134.
107 See discussion of the difference between 'consultation' and 'consent' in the case of indigenous communities in Westra, L. (2007), op cit Note 58, Chapter 4.

CHAPTER 5

Ecological Refugees: Protection and Rights in International Law

1. STATE PROTECTION – REFUGEES AND THE RIGHT TO HEALTH AND NORMAL FUNCTION

No state, acting alone, can insulate itself from major health hazards. The determinants of health (pathogens, air, food, water, even lifestyle choices) do not originate solely within national borders. Health threats inexorably spread to neighbouring countries, regions, and even continents. It is for this reason that safeguarding the world's population requires cooperation and global governance.[1]

It is an oft-repeated truism that the poorest countries, as well as the poorest peoples, suffer the most. Among the latter, the 'canaries', or the first affected and most vulnerable, are the children – 92 per cent of the children under five who die each year are from low-income countries.[2] Also, mass congregation, migration and travel are the source of the spread of infectious diseases among populations and geographical areas, as people flee situations of famine, violence or war:[3]

The gross unsanitary conditions in refugee camps and other mass settings are deeply troublesome from a public health and humanitarian perspective.[4]

States owe physical protection to all their citizens, according to domestic instruments, such as constitutions. But respect for *all* human beings is an international obligation *erga omnes* and no individual state can impose inhumane conditions and claim legality for its actions when asylum seekers show at their borders. Pre-dating the convention, the Universal Declaration of Human Rights gives priority to 'the recognition of the inherent dignity and the equal and inalienable rights of all members of the human family'.[5]

However, respect for human dignity is normally in short supply when refugee aid is provided. Even when material necessities are provided, refugees may be 'fingerprinted and tagged for identification', and their lives are completely regimented.[6]

According to the World Health Organization,[7] the last century was one of the most violent periods encountered on Earth. I submit that the 21st century is certainly no better, as the 'violence' added is ecological as well as traditionally based on conflict situations. Life in a refugee camp is a life deprived of dignity, and of the conditions required for basic health:

> *In the public portrayal of humanitarian emergencies, massive suffering is often reduced to a charitable appeal. The depiction of morally outrageous situations is trivialized as merely needing benevolent relief.*[8]

In sum, both regular health measures and basic respect are absent, once asylum seekers gain footing in their country of choice, and that is in addition to the grave difficulties they meet in attempting to achieve admission (see Chapter 3). As well as the recognized ecological disasters, the economic aggression/colonization practised by multinational corporations (MNCs) (such as mining and extractive industries) especially in developing countries and in areas inhabited by aboriginal and local communities, impose a grave burden of disease upon these peoples. An even graver problem is the presence of exposures capable of altering their normal function, thus adding yet another irreversible burden:[9]

> *Our topic at this point is that of state protection, and it is widely acknowledged ... the UN's human rights system offered little protection for groups and failed to develop an effective system of accountability.*[10]

In fact, all human rights instruments are not binding on United Nations member states unless each state has ratified the instruments, and the same is true of the two international covenants (ICCPR and ICESCR). Hence, the previous chapter argued for placing the rights of refugees clearly in the category of *erga omnes* obligations of states, rather than simply acknowledging the existence of the 1951 Convention on Refugees (CSR) which, in itself, does not address the needs of ecological refugees, and is therefore insufficient as it stands, even if it were fully implemented.

The repeated references to indigenous peoples appear to address an issue that is incidental to the general question for asylum seekers. For the most part, indigenous communities do not flee their countries: their lands are specifically designated for their use, and the inhabitants are not free to move and resettle, no matter how damaging and unliveable the conditions to which they are exposed. At most, they become internally displaced persons (IDPs) as they rejoin other impoverished groups in various shanty towns, surrounding the cities within their country of origin.

Hence, international laws most often do not apply. This problem will be discussed below in this chapter. Ecological refugees, in principle, include these groups as well as those who are normally understood to fit in that category – that is, the victims of ecological 'natural' disasters, whether or not these are partially or entirely caused by human activity. In the next section we will consider the relation between science and law through a discussion of the use of the precautionary principle.

1a. Ecological harms, human rights and the precautionary principle

> *First, we should do more to highlight the consequences of climate change for human health. Second, we should recognize that the precautionary moment for action on*

climate change – the period in which we might have acted based on something less than scientific consensus on the causes and consequences of climate change – has passed. We are in a post-cautionary world now.[11]

In fact, by the time the precautionary principle was thought to be almost an established (though not binding) principle of international law, not only climate change, but the deleterious effects of hundreds of chemicals had been proven without a doubt.

Unfortunately, 'environmental threats rarely capture the attention of the public and policy-makers unless they are linked to human health'.[12] And the 'environment' is not only our habitat; but it includes all the external substances to which we are exposed, and the noxious effects these produce to our health and to the normal human functioning we would expect under different circumstances.[13]

If we consider what has happened for years – the industry denials, the so-called 'scientific' reports proclaiming tobacco to be harmless[14] – we might be ready to reconsider the 'wait-and-see' attitude present in North America regarding chemical exposures, and consider instead the weak (but existing) European regulatory regime REACH and accept it as necessary.

As a result, the time for 'precaution' has long passed on chemical exposures as well as climate change.[15] The post-cautionary principle should be entrenched in international law as well as in domestic instruments, as required and binding. As the interconnection between climate change and chemical exposure is clearly and unequivocally linked to human health, as Heinzerling argues, certain consequences should follow:

> ... motivating political action, enlarging the number and kinds of governmental institutions involved in the problem, and creating a strong moral case for action.[16]

It is no longer a case of studying whether climate change, on the one hand, and industrial activities, on the other, have specific and well-documented health effects, both directly and indirectly on human beings. Direct effects refer to human health impairments, indirect effects to deteriorating environmental conditions, both of which produce the most harm in impoverished populations, and are often causative of mass migrations as well, as we have argued. The post-cautionary principle is equally appropriate to chemical exposures, where the harms imposed are not only limited to disasters and accidents, such as Bhopal, Seveso or Chernobyl, but include regular industrial operations of 'business as usual' (BAU), where the occurring 'externalities' are well documented. Thus, strict legal limits to both production and diffusion of these substances should be regulated by strict legal limits.[17]

This general argument applies to almost every area of the world, and to all populations. But it applies especially well to refugees, as it is often the case that industrial operations, together with the ecological and public health effects of related exposures, are causative of migrations. Thus, mass refugee flights often occur because of ecological degradation, whether gradual or catastrophic, and this includes conditions of starvation[18] or lack of safe water,[19] and other consequences of desertification, as well as glacial melts,[20] and other weather extremes.

In all these cases, not only are the health conditions of refugees dire at the outset and during their flight, but, as we saw, it is far less than optimal after their arrival at their destination. Furthermore, not only are refugees prone to disease, but they may well introduce various infectious diseases into whatever community they are forced to settle.[21] The reality of these health consequences, as caused most often by the ecological footprint of affluent countries,[22] and as refugees are both victims as well as 'vectors' of disease, represents a vicious cycle that must be broken. It needs swift action *before* it develops, as well as mitigation at each stage of the sequence.

2. ECOLOGICAL REFUGEES: THE EMERGENT REALITIES

> *A further weakness of the new UN system was that outside of the Genocide Convention, it provided few protections from abuses against groups. This appears inconsistent, given that so many crimes associated with World War II were perpetrated against collectives or against individuals by virtue of their perceived membership of national, ethnic or religious groups.*[23]

We need to pause and take stock of the situation in all its aspects before we can attempt to point to the main problems and to attempt to outline what, if any, might be the possible solutions. We have considered the multiple threats, exposures and ecological disasters that are causative of the seemingly insurmountable problems faced by the impoverished populations who tend to become 'asylum seekers' as 'ecological refugees'.

We have also noted the lack of 'fit' between the CSR and the realities on the ground, including the number of novel and constantly changing and emerging issues engendered by globalization in its many oppressive manifestations. Hence we might attempt to list these issues, for clarity:

1. the definition of refugee status in the 1951 Convention Relating to the Status of Refugees (Chapter 1);
2. the legal status and 'rights' of internally displaced persons (Chapter 1);
3. the applicability of the 'five grounds' for well-founded persecution' (Chapter 2);
4. the problem of mass migrations due to ecological degradation (Chapter 3);
5. the impact of climate change on mass migrations (Chapter 3);
6. the problematic case of indigenous and local communities (Chapter 4);
7. the *lacunae* and omissions in international law (Chapter 4);
8. the lack of protection in the domestic instruments of most Western states (Chapters 4 and 5);
9. the treatment of ecological refugees at the border, and the question of illegal detentions (Chapter 3);
10. the responsibility of all states beyond the adherence to conventions: the import of *erga omnes* obligations (Chapters 4 and 5).

Against the background of this formidable list of grave issues, and, in fact, counted among them, is the present 'weakness' of international legal instruments, which appear to be incapable of handling the problem of ecological refugees through its extensive series of treaties. Perhaps the major problem is that the United Nations Commission on

Human Rights is made up of state representatives 'whose first duty is to their national interest'.[24] It is because of this inherent weakness, as well as the fact that conventions develop slowly and only through debate among delegates, that the best source for the defence of human rights lies in the Vienna Law of Treaties (1969) and with it, the introduction of *jus cogens* norms, discussed in the previous chapter. Yet, even these norms do not include clear principles of minority protection, or even the official definition of 'minorities': the United Nations Declaration of Human Rights itself does not address this general question.[25]

Nevertheless, there are several conventions that attempt to treat this problem: for instance, the Convention on the Prevention and Punishment of the Crime of Genocide (1948) addresses the protection of minorities; Article 27 of the ICCPR addresses the individual rights (cultural, religious and linguistic) of minorities; the Committee on the Right of the Child (1989) also deals with similar issues, despite its own incompleteness regarding environmental concerns,[26] and the Committee on the Elimination of Racial Discrimination (CERD) addresses collective issues as well.

Despite the work of other commissions and sub-commissions addressing racial, ethnic, cultural and religious issues,[27] there are grave impediments to any attempt to categorize the protection of minority collectives under the strongest *jus cogens* norms: the prohibition of genocide, despite the long life of that question still technically requires clear intent. Raphael Lemkin in 1947 stated:

> *By declaring genocide a crime under international law and by making it a problem of international concern, the right of intervention on behalf of minorities slated for destruction has been established.*[28]

But genocide is not a crime whether it is committed in peace or war,[29] and the question of intent remains a stumbling block to its application.[30] I have argued that several legal categories could now be applied to the protection of minority groups who are faced with elimination without the malicious intent required to raise the attacks against them to the highest level, that is, to genocide.

Without trivializing genocide by lowering the standards needed to identify the crime, the category of 'wilful blindness' in Canadian criminal law, as currently applied to sexual attacks such as rape,[31] or simply using 'knowledge' of the circumstances that will result after certain actions or omissions, might be sufficient.

In addition, even the category of 'crimes against humanity', especially if it is understood as 'an actual offense against humankind',[32] might be appropriate and sufficient to raise the situation of ecological refugees to the level of protection demanded by *jus cogens* norms. At any rate, despite the presence of assorted instruments and related jurisprudence, the situation of all refugees, and especially that of ecological refugees, remains precarious. Hamilton points out that:

> *Given the way in which collectivities were subjected to attacks in the period immediately preceding the creation of the UN, the international community's emphasis on individuals in undertaking measures to protect minorities for serious or large scale violations of human rights or humanitarian law, and to prevent their becoming refugees seems anomalous.*[33]

By invoking the question of 'prevention', I believe Hamilton has reached an important conclusion that will need to be fleshed out below.

2a. The protection of ecological refugees: Legal realities beyond the 1951 convention

Advances in refugee rights since 1951 have, however, largely occurred outside refugee law itself. While alien law has yet to evolve as a meaningful source of protection, the development of a pervasive treaty-based system of international human rights law has filled many critical gaps in the refugee convention's rights regime.[34]

The first part of this paragraph is the most significant: refugee law, as such, is covered primarily in the CSR and the *Handbook on Procedures and Criteria for Determining Refugee Status*.[35] The *Handbook* has 'no binding force either in municipal or international law'.[36] Along with the *Handbook*, as of September 2004, six sets of guidelines had been issued by the United Nations High Commissioner for Refugees (UNHCR);[37] yet none of these even attempt to deal with mass migrations or IDPs. The present lack of clear codified guidelines is a source of a great deal of confusion, and the need for 'principled consensus' is obvious today even in traditional refugee law,[38] aside from the lack of awareness of the issue of ecological refugees.

The convention was preceded by the equally unenforceable Declaration of Human Rights and the binding Convention on the Prevention and Punishment of the Crime of Genocide.[39] Aside from the two Covenants, the UNHCR Executive Committee Conclusion No. 81, 'General Conclusion on International Protection' (1999), urges states:

> *... to take all necessary measures to ensure that refugees are effectively protected, including through national legislation, and in compliance with their obligations under international human rights and humanitarian law instruments bearing directly on refugee protection.*[40]

Hence, the committee itself urges that the *lacunae* present in the CSR be supplemented by the use of international human rights and humanitarian law in order to achieve 'effective protection'. Whether or not it is sufficient to borrow the norms of other instruments at least this paragraph opens the door for appeals to other legal regimes that may be better for the needs of refugees.

The question of environmental racism and, in general, of non-discrimination was discussed in Chapter 4, and this appears to be one of the strongest principles in defence of refugees. It might also be helpful to consider the duty 'of equal protection of non-citizens'.[41] Article 26 of the ICCPR, according to the General Comment 18 of the Human Rights Committee, is particularly strong on this issue:

> *Article 26 does not merely duplicate the guarantee already provided for in Article 2 [of the Civil and Political Covenant] but provides in itself an autonomous right. It prohibits discrimination in law or in fact in any field regulated by public authorities.*[42]

It is important to acknowledge the need for protection based on non-discrimination because what is advocated is more than simple 'equality', as 'formal equality of treatment may itself result in discrimination';[43] hence, it goes even beyond 'equal protection of the law' as it extends to non-citizens. The Human Rights Committee states that 'each of the rights of the covenant must be guaranteed without discrimination between citizens and aliens'.[44]

The guarantee of non-discrimination in international law can be found in the Civil and Political Covenant (Article 26, as we saw, as that is the most far-reaching provision on this issue presently in existence):

> *All persons are equal before the law and are entitled without any discrimination to the equal protection of the law. In this respect, the law shall prohibit any discrimination and guarantee to all persons equal and effective protection against discrimination on any grounds such as race, colour, sex, language, religion, political or other opinion, national or social origin, property, birth or other status.*

Thus, this article guarantees more than equality before the law, a procedural assurance that may not reach far enough as, arguably, even the government of South Africa under apartheid might have made a similar claim. The question of the protection of the law, however, is a substantive issue, not a purely procedural one, as it ensures that aliens will be protected as citizens are, rather than suffer a treatment that might set them apart.[45] What is prohibited is discrimination, however, not differential treatment, as long as it is based on 'reasonable and objective criteria', although not everyone agrees on what constitutes 'reasonableness', and on whether differentiation on the basis of citizenship fits that definition.[46]

Often, the analysis required to assess the 'reasonableness' of a judgement or a decision is highly superficial as in the case of *AS versus Canada*, where a request for family reunification was rejected 'in conformity with the provision of existing Canadian law', despite the fact that 'family reunification' should rank high among the rights of refugees.[47] In general, most of the Human Rights Committee's decisions tend 'to assume the reasonableness of many state-sanctioned forms of differentiation, rather than to condition a finding of reasonableness on careful analysis'.[48]

Essentially then, aliens, do not enjoy the same rights as nationals today, any more than they appeared to do so when Special Rapporteur of the International Law Commission F. V. Garcia-Amador states that they did in 1974.[49] Furthermore, Baroness Diana Ellis, as Special Rapporteur of the Sub-commission on Prevention of Discrimination and Protection of Minorities, pointed out that the Declaration of Human Rights itself 'was not a binding instrument', and that 'many exclusions and permissible limitations in international instruments' do not ensure alien's rights.[50] More recently, David Weissbrodt was appointed Special Rapporteur on the Rights of Citizens, and he also lists many aspects of *de facto* discrimination against non-citizens.[51]

Yet, Hathaway notes that 'the report does not aspire to provide solid answers to the underlying challenge of the exclusion of non-citizens from key parts of human rights law, including by the legal prerogative of less developed states to deny economic rights to non-citizens'.[52] Hence, we can conclude that, even though there has been a great deal of development in human rights law since the convention, the rights of refugees are still not well protected. This situation makes the position of ecological refugees or

IDPs still more precarious, as even the few protection rights available to the convention refugees are not available to them.

It is because of this weakness in the relevant conventions that we have sought to connect the situation of ecological refugees to the strongest obligations of states as obligations *erga omnes*. That entails that the harms suffered by these migrants must rise to the level of the most grave of human rights violations, according to *jus cogens* norms. We need to examine this claim in detail: for the most part the deliberate intent to eliminate these groups (as required by the definition of genocide) is not present. Yet the results of ecological disasters or progressive ecological degradation that eventually render some areas and regions uninhabitable result in such harms that mass atrocities and even crimes against humanity may represent appropriate designations to describe the plight of such migrants.

3. ECOLOGICAL AND ECONOMIC OPPRESSION AS CRIMES AGAINST HUMANITY

> *While millions of innocent human beings have been killed and maimed in the last century in armed conflict and by mass killing, the overwhelming majority of those who fall victim to adverse human agency, are not injured by proximate violence, but as a result of being compelled to live in sub-human conditions… Compelling a person to live in inhumane or degrading conditions amounts to inhumane treatment, a violation of customary international law. Such conditions are defined … as those that do not fulfil minimal humanitarian standards applicable to prisoners of war.*[53]

Extreme poverty and hunger, and the living conditions that they engender, have been indicted by moral and political philosophers from many perspectives: from an approach that critiques 'the problem of world hunger', when it is viewed primarily as a 'problem of famines that should be addressed by donations of food or money';[54] or as our moral obligation 'to prevent evil from happening' anywhere – that is, whether or not we are proximate to it;[55] or as a matter of global justice on the part, primarily, of affluent states;[56] or because of the moral obligations imposed by cosmopolitanism as 'the same scope of principles of justice is said to be universal or cosmopolitan, encompassing all humans';[57] or as the major problem of global governance, as it is essentially the overall dominance of major multinational corporations that eliminate the possibility of a human face, or justice, in the regimes of globalization;[58] and, finally, the acknowledgement of the existence of 'basic rights', which impose an obligation on us all.[59]

When we couple this variety of major philosophical approaches, and moral arguments, with the atrocities that take place on the ground,[60] we can, indeed, agree that our 'moral blindness' is complicit in what represents an ongoing moral outrage. Speaking of Africa, Davidsson says:

> *Most of the deaths are attributable to sickness and famine.*[61] *Yet the civilized world has chosen to look the other way regarding a conflict that has taken more lives than any other since World War II and is the deadliest documented conflict in African history.*[62]

In law, a 'cause' is something that interferes with or intervenes in the course of events which should normally take place.[63] But a cause may well be an omission as well as an action and 'complicity' is, indeed, a complex concept.

A recent paper by Judith Lee Kissell (1999) analyses complicity as a multifaceted concept. 'Complicity' includes 'encouraging', 'enticing', 'enabling', 'ordering' and 'failing to intervene', and one can cite examples from antiquity to the present that all fit loosely under the general heading of complicity.

Kissell says:

> *For example, we count as accomplices Aeschylus/ Aegisthus, who encourages Clytemnestra to kill her husband, Agamemnon; Shakespeare's Iago, who entices Othello to kill his beloved Desdemona; the mother who enables her child to become an alcoholic; the gangleader who orders a beating of a victim; the Western powers who, according to Margaret Thatcher, were complicit for failing to intervene in the former Yugoslavia.*[64]

Kissell defines conspiracy as 'an offence in which one agent, the accomplice, becomes responsible for the acts of, and the harm caused by, another agent, the perpetrator'.[65] Following this definition, she adds: 'complicity is an *offence* and not simply a collaborative action'. Nevertheless, it is clear that 'planning', 'encouraging' or even 'enabling' are not in and of themselves harming anyone, when just two are involved: the accomplice and the perpetrator. It seems as though the situation is totally different when a group is involved. The one who delivers a hate speech to a group cannot claim innocence when the inflamed group acts violently in consequence of hearing the encouragement to hate. The speaker cannot just claim he did not participate in the violence, and stood aside from it.

Speaking of the relationship between accomplice and perpetrator, Kissell emphasizes their 'asymmetric relationship to the harm'; but when group complicity is at stake, the case is not so clear. It is not obvious that one can always distinguish between 'cause' and 'contributions' when a group conspiracy is at issue. Hitler at first 'encouraged', then 'planned' and finally 'ordered' and 'enabled' the killing of millions of Jews. He can certainly be seen as a perpetrator anyway, although he probably never personally, actively perpetrated a single violent crime, or killed a single Jew.

For all that, we can (and must) say that Hitler was indeed blameworthy and personally responsible for causing the atrocities that he did not personally perpetrate. Nevertheless, his causal agency is far more than a contributing factor. Because of the authority he represented, his beliefs and his expressions, aside from the laws he enacted, were directly causative of the harms that ensued. In that case, it seems that Kissell is mistaken when she claims that causation and complicit conduct cannot be equated. She says:

> *I can think of contribution as causal in the broad sense of being the object of inquiry that justifies censure. However, because it is not the same thing as a physical cause, it need not satisfy the necessity requirement, which in any case complicit conduct cannot do.*[66]

Richard Wasserstrom provides a clearer understanding of group dynamics in violent situations,[67] so that the mere joining of certain groups when these are known to promote a specific explicit agenda is sufficient to ensure the personal responsibility of all who join for the ensuing violence. An example might be joining the Ku Klux Klan in the southern US, hence participating in its hate propaganda and its crimes.

For cases of institutionalized eco-violence or ecological violence perpetrated against vulnerable people, we have no centralized 'evil' authority we can point to, although, for instance, the demonstrators at the 1999 WTO protests had crystallized their movement against an organization, including corporations, at least, if not against a specific person. At any rate, a thorough understanding of both causality and complicity forces us to acknowledge the truth of what the former UN Secretary-General's Special Envoy for HIV/AIDS in Africa, Stephen Lewis, termed 'the lack of resources to fight the epidemic "mass murder by complacency"'.[68] We can surely extend this understanding to the lethal consequences of extreme poverty and starvation.

In the next section we will examine the definitions of the Charter and the Trial of Nuremberg, as well as the language of the Statute of the International Criminal Court (ICC) on what constitutes a crime against humanity.

3a. Crimes against humanity: From Nuremberg to the Statute of the International Criminal Court

Crimes against humanity – namely, murder, extermination, enslavement, deportation and other inhuman acts committed against any civilian population, before or during the war or persecution on political, racial or religious grounds in execution of or in connection with any crime within the jurisdiction of the tribunal, whether or not in violation of the domestic law of the country where perpetrated.[69]

Here we find many of the familiar prohibitions regarding refugees; but, at this time, we need to highlight the most important aspect of crimes against humanity. The question of 'persecution' is present and the expected 'grounds'; but so is 'deportation', 'enslavement' and, in general, 'inhuman acts against civilian populations'. In this regard, we must consider the effects of diffuse economic oppression, characterized by the total disregard for the rights of affected populations when climate change and trade-related harms combine to wreak havoc on the lives of land-based communities and indigenous populations. Wolfgang Sachs says:

Indeed, it would be hard to understand why disease and malnutrition should be less important than press censorship and religious persecution in affecting people's ability to act... A minimalist conception of human rights that refers only to the negative political freedoms, therefore, discriminates against the have-nots and those whose livelihood is threatened; recognition of their dignity requires the protection of economic, social and cultural rights.[70]

This incomplete understanding of human rights ignores the generally accepted existence of 'basic rights':[71] the fact that the interdependence of all human rights is now an accepted principle in international law;[72] and the fact that the 'rights-centred approach' is now accepted by UN organs, such as the World Health Organization (WHO), the United Nations Children's Fund (UNICEF) and the United Nations

Development Programme (UNDP), despite the fact that even if these rights are indeed accepted, the corresponding obligations are not as clear:

> *Just as the violation of the right to food, health or shelter can often not be traced back to the action of a clearly identifiable duty-bearer ... climate effects cannot be attributed to a culprit with a name and address.*[73]

The right to food, like the right to water,[74] and the right to a living environment and to health[75] are part and parcel of human rights; together with the right to shelter, they are all the most basic and necessary rights to ensure human survival and the presence of human agency.[76] These rights are recognized by UN organs and committees:

> *Governments must recognize their extra-territorial obligations toward the right to food: they should refrain from implementing any policies or programs that might have negative effects on the right to food of peoples living outside their territories.*[77]

In the case of all these rights and corresponding obligations, it is impossible to pinpoint the 'perpetrator(s)' – that is, precisely who is depriving a specific community of their basic necessities of life; but the responsibility must be ascribed to those who have the power to initiate and support change and activities in the area where such a community lives: local and national governments, multinational corporations, national enterprises, financial institutions who are prepared to finance these enterprises. For all, it is far more than the 'complacency' of the general public mentioned above: we have noted the presence of racist attitudes,[78] as well as 'gross negligence, wilful blindness and recklessness'.[79]

As most of these conditions are linked to extreme poverty, it is clear that every time that environmentally destructive policies are condoned,[80] and when socially regressive policies are imposed and facilitated by local governments, then protection for the poor is absent and, although the names of specific perpetrators may not be in evidence, the existence of complicity by several of these actors is.

Through a combination of omission and committed acts, the conditions that lead to mass migrations and yield the largest numbers of refugees are created by identifiable groups, organizations and institutions, although, no doubt, the intent to destroy is not on their agenda:

> *Substantial analytic efforts are required to deconstruct the ideological assumptions underlying economic theories and translate euphemisms used by international financial institutions and the Security Council into ordinary language, in order to expose such policies' inhumane consequences.*[81]

The results of these policies deprive whole communities of their basic necessities of life, even of the bare minimum that cannot be denied to prison inmates, for instance. These are the minimal civilized measures of life's necessities, and this deprivation may be judged to be 'cruel and degrading punishment' in US municipal law.[82] In addition, inhumane conditions of confinement may also be a category that can be applied to the conditions of asylum seekers after the ecological and economic oppressions they were subjected to in their communities.

Hence, their flight originates from and is based on the consequences of the commission of crimes or acts of omission, even though multiple actors might be involved in the facilitation and 'enabling' of the crimes. The end result of their flight is also no 'solution' because the conditions of treatment and confinement are also unacceptable. Articles 16 and 17 of the ICCPR guarantee the right of recognition of everyone, everywhere, 'as a person before the law', and the right not to have his family and home interfered with. The ICESCR and the United Nations Declaration of Human Rights are also intended to promote human rights (see Articles 55 and 56). Article 11 of the ICESCR ensures the right to an 'adequate standard of living', and Article 12, the right 'to the highest attainable standard of physical and mental health'. Davidsson adds:

While the obligation to 'ensure' these rights is of a progressive character, the correlative obligation to refrain from violating pre-existing standards of living and the other listed rights is immediate.[83]

Against these violent deprivations of the rights guaranteed by international instruments, especially the right to life, which should obviously include the conditions basic to life (Article 6 of the ICCPR), and the right not to be subjected to inhuman and degrading treatment (Article 7), there should be a guarantee that the actions leading to such deprivations should cease immediately and reparations be made, as far as these are possible. From the time an area inhabited by groups that will become asylum seekers becomes progressively unliveable, to the time they flee to seek refuge elsewhere or in another area or city in their own country of origin, through the flight, and after their arrival, the inhumane conditions persist.

It is tempting to reach to the highest international crime and deem it appropriate – that is, to claim that genocide is occurring or has occurred. But because of the lack of clear intent (despite the presence of gross negligence, wilful blindness and recklessness, as previously argued), another category is needed: the category of crimes against humanity. Many years after the Charter of Nuremberg and the Trial of Nuremberg, the Statute of the International Criminal Court (Rome), describes this crime as follows (in part) in Article 7:

Article 7 – Crimes against Humanity

1 For the purpose of this statute, 'crimes against humanity' means any of the following acts when committed as part of a widespread or systemic attack against any civilian population, with knowledge of the attack ...
   (c) enslavement;
   (d) deportation or forcible transfer of population;
   (e) imprisonment or other severe deprivation of physical liberty in violation of fundamental rules of international law;
   (h) persecution against any identifiable group ...
   (j) the crime of apartheid;
   (k) other inhumane acts of a similar character intentionally causing great suffering or serious injury to body or to mental or physical health.

Several of the listed categories fit well the plight of refugees, from 'imprisonment' (e), to 'persecution' (h); from the crime of 'apartheid' (j) to 'other inhuman acts' (k). The most salient point, however, is the fact that under point 1, only 'knowledge of the attack' is required – hence, the crime is committed even without the 'intent to destroy'. We will return below to this question and to the appropriateness of this category of crime to what happens to refugees, before and after they become asylum seekers. Now we need to examine another aspect of their condition, one that is seldom if at all discussed in the legal literature: what are the differences applicable to land-based communities and indigenous peoples.

4. ECOLOGICAL REFUGEES AND INDIGENOUS REFUGEES: SIMILARITIES AND DIFFERENCES

Principles of justice can be derived from the requirement of rejecting inclusive principles of injury, which are not [universal] across the domain of connected others. An analogous pattern of derivation shows that inclusive principles of indifference to and neglect of others also cannot be universalized.[84]

Perhaps the reasons why the interface between ecological refugees and displaced indigenous peoples seems to remain invisible to both legal scholarship and the general public is that the two issues appear to be so different. Refugees, including ecological refugees, by definition, are people who have been displaced by natural disasters, by economic oppression, by hazardous operations or accidents or by a combination of factors that have forced them to flee their habitual places. Their problems are: can they qualify as 'convention refugees' to benefit in some way from convention rights; and can they be admitted to the country they seek to enter and, once admitted, can they have their rights to safety, *non-refoulement* and protection respected and implemented in their new locality?

Ecological refugees, in addition, have an even harder situation with which to cope: they are at the fringes of the world of refugees, one might say, looking in from outside, hoping to gain a foothold in the meagre protection to which regular refugees can aspire. But aboriginal communities, although they are exposed to the same combination of multiple harms, from climate change to chemical exposure to economic oppression of various kinds, are facing a completely different situation from several perspectives.

Essentially, the presence of indigenous peoples entails significant changes to both the situation we have described, and to the possible 'solutions' offered by municipal and international law. It will help to view each of the grave problems that cause the flight or the intolerable conditions of indigenous peoples separately.

The first issue to note is that, no matter how grave the harms, how serious the results discussed above in a general sense, most often indigenous communities may be decimated, they may lose their chosen lifestyle; but the members of the community do not flee, unless the harms originate is a grave environmental disaster. The question that arises, then is *why* are indigenous community members not only included as refugees or IDPs, but even here singled out for special consideration?

The answer is both simple and complex: indigenous groups are exposed to all the aspects of ecological and economic oppression we have listed, and they are among the most vulnerable, but they also suffer an additional injustice, as their rights are at best limited to a specific territory that is theirs, traditionally and originally. This claim is confirmed and rendered legal by treaties, proclamations and often by hard-fought case law, at least in North America.[85]

Yet, despite their inability to move, unless it is after a natural catastrophe, their flight is mostly internal within their own country. A clear example is that of the Arctic peoples as they become progressively 'strangers in their own land' because of the glacial melts and other results of climate change.[86] Thus, for the most part, indigenous peoples' *sui generis* plight is that of IDPs. In many cases, they remain as prisoners of a circumscribed area where the conditions are extremely harmful: despite the possibility of internal self-governance, however, there are no buffer zones around the territories to protect them,[87] and they have little or no control on what happens at their borders, or even at times, inside their own lands. These grave circumstances therefore render them ecological refugees '*par excellence*': the most typical and intractable examples of the specific category of IDPs and ecological refugees.

4a. Climate change and indigenous peoples

> *The result of these increasingly unmanageable hazards give rise to... an even more pressing concern ... [which is] the social fallout from the transformation of these traditional subsistence-based societies to 'Southern' wage-based economies.*[88]

The impact of climate change is seen most clearly in the Arctic as described in this opening passage, and in coastal areas and island states.[89] There is no need to repeat the scientific findings regarding climate change, listed with their impacts on human health in the work of Liza Heinzerling discussed in the early sections of this chapter.[90]

Instead, we need to consider once again the effects of climate change on the availability of food, water, shelter and, in general, on the way of life of indigenous communities. The clearest example of the combination of all these factors and the results that ensue can be seen in the Arctic. Any change in temperature affects the local ecosystems, including not only their normal functioning, but also their flora and fauna. Even a small increase in temperature entails species loss, with the expected cascade effects that it brings.[91] This means that the animals that represent the bulk of the Inuit diet are no longer plentiful or, in some cases, not even available.

In addition, the ice melts and warmer conditions mean that it is increasingly unsafe for hunters to venture out 'on the land' – that is, to travel outside settlements on the ice, which is currently shrinking and unsafe. If the traditional 'hunt' can no longer provide for them, not only must the Inuit provide in a different way for themselves and their families, they must change their way of life completely. They must now depend on handouts from the local self-government – for instance, in the Canadian Territories of Nunavut and the Northwest Territories.

When the traditional way of life is no longer possible, the social hierarchy (with the corresponding importance of hunters in that society), as well as the traditional feasting after a successful hunt and sharing of the spoils are all eliminated.[92] The importance of both the hunt and the rituals and social activities it generates cannot be overestimated. Hence, the issue is larger than just depriving these peoples of their livelihood, through the effects of climate change, it is the deprivation of their identity, of who they are as a people, even if there are ways to prevent the starvation of individuals.

The result is the denial of the rights to their 'cultural integrity'.[93] Essentially, this represents what Raphael Lemkin termed 'cultural genocide'.[94] Whether they stay in the same area where they used to live traditionally, on the land, or they decide to seek their livelihood elsewhere, they are 'ecological refugees' or internally displaced persons, even though they may not be detained at some camp at another state's borders.

As their specific traditional lifestyle is eliminated, so are their traditional religious practices, also tied to the land and the animals. They are therefore deprived of their livelihood, most often their health, as their traditional food choices and active lifestyle are no longer available to them; but they are also deprived of their culture and their right to their chosen religious practices. No amounts of handouts or insurance payments can make up for that situation; in fact, their disappearance as 'peoples' is clearly in breach of all the municipal and international legal instruments where *all* these rights are explicitly guaranteed.

The work of Biermann and Boas[95] represents an important and novel addition to the limited amount of works on this topic. However, this work, although excellent within its limits, ignores the effects of climate change on Inuit and other Arctic peoples with the implications discussed above; and it also ignores the additional migrations and displacements engendered by hazardous industrial operations. In fact, the argument by Biermann and Boas for the responsibility of developed/industrial countries[96] is further strengthened by the addition of these further attacks on communities in developing countries, or indigenous groups in the West. These attacks will be the topic of the next section.

4b. Chemical/industrial exposures and indigenous peoples

> While most studies currently focus on the year 2050, the Secretariat of the United Nations Framework Convention on Climate Change offers a more immediate estimate for 2010, of possibly 50 million 'environmentally displaced people'.[97]

There are two major problems with the United Nations Framework Convention on Climate Change's (UNFCCC's) assessment. First, by ignoring the disasters, the catastrophes and even the simple impact of hazardous industrial operations and their impact on vulnerable people, the report/press release ignores a significant (though currently unreported), additional number of refugees. As a result, the appellation of 'climate refugees' is not synonymous with 'environmentally displaced people' or with what I term ecological refugees. Their assessment is therefore incomplete.

I cannot offer any additional figures; but I might suggest that until some scientific research is done beyond the well-known disasters and uninhabitable locations they created (e.g. Chernobyl and Bhopal), simple review of current jurisprudence, especially in North and South America, as well as present and ongoing conflicts in India, Indonesia and other countries in Asia and Africa, might indicate the magnitude of the problem that is additional to that of climate refugees. A few examples will suffice.

Chapter 3 presented several 'classic' cases of Alien Torts Claims Act (ATCA) jurisprudence discussed under the category of state responsibility. These were chosen especially in order to demonstrate how the conditions of people in the affected communities were similar to those of persecuted groups, according to the definition of the CSR. Now we need to shift our focus somewhat to consider such cases as those that involve gold,[98] or uranium mining,[99] or oil extraction,[100] or mercury exposures from pulp and paper plants.[101]

Briefly, then, gold mining entails using a great deal of water – a very scarce resource in many areas (increasingly so with climate change) and especially grave in the 'altiplano' region of Guatemala, where an indigenous group, the Sipakapa of San Marcos, used to live peacefully practising agriculture and animal husbandry.

In 2005, Montana Exploradora, a subsidiary of the Canadian/US transnational corporation Glamis Gold, received US$45 million from the World Bank Group to exploit an open-pit gold mine in their area.[102] The original video with English subtitles demonstrates clearly the vast gulf between the arguments and proposals of the mine representatives, and the responses of the local people. In the final analysis, the people's 'no' should have meant just that. International Labour Organization (ILO) Convention No. 169 and even the Constitution of Guatemala demand a consultation with the indigenous peoples; the result was *not* consensus but a resounding 'no' to the project. However, this was not respected and the exploration and work continued.

While the Guatemalan courts are still to pronounce on the topic, in April 2006 the open-pit mining was in full operation with its highly toxic cyanide ponds required by that operation, and its heedless use of scarce local water for industrial activities. Repeated in the video, the people ask 'what is *our* advantage?' The answer to this question remains unclear, while the damages inflicted emerge clearly, and the courts deliberately proceed at a slow pace, while the corporation continues with its unwanted and harmful 'development'.

This 'development' represents a clear breach of multiple rights: the right not to be deprived of one's own resources, the right not to be deprived of one's livelihood, and the right to both life and family life were not respected. Nor was their tradition and right to their own social organization. Their life was disrupted for an unwanted hazardous activity that would have never been permitted in the home countries of Glamis Gold (i.e. Canada and the US).

Another example might be the highly hazardous operations of uranium mining. The history of uranium mining in the four-corner area (Utah, Colorado, Arizona and New Mexico, and the Navajo Reservation between the Grand Canyon and the Petrified Forest National Park) appears to have been written in blood. The evidence of the narrative is unequivocal. It is consistently one group and one group alone that is targeted. I have termed this approach 'institutionalized ecological violence', and Peter Eichstaedt is correct in pointing out that this form of violence does more than destroy the unfortunate miners who are working in hazardous unventilated 'dog holes', accumulating in one week multiple doses of the yearly maximum 'safe' radiation exposure in their bodies, and eventually succumbing to untreatable cancer and other diseases.[103]

Some mill workers also had up to 60 micrograms of uranium in their urine samples. The yellowcake dust they inhaled and swallowed was making them radioactive from the inside out.

This intolerable violence also destroys families who attempt to survive on the pitiful sums allotted to them, or with no compensation at all for surviving wives and children. Finally, this same violence, discriminating against Native Americans, also attacks their survival as people – hence, the appeal to genocide in this case. Although we all depend on a healthy, non-toxic environment, native people have a particular right and claim to the lands they inhabit and from which they assert their identity as a nation.

Hence, when the Navajo miners, their families and supporters took on the 'fight for justice', requesting child support and simple compensation to survive, they were asking far less than what should have been theirs by right:

> ... at the age of 40, Peter Yazzie knew the end was near and was driven to a hospital in Albuquerque. He died eight days later, on 6 June 1970. He left a home that was a simple adobe hogan heated with wood, a wife Dolores, age 36, and ten children ranging in age from 2 to 18. His wife began to collect US$250 a month on which to raise a family.[104]

The final injustices were disclosed in February 1993, when even the evident physical damages to the miners were shown to have been calculated improperly:

> [Dr Louise] Abel demonstrated to the assembled doctors, lawyers and government officials that the medical tests are inadequate.[105]

This resulted in hundreds of miners being excluded from 'compassion payments' ordered by the Radiation Exposure Compensation Act of 1990. When a group is singled out for special treatment that effectively eliminates most of their basic rights to life, health, and their rights to free information and consent, then all those involved are guilty of complicity in the crimes perpetrated against them. Through each sad interview describing the story of individual miners and their families, and through the appendices detailing the hearing on radiation exposure and, finally, the Radiation Exposure Compensation Act of 1990, the story that unfolds is one that should fill everyone with shame.[106] Nor is the US the only country with that problem. A 2006 report from Australia relates a similar story:

> Cancer rates among Aborigines near Australia's biggest uranium mine appear to be almost double the normal rates, according to a study by the federal government's leading indigenous research body. The study also found there had been no monitoring in the past 20 years of the ranger mine's impact on the health of local indigenous peoples. Yet since 1981 there have been more than 120 spillages and leaks of contaminated water at the mine located in the World Heritage listed Kakadu National Park.[107]

Energy Resources of Australia (majority owned by Rio Tinto), which operates the mine, denied that the aboriginal peoples in the area were exposed to radiation and announced that the mine would continue to operate until 2020, despite the fact that:

> ... [a] study compared Aborigines diagnosed with cancer in the Kakadu region with the cancer rate among all Aboriginal peoples in the Northern Territory from 1994 to

2003. It found the diagnosis rate was 90 percent higher than expected in the Kakadu region.[108]

In this case as well, neither the corporation(s) responsible for the extractive activities, not the Australian government that allowed and, in fact, defended this operation, accepted responsibility for the harms they had perpetrated, or attempted to close the mine and redress the injustice for which they shared responsibility.

Examples can be multiplied, and the factual recitations of aboriginal groups in the ATCA cases reviewed earlier bear witness to a number of similar exposures. Thus, it is neither the facts nor the science that are lacking, but the functionalist approach of industry and institutions that needs to accept the scientific reality and enact the required corrections.

Yet another extractive industry that is harmful to both human health and ecology is oil extraction. In Canada, the Province of Alberta is enjoying an unprecedented and well-known economic boom. However, the other side of the coin – the grave health hazards associated with tar sands operations – is not as well publicized. In fact, when Dr John O'Connor started working in northern Alberta in 2003, what he saw and studied first hand led him to become a whistleblower, with dire consequences for his professional life:

> *In 2003, Dr O'Connor first started regularly flying from his home in Fort McMurray to see patients in the northern Alberta town of Fort Chipewyan's small, largely native population of 1200. He was startled to find a string of cases of cholangiocarcinoma, an uncommon cancer of the bile duct.*
>
> *Normally the disease affects one in 100,000 people. Dr O'Connor saw six patients in a row he suspected had cholangiocarcinoma and by the time he'd sent three or four referrals to the local toxicologist's office, they jokingly asked: 'What are you doing to those patients up there in Fort Chip, doctor?'*

He went through the health histories of the town's residents and found a striking number of residents who had already had brushes with cancer. He saw high incidence of colorectal cancer and, in the last four or five years, an abnormally high number of gastrointestinal cancers. Dr O'Connor documented what he was seeing and called for a thorough health study of Fort Chip's residents.

After Dr O'Connor's concerns about the oil sands–cancer link were widely publicized last year, the provincial government moved to test the water, almost a decade after scientists first raised warnings of the health dangers. The government held a press conference to say everything was fine; but after everyone left, says Dr O'Connor, officials told the community there may be an issue with arsenic in the water; levels were 17 to 33 times the upper limits in some samples. When asked if it would be monitored, officials said no, and when asked if it was safe to eat the food, they said 'we have no information to say it's unsafe'.

Dr O'Connor's findings are supported by a recent study of the water around Fort Chip. The report, issued by Dr Kevin Timoney, an Alberta ecologist who has studied the Athabasca River for the past 14 years, suggests that arsenic isn't the only issue: 'the level of polycyclic aromatic hydrocarbons are significantly high enough to raise the risk of cancer', he says.

Dr O'Connor was accused of misconduct, 'engendering mistrust' by both Health Canada and Alberta Health and Wellness.[109]

In the same general area, the ongoing case of the Lubicon Cree is also instructive. The Lubicon Cree Nation had been asking the Alberta government 'to demarcate their lands' in the boreal forests of Alberta for many years, to no avail, as 'mining, lumbering and agriculture' were increasingly taking over their traditional lands.[110] Eventually, the Lubicon Cree decided to abandon their efforts at gaining recognition in the courts, and decided instead to 'erect checkpoints on all roads entering their traditional territory'.[111] Chief Ominayak decided they had the right to protect their territories; he said:

> ... the Lubicon Nation intends to assert and enforce its aboriginal rights and its sovereign jurisdiction as an independent nation.[112]

The Lubicon Cree need the boreal forest in order to continue hunting, fishing and trapping, their traditional pursuits; but the provincial courts not recognize their claim, and the provincial government sent in the Royal Canadian Mounted Police, who 'arrested 27 people' at the checkpoint where the Lubicon were blocking the highway,[113] thus justifying the Lubicon's lack of trust in Canadian legal institutions and the promises of the Alberta government.

In 1984, the Lubicon took their case to the United Nations Human Rights Committee:[114]

> *In March 1990, the United Nations Human Rights Committee (UNHRC) concluded that 'historical inequities' and 'more recent developments' have endangered the way of life and the culture of the Lubicon Cree. The committee ruled that 'so long as they continue' these threats are a violations of the Lubicons' fundamental human rights.*[115]

Yet, the rights to the traditional territory of the Lubicon Cree had not been extinguished by any treaty that might affect them as they live within Treaty 8 territory, but had not signed that treaty. The Canadian government assured the committee that it was working to find a way to settle with the Lubicon in a mutually satisfactory way. Since the time when this commitment was made, until 2007, no settlement has been reached. In contrast, while the Lubicon Cree live in squalor, with no running water in their homes, 'billions of dollars more in oil and gas resources have been extracted from Lubicon territory'.[116]

It is vital to keep two points in mind: the first is that as long as Canada stalls by saying it is 'negotiating', or 'trying to settle', somehow it continues to avoid taking any concrete action on this urgent matter; however, since there have been no negotiations since 2003, this is no longer valid. The other point is that what is being taken away from the Lubicon is far more than revenues, although an equitable share of the profit being made by Alberta might be at least a beginning. Nevertheless, the harms they are suffering cannot be compensated for, and even if they were offered a fair share of the profits of those industries, still it would not be right to continue the present rate and mode of resource extraction and 'development', given the irreversible effects of those operations, as we shall see below.

Although eventually the UN decision came down in favour of the Lubicon, their territory has yet to be demarcated. The problem originated because they lived isolated north of the area where treaties such as Treaty 8 had been negotiated, so that the Lubicon Cree were essentially missed when other treaties were signed that affected other aboriginal people in Alberta and Saskatchewan.[117] But the main problems began after the discovery of what some believe are among the most extensive petroleum fields in America, so that it was not only agriculture and various settlements that already posed threats to their traditional lifestyle; the exploitation of timber and mining were especially hazardous. 'The Story of the Lubicon Case shows what can happen in Canada when a native community tries to assert rights to a territory rich in oil.[118] Oil companies were especially pressing, and by 1979:

> *The Province of Alberta completed the construction of an all-weather road to the previously remote Lubicon territory.*[119]

The road was built without ever solving the question of the legal boundaries of the Lubicon territory, yet:

> *Since the all-weather road completion in 1979, more than 400 oil wells have been installed by more than one hundred oil companies, all within fifteen miles of the main Lubicon community of Little Buffalo.*[120]

Hence, the issue is even more complex than the lack of aboriginal title or the recognition of the appropriate boundaries of the Lubicon territory.

Huff lists several of the attacks on the life and health of the Lubicon: first, the proximity of operating oil wells to the Cree settlement, noted above. Second, 'gasoline and motor oil spills have fouled many traditional gathering areas';[121] hence, traditional gathering and trapping are much reduced, while market demand for pelts has also decreased. This reality has affected the Lubicon in several ways. On the one hand, the elimination of the income from trapping has forced most families in the community to depend on welfare for their survival; on the other, traditional kills of moose or other animals were followed by a feast and by the distribution of extra meat to people in need.

This lack of favourable hunting conditions means more than a reduction in income for the Lubicon: it also implies an unravelling of their traditional social interaction. Chief Ominayak explains:

> *On welfare groceries, one is embarrassed because he or she cannot share food with kin – who wants hot dogs and a half can of spam? As the inability to share continues, social relations deteriorate because one is embarrassed to visit empty-handed.*[122]

The third problem reflects a combination of direct and indirect harms. The disappearance of the traditional lifestyle and demands of subsistence resulted in a 'dramatic rise in alcoholism, domestic violence, fights, car accidents, theft and suicide' as well as a series of health problems.[123] Some of the harms described represent a threat to their life as a people; others attack their life as human beings whose health and normal function has not been considered or protected by a government who had the fiduciary duty to do so. The extent of these harms must be fully understood before laws that reflect that reality might be designed and implemented:

> ... since 1978, when the first road was constructed on Lubicon territory, the moose population – the staple of the Lubicon diet – swiftly declined. Moreover, environmental pollutants caused by oil and gas companies have created numerous health problems including a high number of still births, birth defects, asthma, tuberculosis, and various cancers.[124]

When the case of the Lubicon Cree is viewed together with the plight of Dr O'Connor, the almost insurmountable difficulties faced by anyone attempting to document the reality of what is being done to these communities and their territories become clear.

The final example is taken from Canada, once again, where an important dispute took place in northern Ontario, in the vicinity of pulp and paper mills in the Grassy Narrows and White Dog Reserves:

> ... the settlement and the events leading up to it provide a striking example of the fragility of Canadians' environmental rights in the face of environmental wrongs. Access to justice has been difficult to achieve for victims of environmental catastrophes. The substantive, procedural and evidentiary rules in private environmental actions appear biased in favour of the polluter.[125]

The first point to note is that even a 'mediated settlement' is, at best, a fought and won measure based on laws intended to *prevent* the occurrence of multiple harms. The case involves methyl mercury pollution, contaminating the 'English-Wabigoon River system downstream from Dryden, Ontario':

> Two pulp and paper plants in the area, the Dryden Paper Company Ltd and Dryden Chemicals Ltd, both subsidiaries of Reed Paper Ltd of England, used mercury cells in sodium chloride electrolysis to produce caustic soda and chlorine.[126]

The harm from mercury pollution is not a new discovery, as alternative technologies had already been discovered in the 19th century;[127] scientific evidence about the toxic effects of methyl mercury poisoning have also been known since the early 1960s.[128] In fact, the Ontario government had sent a team to the Japanese courts.[129]

In this case, similar effects were observed in the Ojibway communities, as the ravages of mercury pollution affect all aspects of the health and the life of the inhabitants. West lists some of the grave problems they encountered:

> ... in the years immediately preceding and following the pollution, the unemployment rate quadrupled from twenty percent to eighty percent... Statistics indicated increases in violence, alcohol-related deaths caused by pneumonia, exposure, and suicide.[130]

In addition, what emerged was 'the link between mercury poisoning and the increase in deviant and violent behaviour'.[131]

The scientific evidence has been available for years; yet in 1985, when the federal Department of Indian affairs contacted Justice Emmett Hall (former Supreme Court of Canada justice), who visited Grassy Narrows and studied a '211-page legal brief prepared for the Indian Bands by Robert Sharpe, a University of Toronto professor and expert in such litigation',[132] what emerged persuaded him not to recommend going to trial. He believed that the results of the complex and time-consuming litigation would be uncertain – hence, that the best interests of the Ojibways would be served by 'a negotiated settlement outside the court system'.[133]

There is no question about the connection between mercury pollution and the diseases that follow upon that poisoning; yet Justice Hall was correct in stating the following, among his many concerns, in his affidavit at points (vi) and (vii):

(vi) I was concerned about the Plaintiff's ability to establish their claim that mercury poisoning posed a potential hazard to the health of the unborn because of mercury induced genetic damage in one or both parents.

(vii) In general, I was concerned about the likelihood of legally establishing the link between mercury pollution and health damages because the symptoms of mercury poisoning, such as tremor, ataxia, and sensory abnormality are also the symptoms of conditions such as alcoholism.

Hence, to ensure some degree of success for the First Nations involved, Justice Hall decided to negotiate a settlement outside the court system. Because of the problems existing in the evidentiary and regulatory framework in environmental cases, 'the Ojibways Bands really did not have an alternative to settlement', and the Cdn$14 million they received helped them to cope with the problems they were facing, although, to be sure, 'no level of compensation exists which can ever redress the harms caused by the poisoning'.[134]

Again, gross breaches of human rights are not recognized and neither the guilty corporation nor the complicit government officials receive the punishment they deserve.

Although the effects of climate change on human rights and on the survival of affected populations on location is far better known than these issues are, it remains short-sighted to simply consider the former (climate change) without the latter (industrial/chemical effects) on both humans and their habitats. The conditions described in this section show how the indigenous communities are exposed to unacceptable risks and to unbearable living conditions. These industrial effects are either impossible to escape, or, at best, force the members of these groups to other areas, to cities, or to other Canadian provinces, thus becoming IDPs.

In both cases – that is, their *forced* stay in an unliveable area, or the *forced* flight to another area where their credentials and education are viewed as lacking – their rights are not protected. Neither option is fair or appropriate; radical change should be implemented to their local situation and to the CSR or other international instrument in order to be better able to address their plight today than a convention that is over 57 years old.

NOTES

1. Gostin, L. O. (2008) 'Meeting basic survival needs of the world's least healthy people: Toward a framework convention on global health', *Georgetown Law Journal*, vol 96, no 2, January, p333.
2. Ibid, p337; see also Westra, L. (2007) *Environmental Justice and the Rights of Indigenous Peoples*, Earthscan, London; Kunitz, S. J. (2000) 'Globalization, states, and the health of indigenous peoples', *American Journal of Public Health*, vol 90, no 10, p1531.
3. Gostin (2008), ibid, pp347–348.
4. Ibid, p348; see also Thomas, S. L. and Thomas, S. D. M. (2004) 'Displacement and health', *British Medical Bulletin*, vol 69, pp115–127.
5. UDHR, G. A. Res. 217A (III), 10 December 1948.
6. Martone, G. (2006) 'Life with dignity: What is the minimum standard?', in A. Bayefski (ed) *Human Rights and Refugees, Internally Displaced Persons and Migrant Workers*, Martinus Nihoff, The Hague, pp129–144.
7. WHO (2002) 'Summary', in *World Report on Violence and Health*, WHO, Geneva.
8. Martone (2006), op cit Note 6, p133.
9. Westra, L. (2006) *Environmental Justice and the Rights of Unborn and Future Generations*, Earthscan, London, Chapter 4.
10. Hamilton, B. F. (2006) 'Human rights, refugees and the fate of minorities', in A. Bayefsky (ed) *Human Rights and Refugees, Internally Displaced Persons and Migrant Workers*, Martinus Nihoff, The Hague, pp235–247.
11. Heinzerling, L. (2008) 'Climate change, human health and the post-cautionary principle', *Georgetown Law Journal*, vol 96, no 2.
12. Ibid, p453.
13. Grandjean, P. and Landrigan, P. (2006) 'Developmental neurotoxicity of industrially chemicals', *The Lancet*, November.
14. Taylor, A. (2005) 'Trade, human rights and the WHO Framework Convention on Tobacco Control: Just what the doctor ordered?', in T, Cottier, J. Puwelyn and E. Burgi Bonanomi (eds) *Human Rights and International Trade*, Oxford University Press, New York, pp322–333.
15. WHO (2002) 'Summary', in *World Report on Violence and Health*, WHO, Geneva; Licari, L., Nemer, L. and Tamburlini, G. (eds) (2005) *Children's Health and the Environment*, World Health Organization Regional Office for Europe, Copenhagen, Denmark.
16. Heinzerling (2008), op cit Note 11.
17. Westra, L. (2006), op cit Note 9.
18. Pogge, T. W. (2008) 'Aligned: Global justice and ecology', in L. Westra, K. Bosselmman and R. Westra (eds) *Reconciling Human Existence and Ecological Integrity*, Earthscan, London, pp147–158.
19. J. Dellapenna (2008) 'A human right to water: An ethical position or a realizable goal?', in L. Westra, K. Bosselmman and R. Westra (eds), *Reconciling Human Existence and Ecological Integrity*, Earthscan, London.
20. Westra, L. (2007), op cit Note 2, Chapter 8.
21. Heinzerling (2008), op cit Note 11.
22. Rees, W. and Westra, L. (2006) 'Environmental justice in a resource-limited world', in J. Agyeman, R. D. Bullard and R. Evans (eds), *Just Sustainabilities*, Earthscan, London, pp99–124.
23. Hamilton (2006) op cit Note 10, p237.
24. Ibid.
25. Ibid, p239.
26. Westra, L. (2006), op cit Note 9.

27 World Conference against Racism, Racial Discrimination, Xenophobia, and Related Intolerance, Declaration and Programme for Action, A/Conf. 189/12 (8 September 2001).
28 Lemkin, R. (1947) 'Genocide as a crime in international law', *American Journal of International Law*, vol 41, no 1, p145.
29 G.A.Res.260(III) A, adopted 9 December 1948.
30 Schabas, W. A. (2000) *On Genocide in International Law*, Kluwer Publishing, The Hague; see also Westra, L. (2007), op cit Note 2, Chapter 7, for a discussion of this problem.
31 *Pappajohn versus the Queen*, 1980, S.C.C.; see also Westra, L. (2004) *Ecoviolence and the Law*, Transnational Publishers Inc., Ardsley, NY, Chapter 4, for a discussion of this category.
32 Schwelb, E. (1949) 'Crimes against humanity', *British Yearbook of International Law*, vol 23, no 8, p181.
33 Hamilton (2006), op cit Note 10, p247.
34 Hathaway, J. C. (2005) *The Rights of Refugees under International Law*, Cambridge University Press, Cambridge, p110.
35 UNHCR (1979) *Handbook on Procedures and Criteria for Determining Refugee Status*, UNHCR, Geneva.
36 *R. versus Secretary of State for the Home Department ex parte Bugdaycay*, [1987] AC 514 (UK HL, Feb.19, 1987) per Lord Bridge of Harwich @525.
37 Hathaway (2005), op cit Note 34, p116.
38 Ibid, p118.
39 UNGA Res. 260A(III), 9 December 1948, into force 12 January 1951.
40 At paragraph (e); www.unhcr.ch.
41 Hathaway (2005), op cit Note 34, p123.
42 UN Human Rights Committee 'General Comment No. 18: Non-discrimination' (1989), UN Doc. HRI/GEN/1/Rev.7, 12 May 2004, at 146, paragraph 12.
43 Hathaway (2005), op cit Note 34, p124.
44 UN Human Rights Committee 'General Comment No. 15: The position of aliens under the Covenant' (1986), UN Doc. HRI/GEN/IRev.7, 12 May 2004, at 140, paragraph 2.
45 See, for instance, Clark, T. and Niessen J. (1996) 'Equality rights and non-citizens in Europe and America: The promise, the practice and some remaining issues', *Netherlands Quarterly of Human Rights*, vol 14, no 3, p245.
46 Hathaway (2005), op cit Note 34, pp129–130.
47 UNHRC Comm. No. 68/1980, decided 31 March 1981; see also Hathaway (2005), op cit Note 34, p135.
48 Hathaway (2005), op cit Note 34, p139.
49 Garcia-Amador, F. V. et al (1974) *Recent Codification of the Law of State Responsibility for Injuries to Aliens*, p129.
50 Ellis, D. (1974) 'Aliens and activities of the United Nations in the field of human rights', *Human Rights Journal*, vol 7, no 291, pp314–315.
51 Weissbrodt, D. (2003) 'The rights of non-citizens: Final report of the Special Rapporteur', UN. Doc. E/CN.4/Sub.2/2003/23, 26 May.
52 Hathaway (2005), op cit Note 34, p151.
53 Davidsson, E. (2005) 'Economic oppression as an international wrong or as a crime against humanity', *Netherlands Quarterly of Human Rights*, vol 23, no 2, pp173–212.
54 Nickel, J. W. (1996) 'A human rights approach to world hunger', in W. Aiken and H. LaFollette (eds) *World Hunger and Morality* (second edition), Prentice Hall, Upper Saddle River, NJ, pp171–185.
55 Singer, P. (1996) 'Famine, affluence and morality', in *World Hunger and Morality* (second edition), Prentice Hall, Upper Saddle River, NJ, pp26–38.
56 Pogge, T. (2001) 'Priorities of global justice', *Metaphilosophy*, vol 32; see also Pogge (2008), op cit Note 18.

57 O'Neill, O. (2001) 'Agents of justice', in T. Pogge (ed) *Global Justice*, Blackwell Publishers, Oxford, UK, pp188–203.
58 Barlow, M. and Clarke, T. (2002) *Global Showdown*, Stoddard Publishing Co. Ltd, Toronto, Canada.
59 Shue, H. (1996) *Basic Rights: Subsistence, Affluence and American Foreign Policy*, Princeton University Press, Princeton, NJ.
60 UNDP (1999) 'Facts and figures on poverty', www.undp.org/teams/english/facts.htm; see also Sogli, S. (2001) 'The elaboration of a declaration on human rights and extreme poverty', UNHCR, Geneva, 7–9 February 2001, UN Doc. HR/GVA/Poverty/SEM/2001/BP, p1.
61 Petersen, K. (2003) 'Mass murder by complicity', in *Africa Forgotten*, 11 April, www.dissidentvoice.org/Aritlces 4/Petersen Africa.htm.
62 Davidsson (2005), op cit Note 53, p174.
63 Hart, H. L. A. and Honoré, T. (1985) *Causation in the Law* (second edition), Clarendon Press, Oxford, UK.
64 Kissell, J. L. (1999) 'Causation: The challenge for complicity', paper presented at the Eastern Meeting of the American Philosophical Association, p1.
65 Ibid, p2.
66 Ibid, p5.
67 Wasserstrom, R. (1985) 'War, nuclear war and nuclear deterrence: Some conceptual and moral issues', in R. Hardin, J. Mersheimer, G. Dworkin and R. Goodin (eds) *Nuclear Deterrence, Ethics and Strategy*, University of Chicago Press, Chicago, IL, pp15–31.
68 Davidsson (2005), op cit Note 53, p174.
69 Nuremberg Trial Proceedings Vol. 1: Charter of the International Military Tribunal (1945), Article 6.
70 Sachs, W. (2007) *Climate Change and Human Rights*, WDEV Special Report 1, World Economy and Development In Brief, Luxembourg, posted at www.wdev.eu, 2 January; the report has been published also (2006) in 'Scripta Varia' 106 of the Pontifical Academy of Sciences, Vatican City.
71 Shue (1996), op cit Note 59.
72 Steiner, H. J., and Alston, P. (2000) *International Human Rights in Context* (second edition), Oxford University Press, Oxford, UK.
73 Sachs (2007), op cit Note 70.
74 Dellapenna, J. (2008) 'A human right to water: An ethical position or a realizable goal?', in L. Westra, K. Bosselmann and R. Westra (eds) *Reconciling Ecological Existence with Ecological Integrity*, Earthscan, London, UK.
75 Westra, L. (2006), op cit Note 9; Gostin (2008), op cit Note 1.
76 Westra, L. (2004) 'Environmental rights and human rights: The final enclosure movement', in Roger Brownsword (ed) *Global Governance and the Quest for Justice, Volume 4: Human Rights*, Hart Publishing, Oxford, UK; in which I argue that the preconditions of human agency are necessary for the rights supported by the ICCPR; see also McMichael, A. et al (2003) 'Climate change and human health-risks and responses', WHO/UNEP/WMO, Geneva; Parry, M. L. C., Rosenzweig, A., Igelsias, M., Livermore, G. and Fischer, J. (2004) 'Effects of climate change on global food production under SRES emission and social economic scenarios', *Global Environmental Change*, vol 14, no 1, April; Patz, J. A., Campbell-Lendrum, D., Holloway, T. and Foley, J. A. (2005) 'Impact of regional climate change on human health', *Nature*, vol 438, pp310–317.
77 UNHCR (2005) Report of Special Rapporteur Jean Ziegler on the right to food, 25 January, E/CN.4/2005 47.
78 Westra, L. and Lawson, B. (2001) 'Introduction', in *Faces of Environmental Racism* (second edition), Rowman Littlefield, Lanham, MD; Bullard, R. (2001) 'Decision making', in Westra

and Lawson (eds) *Faces of Environmental Racism* (second edition), Rowman Littlefield, Lanham, MD.
79 Davidsson (2005), op cit Note 53; see also Westra, L. (2004) op cit Note 31, especially Chapter 4.
80 Brown, P. (2003) 'Refugee warning to global polluters: Up to 20 million likely to flee environmental damage, report predicts', *The Guardian*, 30 September, p13.
81 Davidsson (2005), op cit Note 53, p176.
82 *Wilson versus Seiler* (89-7376) 501 U.S. 294 (1991); see also *Rhodes versus Chapman* 452 U.S. 337 (1981).
83 Davidsson (2005), op cit Note 53, p179.
84 O'Neill, O. (1996) *Towards Justice and Virtue*, Cambridge University Press, Cambridge, UK, p193.
85 Westra, L. (2007), op cit Note 2, Chapter 4.
86 Ford, J., Smit, B. and Wandel, J. (2006), 'Vulnerability to climate change in the Arctic: A case study from Arctic Bay, Canada', *Global Environmental Change*, vol 16; see also, Westra, L. (2007), op cit Note 2, Chapter 8.
87 Noss, R. and Cooperider, A, (1994) *Saving Nature's Legacy*, Island Press, Washington, DC; Westra, L. (1998) *Living in Integrity*, Rowman Littlefield, Lanham, MD.
88 Ford et al (2006), op cit Note 86.
89 Biermann, F. and Boas I. (2007) 'Preparing for a warmer world towards a global governance system to protect climate refugees', Global Governance Working Paper no 33, November, www.glogov.org.
90 See sections 1, 1a, and 2; see also Biermann and Boas (2007), ibid.
91 Noss and Cooperrider (1994), op cit Note 87; Ford et al (2006), op cit Note 86.
92 Ford et al (2006), op cit Note 86.
93 Anaya, S. J. (2004) *Indigenous Peoples in International Law*, 2nd edition, Oxford University Press, Oxford, UK; Westra, L. (2007), op cit Note 2, Chapter 2.
94 Lemkin, R. (1944) *Axis Rule in Occupied Europe*, Carnegie Endowment for International Peace, Washington, DC.
95 Biermann and Boas (2007), op cit Note 89.
96 Ibid, p16.
97 Ibid, p10; see also UNFCCC Executive Secretary press release of 6 April 2007, http://unfccc.int/files/press/news_room/press_releases_and_advisories/application/pdf/070406_pressrel_english.pdf.
98 Caracol Production, Guatemale (2005) 'Sipakapa no se vende', video documentary, www.sipakapanosevende.org.
99 Eichstaedt, P. H. (1994) *If You Poison Us: Uranium and Native Americans*, Red Crane Books, Santa Fe.
100 *Dashowa, Inc versus Friends of the Lubicon* (1998), 158 DLR(4) 699 (Ont.Gen.Div.); *Omynayak versus Canada*, UN GAOR, 45 Sess., Supplement No. 40, Annex 9 at 27, UN Doc.A/45/40 (1990).
101 West, L. (1987) 'Mediated settlement of environmental disputes: Grassy Narrows and White Dog revisited', *Environmental Law*, vol 18, pp131–150.
102 Caracol Production, Guatemala (2005) op cit Note 98.
103 Eichstaedt, op cit Note 99.
104 Ibid, p94.
105 Ibid, p151.
106 Ibid.
107 Minchin, L. and Murdoch, L. (2006) 'Aboriginal cancer doubles near uranium mine', www.theage.com.au/news/national/aboriginal-cancer-doubles-near-uranium-mine/2006/11/22/116387182163.html, 23 November.

108 Ibid.
109 Lanktree, G. (2008) 'Oilsands whistleblower MD cleared', *National Review of Medicine*, vol 5, no 1, 15 January.
110 Huff, A. I. (1999) 'Resource development and human rights: A look at the case of the Lubicon Cree Indian Nation of Canada', *Colorado Journal of International Environmental Law Policy*, vol 1, no 120, pp161–174.
111 Goddard, J. (1991) *Last Stand of the Lubicon Cree*, Douglas and McMillan, Vancouver, BC, p171.
112 Ibid, p170.
113 Huff (1999), op cit Note 110, p162.
114 *Bernard Ominayak, Chief of the Lubicon Cree Band versus Canada*, Communication No. 167/1984, Report of the Human Rights Committee, UN GAOR, 45th Session, Supplement No. 40, Vol. 2, at 10, UN Doc. A/45/40, Annex IX (A) (1990), view adopted on 26 March 1990 at the 38th Session.
115 See 'Sign the petition in support of the Lubicon', 6 March 2006, http://lubicon solidarity.ca.
116 Support Lubicon Presentation to the United Nations, 17 October 2005; see also Goddard (1991), op cit Note 111, pp2–4.
117 Huff (1999), op cit Note 110, p163; Goddard (1991), op cit Note 111, describes in detail the confusions and misunderstanding that led to the exclusion of the Band from Treaty 8, pp9–20.
118 Goddard (1991), op cit Note 111, p6.
119 Huff (1999), op cit Note 110, p165.
120 Ibid; see also Goddard (1991), op cit Note 111, p76.
121 Huff (1999), op cit Note 110, p166.
122 Chief Ominayak's Affidavit.
123 Ibid.
124 Fred Lennerson in Huff (1999), op cit Note 110.
125 West (1987), op cit Note 101, p132.
126 Ibid, p133; see also Charlesbois, C. T. (1977) 'An overview of the Canadian mercury problem', *Science*, vol 10, pp17–20.
127 Charlesbois (1977), op cit Note 126.
128 West (1987), op cit Note 101, p133.
129 See the *Toyama Itai-tai* case, 635 Hanji 17 (Toyama District Court, 30 June 1991); the *Niigata Minimata* case, 642 Hanji (Miigata District Court, 29 September 1971); the *Yokkaichi Asthma* case, 672 Hanji 30 (Tsu District Court, Yokkaichi Branch, 24 July 1972); the *Kumamoto Minimata Disease* case, 696 Hanjil 5 Kumamoto District Court, 20 March 1973, reprinted in Gresser, J., Fugikura, K. and Morishima, A. (1981) *Environmental Law in Japan*, MIT Press, Cambridge, MA.
130 West (1987), op cit Note 101, p135.
131 Ibid; see also Troyer, W. (1977) *No Safe Place*, Clark Irwin, Toronto, p5; Charlesbois (1977), op cit Note 126, p24.
132 West (1987), op cit Note 101, p136.
133 Ibid; see also Mr Justice Hall's Affidavit before the Supreme Court of Ontario, 14716/77, No. 13.
134 West (1987), op cit Note 101, p145.

PART THREE

The Way Forward: Existing Legal Instruments and New Provisions

CHAPTER 6

International Law beyond the Convention on the Status of Refugees

1. INTRODUCTION: GENOCIDE OR CRIMES AGAINST HUMANITY?

> *International crimes derive mainly from international customary law and sometimes treaties ... Genocide, however, encapsulated in the Genocide Convention of 1948,[1] and excruciatingly slowly ratified over the next 50 years, has remained textually static though interpretatively somewhat fluid. Unlike national criminal codes, international crimes do not lend themselves so easily to periodic re-examination and codification under the goal of establishing an integrated body of law.[2]*

In the previous chapters we argued, as does Wolfgang Sachs, that the results of the present economic oppression of local communities in developing countries, are akin, if not equal, in their effects to the consequences of many crimes against humanity; that starvation and the other deprivations of extreme poverty should be treated as belonging to the same category. 'Climate refugees'[3] as well as other ecological migrants suffer the worst consequences, as they are among the most vulnerable, without either domestic or international protection.

Even when a specific group suffers extreme harms because of the activities of corporate enterprises, with the complicity of local governments, and they are forced to flee unbearable living conditions, the lack of provable intent on the part of any of the perpetrators or co-conspirators renders them ineligible to be viewed as victims of genocide. Hence Elias Davidsson's proposal to view their plight as having been caused by the commission of crimes against humanity appears logical. That is a 'lesser' crime than genocide; but it remains a grave crime, even though an exhaustive definition is currently unavailable.[4] The most recent definition of that crime in the 2005 Statute of the International Criminal Court is more inclusive than the previous definition; hence it might, indeed, be used to categorize the nature of the present crimes against refugees, in general.[5]

To recapitulate the argument proposed above, the Genocide Convention of 1948 defined that crime as requiring 'an intent to destroy in whole or in part a religious, racial, national or ethnic[al] group as such'. However, it is arguable that to cause the destruction of a community 'in whole or in part', through wilful blindness, recklessness, negligence, or plain indifference, or as the crime defined in US law as 'depraved indifference',[6] should not define a lower level of offence, one that might merit less disapprobation or punishment. Deliberate hatred sees the 'other' as hateful, but as existing and real. The mental element and the act of the crime of genocide taken together are viewed as the grave act. But, in some sense, the cruel and inhumane indifference to their plight considers racial or ethnic groups as simply 'in the way' of a proposed plan or project, as a faceless and correspondingly invisible obstacle, no more.

As well, they may not be worthy of consideration as the activities that engender and enhance climate change are not viewed from the standpoint of the effects that these activities produce on developing countries and poor land-based peoples. This is also true of other hazardous circumstances arising from industrial activities, in general, despite the fact that they will generate thousands of impoverished migrants. All of these activities should be viewed as offences against all humanity:

> *Crimes against humanity are crimes of a special nature to which a greater degree of turpitude attaches than to an ordinary crime.*[7]

1a. Ratner's approach: Comparing 'evils'

> *The [Genocide] Convention was the first treaty since those of slavery and the 'white slave traffic' to criminalize peacetime actions by a government against its citizens. Since that time, customary international law has recognized the de-coupling of crimes against humanity from wartime.*[8]

In his timely discussion of this problem, Ratner observes that the general public views genocide as the worse crime in comparison, and, in response to this public perception, governments prefer not to speak of genocide as they are aware that there will be an outcry for the punishment of that crime, once its presence is acknowledged. However, not all legal scholars and philosophers embrace that view.

Its major supporter is William Schabas (2000), who applies carefully the definition of genocide, with its emphasis on the *dolus specialis*, the special intent that characterizes the crime, so that it will be applicable only to a 'small set of atrocities'.[9] The opinion of the *ad hoc* Tribunals, such as the International Criminal Tribunal for Rwanda (ICTR), and the International Criminal Tribunal for the Former Yugoslavia (ICTY), take a similarly uncompromising position.[10]

Ratner suggests that because of the position taken by the *ad hoc* tribunals (i.e. that the intent requirement can also include the will to destroy 'groups' who are 'perceived as such' by the perpetrator(s) of the crime), this is an additional understanding beyond the sense of 'groups' as understood in general.

Hence, David Luban argues that the definition of genocide should also include the crime against humanity of 'extermination' in order to render the crime's definition closer to our present understanding.[11] The crime of 'extermination', however, is not based upon a special intent; thus it would seem as though the incorporation of this change to the Genocide Convention would represent an excellent 'step forward' from our standpoint, especially when the perpetrators, as well as the victims, represent groups where individual intent might be less than clear cut. In addition, the perception of a community as a group to be exterminated may not be obvious to an outsider.

Finally, Ratner lists, but is not prepared to consider, yet another possibility: the position that 'all evil acts against civilians are genocide'. He says:

> *Under this view, genocide means many acts beyond physical extermination, such as the destruction of culture and environmental degradation. I will not discuss this position further because the view moves genocide too far about its core, which is cide, from the Latin caedere, 'to cut (down), strike, beat ... to kill'.*[12]

But the definition of genocide does not refer to 'immediate killing', although it does refer to the intention to do so. Ratner's own explanation for the rejection of this option is therefore flawed in two senses: in the first sense 'beat ... to kill' envisions the possibility of exposing a population to harmful activities that will (or may?) result in death. However, neither 'cutting down' nor 'striking' is necessarily an act that results in immediate death. Similarly, some environmental degradation or exposure to industrial toxins may kill slowly, yet just as inexorably as a gun or a bomb.

One is reminded of the classic Agatha Christie mysteries, where poison is administered a little at a time to the intended victim, nevertheless resulting in murder. As well, Ratner's position does not reflect the current understanding of the effects of 'ecocide'.[13] Because of the oil extraction operations, the whole area of Ogoniland in Nigeria became so polluted that the local population can no longer survive: neither agriculture nor fisheries can take place to ensure their survival. Eventually, eco-martyr Ken Saro-Wiwa referred to the results of those extractive operations as producing 'omnicide'.

But the most telling evidence in an understanding of genocide is the fact that it must involve intentional killing, but without any specific timeframe – the first example that prompted the drafting of the convention itself also indicates a definite time lag before the initial intentional acts leading to the killing, and the killing itself. During the Nazi regime, Jewish people, Roma people and many others were first picked up then put on trains that took them to concentration camps. There, it might have been a matter of weeks or months before they were actually killed. Hence, there was no requirement that the persecuted people had to die immediately after they had been targeted: the time element was therefore *not* an integral aspect of the crime of genocide.

In the second sense, when the victimized community is a 'people', distinct from the society in the country where they reside, their forced displacement from their traditional territories represents a form of 'cultural genocide', or, in other words, their elimination as a 'people', in all cases of land-based minorities. This occurs regularly when climate change or other hazardous conditions (see Chapter 5) force the exodus of whole communities, or where partial groups of the community seek asylum elsewhere, perhaps as internally displaced persons (IDPs). Those who might remain, because unable or unwilling to leave, may *also* be incapable of functioning as a 'people' as they did before their climate was changed or their land was exposed to hazardous effluents. This situation applies to all land-based minorities. Hence, while Ratner is correct in assuming that there is no jurisprudence at this time to support the extension of 'genocide' to ecological and cultural categories, one ought not to dismiss too hastily the possibility that a revision of that original definition, now 60 years' old, or at least the addition of 'extermination' to it, would render the definition more flexible, perhaps even able to accommodate present-day mass atrocities.

1b. Crimes against humanity reconsidered

At any rate, as long as definitional changes are not even envisaged for the Genocide Convention, the category of crimes against humanity appears to be the best category to fit what is happening to thousands of people who form the mass of today's refugees, including ecological refugees.

Patricia Wald notes that the Rome Statute of the International Criminal Court 'includes murder, deportation (all derived from Nuremberg), but also forcible transfer of populations (internal to a country)'.[14] Other 'inhumane acts of a similar character' include 'persecution' (based on the familiar grounds we have discussed, plus gender), but also 'apartheid' and 'acts intentionally causing great suffering or serious injury to body or mental health'. The need for intent is present; but the 'intentionality' aspect does not seem to be necessary, either logically or morally, because:

> As a jus cogens *crime, crimes against humanity carry an obligation on the part of states to prosecute or extradite perpetrators found within their borders, regardless of where the crime was committed, or who the immediate victims were.*[15]

Not all *jus cogens* norms have a *mens rea* requirement, and the crime of persecution needs to be re-examined as reaching beyond 'the territory of the former Yugoslavia', as Wald recognizes:

> *Because of its breadth of coverage, crimes against humanity had become the growth stock of Tribunal jurisprudence. Except for the ICTY, crimes against humanity no longer requires any nexus with armed conflict, it encompasses discriminatory acts against a much wider range of groups than genocide, and many more kinds of acts than the five listed in the Genocide Convention and Charters, and it carries still a heavier component of international shame than war crimes.*[16]

Hence, the situation of mass migrants and ecological refugees appears to fit quite closely the category of crimes against humanity, from their origin through careless, negligent or morally blind acts that force their flight, to the reception they receive and the conditions of their detention as asylum seekers.

It is worthy of note that 'persecution is perhaps the most widely charged crime against humanity';[17] therefore the basis of the five grounds is also basic to crimes against humanity, and this is what makes a refugee or even an IDP. The required weight of evidence to prove 'persecution' is that it must be shown to be specific to one group and to specific issues in that regard.[18]

Crimes against humanity, then, is, increasingly, a catch-all appellation, and one which may indeed 'grow' to include our present victims far better than what happens when they are left to the mercies of tribunals who must fit their individual (or group circumstances) to the tight definition provided by the CSR.

However, the magnitude of the problem of refugees and IDPs is not only a problem for these increasingly large numbers of people, it is also a problem for international law itself, as many of the accepted categories no longer fit the variety of mass atrocities that face the international community today. Hence, while the law represents a problem for asylum seekers in its present state, the sheer number and variety of asylum seekers present a novel and thorny problem for the practice and regulatory regimes of international law as well.

2. THE NEED TO RE-CONCEPTUALIZE THE RULE OF LAW

> ... *mass violence is constructed as something extraordinarily transgressive of universal norms. Transgressions of this ilk call out for investigation, prosecution, and punishment leading perhaps intractably to the emergence of a relatively new branch of law – the law of atrocity.*[19]

The call is for either a 'new branch' of law, or at least the acknowledgement of the expansion of humanitarian law from 'law of war' towards human rights law (as evidenced, for instance, in the definition of Crimes Against Humanity in the Rome Statute of the ICC; and the move from an entirely statist conception of international law, to the application of humanitarian law to intrastate conflicts, as well as its emerging concern with persons and peoples. Ruti Teitel notes that, traditionally, the rule of law was largely limited to 'the protection of territorial sovereignty':

> *In contrast, the new paradigm weds traditional humanitarianism with the law of human rights, causing a shift away from states as the dominant subjects of international law to include 'persons' and 'peoples'.*[20]

Viewed from this perspective, the Refugee Convention is entirely anachronistic since it pits the 'sanctity' of borders and the sovereignty of state against a mounting humanitarian crisis, with which it is not capable of coping. However, the newer *ad hoc* tribunals, such as the ICTR, 'prosecuted solely intrastate crimes committed in the Rwandan genocide',[21] thus – in a sense – showing the way towards an expansion of the combined reach of humanitarian and human rights law.

As a result, the very presence of mass migrations, due not only to conflict situations within or between states, but also to ecological disasters and the impact of global change and of globalized industrialization, confronts present legal categories and regimes and, in a sense, demands radical changes. Drumbl proposes the emergence of a 'law of atrocity', one that reaches beyond the laws that follow the general pattern of 'municipal criminal law', which is already imperfectly dealing with ordinary crime; instead, what is needed is a law that is suitable for 'extraordinary international crime'.[22]

Perhaps the mass migrations of ecological refugees presents yet another 'disruption' to the categories of international law, as does terrorism, according to Antonio Cassese:

> *Indeed, that atrocious action exhibits all the hallmarks of crimes against humanity: the magnitude and extreme gravity of the attacks as well as the fact that it targeted civilians is an affront to all humanity and part of a widespread or systematic practice.*[23]

It is clear that terrorism raises even more questions about its proper place in the law than does the question of ecological refugees, such as its proper definition, the traditional law of self-defence, and the like.[24] But the nexus between Cassese's argument and the ecological refugee question rests on the possibility of a new role for the legal category of 'crimes against humanity'.[25] With the expanded definition present in Article 7 of the ICC, it seems that this is one of the avenues that should be explored to address a problem that appears intractable under the present legal categories.

As Drumbl argues: 'collective violence', in general, is a category that needs to be re-examined as the present treatment in law ends, at best, with individual punishment, which does not address properly the 'criminality of mass atrocity'.[26] I have argued that the presence of environmental harms and their consequences for human rights are best defined as 'institutionalized eco-violence',[27] and that concept encompasses several international crimes, including 'crimes against humanity', although I did not address the question of the appropriate punishment for those guilty or complicit in those crimes, as Drumbl does.[28]

The previous chapters describe the situation of ecological refugees from the causative origin of their plight, through the flight, their arrival and the conditions of their reception and relocation: it seems clear that, in most cases, their human rights are not respected, and that, in a significant number of cases, the appellation of 'mass atrocities' is entirely appropriate.

Refugee 'camps' in Darfur in 2008 Kenya, in Palestine's Gaza strip and in many other regions represent an ongoing criminal disregard for human rights, and the harsh situation faced by these refugees, in each case, has some root in ecological distress, from desertification in African countries to the lack of water in Palestine. Of course, many of these areas are also the locale of vicious ethnic conflicts. But the ecological dimensions should not be forgotten, and we will consider the situation in Palestine below.

The main point to keep in mind at this time is that while these situations are extraordinarily terrible, the way in which they are treated does not do justice to the problem, even when international institutions 'putatively representative of the global community' deal with the situation:

> *These international institutions, therefore, drift into what Michel Foucault called the 'political economy of punishment'. This political economy bureaucratizes and normalizes punishment, thereby inserting it deeply into the now-globalized social body.*[29]

These institutions eventually pass judgement and the punishment remains, however, an unexceptional and 'uninspiring' incarceration of one person: the 'enemy of all human kind is punished as no different than a car thief, armed robber or cop killer'.[30]

At this stage it is much too soon to start considering what might be an appropriate punishment; but it is not too early to view the plight of ecological and climate refugees as a form of crime against humanity, perpetrating mass atrocities upon individuals who are both innocent and vulnerable, without proper attention to the origin and the proximate and long-term causal development of the reasons for their condition, let alone any attempt to isolate the direct and indirect perpetrators and accomplices. The issue of climate change, for instance, is at the forefront of public and private discussions at this time, and it has been referred to repeatedly in these pages. It might be useful to return to that topic's interface with public health as a possible avenue towards a desirable new category of international law.

3. CLIMATE CHANGE AND PUBLIC HEALTH: NEW CATEGORIES OF INTERNATIONAL LAW

Characterizing environmental harm to human populations in legal terms is always a complex task. The complexity and global nature of climate science make climate change particularly difficult to translate into legal terms.[31]

The best-known attempt to translate human harm into a justifiable legal category is the Inuit Circumpolar Conference Petition, whereby the Inuit, under the leadership of Sheila Watt-Cloutier, alleged human rights violations with the Inter-American Court of Human Rights (IACHR), with the support of the Centre for International Environmental Law (CIEL) and Earthjustice.[32] I have detailed the extent and reach of the Inuit problem in my study of the situation in the Canadian territory of Nunavut, home of Sheila Watt-Cloutier.[33]

Essentially, the IACHR presented grave procedural obstacles to the Inuit Petition – namely that the Inuit do not live in Organization of American States member states (but CIEL and Earthjustice, as NGOs, had the standing to submit a petition on their behalf), and that the US 'is not party to the American Convention on Human Rights'.[34] In contrast, the Arctic Climate Assessment (headed by US scientists) had provided important data on climate change in the Arctic at that time. Hence:

The applicants believed that if the United States could not be held accountable for its emissions under international human rights law, no country could be held accountable.[35]

The procedural blockage of any consideration of human rights violations is a constant aspect of litigation involving environment, human rights and the US courts. It is a repeated problem in the ATCA jurisprudence discussed above (see Chapter 3). But the reality of the gross human rights violations that ensue emerges from the consideration of both the Arctic and small island states, as well as coastal cities, even in Western industrialized countries, as we saw in the consequences of Hurricane Katrina in New Orleans.

But the Arctic is, indeed, a case apart, because if the Arctic territories increasingly become uninhabitable, neither compensation nor relocation are acceptable solutions. This is also true in the case of other land-based minorities.

3a. The case of Nunavut: Global warming and vulnerability in the Canadian Arctic

The world can no longer carry on 'business as usual' when the basic rights of the vulnerable are being diminished and often destroyed, due to a 'disconnect' between development and environmental protection.[36]

While Western developed nations debate about the existence of global warming and what to do about it, the Inuit have been plunged right into the effects of it, with no way out:

> *In 2004 scientists with the Arctic Climate Impact Assessment, a comprehensive study of climate change in the Arctic, reported that the region as a whole has undergone the greatest warming on Earth in recent decades with annual temperature now averaging 2° to 3° Celsius higher than in the 1950s.*[37]

This change affects the region's ice, as the 'late summer Arctic sea ice has been thinned by 40 per cent in some parts, and shrunk in area by roughly 8 per cent over the past 30 years'.[38]

What are the major effects of these drastic changes? The first thing to note is that Arctic people are particularly vulnerable to these changes, as a recent study of the Inuit in Arctic Bay, Nunavut, indicates.[39] For that study, Ford and his collaborators took an approach to the issue based on the 'conceptual model of vulnerability', as indicated by the United Nations Framework Convention on Climate Change (UNFCCC).[40] The latter defines vulnerability 'as a function of the climate conditions to which a system is exposed, its sensitivity, and its adaptive capacity'.[41]

The special vulnerability of the Inuit arises principally because of their dependence on the land and sea for their subsistence, a condition they share with most indigenous peoples' communities. Their main, defining activity, in fact, is the hunt:

> *Considerable time is spent by most community members 'on the land' (a term used by Inuit to refer to any traditional activity, camping, hunting, or travelling) that takes place outside the settlement.*[42]

There are several main issues that manifest the basic vulnerability of the Inuit hunting and gathering activities, when either preparing to go, or already out 'on the land', in relation to global warming. The first is the ability to predict weather-related dangers and to be able to adjust plans according to that knowledge. But, as Lisha Levia, a resident of Arctic Bay, puts it:

> *Normally, when the wind starts coming, it comes gradually, then it gets stronger later on. But today when it starts getting windy, it comes on really strong. I cannot predict the weather through looking at the clouds when I used to.*[43]

Eva Inukpuk reports a similar experience of her 70-year-old mother, who used to live in igloos and could predict accurately what the next day's weather would be like. She adds:

> *Now, it could be anything: all her knowledge counts for nothing these days.*[44]

Hence, what we are witnessing in the Arctic is much more than climate change, it is – as the people in Nunavik describe it – 'climatic disruption'.[45] It is more than just warmer temperatures. It is the total unpredictability those changes produce, the related elimination of the Inuit's knowledge base and the severe impact on their cultural life.[46]

If the Inuit are traditionally dependent on their hunting activities, the ability to predict the weather, in order to prepare ahead of each trip is much more than the source of convenience in their travel: it could be, and often is, a matter of life and death. For instance, if the expectations are for spring temperatures, that might be too warm to build igloos, so that tents might be a better alternative; making this decision ahead of a trip may well prove fatal if the temperature drops suddenly in the night and the hunters may then freeze to death.

Similarly, the arrival of freak blizzards and sudden snowmelts may prove equally fatal to hunters unexpectedly falling through thinner ice.[47] Thus, the importance of traditional knowledge is drastically diminished, as is the respect due to experienced hunters. Hunters were formerly the keepers of the 'collective social memory'.[48]

When this IQ or knowledge base fails, and this failure is combined with climatic conditions that change the historically known accessibility of hunting grounds, this gravely undermines the very existence of their cultural integrity, as rising weather unpredictability forces changes in lifestyle on local inhabitants.

Nor does the addition of modern technology guarantee mitigation of the increasingly hostile environmental conditions we have described. Traditional travel involved dog sleds, and these animals' instincts as well as their own knowledge base ensure safety for hunters, for the most part. Modern snowmobiles, instead, often permit sudden plunges through thin ice, hidden under snow.[49] Perhaps the use of global positioning systems (GPS) might help to preserve, at least in part, the continuity of traditional ways. Yet, when these man-made devices fail, as they often do, the stranded hunters are left with neither technology nor traditional knowledge to guide them to safety:[50]

> *The results of these increasingly unmanageable hazards give rise to ... an even more pressing concern ... [that is] the social fallout from the transformation of these traditional subsistence-based societies to 'Southern' wage-based economies. Unemployment in both Arctic Bay and Igloolik stands at over 20 per cent, and alcoholism is a major problem. Nunavut's suicide rate, at 77 deaths per 100,000 people, is one of the highest in the world, and six times higher than in the rest of Canada.*[51]

The inability to continue traditional practices leads to dependence on waged positions – hence, the change to a 'dual economy' or 'mixed economy', where both traditional living and market-based activities coexist.[52]

In addition, during the 1960s, the government promoted 'fixed settlements', which further complicated traditional access to hunting areas.[53] Finally, the dependence on a 'mixed economy' implied the reduction of traditional foods and increased dependence on store-bought and fast food, with the expected rise in obesity and diabetes, as the expected results of unhealthy diets.[54]

The corollary of this change is not only a grave threat to the health of the Arctic Bay Inuit, but also, increasingly, to the cultural survival of those Inuit as a people. The 'social networks' typical of these societies are seriously eroded. As Lisha Qavavang puts it: 'that's the only way we survive, by supporting one another'.[55] But the existence of a 'mixed economy' does not facilitate the redistribution and transfer mechanisms of food sharing.[56]

Furthermore, as the difficulties encountered in the changed physical environment dissuade the present and older generations from persisting in their traditional ways, the results have been even worse in the younger generation:

> *English has replaced Inuktikut as the dominant language among younger generations, older generations think the young Inuit are not interested in learning the traditional ways, and the Euro-American social norms of youth are far removed from the traditional upbringing of older generations.*[57]

Many younger people have lost the traditional skills necessary for successful hunting; but without those skills, on the one hand, their abilities are insufficient to ensure their safety; and, on the other, their economic prospects are bleak, as they depend now on elusive monetary resources to acquire the technology and the gadgets they would need to survive while there are only limited private sector jobs, and high unemployment is a fact of life.

3b. Self-governance in defence of Nunavut's people?

> *People form governments for their common defence, security and welfare. The first thing that public officials owe their constituents is protection against natural and man-made hazards.*[58]

Lawrence Gostin stresses the most important function of a government: the security of citizens and the protection of public health. And that is the question that needs to be answered at this point: can self-government, even one based on a separate territory such as Nunavut, do enough to help alleviate or even eliminate the threats against the Inuit people?[59]

We have noted the grave problems that beset them: loss of cultural integrity and identity, primarily, based not only on the loss of an appropriate land base, but also on the erosion of their traditional knowledge. Consequently, even on the land, under conditions of changing climate and altered geographical characteristics, the Inuit are becoming strangers in their own lands, without the reassuring presence of their age-old skills to guide them.

Even established self-governance institutions can do little for these problems, although, as we shall see, by confirming the existence of Nunavut as a nation, these institutions can reinstate a First Nation's presence as a subject of international law – and are thus, presumably, open to the protection available through those instruments from transboundary harms,[60] although there is no present case law to support my proposal.

Nevertheless, the problems the Inuit are facing are not open to internal solutions: they are both systemic and collective at the same time.

The systemic problems arise from the presence of globalization and its protection of trade and economic interests, above public health: this is in evidence in the sheer numbers of untested chemicals,[61] particularly grave in the Arctic, as they bio-accumulate in large mammals, which represent the basis of the Inuit diet: DDT is a prime example as it is strongly present in polar bears and whales.[62]

A further corollary of the unrestrained presence of industrial chemicals is that all the treaties and proclamations that are intended to ensure a certain territory for these peoples define its borders and hence, at best, ensure the quantitative aspects of the territories to which a community has a right. But their rights include the right to live their traditional lifestyle and practise their religion: both require the presence of animals, trees and other natural features of the region in their original condition. As a result, they ought to also require the integrity of their land in its qualitative aspect.[63]

The collective aspects of the problem build on the systemic difficulties here outlined. The exercise of the indigenous traditional rights are basic to who they are as a people. When the conditions that support the practice of their traditional culture no longer exist, they cannot simply be placed as 'refugees' somewhere else, as resettlement, in their case, amounts to the elimination of their culture. In fact, as argued above (see also Chapter 5) the result would be their elimination as a people.

3c. The right to life and the right to health and family life

> *The consequences of global warming on human migration are distressing since areas particularly vulnerable to natural disasters will face an increase in the occurrence and severity of sudden natural environmental disruption. However, the phenomenon that may trigger the most important number of migrants is the rise in sea level. Considering the fact that one third of the world's current population lives within 60km of a coastline and that the global population is increasing, the rise in sea level will have devastating implications.*[64]

Although this aspect of the problem is not often emphasized, the right to life must include the right to a safe 'habitat', including the means to survive. According to B. G. Ramcharan, the right to life includes 'the right to have access to the means of survival; realize full life expectancy; avoid serious environmental risks to life; and to enjoy protection by the state against unwarranted deprivations of life'.[65]

The protection of the right to life in relation to the environment does not have a long or rich legal history. A recent case decided by the European Court of Human Rights[66] has the distinction of being the first case involving 'death by environment' thus far. The case involved a man living in a poor quarter of Istanbul, near a rubbish dump, where a lethal methane explosion occurred. The explosion buried 11 houses under refuse, including Oneryildiz's house, and he lost nine members of his family to that explosion. According to Article 2 of the European Court of Human Rights (ECHR), the right to life was breached by the negligence of the local authorities.[67] It is instructive to read the court's decision:

> *Held (1) The positive obligation to take all appropriate steps to safeguard life for the purpose of art 2 of the convention entailed, above all, a primary duty on the state to put in place a legislative and administrative framework designed to provide effective deterrence against threats to the right to life. That obligation indisputably applied in the particular context of dangerous activities where, in addition, special emphasis had to be placed on regulations geared to the special features of the activity in question, particularly with regard to the level of potential risk to human life.*

In addition, 'those responsible for endangering human life' are indicted with having committed a criminal offence, in the second point of the court's decision. Neither of these points is easily found in the legal literature and the case law. It is not surprising that they are found first in European jurisprudence, where cases defending the right to health and family life can also be found.[68]

The right to health and to family life (see Article 8) has been successfully argued in *Lopez-Ostra versus Spain*[69] and in *Guerra versus Italy*;[70] both involve environmental issues and industrial activities.

Both cases were brought to the court after the plaintiffs failed to receive satisfaction from their respective countries. For the *Guerra* case, although at first the Italian government expressed a preliminary objection based on 'non-exhaustion of domestic remedies', the court did not accept their argument: had they pursued such remedies, at best they might have caused a temporary closure of the plant, perhaps even a criminal conviction of the factory's managers. However, such a course of action would not have provided them with the information they sought, or any redress:

The court judged, in the merits of the complaint that the state had failed to act:

Direct effect of toxic emissions on applicant's right to respect for private and family life meant that Article 8 was applicable. Applicants complained not of an act of State, but of its failure to act – object of Article 8 was essentially that of protecting individuals against arbitrary interferences by public authority – it did not merely compel State to abstain from such interference: in addition to that primarily negative undertaking, there might be positive obligations inherent in effective respect for private or family life.

This case concerns a group of citizens of Manfredonia, located 1km away from Erichem Agricoltura, a chemical factory involving the release of large quantities of inflammable gas. Often the operation caused chemical explosions that spewed highly toxic substances into the air. In 1988 the factory was classified as 'high risk' according to European Union Directive (EEC) 82/501m – that is, the major accident hazard of industrial activities, 'dangerous to the environment and the well being of local populations'.[71]

Forty citizens complained to the European Commission of Human Rights that the action and especially the omissions of the Italian authorities had violated Article 10, as well as Articles 8 (Respect for Family and Home) and 2 (Right to Life) of the ECHRTC (Council of Europe)'s Convention on Human Rights. Article 10, Freedom of Expression, emphasizes something on which this work has focused: the exercise of freedom is, and must be, limited by responsibilities and duties:

Article 10(2) – Freedom of Expression

The exercise of these freedoms, since it carries with it duties and responsibilities, may be subject to such formalities, conditions, restrictions and penalties as are prescribed by law and are necessary in a democratic society, in the interests of national security, territorial integrity or public safety, for the prevention of disorder or crime, for the protection of health or morals, for the protection of the reputation or rights of others, for preventing the disclosure of information received in confidence, or of maintaining the authority and impartiality of the judiciary.

This article is outstanding among other international human rights instruments because of the thorough and painstaking way it outlines the 'duties and responsibilities' that balance and limit all 'freedoms', not only freedom of expression, but also 'freedom of thought, conscience and religion' (Article 9): 'public safety', 'the protection of health and morals' and, in Article 9 (a), 'the protection of the public order'. Hence, the freedom of the corporate enterprise is by no means absolute, and it does not appear to extend as far as it does in North American instruments, as it is clearly limited even in the realm of legally sanctioned activities.

In turn, the freedom of citizens to be safe in their homes and to retain their health is openly considered to have been under attack. The right to protection extends, according to Article 8, to the right of respect for the 'well-being' of persons, and the 'respect for their private and family life'. The failure of the Italian authorities to protect the 'right to life' extends to the protection of 'physical integrity,' as guaranteed by Article 2 of the European Convention (1950). Although this extension is not explicitly spelled out in the language of the convention, it appears to represent a juridical extension by analogy. The logic of this extension has also been argued as the necessity for micro-integrity given its clear connection to ecological (macro-)integrity, in my earlier work.[72]

Returning to *Guerra* (1998) 26 EHRR 357, eventually several steps were taken to impose government restraints on the corporation because of the status of the latter under Council Directive (EEC) 82/501 (under the Seveso Directive). In 1993, the Ministry of the Environment issued an order, jointly with the Ministry of Health, prescribing measures to be taken (at para 17), and in 1994 the factory permanently stopped the production of fertilizer (at para 18).

But already in 1985, 420 residents of Manfredonia complained of the health effect of the air pollution, and criminal proceedings had been brought to bear against seven directors of the company (at para 19). The court declared that 'a complaint is characterized by the facts alleged in it and not merely by the legal grounds or arguments relied on' (at para 44); hence, despite objections on various legal points, it concluded: '46. Having regard to the foregoing and to the commission's decision on admissibility, the court holds that it has jurisdiction to consider the case under Articles 8 and 2 as well as under Article 10.' Aside from the disposition of the case ordered by the court in favour of Guerra and the other citizens, it is instructive to read a paragraph in the 'Concurring Opinion of Judge Jambrek' since he and Judge Walsh hold that this case clearly represents a violation under Article 2:

> *Article 2 states that 'Everyone's right to life shall be protected by law. No one shall be deprived of his life intentionally.' The protection of health and physical integrity is, in my view as closely associated with the 'right to life' as with 'respect for private and family life'. An analogy may be made with the Court's case law on Article 3 concerning the existence of 'foreseeable consequences' where* – mutatis mutandis – *substantial grounds can be shown for believing that the person(s) concerned face a real risk of being subjected to circumstances which endanger their health and physical integrity, and thereby put at serious risk their right to life, protected by law. If information is withheld by a government about circumstances which foreseeably, and on substantial grounds, present a real risk of danger to health and physical integrity, then such a situation may also be protected by Article 2 of the Convention: 'No one shall be deprived of his life intentionally.'*

This case, I believe, demonstrates, without a doubt, the strength of the European Convention and the position of the European Court of Human Rights, in contrast with other venues. What is striking is the lack of any effort to 'balance interests' and the lack of any argument citing the 'economic and social interests' of the legal persons involved in maintaining a noxious operation, despite its effects on the health of citizens.

This is a major consideration in our quest for a blueprint for an improved regime, based on a supranational regulatory framework. Another case offers further evidence of the judicial superiority of the European Court of Human Rights: the case of *Lopez-Ostra versus Spain* (1995) 20 EHRR 277, (1994) ECHR 16798/90. Mrs Lopez-Ostra lived in Lorca (Murcia), a town with a high concentration of leather industries, all of which belonged to SACURSA, a company that also had a plant for the treatment of liquid and solid waste, built with a state subsidy on municipal land, 19km from Lopez-Ostra's home, in July 1988 (at para 8).

The gas fumes and other contamination, arising from the tanneries and the waste treatment operation, caused health problems to many in Lorca, and in September 1988 health authorities and the Environmental and Nature Agency (Agencia para el Medio Ambiente y la Naturaleza) forced the company to cease some of its activities and relocated a number of residents elsewhere. However, some of the practices of the operation were allowed to continue, such as the treatment of wastewater contaminated with chromium (at para 9). Mrs. Lopez-Ostra sought protection of her fundamental rights, and the language of her complaint is worthy of note (at para 10):

> *She complained, inter alia, of an unlawful interference with her home and her peaceful enjoyment of it, a violation of her right to choose freely her place of residence; attacks on her physical and psychological integrity, and infringements of her liberty and her safety.*[73]

Despite the strong evidence available, both the Municipal and the Supreme Court of her country dismissed both her case and her appeal, respectively. Evidence was eventually accumulated by the National Toxicology Institute, the Ministry of Justice Institute of Forensic Medicine (Cartagena) and even by three police offices called to the home. The health effects were listed as 'a clinical picture of nausea, vomiting, allergic reactions, and anorexia', in addition to acute symptoms of 'bronchopulmonary infections' (at para 19), all in clear conflict with Article 15 of the Spanish Constitution: 'Article 15: Everyone shall have the right to life and to physical and psychological integrity'.

Hence, once again, we see the protection of fundamental human rights and environmental protection provisions, coupled explicitly in a way that justifies the imposition of severe penalties, including imprisonment and hefty fines, and allowing the temporary or permanent closure of the establishment in question. Under the European Court of Human Rights, the court found that there had been a breach of Article 8 and awarded 4 million pesetas for damages, and 1.5 million pesetas for costs and expenses to Mrs Lopez-Ostra.

In sum, not only are the relevant articles of the European Convention on Human Rights progressively and analogically applied and understood, but there is little or no effort to view as comparable economic (corporate) rights, on the one hand, and health/life rights (individual or group based), on the other. Therefore, the Council of Europe appears to be far ahead of other similar courts.

4. ENVIRONMENTAL PROBLEMS AND HEALTH IMPACTS: A MISSING LINK

At present, in a large number of states the systematic and deliberate violation of human rights is an integral part of the governing process. Such violations include genocide, official racism, large-scale terrorism; totalitarian governance; deliberate refusal to satisfy basic human needs, ecocide, and war crimes.[74]

The last several sections appeared to move away from internally displaced persons (IDPs) or ecological refugees, as we have considered the related rights to life, to health and, essentially, to survival. It is clear that the limited available jurisprudence comes primarily from the Court of Human Rights of the European Union: neither Canada nor the US has anything comparable.

The situation of migrants includes most, if not all, of the human rights violations listed above by Richard Falk. The previous chapters discussed most aspects of their plight, from the inception of the problems that cause the flight (e.g. 'official racism', 'ecocide' and 'deliberate refusal to satisfy basic needs'), to their arrival and subsequent detention (e.g. 'genocide', or at least crimes against humanity). But in order to make this case, even in principle, we need to acknowledge the true reach of human rights that have been breached to create ecological or climate migrants, who are then ignored and, finally, when they attempt to flee to survive, are eventually detained like common criminals, rather than the victims that they are.

Many have noted the 'disconnect' between environmental issues, including climate change, and human rights.[75] That 'disconnect' is the root of the present problem of ecological refugees, and it represents a grave obstacle to the protection of the most basic rights of great numbers of people. From the United Nations High Commissioner for Refugees (UNHCR) estimating that there were 1.2 million IDPs in 1982, rising to 24 million in 1992, to the estimates of the first scholar to consider 'environmental refugees', Essam El Hinnawi, who in 1985 thought the number could reach 50 million; then the Almeria Statement in 1994, which suggested there were already a total of 135 million; then Norman Myers (2005) estimating 150 to 250 million, and the Stern Review (2006) anticipating 200 million by 2050, estimates roughly agreed also by Friends of the Earth (2007); and, finally, the Christian Aid's estimate of 250 million IDPs due to climate change out of a total of around 1 billion from all causes – this is not a negligible problem.[76]

As such, and in response, some have proposed creating a new 'Convention to Protect Environmentally Displaced Persons, specifically designed to address the rights of these migrants'.[77] It is obvious that, as climate disasters intensify and sea levels rise to 'foul freshwater supplies for millions of peoples and spur mass migrations',[78] some islands are already disappearing.[79]

The missing link between the protection of international law and hazardous environmental conditions, including climate change, is the connection between human rights and environmental impacts:

> *There are admittedly many obstacles to using a human rights approach. As one scholar noted, 'existing right(s) must be reinterpreted with imagination and rigor in*

the context of environmental concerns which were not prevalent at the time existing rights were first formulated'.[80]

That is precisely the problem encountered by those seeking redress under ATCA; if the environmental problems that affect them are not considered serious enough to reach the level of international law, then the connection to their rights as human beings is not acknowledged. Rodriguez-Rivera states:

The logical question raised by the articulation of a human rights approach to environmental protection is whether a human right to live in an environment of such a quality that is consistent with the life of dignity and well-being, is recognized in international law.[81]

This appeal to 'dignity' and human rights merits a separate discussion given its importance, and given the fact that a different understanding of 'simple human moral rights' is possible.

4a. An aside on human rights: Dignity and agency

Most people who defend the existence of human rights minimally tie such rights to human dignity.[82] John Gardner terms these 'plain moral rights'[83] to distinguish them from institutionalized rights – that is, from rights that are defined by a specific legal system. It is possible to judge these to be unfit as rights, or to have disagreements about them, and this detracts from the universality; but 'plain moral rights' can be used as intermediate steps in arguments about how their holders are to be treated, in general:[84]

... rights are justified by those interests of right-holders that are served by the possession of a right combined with the interests of others that are served by serving the interest of right-holders through their possession of a right.[85]

It is useful to start at the beginning to consider the existence of moral rights because the CSR is a prime example of legal rights (or 'institutional rights') which, 'simply ... sometimes defy justification'.[86] The situation of refugees is such that their simple moral rights, starting with the right to life, appear to be universally ignored. Yet, those rights should be considered universal (i.e. applicable to all humans).

I use the term 'humans' advisedly because to speak of human 'persons' regarding the right to life implies too much. For instance, people in a coma, or asleep, for that matter, those suffering from Alzheimer's disease or dementia, or the mentally challenged would be hard pressed to meet the requirements of 'personhood' as that expression is used primarily in partisan arguments against the right to life in pro-abortion literature.[87]

Moving 'forward' – looking at personhood's implications after birth – Gardner suggests that the moral right to life, in itself, is not a right that promotes 'human flourishing', but merely what is needed for 'human status'. Gardner says:

> *To spell the point out: there is a gap between treating me as a human being is to be treated and making sure that my life as a human being goes well.*[88]

While this second set of human rights is both appropriate and praiseworthy, generally speaking, Gardner is correct in saying that other rights do not properly belong to the right to life. What happens is that other rights try to attach to the right to life by 'fattening up the idea of what it means to be human so that it becomes implausible as a universal picture'.[89]

Yet Gardner himself seeks universality in the notion of 'human dignity', which, however, he leaves largely undefined.[90] I find the proposal of Beyleveld and Brownsword somewhat more convincing on this issue. The authors argue that human dignity may have an important role to play but other basic options are possible:

> *… we can see the new bioethics in Europe, as aspiring to do much more than put human dignity back on the map. It aspires to represent Europe as a community that stands for a certain vision of human dignity; and, what is more, it is this particular vision of human dignity that identifies Europe as the particular community that it is.*[91]

However, this understanding may limit the application of 'dignity' and threaten the universality of the concept.

In contrast, under the Principle of Generic Consistency (PGC), we can grant intrinsic moral status and hence, perhaps, the right to life 'to all living beings (biologically defined) (because there is sufficient evidence that all living beings are at least partial agents)'.[92] The authors conclude:

> *Consequently, if our argument for the PGC for the acceptance of human rights is valid, then the human rights conventions and instruments logically should grant protection (Though not necessarily will claim rights) not only to human agents, but also to all living humans, animals, even plants to at least some degree.*[93]

Leaving aside for now the strong environmental implications of this argument, I have accepted this conclusion together with Alan Gewirth's argument for the preconditions of agency[94] to 'fatten', in a sense, the right to life to include the preconditions of agency, included in the right to normal pre-birth development.[95]

Simply put, it seems to me that the right to life includes the right to be born as you could be and would be, given your own genetic history and predispositions, but without having been affected by industrial chemical exposures[96] or other exposures involving endocrine disruptors.[97] These exposures lessen one's personal mental ability or predispose one to a number of altered characteristics or later diseases, all of which impede a person's otherwise normal development.

Hence, perhaps, the presence of even limited agency, together with its own preconditions, might strengthen the right to life as currently understood, without, however, adding undue 'fattening' on life-project conditions that might be best defended under separate rights instead.

It is worthy of note that those who become asylum seekers start, most often, by being subjected to these exposures or to life-affecting climate conditions, all of which are felt most gravely by the most vulnerable among them: pregnant women and the preborn.[98] When these catastrophic exposures are later coupled with the conditions of deep deprivation that occur both in flight, and in detention, the intergenerational consequences are incalculable; but even in their imprecision, they must be included in the institutionalized rights that are eventually formulated for the protection of refugees.

5. ECOLOGICAL REFUGEES AND ECOLOGICAL RIGHTS IN INTERNATIONAL LAW: *LACUNAE* AND UNDER-INCLUSIONS

The Handbook on Procedures and criteria for Determining Refugee Status (Handbook), which is undoubtedly the most authoritative interpretation of the 1951 Refugee Convention and the 1967 Refugee Protocol, affirms that 'there is no universally accepted definition of 'persecution' and various attempts to formulate such a definition have met with little success.[99]

Another approach to the issue we are attempting to analyse would be to return to the CSR itself. Based, as it is, on persecution as the central point defining refugee status, it might be easier to establish that extreme environmental degradation may be a form of persecution. However, 'persecution' is primarily an act of governments against individuals, although many cases are based on group persecution that does not originate exclusively from governmental activities (although the question of complicity, or of enabling remains), and we will return to this topic below.

At this point, we are most concerned with the situation of IDPs and other forced migrants. The urgency and the complexity of the situation cannot be overestimated; it seems as though the lesson that should have been learned through the refusal of states to freely welcome the Jewish victims of persecution in the Nazi era has not been accepted.[100]

If 'persecution' has, admittedly, never been thoroughly defined, then the all-encompassing concept of 'forced migration' might be a more useful category, including those who 'might not meet the narrow convention refugee definition'.[101] Originally limited to those refugees whose situation arose because of European events prior to January 1951, the 1967 protocol[102] removed these temporal and geographical limitations, but did nothing that might have been used to develop the original definition of refugees in order to render it more consonant with the problems arising from climate change and other globalization issues.

We noted that both of the international covenants of 1966 (ICCPR and ICESCR) appear to be more useful through some of the articles that are applicable to refugee problems; but neither implies that the member states will, in fact, apply the human rights prescribed therein, or that either possesses an appropriate enforcement mechanism. In fact, what has emerged thus far is precisely the under-inclusiveness of most international instruments, starting with the CSR, given the multiple *lacunae* that it manifests regarding the situation of refugees that do not fit its dated and strict definition. Helton and Jacoby define these limitations as follows:

First, several terms of the definition are ambiguous and result in inconsistent interpretation and application. Second, the omission of those who have not yet crossed an international border, but are internally displaced, denies protection to an equally vulnerable group. Third, persons who have been externally displaced for reasons other than individualized persecution – including armed conflicts and civil strife or simply invidious and wide-spread discrimination – have been omitted from the definition.[103]

However, even this expanded analysis leaves untouched forced migrations due to environmental reasons despite the fact that many of the asylum seekers today belong to this category. The question then remains: where can we find an international law instrument that might at least acknowledge the 'missing link' discussed above (see section 4 of this chapter), or provide a way to move forward towards the recognition of the gravity of environmental destruction and of its consequences.

The Protocol to the Geneva Convention considers environmental protection only in the context of warfare. Article 55 of the protocol states:

Care should be taken in warfare to protect the natural environment against widespread, long-term and severe damage. This protection includes a prohibition of the use of methods and means of warfare which are intended or may be expected to cause such damage to the natural environment and thereby to prejudice the health and survival of the population.[104]

The environmental attacks we have discussed are part of economic aggression and oppression, rather than of warfare; but as Weinstein remarks, 'Article 55, on the other hand, establishes that the environment is a protected object and recognizes the link between environment and human survival'.[105]

This is precisely an acknowledgement of the 'link' we were seeking to find. This article envisages a different situation than the ones that normally give rise to forced migrations. Yet, the presence of this 'link' – that is, this connection which is seldom recognized – shows the possibility of a clear appeal to humanitarian law. In fact, this is a protocol of the Genocide Convention that we had dismissed earlier at the start of this chapter because of the *mens rea* requirement (the *dolus specialis*), which for the most part cannot be proven either in environmental disasters, or in other environmental attacks that may produce mass migrations.

In addition, although it is both appealing and suggestive to speak of economic oppression as 'an attack' and, perhaps, even as a form of warfare leading to mass atrocities, the concept of 'aggression' in international law does not yet permit us to rely fully on this interpretation, as the concept is still undefined even in the Rome Statute of the ICC. In contrast, Weinstein argues that the environment itself has been used as a tool of aggression from time immemorial:

Whether intentional or unintentional, the destruction of the environment has always been a consequence of armed conflict. Warfare can leave landscapes littered and contaminated with bomblets, landmines, and other weapons. In particular, purposeful environmental modification as a tool of war is as ancient as civilization and widespread throughout Asia, Europe and North America.[106]

From the 'scorched earth' policy practised by the Scythians against the Persians in 512 BC to the American use of Agent Orange in Vietnam, and the Iraqi government actions to ignite the oil fields in Kuwait during the Gulf War to the destruction of 'the marshes in southern Iraq following the 1991 'Shi'a rebellion',[107] environmental destruction is a constant refrain as a tool or a consequence of warfare.

In fact, after the Vietnam War, a treaty was created to deal with the issue: the Convention on the Prohibition of Environmental Modification Techniques (ENMOD),[108] prohibiting *states* from using 'hostile environmental modification techniques'[109] that have 'widespread, long-lasting or severe effects as the means of destruction, damage or injury to any other state party' (Article 1, ENMOD).

Somehow, despite these instruments, both of which can be used *post hoc* rather than as preventive measures, and only one of which (Article 55 of Protocol I) considers acts by individuals rather than only states, the international community did not move to the next stage – that is, to the disastrous effects these activities must have on local populations. In fact, *if* the environment is thus used as a tool of violence, then the intentional aspect of these actions could be used to indicate not only persecution, but even the possibility of returning, better armed, to the notion of genocide in these cases. The appellation of war crimes, to say the least, seems unavoidable.

Whatever the force of these arguments, there is a category of ecological refugees/ IDPs, or simply 'forced migrants', that we have not considered yet: the victims (or potential victims, should they be able to flee) of warfare, especially of armed conflicts initiated or ongoing, even in part, because of the scarcity of resources in their region, whether or not this scarcity is fostered by various aspects of global change. Thus far there has been little or no prosecution either at the International Criminal Tribunal for Yugoslavia (ICTY) or the International Criminal Tribunal for Rwanda (ICTR):

> *... although the ICTR has jurisdiction over the crime of pillage and violence to health and life, the tribunal has never brought charges for those crimes. Similarly, despite the environment destruction, the ICTY has virtually no jurisdiction for crimes against property or the environment.*[110]

Nevertheless, the Rome Statute, like the Iraqi Statute,[111] requires that the environmental damage should be part of an international conflict, and 'the protection of the environment during international conflict or insurrection is limited at best'.[112] Weinstein adds:

> *The elements of the crime – knowledge and intent; widespread, long-term, and severe damage; and the damage clearly excessive to military advantage – all pose obstacles that make successful prosecution unlikely.*[113]

This assessment also demonstrates the inadequacy of any of these instruments intended for the protection of the environment, and their obvious *lacunae* to further extend that protection to the migrants, true ecological refugees that originate from these often willed and acknowledged disasters. The grave difficulties that ensue are perhaps most obvious in the ongoing tragedy in the Middle East and the case of the Palestinian refugees.

6. THE WATER CONFLICT IN THE MIDDLE EAST AND THE QUESTION OF PALESTINIAN REFUGEES

> *The problem is that there are no legal criteria for applying the guidelines of international water law, in order to establish ownership over water sources.*[114]

Although Palestinians were originally 'British protected persons' and entitled to a British passport issued by the government of Palestine,[115] after the conflict beginning in 1948:

> *Palestinian refugees were not only barred from returning to their homes, but were also effectively and retroactively deprived of their citizenship.*[116]

According to international law, states make decisions regarding who are its citizens, but they do not have the right to 'denationalize their nationals in order to expel them as non-citizens'.[117] Yet Israeli courts decided that Palestinian citizens lost their previous citizenship when the British Mandate terminated; but they did not acquire any other citizenship, as they are effectively denied Israeli citizenship.[118] Despite their statelessness and the obvious and illegal loss of their territories:

> *Palestinians are the only group effectively placed outside the protection regime established by the UNHCR Statute and the 1951 Convention.*[119]

At any rate, although initially assistance to Palestinian refugees was provided by the United Nations Relief and Works Agency (UNRWA), it is unclear which organization should protect and assist the descendants of the refugees from the 1948 war, or those displaced by further and later hostilities.[120] Essentially, then, neither the historical background nor the applicable international legal instruments provide a clear answer to the problem of the status of Palestinian refugees.

The most significant article of the 1951 Convention on Refugee Status in regard to Palestinian refugees is Article 1D of the CSR:

> *This Convention shall not apply to persons who are at present receiving from organs or agencies of the United Nations other than the United Nations High Commissioner for Refugees protection or assistance.*
>
> *When such protection or assistance has ceased for any reason, without the position of such persons being definitely settled in accordance with the relevant resolutions adopted by the General Assembly of the United Nations, these persons shall ipso facto be entitled to the benefits of this Convention.*

Nevertheless, the situation of Palestinian refugees is an extremely complex one at this time,[121] as the question of their statehood has not been settled:

> *Notwithstanding the changed and changing political situation, UNRWA retains competence with respect to those who left Palestine as a result of the 1948 conflict;*

their dependants and descendants, as well as those who fled for reasons of later conflicts.[122]

Environmental issues are seldom mentioned in the largely political and ethnic debates surrounding the plight of the Palestinian refugees as they appear to be overshadowed by the ongoing violence, especially after the 1967 war. At that time, the United Nations Security Council Resolution 237 stated that Israel should:

> *... facilitate the return of these inhabitants who have fled the area since the outbreak of hostilities.*[123]

This resolution came long after the 1948 UN General Assembly Resolution 194 (III):

> *... the (1948) refugees wishing to return to their homes and life at peace with their neighbours should be permitted to do so at the earliest practicable date, and that compensation should be paid for the property of those choosing not to return and for the loss of or damage to property which, under principles of international law or in equity, should be made good by the governments or authorities responsible.*[124]

In some sense, Palestinian refugees appear to be refugees '*par excellence*': their situation endlessly dangerous, complicated and, increasingly, recalcitrant to any equitable solution, as they continue to live, for decades now, in an 'extremely difficult situation, with poor and crowded housing, few economic opportunities, and inadequate security'.[125] Even the possibility of improvements or development for Palestinians is severely curtailed as 'Israel also maintains control of the West Bank and Gaza aquifers through the location of the colonies and military zones, as well as restrictive drilling regulations'.[126]

6a. An Overview of Water Issues and Water Law in the Region

> *The right to water has been recognized in a wide range of international documents including treaties, declarations and other standards.* (General Comment 15, the Right to Water)[127]

In addition to Comment No. 15, there are many basic human rights instruments from which a human right to water may be inferred, although it is not explicitly articulated in those instruments.[128]

The right to water is intimately linked to the right to life, yet the language of the ICESCR Human Rights Committee implies that the rights it defends must be implemented by states only 'progressively':

> *... the right of every human being to have the appropriate means of subsistence, and a decent standard of life (preservation of life, right of living).*[129]

In addition, 'state parties to the ESC Covenant must prevent any third parties that operate or control water services from "compromising" equal, affordable, and physical access to sufficient, safe and acceptable water'.[130]

Against this background in international law, in order to better understand the specific situation in the Middle East, between Palestine and Israel, it will be useful to consider the laws and customs governing water law in both Israel and Palestine.

Israeli laws governing the status and the use of water can be traced back to the Bible: 'And ye shall serve the Lord they God and He shall bless ... thy water.'[131] Under Talmudic law, 'Rivers and streams forming springs, these belong to every man',[132] although Maimonides acknowledges that, though upstream riparians have greater rights than downstream ones, in any dispute, 'the stronger one is superior'.[133] There is also an order of priorities: the citizens who own a spring in common have priority in the use of water over those outside the city; priority is also given to animals belonging to the citizens over the needs of other animals. As for other uses, such as laundering, the lives of 'others' (non-citizens) take precedence over all other uses of the citizens themselves.

When we turn to the Palestinian side, their water laws initiated with the Ottoman Civil Code;[134] Dante Caponera lists the following:

1 *All waters were declared as vested in the state, the crown or incorporated in the public domain, the state thus taking the place of the Moslem community.*
2 *Every use of water (other than for drinking or animal watering purposes) left free under colonial legislation and Shari'a was placed under government control.*
3 *Water commissions were set up to survey and recognize established water rights.*
4 *Land registers were compiled in order to keep a written record of duly recognized land and water rights.*[135]

That code recognized that water for drinking (both human and animals) is (and should be) available to everyone, including water for irrigation as well – hence the general public could take water from for all 'rivers and streams in the public domain' without, however, exhausting these supplies or lowering water levels, thus interrupting the passage of boats.[136] In general, ground waters belong to the community as 'water [is] a non-saleable, publicly owned commodity'.[137] Similarly, the Medjelle Code proscribes 'upsetting the natural order through pollution':

> *As distinguished from land pollution liability, which may hinge on intent, liability from groundwater pollution does not – the owner of the land with polluted groundwater is liable without inquiry.*[138]

Thus, it is easy to see that both groups already possessed regulatory regimes and strong principles regarding water, long before any conflicts between Israel and Palestine initiated. In fact, Caponera notes that:

> *It is interesting to note that many legal principles set forth in the Talmudic Law are similar to those later developed under Moslem water law, particularly with regard to the order of priorities in the uses of water, to the maintenance of waterworks, and their protected area.*[139]

At any rate, in recent times Israel concluded the Israel–Jordan Treaty of Peace.[140] Article 6 (Water) and Article 18 (Environment) are the most relevant in that document, although the parties' main concern appears to have been achieving 'a comprehensive and lasting settlement of the water problem' between those states, rather than simply the conservation of water.[141] McCaffrey points out that:

> *Since 1967 Israel has controlled the areas in which these...streams are located, giving it complete control of the headwaters of Jordan... Thus 77 per cent of the Jordan water originates in Arab countries.*[142]

However, the assumption underlying the water treaty, that additional water may be found, is unrealistic: providing the 1990 population of Israel, Jordan and the West Bank with a minimum of 50 litres per day, including drinking, sanitation, bathing and cooking needs, but not industrial or commercial needs,[143] 'would require 180 million cubic metres of water a year', and the UN population projections for 2025 would raise that figure to 400 million cubic metres, a totally unrealistic expectation of increased water availability.[144]

In addition, today Israel retains control of the Mountain Aquifer (which underlies the West Bank as well as Israel); it also controls 'large portions of the Gaza Aquifer and Jordan River', while, since 1967, Palestinians have been unable to use that river's water, and Israel has 'declared the river a Closed Military Area and destroyed 140 Palestinian pumps in the closing process'.[145] Nor is this situation likely to improve as population increases and future and ongoing refugees only render the water issue more precarious, as the competition for water resources rises.[146]

Many of these issues are discussed in detail in the literature today and, although no specific right to water is present in any binding international law instrument, the language of the ICESCR is basic to our understanding of the right to water:

> *A right to water based on the right to develop would require that access to affordable water supplies not place a disproportionate economic or physical burden upon any segment of society. This access-based right to development is not explicitly covered by other human or socio-cultural rights though it may be implied from other rights.*[147]

This section has compared briefly the principles concerning water and its allocation in Jewish and Moslem areas, and found a great deal of general agreement on the humanitarian aspects of the problem. A thorough review of all instruments supporting the right to water, however, would require an in-depth discussion, beyond the scope of the present section. At any rate, the situation on the ground appears to be increasingly problematic, as those who hold the power to make decisions tend to put state interest above humanitarian concerns – hence, the water issue is one of the gravest problems faced by Palestinian refugees. In the next section we will consider one of the rights of CSR refugees: the right to '*non-refoulement*' as it applies to them.

6b. The question of *non-refoulement*

The current emphasis on the 'right to return' of these refugees makes their position entirely anomalous and *sui generis*: normally, convention refugees have the right to '*non-refoulement*'.[148] In fact, although it has been argued that in the case of a mass exodus or mass migration, the sheer number of refugees might pose a grave threat to the host state (hence the latter *might* be justified in refusing access), Article 33 of the Refugee Convention, Article 3 of the Torture Convention, and Article 6 and 7 of the Civil and Political Covenant all support the conclusion that '*non-refoulement* must be regarded as principle of customary international law'.[149]

This contrast with normal refugee rights represents the first of the anomalies and contentious issues that form part of the complexities of the situation of Palestinian refugees. We will consider these in turn below.

6c. Palestinian refugees and the first anomaly: *Non-refoulement*, or the right to return?

> *Temporary protection also specifically addresses the fear of both Arab and other states that they would either have to grant asylum or some more permanent type of status to the refugees, or else expel them. Finally, temporary protection addresses the ongoing concern of Palestinian refugees and the POL [Palestinian Occupied Lands] that the post-Oslo process might violate the international consensus so firmly embodied in the UN General Assembly Resolution 194 and in customary international law, that the durable solution for Palestinian refugees is return to their place of origin, restitution and compensation.*[150]

Hence, in contrast to the common right to *non-refoulement*, Palestinian refugees fight for the 'right to return' to their homelands despite the fact that, for many, their villages and territories are now under Israeli domination, and any evidence of their former presence has long been erased.[151] Ghannam reports:

> *When refugees recite their histories, their point of departure is their ancestral village, which may no longer appear as it once did on maps.*[152]

In contrast, Jewish sources, such as Joel Singer, respond that:

> *Resolution 194 (III) like all UN General Assembly Resolutions is non-binding and not part of international law.*[153]

The opening paragraph of this section reproduces the closing paragraph of an important recent on-site study, which complements fully the UN General Assembly Reports of 2004 and 2005 by Special Rapporteur John Dugard,[154] of which more below.

Essentially, these studies indicate clearly the *sui generis* position of Palestinian refugees, and the difference between their case and that of refugees in general. Before any attempt can be made to assess the legality of the positions on either side of the conflict, what must be noted is the refugee right *not* to be returned especially to situations where they will find unacceptable conditions and ongoing persecution. Thus, the situation of Palestinian refugees renders them akin to IDPs, especially to the similar position of displaced indigenous and local populations elsewhere, whether the displacement is caused by a catastrophic environmental event, or by deliberate hazardous corporate practices as economic oppression, resulting in 'ethnic cleansing' in a specific area to be mined or otherwise exploited, or any similar situation.

Any of these peoples would desperately want to return to their territories, if only corporate or other oppressors were not intent on making their return an impossibility.

John Dugard[155] details both the sheer numbers and the terrible situation of Palestinians, whose suffering is starkly enumerated in the 2004 report, summarized below:

- *Death and injuries ... of over 3850 Palestinians (including over 650 children below the age of 18) ... since September 2000; ...*
- *Assassinations ... some 340 persons have been killed in military excursions ... of which 188 were targeted persons and 152 innocent civilians [the latter viewed as 'collateral damage']; ...*
- *Incursions ... the IDF [Israel Defense Forces] have frequently engaged in military incursions ... [with] civilians killed in indiscriminate gunfire; ...*
- *Prisoners – there are some 7000 Palestinian prisoners in Israeli prisons or detention camps, of whom 380 are children and over 100 are women ... many ... report being subjected to torture or inhuman and degrading treatment; ...*
- *Curfews ...*
- *Humanitarian crisis ... [according to] the International Labour Organization (ILO) ... an average of 35 per cent of the Palestinian population is unemployed. 62 per cent ... live below the poverty line.*[156]

In addition, 'Israel has engaged in a massive destruction of property in Gaza', and although some reasons are adduced for each instance of destruction, often that destruction is wanton and unjustified:

Caterpillar bulldozers have savagely dug up roads with a 'ripper' attachment, which has enabled them to destroy electricity, sewage and water lines in a brutal display of power.[157]

Conditions in refugee camps are equally brutal, and 'punitive' actions against refugees and their property are a regular occurrence, contrary to international law:

The demolition of houses in Rafal, Jabalyia and other parts of Gaza, probably qualify as war crimes in terms of the Geneva Convention relative to the protection of civilian persons in times of war.[158]

While the sheer listing of these dehumanizing conditions explains fully the desire of Palestinians to escape and return, the magnitude of the problem coupled with the increasing Israeli settlements[159] show the grave difficulty involved:

Despite assurances from the Government of Israel that settlement growth has been frozen or limited to natural growth, the reality is that the settler population has grown more than the Israeli population itself.[160]

This growth represents an enormous obstacle, not only political and administrative, but also environmental, to any possibility of returning for the Palestinians.[161] The United Nations General Assembly[162] produced yet another report on *The Human Rights*

Situation in Palestine and the Occupied Arab Territories by Rapporteur John Dugard. The situation has deteriorated since the last report, rather than improved. At this time, the rapporteur explains the one-sidedness of his position: his mandate and his reports have been criticized as repetitious, as one sided, especially regarding various acts of terrorism in the region. He responds that:

> ... *while such acts cannot be justified, they must be understood as being a painful but inevitable consequence of colonialism, apartheid and occupation.*[163]

In fact, Dugard clearly adds that:

> *The mandate of the Special Rapporteur therefore requires him to report on human rights violations committed by the occupying power, and not by the occupied people.*[164]

At any rate, this report states that 80 per cent of the population, mostly refugees or IDPs, depending on our understanding of the situation, live below the poverty line, while farmers, for the most part, cannot farm their lands because of various blockages and the closure of roads, and fishermen cannot fish 'because of the Israeli ban on fishing along the Gaza coast'.[165] Water resources have also been affected, so that 210,000 people are able to access drinking water supplies for only one to two hours a day, and sewage is increasingly problematic, as repairs to plants have become impossible since 'metal pipes and welding machines' have been prohibited by Israel as 'they may be used for making rockets'.[166]

The whole situation requires a strong approach on the part of the international community, based on the rule of law and, especially, on clear normative principles.

6d. Palestinian refugees or internally displaced persons?

> *Under UNRWA's operation definition, Palestine refugees are persons whose normal place of residence was Palestine between June 1946 and May 1948, who lost both their homes and their means of livelihood as the result of the 1948 Arab–Israeli conflict... UNRWA's definition of a refugee also covers the descendants of persons who became refugees in 1948. The number of registered Palestine refugees has subsequently grown from 914,000 in 1950 to more than 4 million in 2002, and continues to rise due to natural population growth.*[167]

These refugees live in camps 'ranging in size from 20,000 to more than 100,000 people'.[168] Without returning once again to the material conditions of these refugees, we need however, to add the chronic malnutrition of children and others, despite the fact that 'some 125,000 families in Gaza', for instance, 'received emergency food aid from the United Nations'.[169] The Israelis are withdrawing from Gaza; and when the Israeli settlements are fully evacuated, the Palestinians will regain 'control of the Gaza aquifer, the only freshwater source in Gaza, which has a sustainable yield of roughly ninety-six million cubic meters per year'.[170]

162 ENVIRONMENTAL JUSTICE & THE RIGHTS OF ECOLOGICAL REFUGEES

However, even with a complete evacuation of Gaza:

> *Israel will guard and monitor the external land parameter of the Gaza Strip, will continue to maintain exclusive authority in Gaza air space, and will continue to exercise security activity in the sea off the coast of the Gaza Strip... Israel will continue to maintain a military presence along the border between the Gaza Strip and Egypt (Philadelphia Route).*[171]

Hence, it remains somewhat unclear whether Palestinians are refugees in an occupying country (Israel) despite the illegality of Israel's present borders after 1967; or, perhaps, whether they are IDPs – that is, fleeing to a different part of their own country after a conflict and a violent eviction or forced displacement, away from their original territory. When the conflict persists, they remain in a 'protracted refugee situation', and this is not unique to this area since in Africa, for instance, over 3 million refugees have 'spent more than a decade in refugee camps'.[172] According to Crisp, so far, the only possible solutions for refugees are:

> *... firm resettlement offered by a third country, local integration that occurs when the first refugee haven permits the new arrivals to remain as legal residents and potential citizens, and repatriation in safety and dignity when the conditions that caused flight presumable have changed.*[173]

Given the increased dangers, hostility and other insecurities, the preferred solution of Palestinians does not appear to be even remotely achievable under the present political realities. In addition, neither the first nor the second are fully viable options, although the second one appears to present some hope, at least for the present.

6e. Palestinian refugees after a conflict including basic resources: Humanitarian law or human rights protection?

> *In the West Bank, the continuation of the Wall ... has continued despite a ruling by the International Court of Justice (ICJ) that the Wall is illegal and Israel is obliged to cease the construction of the Wall and to dismantle it. Neither the advisory opinion of the court on the Legal Consequences of the Construction of a Wall in Occupied Palestinian Territory, rendered on 9 July 2004, nor the subsequent resolution of the General Assembly approving the advisory opinion (ED/10-15) have succeeded in curbing Israel's illegal actions.*[174]

It is important to examine exactly what were the specific conclusions of the International Court of Justice in accepting and responding to the request for an advisory opinion. It is remarkable that the Summary of the Advisory Opinion of 9 July 2004 (regarding the Israeli-built wall) notes that:

> *There have been serious repercussions for agricultural production and increasing difficulties for the population concerned regarding access to health services, education establishments and primary sources of water.*[175]

Hence, the erection of the wall, in addition to other provisions regarding the Occupied Palestinian Territory, have led the court to express the opinion that the wall contributed to a number of breaches of international legal instruments, including:

> ... articles of the 1907 Hague Regulations, the Fourth Geneva Convention, the International Covenant on Civil and Political Rights, the International Covenant on Economic, Social and Cultural Rights, and the United Nations Convention on the Rights of the Child ... it also refers to the obligations relating to guarantees of access to their Christian, Jewish and Islamic Holy Places.[176]

Palestinian refugees escape an intolerable occupation and war situation, only to find themselves in an ongoing situation of violence that includes physical aggression, economic oppression, deprivation for basic rights, including the right to subsistence and the right to survival for themselves and for their families.

The first response of the international community is usually humanitarian relief, as the situation warrants it. But an overly speedy 'movement from humanitarian aid to development assistance'[177] is not desirable for Palestinian refugees who, despite flight, are still enmeshed in a situation where illegal aggression dominates. This aggression includes the imposition of indiscriminate punitive measures to civilians, the erection of an illegal 'wall' that divides Palestinian communities (such as those in Eastern Jerusalem, according to Dugard),[178] but also that separates Palestinians from fertile soils closer to the green line – hence to the subsistence to which they have a clear right in international law: these actions and situations imply that the war has not fully abated, as conflict and hostilities remain.

The conflict is not likely to abate in the near future, if one considers the remaining roadblocks to peace and a legal two-state solution. Dugard explains why the present reforms:

> ... fail to address the principal institutions and instruments that violate human rights and humanitarian law in the Occupied Palestinian Territory – settlements, the Wall, checkpoints and roadblocks, the imprisonment of Gaza, and the continued incarceration of over 7000 Palestinians.[179]

The presence of 'closed zones' with only one gate 'seriously curtail[s] access to health services, education, basic consumer goods, food and water in the West Bank'.[180] Setting up additional 'annexed' territories,[181] through the location of the illegal wall, represents clear evidence of the Israeli plans regarding Palestine, plans that do not appear to include mutual respect between two sovereign states.

The laws regarding permits from Israeli military authorities for movement of Palestinian East Jerusalem residents towards Ramallah, where most of these people have 'strong work, family and cultural links',[182] is also representative of a brutally repressive regime, especially when one considers that those in East Jerusalem must choose between maintaining their cultural ties outside of the city or possibly losing their homes there, according to 'an absentee property law' that would have enabled Israeli to confiscate property in East Jerusalem without compensation on the grounds that 'the owner was not resident in Jerusalem'.[183] That law has been halted temporarily; but there is no guarantee that it will not be reinstated at a later time.

These refugees, therefore, often resemble war-zone civilians, rather than convention refugees or IDPs. The international human rights laws that are breached daily are too numerous to list: as Dugard suggests, this is the time to ensure that the UN decisions be respected and implemented without delay. For the rest of the international community, 'the time for appeasement has past'.[184] It is interesting to note that the conclusions of Israeli philosopher Shyli Karin-Frank, cited at the start of this section, are similar, even in 2000 when several of these conditions were not present (e.g. the wall): as she speaks of the right time for international intervention, based strictly on environmental grounds and the lack of water for Palestinians.[185]

The current disregard for the refugees' racial, economic, cultural and religious rights may be seen in a sentence describing just some of the many such situations encountered by the UN rapporteur:

> ... [he] met with a man in Anata who was compelled to watch a Caterpillar bulldozer destroy his land for the construction of the wall, despite a court injunction to stop construction; spoke with a family in Abu Dir whose hotel on the Jerusalem side of the wall had been seized by the IDF as a security outpost and witnessed the monstrous wall around Rachel's Tomb, that has killed a once vibrant commercial neighbourhood of Bethlehem. Although Rachel's Tomb is a site holy to Jews, Muslims and Christians, it has effectively been closed to Muslims and Christians.[186]

The UN reports used here are somewhat dated. Also, they appear cautiously hopeful about the possibility of change for the better. On 6 March 2008, Amnesty International UK, CARE International UK, CAFOD, Christian Aid, Médecins du Monde UK, Oxfam, Save The Children and Trocaire issued a new combined report, *The Gaza Strip: A Humanitarian Implosion*.[187] Their key statistics are summarized in the box opposite.

Even in March 2008, the need for prompt intervention by the international community appeared urgently needed. The unique position of Palestinians, refugees or IDPs, seems to require a strong and novel approach, beyond the attempts at 'peace-building'. Dugard put it well:

> In the opinion of the Special Rapporteur negotiations should take place within a normative framework, with the guiding norms to be found in international law, particularly international humanitarian law and human rights law, the advisory opinion of the International Court of Justice and Security Council Resolutions. Negotiations on issues such as boundaries, settlements, East Jerusalem, the return of refugees and the isolation of Gaza should be informed by such norms and not by political horse-trading.[188]

On 26 March 2008 the United Nations Human Rights Council (UNHRC) appointed Richard Falk for a six-year term as United Nations Special Rapporteur, to replace John Dugard. On 14 December, Falk landed at Israel's Ben Gurion Airport with staff members from the UN, but he was not allowed into the West Bank and Gaza: he was detained for 30 hours, before being released to a flight back to Geneva.[189] On 27 December 2008 the army of the Israel Occupation Forces (IOF) initiated a war against Palestine, by opening heavy machine-gun fire in the Talet-Az-Zaitoun area of the Jabalia Refugee

Key Gaza statistics (March 2008)

Poverty

80 per cent of families in Gaza currently rely on food aid compared to 63 per cent in 2006. This amounts to approximately 1.1 million people.[190]

In 2007, households were spending approximately 62 per cent of their total income on food compared with 37 per cent in 2004.[191]

During the period of May–June 2007 alone, commodity prices for wheat flour, baby milk, and rice rose 34, 30 and 20.5 per cent, respectively.[192]

During the period of June–September 2007, the number of households in Gaza earning less than US$1.2 per person per day soared from 55 to 70 per cent.[193]

Economic collapse

In September 2000, some 24,000 Palestinians crossed out of Gaza every day to work in Israel.[194] Today that figure is zero.

Unemployment in Gaza is close to 40 per cent and is set to rise to 50 per cent.[195]

In the months before the blockade began, around 250 trucks a day entered Gaza through Sufa with supplies; now it is only able to accommodate a maximum of 45 trucks a day. In most cases, this number is barely reached.

95 per cent of Gaza's industrial operations are suspended due to the ban on imported raw materials and the block on exports.[196]

Basic services

A total of 40 million to 50 million litres of sewage continues to pour into the sea daily.[197]

As a result of fuel and electricity restrictions, hospitals are currently experiencing power cuts lasting for 8 to 12 hours a day. There is currently a 60 to 70 per cent shortage reported in the diesel required for hospital power generators.

Health

18.5 per cent of patients seeking emergency treatment in hospitals outside Gaza in 2007 were refused permits to leave.[198]

The proportion of patients given permits to exit Gaza for medical care decreased from 89.3 per cent in January 2007 to 64.3 per cent in December 2007, an unprecedented low.[199]

During the period of October to December 2007, the World Health Organization (WHO) confirmed the deaths of 20 patients, including 5 children, among people awaiting visas.[200]

Source: 'Media briefing: Key Gaza statistics', Press release issued by Amnesty International UK, CARE International UK, CAFOD, Christian Aid, Médecins du Monde UK, Oxfam, Save The Children and Trocaire on 6 March 2008, summarizing information presented in their report *The Gaza Strip: A Humanitarian Implosion* (see note 185)

Camp. The war lasted until 17 January 2009, and on 21 January Israel completed its withdrawal from Gaza.

On 12 January 2009 the UN Human Rights Council in its 9th Special Session adopted a resolution on the 'grave violations of human rights in the Occupied Palestinian Territory, particularly due to the recent Israeli military attacks against the occupied Gaza Strip'.[201]

The council stated that it:

> *1. Strongly condemns the ongoing Israeli military operation carried out in the Occupied Palestinian Territory, particularly in the occupied Gaza Strip, which has resulted in massive violations of the human rights of the Palestinian people and systematic destruction of Palestinian infrastructure;*[202]

and

> *14. Decides to dispatch an urgent, independent international fact-finding mission, to be appointed by the President of the Council, to investigate all violations of international human rights law and international humanitarian law by the occupying Power, Israel, against the Palestinian people throughout the Occupied Palestinian Territory, particularly in the occupied Gaza Strip, due to the current aggression, and calls upon Israel not to obstruct the process of investigation and to fully cooperate with the mission; …*[203]

At time of writing (April 2009) there have been no further official reports, but the effects of the recent events have been widely reported in the various international press organs. In this chapter our main concern has been the living conditions of Palestinian eco-refugees. Hence, we will not discuss whether the war itself and its conditions (that is, *jus ad bellum* and *jus in bello*) have given rise to what many now term war crimes.[204] Nor will we dwell on the allegations that Israel's war involved the use of illegal weapons, including white phosphorus.[205]

Here we merely record that the latest reports indicate that over 50,000 Gazans are homeless, while 400,000 are without running water.[206] Many hospitals and clinics have been shelled and are unavailable; of the 122 facilities assessed by the WHO, 48 per cent were found to be damaged or destroyed.[207] Thus, for the Palestinian people in the Gaza Strip, the intervention of the international community is needed more than ever before.

NOTES

1 Convention on the Prevention and Punishment of the Crime of Genocide, 9 December 1948, 102 Stat. 3045, 78 UNTS 277.
2 Wald, P. M. (2007) 'Genocide and crimes against humanity', *Washington University Global Studies Law Review*, vol 6, no 3, p621.
3 Sachs, W. (2007) *Climate Change and Human Rights*, WDEV Special Report 1, World Economy and Development In Brief, Luxembourg, posted at www.wdev.eu, 2 January; the report has been published also (2006) in 'Scripta Varia' 106 of the Pontifical Academy of Sciences, Vatican City.

4 Davidsson, E. (2005) 'Economic oppression as an international wrong or as a crime against humanity', *Netherlands Quarterly of Human Rights*, vol 23, no 2, pp173–212.
5 Rome Statute of the International Criminal Court, 17 July 1998, 2187 UNTS 90.
6 See Corpus Juris Secondum, database updated April 2008, 40 CJS Homicide &42.
7 *Prosecutor versus Duko Tadic*, Case No. IT-94-I-A, Judgement, para. 271, 15 July 1999.
8 Ratner, S. R. (2007) 'Can we compare evils? The enduring debate on genocide and crimes against humanity', *Washington University Global Studies Law Review*, vol 6, p583.
9 Ibid, p584; Schabas, W. A. (2000) *Genocide in International Law: The Crime of Crimes*, Kluwer Publishing, The Hague; see also May, L. (2005) *Crimes Against Humanity: A Normative Account*, Cambridge University Press, Cambridge, UK, pp80–90.
10 *Prosecutor versus Akayesu*, Case No. ICTR-96-4-T, paras, 510–516 (2 September 1998); *Prosecutor versus Jelisic*, Case No. IT-95-10-T paras 69–72 (14 December 1999).
11 Luban, D. (2006) 'Calling genocide by its rightful name: Lemkin's word, Darfur, and the UN report', *Chicago Journal of International Law*, vol 7, p303; see also Ratner (2007), op cit Note 9, p585.
12 Ratner (2007), ibid.
13 As Ken Saro-Wiwa termed it in his Right Livelihood Award acceptance speech on 9 December 1994 in Stockholm, referring to the conditions in his country, Ogoniland, following upon Royal Dutch Petroleum's operations in the area; see also 'Appendix 2: Development and Environmental Racism: The Case of Ken Saro-Wiwa and the Ogoni', in Westra, L. (2007) *Environmental Justice and the Rights of Indigenous Peoples*, Earthscan, London.
14 Wald (2007), op cit Note 2.
15 Ibid; see also Bassiouni, C. (1998) 'The normative framework of international humanitarian law: Overlaps, gaps, and ambiguities', *Transnational Law and Contemporary Problems*, vol 8, pp201–202.
16 Wald (2007), op cit Note 2.
17 Wald (2007), op cit Note 2.
18 *Prosecutor versus Kupresic*, Case No. IT-95-16-A, Judgement (23 October 2001).
19 Drumbl, M. A. (2005) 'Collective violence and individual punishment: The criminality of mass atrocity', *Northwestern University Law Review*, vol 99, p539.
20 Teitel, R. (2002) 'Humanity's law: Rule of law for the new global politics', *Cornell International Law Journal*, vol 35, pp356–387.
21 Ibid.
22 Drumbl (2005), op cit Note 19, p545.
23 Cassese, A. (2001) 'Terrorism is also disrupting some legal categories of international law', *European Journal of International Law*, vol 12, p993.
24 Ibid.
25 Wald (2007), op cit Note 2.
26 Drumbl (2005), op cit Note 19.
27 Westra, L. (2004) *Ecoviolence and the Law*, Transnational Publishers Inc., Ardsley, NY.
28 Ibid, Chapter 7.
29 Drumbl (2005), op cit Note 19, p541; see also Foucault, M. (1975) *Discipline and Punish: The Birth of the Prison*, New York, Pantheon (translation by Alan Sheridan from the French *Surveiller et Punir: Naissance de la prison*, Paris, Gallimard, 1975).
30 Drumbl (2005), op cit Note 19, p542; see also Luban, D. (2004) 'A theory of crimes against humanity', *Yale International Law Journal*, vol 29, pp85–90.
31 Aminzadeh, S. C. (2007) 'A moral imperative: The human rights implications of climate change', *Hastings International and Comparative Law Review*, vol 30, p231–233.
32 Aminzadeh (2007), op cit Note 31, p239.
33 Westra (2007), op cit Note 13, Chapter 8.
34 Ibid, p240.
35 Ibid.

36 Sheila Watt-Cloutier, comment on back cover of Westra (2007), op cit Note 13.
37 Ford, J. (2005) 'Living with change in the Arctic', *WorldWatch*, September/October, p18.
38 Ibid; Kattsov, V. M. and Källén, E. (2005) 'Future climate change: Modeling and scenarios for the Arctic', in ACIA (ed) *Arctic Climate Impact Assessment: Scientific Report*, Cambridge University Press, Cambridge, UK, pp99–150, available for download at www.acia.uaf.edu/pages/scientific.html.
39 Ford, J., Smit, B. and Wandel, J. (2006) 'Vulnerability to climate change in the Arctic: A case study from Arctic Bay, Canada', *Global Environmental Change*, vol 16, pp145–160.
40 UNFCCC (UN Framework Convention on Climate Change), adopted 29 May 1992, entered into force, 21 Mar 1994, 31 I.L.M. 849 (1992).
41 McCarthy, J., Canziani, O. F., Leary, N. A., Dokken, D. J. and White, K. S. (2001) 'Climate change 2001: Impacts, adaptation, vulnerability', contribution of Working Group II to the *Third Assessment Report of The Intergovernmental Panel on Climate Change*, Cambridge University Press, Cambridge, UK.
42 Ford et al (2006), op cit Note 39, p149.
43 Ford (2005), op cit Note 37, p19.
44 Kendall, C. (2006) 'Life at the edge of a warming world', *The Ecologist*, vol 36, no 5, July/August, p26.
45 Ibid.
46 Ford et al (2006), op cit Note 39, p150.
47 Kendall (2006), op cit Note 44, p27.
48 Ford et al (2006), op cit Note 39; the 'memory' is based on the knowledge and skills passed on by elders, and it is known as Inuit *Qaujimajatuqanqit* (IQ), pronounced *cow-yee-ma-ya-tu-kant-eet*.
49 Ford et al (2006), op cit Note 39, p151.
50 Ibid, p155.
51 Ibid.
52 Damas, D. (2002) *Arctic Migrants/Arctic Villagers: The Transformation of Inuit Settlement in the Central Arctic*, McGill-Queens University Press, Montreal, Canada; Chabot, M. (2003) 'Economic changes, household strategies, and social relations in contemporary Nunavik Inuit', *Polar Record*, vol 39, pp19–34.
53 Ford et al (2006), op cit Note 39, p150.
54 Ford (2005), op cit Note 37.
55 Ford et al (2006), op cit Note 39, p153.
56 Ibid; Damas, D. (1972) 'Central Eskimo systems of food sharing', *Ethnology*, vol 11, pp220–240.
57 Kral, M. (2003) *Unikkaartui Meaning of Well-being, Sadness, Suicide, and Change in Two Inuit Communities*, Final Report to the National Health Research and Development Programs, Health Canada.
58 Gostin, L. O. (2004) 'Law and ethics in population health', *Australian and New Zealand Journal of Public Health*, vol 28, no 1, p11.
59 *Nunavut Act*, 1993, c.28 [assented to 10 June 1993]; *Nunavut Land Claims Agreement Act*, 1993, c.29 [Assented to 10 June 1993].
60 *Trail Smelter Arbitration*, 35 American Journal of International Law, 1941 684.
61 Grandjean, P. and Landrigan, P. (2006) 'Developmental neurotoxicity of industrial chemicals', *The Lancet*, November.
62 Colborn, T., Myers, D. and Patterson, J. (1996) *Our Stolen Future*, Dutton (Penguin Books), New York.
63 Westra (2007), op cit Note 13, pp200ff.
64 Lopez, A. (2007) 'The protection of environmentally-displaced persons in international law', *Environmental Law*, Spring, pp371–72; see also Myers, N. (1993) *Ultimate Security: The Environmental Basis of Political Stability*, W. W. Norton, New York, p190.

65 Ramcharan, B. G. (1985) 'The concept and dimension of the right to life', in B. G. Ramcharan (ed) *The Right to Life in International Law*, Martinus Nijhoff, The Hague, p7.
66 *Oneryildiz v. Turkey* (App. no. 48939/99), [2004] ECHR 48939/99.
67 Aminzadeh (2007), op cit Note 31, p251.
68 Westra (2004), op cit Note 27, Chapter 9.
69 *Lopez-Ostra v. Spain* (1995) 20 EHRR 277.
70 *Guerra v. Italy* (1998) 26 EHRR 357; (1994) ECHR 16798/90.
71 *Guerra v. Italy*, 'Head note'.
72 Westra, L. (1998) *Living in Integrity*, Rowman Littlefield, Lanham, MD.
73 Articles 15, 17(1), 18(2) and 19 of the Spanish Constitution.
74 Falk, R. (1981) *Human Rights and State Sovereignty*, Holmes and Meier Publishers, Teaneck, NJ, p153; Falk, R. (1973) 'Environmental warfare and ecocide: Facts, appraisal and proposals', *Belgian Review of International Law*, vol 9, p1.
75 Aminzadeh (2007), op cit Note 31.
76 Loescher, G., Betts, A. and Milner, J. (2008) *The United Nations High Commissioner for Refugees (UNHCR): The Politics and Practice of Refugee Protection into the Twenty-First Century*, Routledge, London, p50; El Hinnawi, E. (1985) *Environmental Refugees*, United Nations Environment Programme, (UNEP), Nairobi, Kenya; International Symposium on Desertification and Migration (1994) 'The Almeria Statement', International Symposium on Desertification and Migration, Almeria, Spain, 9–11 February; Myers, N. (2005) 'Environmental refugees: An emergent security issue', 13th Economic Forum, Prague, 23–27 May; Stern, Sir Nicholas (2007) *The Economics of Climate Change: The Stern Review*, Cambridge University Press, Cambridge, UK; Friends of the Earth (2007) *A Citizen's Guide to Climate Refugees*, Friends of the Earth, Australia, available at www.foe.org.au/resources/publications/climate-justice/CitizensGuide.pdf/view; Christian Aid (2007) *Human Tide: The Real Migration Crisis*, report, May, available at www.christianaid.org.uk/resources/policy/climate_change.aspx. These and other estimates are detailed on page 12 of Boano, C., Zetter, R. and Morris, T. (2008) *Environmentally Displaced People: Understanding the Linkages between Environmental Change, Livelihoods and Forced Migration*, Forced Migration Policy Briefing 1, Refugee Studies Centre, Oxford, available at www.rsc.ox.ac.uk.
77 Falstrom, D. (2001) 'Stemming the flow of environmental displacement: Creating a convention to protect persons and preserve the environment', *Colorado Journal of International Environmental Law and Policy*, vol 1, pp2–32.
78 Aminzadeh (2007), op cit Note 31.
79 Perry, M. (2005) 'Rising seas, disappearing islands to cause environmental refugees in a warming world', Reuters (Sydney), 24 November, available at http://news.mongabay.com/2005/1124-reuters.html (accessed 27 March 2009).
80 Aminzadeh (2007), op cit Note 31, p262; see also Rodriguez-Rivera, L. (2001) 'Is the human right to environment recognized under international law? It depends on the source', *Colorado Journal of International Environmental Law and Policy*, vol 12, pp1–19.
81 Rodriguez-Rivera (2001), ibid, p4.
82 Gardner, J. (2008) 'Simply in virtue of being human: The whos and whys of human rights', *Journal of Ethics and Social Philosophy*, vol 2, no 2, February.
83 Ibid, p7.
84 Raz, J. (1984) 'On the nature of rights', *Mind*, vol 93, no 194, pp208–209.
85 Raz, J. (1992) 'Rights and individual well-being', *Ratio Juris*, vol 5, p127; see also Gardner (2008), op cit Note 82, p12.
86 Gardner (2008), ibid, p13.
87 Warren, M. A. (1973) 'On the moral and legal status of abortion', *The Monist*, vol 57, no 1, 27 March, pp43–61; reprinted in T. Mappes and J. Zembaty (eds) (1991) *Biomedical Ethics*, McGraw-Hill, New York, pp438–444.

88 Gardner (2008), op cit Note 82, p18.
89 Ibid, p20.
90 Ibid, pp21–22.
91 Beyleveld, D. and Brownsword, R. (2001) *Human Dignity in Bioethics and Biolaw*, Oxford University Press, Oxford, UK, p65.
92 Ibid, p126.
93 Ibid.
94 Gewirth, A. (1982) *Starvation and Human Rights: Essays in Justification and Application*, University of Chicago Press, Chicago, IL.
95 Westra, L. (2004) 'Environmental rights and human rights: The final enclosure movement', in R. Brownsword (ed) *Global Governance and the Quest for Justice, Volume 4: Human Rights*, Hart Publishing, Oxford, UK.
96 Grandjean and Landrigan, op cit Note 61.
97 Colborn et al, op cit Note 62.
98 Westra, L. (2006) *Environmental Justice and the Rights of Unborn and Future Generations*, Earthscan, London.
99 Lopez (2007), op cit Note 64; UNHCR (1992) *Handbook on Procedures and Criteria for Determining Refugee Status Under the 1951 Convention and the 1967 Protocol Relating to the Status of Refugees*, Document HCR/IP/4/Eng/REV.1, United Nations High Commissioner for Refugees, Geneva, re-edited January 1992, available at www.unhcr.org/publ/PUBL/3d58e13b4.pdf.
100 Helton, A. C. and Jacoby, E. (2006) 'What is forced migration?', in A. F. Bayefsky (ed) *Human Rights and Refugees, Internally Displaced Persons*, Martinus Nijhoff Publishers, Leiden, The Netherlands, pp3–13.
101 Ibid, p5.
102 Protocol Relating to the status of Refugees, 606 UNTS 267, in force 4 October 1967; to date 145 countries are party to the Convention or the Protocol.
103 Helton and Jacoby (2006), op cit Note 100, p7.
104 Protocol Additional to the Geneva Conventions Relating to the Protection of the Victims of International Armed Conflicts, 8 June 1977, 16 I.L.M. 1391, UN Doc. A/32/144(1977), Article 55.
105 Weinstein, T. (2005) 'Prosecuting attacks that destroy the environment: Environmental crimes or humanitarian atrocities?', *Georgetown Immigration Law Journal*, vol 17, pp697–722.
106 Ibid, pp699–700; Ross, M. A. (1992) 'Environmental warfare and the Persian Gulf War: Possible remedies to combat intentional destruction of the environment', *Dickinson Journal of International Law*, vol 10, no 3, pp515–539.
107 Weinstein (2005), op cit Note 105.
108 Convention on the Prohibition of Military or any other Hostile Use of Environmental Modification Techniques, May 18, 1977, 31 U.S.T. 333, T.I.A.S. No. 9614.
109 Weinstein (2005), op cit Note 105, p701.
110 Ibid, pp704–705; see also Statute of the International Criminal Tribunal for Rwanda, 8 November 1994, Article 4, S.C., Res. 955, UNSCOR 3453 mtg., Art. 4, UN Doc. S/Res/955, 33 I.L.M. 15981, 1600; Statute of the International Tribunal Criminal for the Former Yugoslavia, 25 May, 1993 Art.4, UN Doc. S/25704 (1993), Approved by UNSCOR Res. 827, 32 I.L.M. 1192 (1993).
111 Statute of the Iraqi Special Tribunal (10 December 2003).
112 Weinstein (2005), op cit Note 105, p710.
113 Ibid, p711.
114 Karin-Frank, S. (2000) 'The water conflict in the Middle East: A test case for international intervention', in P. Crabbe, A. Holland, L. Ryszkowsi, and L. Westra (eds) *Implementing Ecological Integrity*, NATO Science Series, vol 1, Kluwer, Dordrecht, The Netherlands; see

also Naff, T. and Matson, R. (eds) (1984) *Water in The Middle East: Conflict or Cooperation*, Westview Press, Boulder, CO; and Lowi, M. (1993) *Water and Power*, Cambridge University Press, Cambridge, UK.
115 Goodwin-Gill and McAdam (2007), *The Refugee in International Law*, (third edition), Oxford University Press, Oxford, UK, p459; see also Takkenberg, L. (1998) *The Status of Palestinian Refugees in International Law*, Clarendon Press, Oxford.
116 Goodwin-Gill and McAdam (2007), ibid, p459.
117 Ibid.
118 Ibid; see *Oseri versus Oseri* (1953) 8 PM 76; 17 ILR III (1950), a decision that enforced the desire of the Tel Aviv District Court not to recognize Palestinians as citizens of Israel, despite the fact that, under international law, they retain a link to their territory, and the UN General Assembly re. 194 (III) recognizes this.
119 Goodwin-Gill and McAdam (2007), op cit Note 115. They add: 'the competence of the High Commissioner in the political issues surrounding the Palestinian question was once thought incompatible with the proclaimed non-political character of the UNHCR's work'.
120 Ibid, pp151–152.
121 See, for instance, the 1993 Declaration of Principles of Interim Self-Government Arrangements in the West Bank and Gaza; 32 ILM 1520 (1993).
122 Goodwin-Gill and McAdam (2007), op cit Note 115, p161.
123 UN Security Council Resolution S.C. Res. 237, 1, UNSCOR, 22nd Sess., 1361 mtg., UN Doc. S/RES/237 (1967).
124 Progress Report of the United Nations Mediator, G.A.Res. 194 (III), UN GAOR, 3d Sess. at §11, UN Doc. A/RES/194(III) (1948).
125 Martin, S., Warner, J. G. and Fagen, P. (2004) 'Palestinian refugees in Gaza', *Fordham International Law Journal*, vol 28, 1457–1458; see also Leinwand, A. J. (2001) 'The Palestinian poverty problem in the era of globalization', *Indiana Journal of Global Legal Studies*, vol 9, pp325–330.
126 Akram, S. and Rempel, T. (2005) 'Temporary protection as an instrument for implementing the right of return for Palestinian refugees', *Boston University International Law Journal*, vol 22, pp1–112; see also Lein, Y. (2000) *Thirsty for a Solution: The Water Crisis in the Occupied Territories and its Resolution in the Final-Status Agreement*, B'Tselem, Jerusalem, July.
127 Article 11 and 12 of the International Covenant on Economic, Social and Cultural Rights, UN Doc. E/C.12/2002/11, 26 November 2002.
128 McCaffrey, S. C. (2005) 'The human right to water', in E. Brown-Weiss, L. Boisson de Chazournes and N. Bernasconi-Osterwalder (eds) *Fresh Water and International Economic Law*, Oxford University Press, Oxford, pp93–116; see also the 1948 Universal Human Rights Declaration, Article 25, which states 'everyone has the right to a standard of living adequate for health and well-being of himself and of his family, including food'.
129 Human Rights Committee, General Comments adopted under Article 40, para 4, of the CP Covenant, UN Doc. CCPR/C/21/Rev.1 (19 May, 1989) at 51-52.
130 McCaffrey (2005), op cit Note 128, p105; see also General Comment 15, para 24.
131 Book of Exodus XXIII, verse 25; see also Caponera, D. A. (1992) *Principles of Water Law and Administration: National and International*, A. A. Balkema Publishers, Rotterdam, pp22–223.
132 As cited in Hirsch, A. (1957) *International Rivers in the Middle East*, PhD thesis, Columbia University, New York.
133 Caponera, op cit Note 137, p22, referring to Moses Maimonides (1135–1204), Jewish philosopher and Torah scholar.
134 Medjelle Code, 1870.
135 Caponera, op cit Note 131, p71.
136 Ibid, pp71–72.
137 Ibid; see also Jabaily, A. (2004) 'Water rites: A comparative study of the dispossession of American Indians and Palestinians from natural resources', *Georgetown Journal of*

Environmental Law, vol 16, p225. Particularly interesting is the injunction from the Qu'ran: 'eat and drink: but waste not ... God loveth not the waster of water'.
138 Jabaily (2004), ibid; see also Ahmad, A. (2001) *Cosmopolitan Orientation of the Process of International Environmental Law: An Islamic Law Genre*, University Press of America, Lanham, MD, pp89–91.
139 Caponera, op cit Note 131, p23.
140 Israel–Jordan Treaty of Peace, 34 I.L.M. 43(1995), 26 October 1994.
141 McCaffrey, S. (1997) 'Middle East water problems: The Jordan River', in E. H. P. Brans, E. J. de Haa, A. Nollkaemper and J. Rinzema (eds) *The Scarcity of Water – Emerging Legal and Policy Responses*, Kluwer Law International, The Netherlands, pp158–161.
142 Ibid, p159.
143 Gleick, P. (1996) 'Minimum water requirements for human activities: Meeting basic needs', *Water International*, vol 21, pp83–92.
144 McCaffrey (1997), op cit Note 141, p164.
145 Jabaily (2004), op cit Note 138, p239; Abouali, J. (1998) 'Natural resources under occupation: The status of Palestinian water under international law', *PACE International Law Review*, vol 10, pp411–428.
146 Jabaily (2004), op cit Note 138, notes: 'For example in 1987, the average water allocation to an Arab villager was 47.4 cubic metres, while the average allocation to a Jewish villager was 134.4 cubic metres'; see also Falah, G. (1999) 'Arabs versus Jews in Galilee: Competition for regional resources', *Georgetown Journal of International Law*, vol 21, pp325–330.
147 Bluemel, E. (2004) 'Human right to water', *Ecology Law Quarterly*, vol 31, pp959–970; see also Allen, J. A. (1998) 'Water in the Middle East and in Israel and Palestine: Some local and global issues', in E. Feitelson and M. Haddad (eds) *Identification of Joint Management Structures for Shared Aquifers*, World Bank, Washington, DC.
148 Hathaway, J. C. (2005) *The Rights of Refugees Under International Law*, Cambridge University Press, Cambridge, UK, pp278–363; see also discussion in section 2.a of Chapter 2 of this book.
149 Lauterpacht, E. and Bethlehem, D. (2003) 'The scope and content of the principle of *non-refoulement*', in E. Feller, V. Türk and F. Nicholson (eds) *Refugee Protection in International Law*, Cambridge University Press, Cambridge, UK, p87.
150 Akram, S. M. and Rempel, T. (2004) 'Temporary protection as an instrument for implementing the right of return for Palestinian refugees', *Boston University International Law Journal*, vol 22, no 1, pp1–43
151 Ghannam, J. (2000) 'Where will they go?', *ABA Journal*, Cover Story/Human Rights Law, December, p40.
152 Ibid.
153 Singer, J. (2001) 'No Palestinian return to Israel', *ABA Journal*, January, p14.
154 *Question of the Violation of Human Rights in the Occupied Arab Territories, Including Palestine*, Report of the Special Rapporteur of the Commission on Human Rights, John Dugard, on the Situation of Human Rights in the Palestinian Territories Occupied by Israel since 1967, UN document E/CN.4/2005/29, 7 December 2004 (henceforth, Dugard, 2004); and an *Addendum* to the same report, UN document E/CN.4/2005/29/Add.1, 5 March 2005 (henceforth, Dugard, 2005).
155 Dugard (2004), ibid.
156 Ibid, pp7–8.
157 Ibid.
158 Ibid, p2.
159 Dugard (2005), op cit Note 154.
160 Ibid, p2.
161 An interesting development on this problem is currently under consideration at Canada's Supreme Court in Quebec (Province of Quebec, District of Montreal, Bil'in (Village Council),

Occupied Territories Palestine), regarding the *Bil'in Village in the occupied lands in Palestine, Ahmed Issa Abdallah Yassin (Head of the Village) versus Green Park International, Inc (Green Mount International, Inc), and Anne Laroche* (sole director and officer of the defendants; Case No. 500-17-044030-081; Mark Arnold, Gardiner, Miller, Arnold LLP, Counsel of the Plaintiffs). The motion initiating a suit describes how the village inhabitants are excluded from cultivating their own lands, or from having a voice in the ongoing construction of apartment blocks (erected by the defendant corporations), which are housing and are intended to house only Israeli citizens, while citizens of Palestine are excluded. These policies render the defendants 'acting agents' of Israel in the illegal occupation of Palestinian territories, as the West Bank lands that were occupied by the State of Israel were never annexed by Israel. The lands therefore are considered by the international community, the United Nations and the State of Israel to be occupied territory and are subject to the rules and obligations of international law, including international humanitarian law. The village pleads (in this regard) and relies on Article 49(6) of the Fourth Geneva Convention, 12 August 1949: 'The Occupying Power shall not deport, transfer parts of its own civilian population into the territory it occupies'; in addition, Article 85(4) (a) of the Geneva Convention Act R.S.C. 1985, c.G-3, provides that the mandates of the Geneva Conventions are applicable in Canada, as part of the Canadian Criminal Code. The defendants are therefore acting as 'agents of the state of Israel because in recent years, and since the Camp David Summit in 2000, Israeli government policy has concentrated in … settlement blocs.' The aims of that state are to ensure that these settlement blocs remain part of the State of Israel 'in any future agreement with Palestine' (ibid, 9.(i)). Given the government of Canada's position with regard to Israeli settlements in the Occupied Territories (ibid, 22(a)), and the Civic Code of Quebec (Article 1457: 'Every person has a duty to abide by the rules of conduct which lie upon him, according to the circumstances, usages or law so as not to cause injury to another'), perhaps the Supreme Court will decide in favour of the Palestinian refugees and/or IDPs, when the case is heard.

162 UNGA, Human Rights Council, 7th Session, Item 7 of the provisional agenda A/HRC/7/17 21 January 2008.
163 Ibid, para 4.
164 Ibid, para 6.
165 Ibid, para 20; see also World Bank (2007) *Investing in Palestinian Economic Reform and Development*, 17 December, Report of the Pledging Conference, World Bank, Paris.
166 *Human Rights Situation in Palestine and Other Occupied Arab Territories: Report of the Special Rapporteur on the Situation of Human Rights in the Palestinian Territories Occupied since 1967*, John Dugard, UN Doc. A/HRC/7/17, 21 January 2008 (henceforth, Dugard, 2008).
167 UN Relief and Works Administration (UNRWA) 'Who is a Palestinian Refugee?', available at www.un.org/unrwa/refugeeswhois.html.
168 UNRWA in figures: figures as of 20 June 2004, available at www.un.org/unrwa/publicatiosn/pdf/uif-June.pdf.
169 Martin, Warner and Fagen (2004), op cit Note 125, p1462.
170 Ibid, pp1463–1464.
171 Dugard (2005), op cit Note 154, para 19.
172 Crisp, J. (2002) *No Solution in Sight: The Problem of Protracted Refugee Situation in Africa*, Center for Comparative Immigration Studies, p1, available at http://respositories.cdlib.org/cgi/viewcontent.cgi article=1010§context=ccis.
173 Ibid, p1.
174 Dugard (2005), op cit Note 154, p6.
175 Summary of the Advisory Opinion on Legal Consequences of the Construction of a Wall in the Occupied Palestinian Territory [2004] *ICJ Rep.*, para 133.
176 Ibid.
177 Martin, Warner and Fagen (2004), op cit Note 125, p1472.

178 Dugard (2005), op cit Note 154.
179 Ibid.
180 Ibid.
181 Dugard (2004), op cit Note 154, p8, terms it 'annexation under the guise of security'.
182 Dugard (2005), op cit Note 154, p10.
183 Ibid, p10.
184 Dugard (2004), op cit Note 154.
185 Karin-Frank (2000), op cit Note 114.
186 Dugard (2005), op cit Note 154, p10.
187 Amnesty International UK, CARE International UK, CAFOD, Christian Aid, Médecins du Monde UK, OXFAM, Save The Children and Trocaire (2008) *The Gaza Strip: A Humanitarian Implosion*, Report issued jointly on 6 March, available for download at www.amnesty.org.uk/news_details.asp?NewsID=17689.
188 Dugard (2008) op cit Note 166, para 58.
189 Keinon, H. (2008) 'UNHRC rapporteur denied entry to Israel', *Jerusalem Post*, 15 December, available at www.jpost.com/servlet/Satellite?cid=1228728204503&pagename=JPost%2FJPArticle%2FShowFull (accessed 1 April 2009).
190 OCHA (2007) 'The closure of the Gaza Strip: The economic and humanitarian consequences', *OCHA Special Focus*, United Nations Office for the Coordination of Humanitarian Affairs, December.
191 World Food Programme (2007) *Food Security and Market Monitoring Report: Report 9*, June World Food Programme, Rome, Italy.
192 OCHA (2007), op cit Note 190.
193 World Food Programme (no further details attributed as cited in Amnesty International UK et al, op cit Note 187).
194 World Bank (2006) *West Bank and Gaza Update*, World Bank, September.
195 The exact figure is 37.6 per cent. Palestinian Bureau of Statistics cited in OCHA (2007), op cit Note 190.
196 World Bank (2007) *Investing in Palestinian Economic Reform and Development*, 17 December, World Bank, Paris.
197 Oxfam, Jerusalem/CMWU, Gaza, February, 2008.
198 World Health Organization (no further details attributed as cited in Amnesty International UK et al, op cit Note 187).
199 Ibid.
200 Ibid.
201 Resolution at 9th special session of the Human Rights Council, 'The grave violations of human rights in the Occupied Palestinian Territory including the recent aggression in the occupied Gaza Strip', adopted on 12 January 2009 by a recorded vote of 33 in favour, 1 against and 13 abstentions (A/HRC/S-9/L.1). Text available from www2.ohchr.org/english/bodies/hrcouncil/specialsession/9/index.htm (accessed 1 April 2009).
202 Ibid.
203 Ibid.
204 See, for example, Hirsch, A. (2009) 'Israeli war crimes allegations: what the law says', *The Guardian*, 24 March, available at www.guardian.co.uk/world/2009/mar/24/israel-war-crime-allegations-law (accessed 1 April 2009).
205 Ibid; see also BBC (2009) 'New Israel phosphorus accusation', *BBC News* website, 20 January, available at http://news.bbc.co.uk/1/hi/world/middle_east/7838598.stm (accessed 1 April 2009).
206 BBC (2009) 'Gaza "looks like earthquake zone"', *BBC News* website, 20 January, available at http://news.bbc.co.uk/1/hi/world/middle_east/7838618.stm (accessed 1 April 2009).
207 WHO (2009) 'Health situation in Gaza – 4 February 2009', available at www.who.int/hac/crises/international/wbgs/sitreps/gaza_4feb2009/en (accessed 1 April 2009).

CHAPTER 7

Towards a Comprehensive Approach to Protecting Refugees and the Internally Displaced

1. UNDERSTANDING THE ISSUES: THE AETIOLOGY OF CRIMES AGAINST HUMANITY

After all, as capital subsumes the economic life of society with the spread of integrated systems of self-regulating markets operating within the geospatial contours of modern nation states, it sunders the historical links between production and consumption that characterized community existence since its dawn.[1]

Unlike the victims of other crimes against humanity, ecological refugees bear a double burden since these groups are suffering from attacks both before and after the 'fact' of their flight. Technically they become refugees or internally displaced persons only after they face the unbearable conditions in which they find themselves for various reasons. Even in the case of 'environmental disasters', the displacement or the conditions that cause the flight are – at least in part – the result of human agency, with or without the intent to harm the affected communities.

Essentially, in this brief review of their situation, we intend to focus on both before flight (BF) and after flight (AF) conditions as both areas clearly show the *lacunae* in the laws that should protect people, first and foremost as human beings (BF), and second, as refugees (AF). The results of today's situation, the steadily increasing number of migrants, and the incremental results expected from global change in the near future, indicate that the best possible solution is one that *prevents* whatever causes the environmental hazards – hence, whatever mitigates the major cause of their migrations.

As we attempt to puzzle out the ongoing causes, starting with the effects of globalization itself, we must also be prepared to envision the additional emerging economic trends that will further aggravate the present situation. Finally, climate change is front and centre on the world's stage, as most countries now acknowledge its existence and recognize its gravity. But the additional problem is that instead of recognizing the unsustainability of both a growth model and of a model that attempts modest adjustments to the ongoing injustice that follows a globalized eco-footprint,[2] government and corporate actors attempt to prescribe a medicine that might be worse than the disease it attempts to cure.

The quest for a 'win–win' situation that might permit a modified version of business as usual (BAU) has brought, for instance, the 'solution' of biofuels to the fore with disastrous results, including 'food inflation' of which more below.[3]

Recently, an unidentified United Nations official termed the use of food for fuel in Brazil 'a crime against humanity'.[4] This 'crime' should be added to the use of grains to feed animals for the meat industry, an equally unconscionable choice in a globalized world, where hunger either kills outright or renders living conditions unacceptable, especially in developing countries, thus forcing migrations and internal displacements.[5]

Similarly, continuing to treat water as endlessly available fits in the same category of crimes against humanity when this approach is applied to industrial agriculture, to careless irrigation for both farming and optional use for lawns or golfing greens, or, once again, to the meat industry.[6]

The mindless approach to the effects of climate change and other environmental abuses is endemic to capitalism. It is magnified through globalization, where the World Trade Organization (WTO) has far more power than the World Health Organization (WHO)[7] and no specific tribunal exists to redress these injustices. These are clearly problems that affect everyone, globally; but they are particularly onerous for the most vulnerable people, including local land-based and indigenous communities, and those affected by climate extremes. In the next section we shall review the sudden events and the ongoing difficulties that result in the eventual flights of people and groups.

2. STATE, CORPORATE AND INTERNATIONAL RESPONSIBILITY BEFORE AND AFTER THE FACT: A REVIEW

Civilization is limitless multiplication of unnecessary necessities. (Mark Twain)

The earlier chapters have discussed one or more of the problems that beset the most vulnerable people and those who will become or already are ecological refugees. In this section I propose to sum up the results of the practices and conditions that lead to forced migrations, as well as the consequences that follow upon the migrations, the topic of the next subsection. The primary source of all the difficulties lies in the combination of capitalism with its endless growth mentality, and globalization, as the imposition of the primacy of economic considerations, with its relentless pursuit, without any regard for the regional/local and the cultural/religious aspects of that goal.

Given the global spread of this situation, it is unlikely that mitigating circumstances will intervene to change the current picture. It is far more likely that the aggregate and cumulative effects will continue to mount, producing increasingly large migrations. Hence, as we review the ecological assaults that will result in unliveable conditions for increasing numbers of people, and the human rights and humanitarian conditions that will ensue, including further ecological damage, the only conclusion that can be drawn is that the ongoing crisis can best be eliminated, or at least mitigated significantly, only at the outset – that is, by restraining the present environmental deterioration. From a social point of view, justice and equality cannot be established as long as the capitalist/globalized paradigm reigns, even when some groups may benefit temporarily:

> *Even when workers' consumption of use-values increases, the activities of human agents are still subsumed under a non-human imperative, the accumulation of capital as an end in itself. As long as this is the case human flourishing and human autonomy are systematically subordinated to the flourishing and autonomy of capital.*[8]

From an ecological viewpoint, the situation is much worse as too many non-renewable resources fall prey to the ongoing march of capitalist growth, increasing exponentially the lack of necessities (clean water, clean air and food), as nature's services are depleted[9] and the basics of life disappear. The most vulnerable are the poor and land-based minorities in the global South, as the ecological footprint of the affluent North appropriates the necessities of the present South, as well as those of the future of all humanity.[10]

Hence, even changing some of the international legal infrastructure and domestic regimes to assist ecological refugees, is necessary, but not sufficient: like the present emphasis on finding 'the cure' for cancer, while continuing to produce and use the chemicals that cause the disease for the most part. These chemicals attack us insidiously, are beyond our control and are beyond the reach of our possible consent; yet the imposition of strict regulations on carcinogenic substances, or restrictions on their proliferation by insisting on proven harmlessness before release, are not even considered in most of the world. Europe, however, has a regulatory regime, REACH, that shows us the way, although it is neither strict enough nor comprehensive enough.[11]

It is not this plastic bottle, that toy or this additive that must be eliminated, but the whole systemic infrastructure that leads to:

- expectations of transparency and social responsibility on the part of corporate actors;
- pre-eminence of business growth, without considering the human costs of that growth; and
- expectations of public policy choices that favour powerful nations over vulnerable communities globally.

All of these expectations must be corrected in order to attack the problem of ecological refugees at the root. We cannot hope to contain and mitigate such a large and unmanageable problem without attacking its basis, any more than we can mop up the water from the floor, as it flows from a sink constantly refilling from an open tap: the tap must be turned off first in order to succeed.

From the standpoint of a moral imperative, I proposed 'living in integrity':[12] abiding by holistic principles and, in general, living as though in a buffer zone, respecting in all our decisions and activities the ecological integrity of the core areas, thus also the biological integrity of other local inhabitants, and that of future and unborn generations that will follow us.[13]

In law, many preambles in conventions, declarations and soft law instruments (such as the Earth Charter) support ecological integrity in varying degrees, and we will return to what is already available in this chapter.

Although this approach sounds idealistic, perhaps even impractical, current realities prove that the consequences of not abiding by a 'principle of integrity' ultimately result in policies and legal infrastructures that protect neither ecology nor human life. The consequences of these policies are even harder to remedy or at least to mitigate than it might have been to correct the wrong-headed economic and environmental policies that generated the problems we face. Global warming and climate change, widespread ecological degradation and depleted resources leading, finally, to large human migrations, for which no place or solution can be found are some of the results of recent and present practices.

2a. Pre-flight conditions conducive to displacement and migrations

States have the responsibility to ensure the protection of citizen human rights, particularly for their physical safety. In Chapter 1 the focus was on several aspects of that safety, from the standpoint of public health and regarding indigenous communities. The reasons for their fights demonstrate the attacks to which they are exposed:

- attacks to their health as states are the 'enablers' of hazardous operations, explained as 'development' (largely enforced);
- attacks on collectives, rather than individuals, through forced removal from traditional territories; and
- attacks on the integrity of such territories; as without the qualitative protection, the purely quantitative aspects of these lands (i.e. their size), whatever the actual condition of the ecosystems within the lands, cannot support either the lifestyle or the culture of these people.

The criminal law categories of 'wilful blindness' or 'reckless endangerment' appear applicable to the positions of enabling governments for the former and to multinational corporations for the latter.

In Chapter 2 we noted the lack of government protection, which affects everyone, not only specific groups or racial majorities. This should be viewed as a form of persecution when it is levied against specific groups or ethnic minorities. In addition, the significant contribution of industrialized affluent countries to climate change also disproportionately affects persons living in the Arctic, as well as on islands and coastal areas, especially those who are poor and/or live 'on the land', and who follow traditional lifestyles.

This form of persecution does not deliberately target a specific ethnic or racial group; but its consequences effectively discriminate on the basis of the group's characteristics. The most vulnerable groups are the poor and those in developing countries, as well as indigenous people in North and South America; thus, belonging to a certain minority somehow invites the neglect of law-makers, government bureaucracies and even legislators as no hazardous facility is ever placed near a wealthy white neighbourhood in a suburban or city area. Similarly, we now apply the label of 'environmental racism' to decisions that place hazardous operations, whether extractive, industrial or disposal facilities, close to African American neighbourhoods in the US[14] and in developing countries in cases too numerous to list.

In addition, climate change and the encroachment of 'development' upon forests and other pristine areas that could provide 'nature's services'[15] increases desertification, soil erosion and the scarcity of water, thus leading to the 'new global menace: food inflation',[16] which now can join the rest of the ecological problems that not only cause grave disasters but also conflicts – hence, eventually migrations.

Increasingly, the new 'painless' way of addressing global emissions by turning to biofuels will lead significantly to this problem instead. Gideon Polya speaks of the 'global food crisis':

> *In summary, current global biofuel production is an obscene perversion that is a major source of greenhouse gas (GHG) pollution and is helping to drive up world food prices with the looming prospect of global famine. Biofuel diversion (e.g. for canola oil- or sugar-derived biodiesel, and grain- or sugar-derived ethanol) is threatening world food production, driving up food prices and threatening lives of billions of people.*[17]

Essentially, the anticipated 6 billion deaths due to the negative effects on agricultural production of global warming[18] will be joined by other millions dying from famine because of food price increases, due primarily to the developed world:

> *The major developed world GHG culprits on a per capita GHG pollution basis are the US, Canada and Australia (the world's biggest sugar producer), Brazil, the UK and the EU [which] are among the worst biofuel culprits.*[19]

Because of these forms of persecution and the inhumane conditions that they impose, we witness the increases in forced displacement and it is hard to see any reduction of these problems in the near future, unless the power of Western capitalist societies is reduced or eliminated. At the same time, new ecological regimes should be designed to prevent the harms and mitigate the disasters, thus achieving improvements in living conditions before the situation forces migrations.

2b. After the flight – mounting human rights breaches: Victimizing the victims

Starting with the practice of 'interception' at sea or on land, unfortunately, the persecution of vulnerable groups continues. In Chapter 1, the description of the Australian response to the request for the asylum of a boatload of refugees manifests a total disregard for the public health component of their rights. In fact, the Australian government went so far as to imperil even the crew of the Norwegian vessel (the *Tampa*) that provided humanitarian aid at sea, as required by international law.

When the Norwegian vessel was rerouted in order to allow others (not Australians) to accept the refugees temporarily, they were greeted with detention, rather than aid. The situation of all refugees in detention camps is highly discriminatory. Chapter 3 details and discusses this issue, starting with procedural rights that are ignored upon their first examination, and on to the conditions prevailing during the prolonged detention that they face, for the most part. Finally, even those who might be admitted to a country as asylum seekers are expected to conform and often to be assimilated as much as possible: this too represents a threat to the survival of a specific ethnic group, particularly to those belonging to an aboriginal community.

Assimilation means, essentially, the loss of the cultural integrity of the community, who therefore can no longer exist as a 'people'. In relation to the detention issue, Chapter 3 also discusses the meaning of 'cruel and unusual punishment or treatment', while Chapter 1 confronts what El Hinnawi terms 'the end of the line' – that is, the circumstances of refugees or IDPs when they find themselves in shanty towns or ghettos at the fringes of large cities in their adoptive country.

Hence, neither those who can avail themselves of the right to *non-refoulement* nor those who would demand their 'right to return' are treated in a way that respects their rights (civil, political, but also social, economic and cultural), let alone their right to a safe and liveable environment. For those seeking the right to return, the situation is especially grave as a safe return is usually impossible within a refugee's lifetime, after grave ecological disasters or other conditions engendered by climate change.

Hence, the situation of too many vulnerable people is extremely grave both before and after flight: it is necessary to reconsider the Convention on Refugees (CSR) itself in order to see whether there might be any hope of extending it to cover ecological refugees. In addition, we will also need to reconsider other human rights and humanitarian instruments that might better provide protection for all those who are under threat.

3. ENVIRONMENTALLY DISPLACED PERSONS: A CONVENTION FOR THEIR PROTECTION

The Yanomani people of the Brazilian rainforest, the Ukrainians around Chernobyl, the Indians affected by the Bhopal disaster, Nicaraguans whose homes were destroyed by Hurricane Mitch, Ethiopians, Rwandans and Somalis suffering from drought and lack of sustainable agriculture, Central Asians harmed by years of poor Soviet agricultural practices, Nigerians suffering from increased pollution and the loss of their land, due to government policies towards oil companies – all these groups of individuals have one thing in common: they have been displaced, forced to move from their homes and traditional habitats due wholly or in part to environmental reasons.[20]

From the theoretical list of possible causes of displacement, to the listing of real situations in all continents above, a comparison between the situation of these asylum seekers and displaced persons and the only existing convention on the status of refugees (1951) is in order. The lack of 'fit' between what we face today and what is covered by the CSR is glaring. Thus, once again, the question is whether there is any other way to protect today's refugees through the only instrument available to them, or whether it might be best to consider what other conventions, new or currently available for other issues and circumstances, might be more appropriate and, hence, more useful.

Jessica Cooper argues that a better understanding and perhaps a difference of emphasis might render the CSR sufficient to address today's needs:

> *Expanding the established refugee definition to encompass environmental refugees may require no more than an easy extension of human rights policy. Since the 1951 refugee definition is heavily imbued with human rights notions and environmental refugees are no less entitled to their basic rights and needs than their traditional counterparts, using human rights concepts to expand the refugee definition has natural appeal.*[21]

The number of environmental refugees is increasing almost daily as both catastrophic events and slowly developing problems add constantly to the present numbers, as 'it is estimated that 150 million environmental refugees will exist in the year 2050'.[22] The present numbers and the projected increases indicate that, even if possible, the simple addition of language to cover these refugees by adding them to the present Convention on Refugee Status would do nothing to address 'the root causes of the environmental changes that caused the displacement'.[23]

At any rate, the plausible category under which ecological refugees might fit (i.e. under 'membership in a particular social group') would not be a useful way of approaching their case as they 'do not have the immutable characteristics required to provide refugee status under the existing definition';[24] in fact, internally displaced persons (IDPs) are explicitly excluded as refugees:

> *... refugees are distinguished by the fact that they lack the protection of their state and therefore look to the international community to provide them with security. Environmentally displaced people, on the other hand, can usually count upon the protection of their state, even if it is limited in its capacity to provide them with emergency relief or long-term reconstruction assistance.*[25]

This might be true if all that is under consideration is a disaster caused suddenly by environmental upheavals, such as an earthquake, a tsunami or a hurricane. In contrast, this work has argued that many, if not most, states are complicit – to say the least – in environmental harms. Whether they ratify agreements that will be harmful to both ecosystems and the land-based minorities who inhabit a specific area, or issue permits for drilling, exploration or deforestation in territories where indigenous peoples do not consent to those hazardous operations, or refuse to ratify instruments that would mitigate the disastrous effect of climate change – it seems obvious that the affected populations 'lack the protection of their state'.

The United Nations High Commissioner for Refugees (UNHCR) only accepts one exception to its pronouncement: when 'acts of environmental destruction, such as poisoning of wells, the burning of crops, or the draining of marshlands are methods purposefully used to persecute, intimidate or displace a particular population'.[26] This 'exception' appears to be flawed, however, since the CSR itself does not require proven intent – that is, 'purposeful' persecution to be proven – before the refugee may be recognized (see Chapter 1), but only the *subjective*, well-grounded (*objectively* known or observable) fear of persecution on the part of the refugee herself.

Therefore, there is no special intent component required. In addition, for the most part, affected persons and communities are, indeed, politically powerless to ameliorate their situation,[27] even when they are not, technically, 'powerless' – that is, when they can vote and perhaps even sue those who inflict harm in the courts, or win their cases. Such *de facto* powerlessness is present in the narrative of the cases litigated under the Alien Torts Claims Act (ATCA) that we considered in Chapter 3. As well, Chapters 5 and 6 describe the economic oppression affecting developing countries, and the powerlessness of self-governing Arctic peoples, such as those of the Nunavut Territory in the Canadian Arctic. Hence, a deeper understanding of the limits of self-determination and of civil and political rights, especially under today's economic power in a globalized world, regulated by capitalist institutions, shows the extent of the flaws in the UNHCR definitions. It might be too difficult to widen the reach of the present CSR, and to ensure a deeper meaning for its present provisions. In that case, it might be best to consider once again what other international law instruments might be useful for the protection of ecological refugees.

3a. Existing international legal instruments for the protection of ecological refugees

> *Around the globe, millions of people are at risk of displacement due to climate change. At the end of last year, it was reported that the first inhabited island was submerged as a result of rising sea levels.*[28] *And island nations across Central Pacific, South Pacific, and from Bangladesh to Egypt, risk partial or complete displacement by the middle of this century.*[29]

It seems obvious from our discussion so far: the issues of ecological refugees are primarily, though not exclusively, ecological issues – that is, unless the interface between human rights and ecological integrity is accepted, it will not be possible to design instruments that will truly address the problem, or even use current existing instruments to the best advantage of present and future migrants. We have appealed to a number of international conventions and declarations in the previous chapters, as our discussion unfolded. We will not try to review them all at this time. Perhaps they might be understood differently, and there might be others worthy of consideration.

Ideally, we would need formally binding treaties to help refugees to find their place in the crowded agendas of the International Criminal Court, or the International Court of Justice. This does not appear to be a likely prospect, at least not until the interface between human and environmental rights is recognized and accepted, as well as codified internationally, and this requirement appears to present an almost insurmountable block. Yet, Falstrom justly repeats:

> *We are all responsible for the environment and the environmental degradation on this planet, and therefore it is our responsibility as a global community to assist those who suffer the most as a result.*[30]

The question is, what can we appeal to most effectively in order to accomplish this task? An appropriate starting point might be the Universal Declaration of Human Rights,[31] Article 14(1) states:

> *... everyone has the right to seek and enjoy in other countries asylum from persecution.*

In addition, Article 25 of the same declaration provides the right to:

> … a standard of living adequate for the health and well-being … including food, clothing, housing and medical care and necessary social services…

Since that declaration, there has been a proliferation of agreements intended to protect individuals, starting with the international covenants of 1966.[32] However, even that impressive list of instruments, for the most part, does not include a serious consideration of environmental issues, nor do these ever rise to the same level of importance as human rights, if they are considered at all.

At best Article 14(1) and Article 25 should protect the ecological rights of citizens within their own country.[33] The exponential growth of ecological migrants clearly demonstrates that even these venerable and well-established principles are not seriously followed in the home countries of refugees. Yet this is what must be done in order to stem the tide of refugees and start mitigating the conditions that cause it.

In international environmental law, the 'lack of international consensus on environmental norms' persists,[34] as does the 'disconnect' between these norms and human rights, in the mind of legislators, judges and even advocates (see Chapter 4).

The approach that should redress this imbalance is one which relies on *jus cogens* norms, which include both human rights and humanitarian law, such as the right to life, the rights of children, the prevention of genocide and crimes against humanity, as well as the prevention of racial and gender discrimination, all of which represent obligations *erga omnes* on the part of the international community, whether or not individual states have ratified the respective conventions. As noted in Chapter 4 (page 87), Article 53 of the Vienna Convention on the Law of Treaties emphasizes the status of *jus cogens* norms:

> A treaty is void if, at the time of its conclusion, it conflicts with a peremptory norm of general international law. For the purposes of the present Convention, a peremptory norm of general international law is a norm accepted and recognized by the international community of States as a whole as a norm from which no derogation is permitted and which can be modified only by subsequent norm of general international law having the same character.[35]

The US has not ratified the Vienna Convention, but recognizes it as a 'codification of the customary international law governing international agreements'.[36] The best-known application of this principle to human/environmental rights is found in the classical 'Dissent' by ICJ Judge Christian Weeramantry in the Gabcikovo-Nagymaros case.[37] All of these difficulties make it desirable to seek some other international instruments. For instance, there is another approach and another convention that should be considered as it alone straddles the realms of nature and culture: the World Heritage Convention.[38]

3b. The World Heritage Convention

> [Member states] should be responsible not only for combating deterioration and damage to the cultural and natural heritage, but also for investigating their causes in order that the evil may be attacked at its root.[39]

Despite this strong directive, the World Heritage Convention (WHC), of which the US is a 'key member', has not addressed the need for strong climate change policies.[40] The World Heritage Convention already represents strong protection for both the cultural and natural aspects of the Heritage of Mankind, and this applies especially well to the plight of aboriginal peoples, although to my knowledge, it has not yet been so used in case law.

Article 1 of this Convention for the Protection of the World Cultural and Natural Heritage defines 'sites' as 'works of man or the combined works of nature and man, and areas including archaeological sites which are of outstanding universal value from the historical, aesthetic, ethnological or anthropological point of view'. Article 2 defines 'natural heritage' thus:

> Article 2: *natural features consisting of physical and biological formations or groups of such formations, which are of outstanding universal value from the aesthetic or scientific point of view; geological and physiographical formations and precisely delineated areas which constitute the habitat of threatened species of animals and plants of outstanding universal value from the point of view of science or conservation; natural sites or precisely delineated natural areas of outstanding universal value from the point of view of science, conservation or natural beauty.*

The duty to identify and protect cultural and natural sites that are part of the world's global heritage accrues to states; but the international community has increasingly recognized its obligation to protect endangered species since many areas that are the habitats of these species, or the location of these natural sites, exceed the boundaries of one state and, often, the state's economic capacity.

Although, thus far, the convention has not been interpreted as providing special protection for indigenous peoples or ecological refugees, the fact that the former are the best existing source of protection for both natural sites and threatened and endangered species should ensure that this connection be noted, and that the convention be extended this way in the future. In addition to the protection of physical elements of sites and the sites themselves, there is also a further component that adds to the appropriateness of this convention to indigenous rights. Speaking of the protection of non-commercial goods, Tullio Scovazzi says:

> *Les Etats peuvent aussi établir un régime spécial visant certain biens-dont les biens culturel-afin d'assurer la jouissance de leurs bénéfices non vénaux (émotionnels ou conceptuels) par les générations présentes et futures, et de partager les sacrifices lies a leur protection. [States may also establish a special regime regarding certain goods, such as cultural goods, in order to ensure the enjoyment of the benefits of non-commercial goods (emotional or conceptual) by present and future generations, and to participate in the sacrifices required for their protection.]*[41]

The cultural/emotional/conceptual special goods here proposed fit well with the cultural/religious aspects of aboriginal rights in international law for the protection of cultural integrity of those communities. Without special reference to indigenous peoples, Scovazzi adds:

Un aspect important de la protection transfrontière est constitué par la préoccupation de l'intégrité des biens naturels, avec la conséquente obligation de restitution des biens, à l'Etat qui en aurait été dépouillé (principe de non-appauvrissement du patrimoine culturels des autres Etats). [An important aspect of transborder protection is the concern for the integrity of cultural goods, with the consequent obligation of restitution of these goods to the state that has been deprived of them (the principle of non-impoverishment of the cultural patrimony of other states).][42]

The deprivations suffered by aboriginal peoples are not as simple as the theft of a statue or a fresco or some other art treasure: no 'restitution' is possible for the devastation of the Arctic lands and the ongoing extermination of the wildlife and the ecosystem services upon which Arctic peoples depend.

Furthermore, it is not only that the exclusive possession of an artefact has been violated, but the violation of Arctic people's rights to their heritage is, *ipso facto*, a violation of our heritage, globally. Hence, the previous arguments insisting that the derogation from the norms of environmental and human rights protection ought to be considered breaches of *erga omnes* obligations:

> *Human right interests ... have worked a revolutionary change upon many of the classic rules of international law as a result of the realization by states in their international practice, that we have a deep interest in the way other states treat their own interest.*[43]

The lack of ecological integrity in the territories of aboriginal peoples *may* be corrected with a lot of restoration work; but it may never be returned to its original condition. That, once again, is not only a problem for the people directly involved in the area: it is an ongoing disaster for humankind, as indicated, for instance, by the interface between the melting of the polar ice and glaciers, and the increase in the number and severity of hurricanes, sea surges and tsunamis, and the hazardous rising of sea levels near island states and sea-level cities. Other cases of eco-crimes on aboriginal territories always include degradation of those lands and surrounding areas, often also involving water scarcity, desertification and alteration of ecosystem function – hence the loss of 'nature's services'.[44]

In all such cases, the problems of 'restitution' are immense as the appropriated territorial integrity is not an object that can simply be put back. The same is true of the industrial operations that result in the loss of biological integrity – hence, in the loss of health and normal function of the indigenous peoples affected.

Aside from the applicability of the WCH to indigenous and local communities, the consequences of climate change and chemical alterations of natural systems have grave consequences for biodiversity that include:

> *... species migrations; local, regional and global extinctions; change in the timing of biological events; and changes in the intensity and frequency of ecological disturbances, such as flooding, wildfires and droughts.*[45]

The 'poster boys' of climate change are polar bears and the ice and glaciers where they reside; but the glacial melts that we are facing are having dire consequences for local people, local fauna and ecosystems, and – in general – for all populations who are facing increasing water scarcity.[46] The 'right to water' is a hotly debated issue,[47] and children's deaths in sub-Saharan Africa and Asia[48] are due to unsafe and insufficient water, as well as to water-borne diseases. The deaths show clearly the grave impact of water shortages from Palestine to Darfur and beyond:

> ... according to UN Secretary Ban Ki Moon, the situation in Darfur 'began as an ecological crisis arising at least in part from climate change, with increasing food insecurity and lack of rainfall – and ultimately insufficient food and water for the population – leading to conflict.[49]

At any rate, the WHC does impose state party obligations, under Articles 4, 5 and 6, although 'Articles 4 and 5 are broad, potentially leaving much more room for state party discretion'.[50] Article 6, however, states that state parties may not 'undertake deliberate measures that might damage world heritage'.[51] Finally, then, we find a binding legal obligation, albeit one which makes no explicit references to environmental refugees or IDPs, or – in general – to populations forced to migrate because of grave damage to their traditional area, including its elimination because of rising sea levels, glacial melts, or desertification and scarcity of food and water.

Not all regions form part of the United Nations Educational, Scientific and Cultural Organization (UNESCO) World Heritage Centre's List of World Sites; but the biodiversity and cultural diversity that are steadily disappearing are surely a central part of the heritage of mankind. Thus, perhaps, this convention might be appealed to for the protection of ecological refugees. In fact, its mandates, if seriously observed, could be used for the most important task of all: to prevent to a great extent ecological disasters and migrations – that of protecting biodiversity and ecological integrity *before* their disappearance engenders mass migrations.

4. A CONVENTION MODELLED ON THE CONVENTION AGAINST TORTURE?

> *This proposed Convention on the Protection of Environmentally Displaced Persons would address the root cause of migration. This crucial element is ignored by those proposing merely to include environmentally displaced persons in the existing refugee structure. As in the Convention against Torture, the Convention on the Protection of Environmentally Displaced Persons should incorporate extensive provisions outlining state responsibility to find, correct, and prevent occurrences of the environmental degradation and destruction that force people to migrate.*[52]

Dana Falstrom proposes a new convention based upon the structure of the Convention against Torture. It would define an environmentally displaced person as 'an individual forced to leave his or her home due to environmental reasons',[53] and the environmental reasons would include much that has been described in these pages (with the exception, perhaps, of extremes caused by climate change, including the water shortages noted in the previous section):

> ... *water shortage due to pollution, food shortages due to desertification or pollution, a sudden environmental disaster such as a hurricane, tornado, etc., or inhabitability of an area due to pollution toxicity, or a sudden disaster such as a nuclear explosion.*[54]

Asylum seekers could receive temporary refugee status, but no permanent rights to residency: the right to *non-refoulement* would be honoured; but it is not clear what could be done about the 'right to return' for the refugees who would want that option. It would be highly desirable to elevate environmental harms to the level of *jus cogens* norms such as the prohibition of torture, and I, too, have been advocating such a move,[55] given the gross human rights violations that ensue. State parties would be required to incorporate explicitly the mandates of such a convention in their constitutions and other municipal infrastructures.

State parties would have the responsibility to prevent the environmental degradation and ongoing toxicity of most industrial operations – hence, to ensure strict regulations and monitoring of all hazards, including all present business operations. Self-monitoring and the procedural systems that now prevail in most corporate activities would have to be eliminated in favour of more robust regulatory regimes. In support of her proposal, Falstrom notes:

- the number of new conventions protecting human rights in recent years;
- the present UNHCR programme designed to assist states that 'take in environmentally displaced persons'; and
- the fact that other UN agencies and non-governmental organizations (NGOs) have been providing humanitarian aid as needed, already for some time.[56]

However, there are powerful blocks in place to halt the emergence of such a document, let alone its ratification: the main one is the inability of legislators and judges to fully appreciate the grave human impact of environmental harms. The environment is still perceived – for the most part – as 'out there', or as separate from human beings, hence unconnected to human rights. Law schools do not provide any training or information on the interface between environment and humanity. Even environmental ethicists at universities concentrate on the moral principles that may be either anthropocentric or eco-biocentric; but when the latter are presented, the relation between such principles and human survival is seldom discussed.[57]

Falstrom's proposal would resonate better when viewed in connection with environmental justice/environmental racism, and the abundant literature that treats those issues (and has done so for some time, particularly in the US, in relation to African American communities).[58] That literature explicitly connects environmental causes to health effects and racial discrimination, particularly evident as hazardous operations are routinely sited in areas inhabited by African Americans and Hispanics.

The research in these cases may be usefully employed to argue for the criminalization of environmental racism,[59] and we will examine the possibility of yet another convention that might be useful to ecological refugees: a Convention on Public Health.[60] The advantage for such a move would be to propose a goal that is hard to ignore or to treat as unimportant – that is, the promotion of health itself. In addition, there is a practical consideration that must not be forgotten: most powerful nations have followed the previous US administration under George W. Bush's presidency in ignoring the *jus cogens* norm against torture itself by appealing to principles of national interest and to the right of self-defence. In this climate, then, any attempt to extend further the meaning of 'torture' may be doomed to failure right from the start.

4a. A Framework Convention for Global Health (FCGH)

> *What is truly needed, and which richer countries instinctively (although not always adequately) do for their own citizens, is to meet what I call 'basic survival needs'... Basic survival needs include sanitation and sewage, pest control, clean air and water, tobacco reduction, diet and nutrition, essential medicines and vaccines, and functioning health systems for the prevention, detection and mitigation of disease and premature death.*[61]

There are two particularly important components of an instrument designed for the protection of environmentally displaced persons or ecological refugees, and both appear to be present in Gostin's proposal:

1. the recognition of the environmental aspects of human health; and
2. the understanding of the right to health as more than the right to medical care when ill, important though that is.

For the former, 'basic survival needs' include 'clean air and water' and 'nutrition'; for the latter, 'health systems for the prevention, detection and mitigation of disease and premature death'. In addition, rather than leaving these aspects of the right to health to the goodwill of individual states, Gostin also proposes that 'the World Health Organization (WHO) or a newly created institution could set ongoing standards, monitor progress, and mediate disputes'.[62]

Such a convention would go to the heart of the environmental justice issue – that is, to the blatant inequalities in life expectancy, the incidence of infectious diseases and chronic diseases disproportionately present among the poor and developing countries, on the one hand, and rich nations, on the other:[63]

> *Chances of living merely to the age of five are low among the world's poor compared with the wealthy. In many developing countries, child mortality rates can be 25 to 30 times higher than the rate in the developed world. In fact, of the 10.8 million children under five who die each year, 10 million are from low-income countries – more than twice the number of children born annually in the United States and Canada combined. As little as one concrete example offers a sense of perspective on the global health gap between the rich and the poor. The World Bank reports that in one year alone, 14 million of the poorest people in the world died, while only 4 million would have died if this population had the same death rate as the global rich.*[64]

These are just some of the statistics that indicate the ongoing injustice that has been viewed as criminal by some.[65] No one denies the pivotal importance of socio-economic status in health statistics, and the conclusion is that the poorer and less powerful are most affected globally:

Vulnerable populations – women, children, and indigenous persons – in the world's poorest countries thus are even less healthy than their peers. In many of the poorest regions, women have little social, political, or economic control over their lives and communities, which are prime indicators of poor health.[66]

Those who will become ecological refugees are among these vulnerable populations, and those whose actions precipitate their flight or contribute significantly to it should have sufficient knowledge to anticipate the consequences of their activities. Not only are information and knowledge spread almost instantly now, but large corporations have research and development departments with larger budgets than many small countries; in addition, the governments that permit or encourage their activities are equally informed agents. Hence, the consequences of the hazardous actions that engender environmental migrations cannot be ignored, nor can ignorance be claimed, even when these consequences occur in areas where they will affect primarily marginalized populations. In fact, one could argue that the activities are kept deliberately from affecting the favoured majority, at the expense of minorities:

Indigenous persons experience an 'epidemiological accumulation', whereby disease and disability are exacerbated due to unmet basic needs.[67]

The situation of local and indigenous communities, as globalization and global change conspire to render their conditions unliveable, demonstrates clearly why, first, nations and corporate agents that contribute to the situation or are directly causative of it cannot and should not claim ignorance and avoid their responsibility; and, second, most often even after migration, the conditions of those individuals and communities remain equally hazardous.

People who migrate in large numbers to 'flee situations of famine, violence, civil unrest or war',[68] added to those who flee a destroyed habitat and ongoing attacks on their health, only to be exposed to 'gross unsanitary conditions in refugee camps',[69] are equally at risk before and after migrations. Hence, not only is the situation of migrants most often *not* ameliorated by their flight, but their presence in a new area 'places a strain on drinking water, food supplies, and sewage systems, providing a breeding ground for infectious diseases'.[70]

Most developed countries are well aware of this dimension of the displacement of large groups as they often cite these or similar concerns as the major reason for not granting asylum, and for viewing refugees in an unfavourable light. It is paradoxical, however, to find that when these circumstances affect poor local communities or indigenous groups within these countries' own borders, the same arguments and concerns are not taken seriously by the same states who acknowledge the issues when migrants arrive at their borders.

At any rate, unlike the precepts of the Convention on Torture, the pronouncements of the WHO are normally accepted by regional and national governments, as are the health-related prohibitions that are given primacy in the media. Recent examples include outbreaks of severe acute respiratory syndrome (SARS) and the effects of the WHO's declarations on the hazards present in the Canadian Province of Ontario,[71] and the emergence of bovine spongiform encephalopathy (BSE) and its effects on meat trade, animal agriculture and meat consumption, in the UK, Italy, France and elsewhere.[72]

Unlike other human rights concerns, health concerns are readily accepted, for the most part, by national infrastructures, and are promoted to the public, although in many cases economy and trade might be affected. In other cases, however, powerful economic interests block or obstruct the appropriate measures: the best example can be found in relation to large chemical interests and their influence on preventative measures for cancer,[73] as well as the ongoing proliferation of untested chemicals, despite their documented effects:[74]

> *The WHO Constitution envisaged an agency that would use law and exercise power to proactively promote the attainment of 'the highest possible level of health'. But the agency has never met these key expectations.*[75]

Many scholars have criticized the WHO's passive/reactive position, and have advocated a much stronger involvement in the right to health on their part than their past performance has demonstrated:

> *WHO's advancement of national and international public health and supervisory institutions is critical to furthering the realization of the right to health. Encouraging countries to develop specific binding legal obligations with respect to the right to health, and publicizing their compliance and non-compliance with those obligations, can powerfully influence states to rethink priorities and redirect national resources to national health care.*[76]

The WHO's mandate of 'Health for All', declared in 1977, was intended to be achieved for all the world's citizens by 2000.[77] Nevertheless, it is hard to find any appeals to science or health in the jurisprudence concerning indigenous people's rights. There appears to be a disjoint between the WHO health mandate, despite its position in the UN, and other documents, which, even if they address the question of health, do so in general terms and with no reference to the WHO, let alone to the possibility of binding regulations. For instance, Article 7 of the Human Rights Council[78] states:

> 1 *Indigenous individuals have the right to life, physical and mental integrity, liberty and security of persons.*
> 2 *Indigenous peoples have the collective right to live in freedom, peace and security as distinct peoples and shall not be subjected to any act of genocide or any other act of violence including forcibly removing children of the group to another group.*[79]

The problem is that, at this time, these articles and the whole draft itself do not represent binding legal obligations. Hence the desirability of involving the WHO – or, better yet, the WHA (World Health Administration) – to add their authoritative voice to the requirements proposed by this report. The WHA has a power that should be exercised in addition to the technical recommendations it normally issues:

> *WHA also enjoys authority to adopt regulations regarding sanitary and quarantine requirements to deter the international spread of disease, and standards for safety, purity*

and potency of biological and pharmaceutical products that move in international commerce, among other things.[80]

Thus, a precedent exists whereby an arm of the WHO – that is, the WHA – its legislative organ, is empowered to limit trade, and also to limit freedom of action of individuals in the usual public health fashion through sanitary regulations and quarantines.

Public health is the mandate and the duty of the WHO, internationally, and they do have a history of speaking for the most vulnerable – for instance, for children's exposures and diseases: all of the signatories of the Convention on the Rights of the Child (CRC) are obliged to report periodically to Geneva how their countries are integrating the mandates of that document within their own domestic laws.[81]

The WHO has been very active organizing ministerial conferences on health in Europe, where the 'silent epidemic' of chemical/toxic exposures are described and presented based on the exhaustive research that the WHO has accumulated.[82] They have also organized a meeting addressing questions of aboriginal peoples' health recently in Vancouver, Canada.[83] As an organ of the UN, their presence ought to make a stronger impact as they indict specific threats, while grave global challenges persist – from the return of drug-resistant tuberculosis, to cholera epidemics and the persistence of malaria, as well as the presence of an ever-growing body of research on exposures.[84] Taylor adds:

> *These global health challenges have not only exposed the inadequacy of national public health systems, but also evidenced the increasing interdependence of world health. Indigenous public health issues can no longer be regarded as purely a matter of domestic concern. Increasingly public health challenges are recognized as transcending national boundaries.*[85]

Essentially, then, the right to health, guaranteed by the International Covenant of Economic, Social and Cultural Rights,[86] Article 12, 1 provides for 'the right of everyone to the enjoyment of the highest attainable standard of physical and mental health'; hence, it recognizes that the right to health 'is an essential element of human dignity'.[87] The 'guarantee' intended, of course, is not for the absence of disease for all, a patently impossible requirement. The right is, instead, intended to ensure certain preconditions for health and normal function, not to healthcare.[88] I have argued elsewhere that the preconditions to physical and mental health as well as that to normal development are specifically based on the requirement to ensure ecological health for all human beings.[89]

Yet, the WHO has recently achieved an important success, despite the powerful interests that have been deployed against it for too long: the Framework Convention on Tobacco Control.[90] Gostin adds:

> *The critical question, however, is whether the WHO can build on these recent achievements to deal with the most important and intractable health problems in the poorest regions of the world.*[91]

Other UN instruments such as the International Covenant of Economic, Social and Cultural Rights (ICESCR) have attempted to deal with these problems in a constructive way;[92] but the power of trade and of the WTO cannot be denied as the International Health Regulations, Article 2, for instance, states that 'health measures must avoid unnecessary interference with international traffic and trade'.

Therefore, it seems that despite the pronouncements of many treaties and declarations of the UN (mostly in their preambular sections), addressing the 'right to health', there is no robust instrument making that aspiration a human right in practice. The primary components of the proposed Framework Convention on Global Health, according to Gostin, will include the following:

- *Build capacity, so that all countries have enduring and effective health systems.*
- *Set priorities, so that international assistance is directed to meeting basic survival needs.*
- *Engage stakeholders, so that a wide variety of state and non-state actors can bring to bear their resources and expertise.*
- *Coordinate activities, so that programmes among the proliferating number of actors operating around the world are harmonized.*
- *Evaluate and monitor progress, so that goals are met and promises are kept.*[93]

This is not the appropriate forum for a detailed discussion of an initiative that Gostin and his collaborators have put together in an excellent and ground-breaking issue of the *Georgetown Law Review* (vol 96, January 2008). But from our point of view, the emergence of such an instrument in international law would represent one of the best possible avenues to stop or significantly diminish the mounting flow of migrants at the start, and to also improve the situation of the ecological refugees who have already been affected and are living in squalid and hazardous circumstances today.

Ecological refugees are, by definition, severely affected by environmental factors; hence, whatever instrument may be devised to include their protection must incorporate strong environmental regulations, together with the clear acknowledgement of the interface between environmental factors and human rights. The question of health as a right is already present in many international law instruments, such as the UN Charter,[94] the Universal Declaration of Human Rights, which requires a 'standard of living adequate for ... health',[95] the International Covenant on Economic, Social and Cultural Rights (ICESCR), mandating the 'highest attainable standard of physical and mental health',[96] as well as the preamble of the WHO's Constitution, which declares health to be a 'fundamental right of every human being'.

Essentially, then, given the presence of strong sentiments in favour of the protection of health, coupled with the general institutional climate favouring human rights, there seems to be a solid ground for the promotion of such a new convention. The convention, if ratified, would serve well the populations that are currently at risk, as we saw in our discussion thus far. Only one aspect of the issue is still missing: the codification of environmental harms as human health harms – hence, as human rights violations.

This basic *lacuna* has been plaguing us in our assessment of the situation of ecological refugees all along. It has also rendered the proposals we have considered equally lacking – that is, the possibility of using an improved, more comprehensive understanding of the present CSR;[97] the present Common Heritage of Mankind;[98] and the formulation of a totally new convention based on the Convention on Torture.[99]

Perhaps the proposed Framework Convention on Public Health might offer the best chance of protection for endangered local populations under present conditions. In fact, many of the problems we have encountered through this work, as well as many of the recommendations that Gostin proposes, are forcefully reiterated in the 2008 final report of the Commission on Social Determinants of Health.[100]

4b. The WHO and social determinants of health

> *Social injustice is killing people on a grand scale.*[101]

The unfair and unequal health conditions faced by people in the North and South are here described as 'the result of a toxic combination of poor social policies and programmes, unfair economic arrangements, and bad politics' and we must therefore 'bring the two agendas of health equity and climate change together'.[102] These problems exist in almost all countries, but also within each country – hence the need to support equitable global governance. It is highly significant that the WHO sees its organization as one of the 'global institutions' which, with civil society and governments, are meant to support and even monitor the implementation of their plans, governed by three 'overarching recommendations':

1 *Improve daily living conditions.*
2 *Tackle the inequitable distribution of power, money, and resources.*
3 *Measure and understand the problem and assess the impact of action.*[103]

These three principles appear to propose an active and involved role for the WHO, rather than limiting it to its usual reactive or purely technical role. Particularly significant is the new emphasis found in this document, on 'equity from the start' – that is, early child development (ECD), as it 'provides one of the greatest potentials to reduce health inequities within a generation'.[104]

The range of circumstances this document considers far exceeds the considerations of diseases, as it indicts climate change, as well as urbanization, migrations, current building and transport patterns, among many other issues and activities, stating that we 'must place health and health equity at the heart of urban governance and planning'. Hence, the summary advocates both 'fundamental health improvement', such as those that would follow upon the major policy issues named so far, but also proposes universal healthcare as a basic social determinant of health.

The second point (the inequitable distribution of power, money and resources), requires 'policy coherence'. For example:

> *trade policy that actively encourages the unfettered production, trade, and consumption of foods high in fats and sugars to the detriment of fruit and vegetable production is contradictory to health policy, which recommends relatively little consumption of high-fat, high-sugar foods and increased consumption of fruit and vegetables.*[105]

Nevertheless, this is an example applicable only to developed wealthy countries. It is worthy of note that, despite the acceptance this document displays of the harms that chemical and other industrial exposures do particularly in relation to the perinatal period, this aspect of health policy is not discussed.

At any rate, the aim to 'place responsibility for action on health and health equity at the highest level of government, and ensure its coherent consideration across all policies'[106] should certainly include the worse harms to communities in developing countries and to indigenous peoples, although neither is explicitly named. These harms should include the exposure to industrial activities of all kinds, including mining and extractive processes, all of which take place primarily in developing countries, near local and indigenous communities, or in developed countries in areas classified as 'brown fields' that are for the most part *de facto* racially segregated, especially in urban settings as 'almost 1 billion live in slums'.[107] Hence, the WHO prescription is to:

> *Ensure that economic and social policy responses to climate change and other environmental degradation take into account health equity.*[108]

Once again, the WHO does not go far enough as there is no evidence here of ensuring that the practices that foster climate change and industrially fostered environmental degradation be eliminated (as in the example of unhealthy food choices listed above). All that is required (and that is a significant improvement in itself) is that 'health equity' should be taken into account and, later, that universal healthcare be adopted. The lack of free healthcare is particularly deplorable in developed countries:

> *Upwards of 100 million people are pushed into poverty each year through catastrophic household health costs. This is unacceptable.*[109]

The section on 'Market responsibility', in addition, offers a clear guideline and plan that should include these issues:

> *Health is not a tradable commodity. It is a matter of rights and a public sector duty. As such, resources for health must be equitable and universal. There are three linked issues. First, experience shows that commercialization of vital social goods such as education and health care produces health inequity. Provision of such vital social goods must be governed by the public sector, rather than being left to markets. Second, there needs to be public sector leadership in effective national and international regulation of products, activities, and conditions that damage health or lead to health inequities. These together mean that, third, competent, regular health equity impact assessment of all policy-making and market regulation should be institutionalized nationally and internationally.*[110]

Aside from the major responsibility of the state, the recommendation to 'Institutionalize consideration of health and health equity impact in national and international economic agreements and policy-making'[111] is excellent, although 'consideration' is a weak term. Given the admitted connection between health equity and human rights, surely the 'primacy' of health and health equity would be a far better term in this regard.

However, as I have advocated repeatedly in my own work,[112] the final recommendation in this section presents a highly desirable goal:

Strengthen WHO leadership in global action on social determinants of health, institutionalizing social determinants of health as a guiding principle across WHO departments and country programmes.[113]

This goal is also spelled out in detail a few pages later:

WHO is the mandated leader in global health. It is time to enhance WHO's leadership role through the agenda for action on the social determinants of health and global health equity. This involves a range of actions, including:

- Policy coherence globally and nationally: *adopt a stewardship role supporting social determinants of health capacity-building and policy coherence across partner agencies in the multilateral system; strengthen technical capacity globally and among member states for representation of public health in all major multilateral fora; and support member states in developing mechanisms for coherent policy and ISA for social determinants of health.*
- Measurement and evaluation: *support goal-setting on health equity and monitoring progress on health equity between and within countries as a core developmental objective; support the establishment of national health equity surveillance systems in member states and build necessary technical capacities in countries; support member states in development and use of health equity impact assessment tools and other health equity-related tools such as a national equity gauge; and convene a regular global meeting as part of a periodic review of the global situation.*
- Enhancing WHO capacity: *build internal social determinants of health capacity across the WHO, from headquarters through the regional offices, to country programmes.*[114]

Nevertheless, we also need to turn to the basis for seeking asylum – that is, ecological degradation and ongoing and sudden ecological disasters, as well as the consequences of the invasive and ubiquitous activities of industrial globalization. In the next section we will attempt to assess what is already available today, both in law, and in some of the declaratory/inspirational documents of soft law, in order to attempt to frame yet another proposed Convention for the Protection of Ecological Refugees, based on the primacy of ecological integrity for global governance.

5. TOWARDS A COMPREHENSIVE APPROACH: ECOLOGICAL INTEGRITY FOR GLOBAL GOVERNANCE

Human well-being is highly dependent on ecosystems, and ecosystems are sensitive to human activities. Ecosystem degradation in one geographic area affects other parts of the world; in this way living systems (e.g. air, sea, forests and soil) are interconnected, as are people and places in the world.[115]

The Framework Convention of Global Health, if it will ever come to be, will be a powerful asset for the protection of ecological refugees and of local and indigenous communities everywhere. Nevertheless, there are a couple of problematic aspects that might render even such a splendid document less than effective. Gostin rightly criticizes the record of the WHO as both too limited and ineffective. But the representatives of that organization respond to that critique by explaining their status as a 'stage', as well as an 'actor', as they are dependent upon the goodwill and the funds of the states that comprise it, and must be accountable to them, as well as being an independent voice. In addition, we must keep in mind the dependence of the states themselves on both voters, easily swayed by spin doctors, and campaigns, well-funded by industry and represented by junk/prostitute science (recall years of tobacco propaganda in that regard).

One of the salient aspects of the proposed Framework Convention for Global Health is the commitment to 'engage stakeholders' so that 'a wide variety of state and non-state actors can bring to bear their resources and expertise'. Unfortunately, as well as resources and expertise, states will also bring their political positions, commitments and economic interest to bear. In that case the FCGH would find itself roughly in the same position as the WHO: a 'stage' where competing interest may play out, thus diminishing significantly the convention's ability to meet its lofty goals. For both the WHO and the FCGH, because of their professional status, I would like to propose that too much 'democratic' involvement may be a disadvantage, not a boon. No doctor involves stakeholders when asked to diagnose or prescribe treatment, although in certain circumstances a second or even a third opinion may be sought, remaining, however, always in the ambit of medical expertise alone. Doctors who are swayed by the interests of pharmaceutical companies, for instance, may be considered as guilty of malpractice, despite the expertise and resources of these corporations.

It is probably too much to hope for this at the present time; but it might be best if the FCGH were to be recognized as protecting 'basic rights',[116] as it actually does, hence as imposing obligations *erga omnes*, rather than accepting stakeholders' input for its decisions. Possible breaches, then, should be treated as other grave crimes, such as torture, crimes against humanity and racial discrimination, and brought to the International Court of Justice (ICJ) or the ICC, if they occur. At any rate, the relations between environment/health/basic rights is well documented:

> *Of the 50 or so armed conflicts currently in progress, approximately 20 have an environmental dimension or are partly environmentally induced. Half of the latter are associated with arid land. Many of these wars are often overlooked by the central governments and the world at large... Evidence is emerging for a correlation between poverty, desertification and conflicts of various kinds in arid and semiarid areas. The common ground is the process of exclusion of vulnerable groups who are subject to suffering and oppression, and who depend on fragile ecosystems under stress.*[117]

This was written in 1994: now, together with all the other climate change issues that result in large migrations, the 'basic rights' of too many poverty-stricken individuals in developing countries are not respected. Minorities in developed countries are also affected as they were, for instance, in the aftermath of Hurricane Katrina. Those were also IDPs, part of what has been termed 'an emerging migration crisis [that] will spiral out of control'. Christian Aid predicts that 'a further 1 billion people will be forced out of their homes between now and 2050'.[118] In addition, it is also widely accepted that projects such as dams, oil and gas pipelines and other activities governed by trade rules contribute significantly to displacements and migrations.[119]

Yet, despite the magnitude and reality of the crisis, and the widely acknowledged contributing causes that produce it, the human right to a healthy environment is – at best – an 'emerging' issue today,[120] as the pivotal connection between trade and environment/public health is largely ignored.[121]

The debate on this issue can never be solved while we attempt to adapt an anthropocentric position, with the dubious 'benefits' of development pitted against vague 'environmental concerns'. What is needed here is to raise clearly the question of justice – that is, *whose* benefits and *whose* choice should have primacy.[122] Atapattu remarks:

> *It must be stressed that this discussion of a possible human right to a healthy environment should not be viewed as advocating an anthropocentric approach to environmental protection… At no point should the anthropocentric approach override or replace an ecocentric approach to environmental protection.*[123]

This has been precisely the position advocated in defence of the principle of integrity:[124] no separation is possible between eco/biocentrism and anthropocentric environmental concern; and an interconnection exists between biocentric environmentalism and human health; hence, human rights are basic to moral concern and should be equally basic to international law. Atapattu's argument hinges on what rights we have in this regard, other than the 'right' to be polluted. As a result, we should consider what is available today in law before proposing a possible new or modified instrument.

There have been many international instruments proposing various environmentally related rights, including, at times, appeals to the right to life, to health and to an adequate standard of living. Prudence Taylor says:

> *How valid is the argument that a human right to a sound environment can be derived from existing right to life, health and adequate standard of living? There is no logical rationale for this argument. These rights are obviously connected to the state of the environment because their realization, in particular, depends upon the protection of the environment. However, this connection alone does not justify recognition of a distinct human right to a sound environment. Protection of the environment is a prerequisite to assuring all human rights. Thus failure to provide environmental protection can amount to a violation of basic human rights. But this may not be sufficient to protect the environment adequately.*[125]

A brief survey of what is available in law for protection of human life and health in relation to the environment shows little awareness of the major issues. In fact, environmental concerns ought to have been placed as binding regulations before hazardous industrial activities proliferated after the 1950s. At best, and in a very limited way, environmental harms may be redressed after they have occurred, either in rare cases in domestic courts or, in even rarer cases, in international law at the European Court of Human Rights. At best, a handful of cases have been recognized in this way. But even if we had a much more developed jurisprudence instead of a few cases, the *nature* of environmental/

health harms is such that redress after-the-fact is patently insufficient: many of the harms that occur may not be compensated for. Grave damages to the health or normal development of children, for instance, may not be remedied, and the destruction of previously healthy habitats, to the point where migrations ensue, demand much more than after-the-fact 'redress'.

Hence, the point is not to permit a victim of environmental harm to vindicate a violation of a right to a clean environment; at best,[126] it is rather to institute strict *erga omnes* obligations on state and non-state actors, *not* to permit the violation of ecological rights in the first place. Nevertheless, it will be useful to review briefly what is available in law today.

5a. IDPs and ecological rights: A brief overview of existing regulatory regimes in regional and international law

> *Sometimes they flee across national frontiers. Sometimes not. To them it makes little difference. They may not even know which country they are in, when they first arrive in a place of refuge. Those who are still in their own country are in just as desperate need of protection and relief as those who are not. And those who have crossed a border sometimes find themselves better off than the 'host' population which gives them refuge, but which does not benefit from the same assistance programmes.*[127]

The previous sections discuss what is currently available for the protection of public health for refugees and IDPs in international law. It is clear that the most important issue is the existence of *lacunae* in law regarding the interface between public health and the environment. The same problem arises in reverse when we start from ecological considerations: the connection between pollution, climate change and human exposures is not explicitly recognized in any legal instrument.

For the most part, 'environmental rights' are not acknowledged, either as right of the environment, or as human rights to the environment. In fact, the ascription of 'rights in this regard, according to Birnie and Boyle, is only the means 'to force lawmakers and institutions to take account of those interests' in the context of existing legal rules.[128] As we have noted repeatedly in the previous pages, this is not sufficient to protect the rights of individuals or the collectives, such as indigenous communities, from the harms caused in and through the environment, despite the fact that these claims are somewhat stronger than those that would protect the environment itself.

One of the most serious problems we encounter is the fact that individual rights include the rights of legal persons such as corporations, and the latter bear a great deal of responsibility for the harms caused, while the natural persons that direct their activities, for the most part, are far removed from the location where the resulting hazards take place; hence, they do not suffer the consequences of their actions, but only reap the resulting profits of their operations.[129]

National laws ought to prevent these harms and the burdens they impose on vulnerable populations by much stricter controls of corporate activities than what is present today. In turn, the role of international law should be to harmonize standards between states, and to control the activities of multinational corporations (MNCs) and international trade, especially, but not exclusively in the resolution of disputes.[130] However, because of the gravity of the human rights/health consequences that result from environmental violations, the question of redress as well as that of public participation – that is, the emphasis on procedural right – should be viewed as secondary. When considered from the standpoint of affected groups, whether these are able to migrate or not, the main issue is not whether there might be instruments or *ad hoc* tribunals to help compensate them in some way after the fact, but whether there might be legal regimes robust enough to avoid the environmental degradation that gives rise to the human/health hazards they encounter before they are forced to flee or suffer the damage.

The history of environmental human rights has been vague, imprecise and weak from the start since the 1972 Stockholm United Nations Conference on the Human Environment:

> *Man has the fundamental right to freedom, equality and adequate conditions of life in an environment of a quality that permits a life of dignity and wellbeing.*[131]

Twenty years later, the Rio Conference on Environment and Development was even less specific:

> *Human beings are at the centre of concerns for sustainable development. They are entitled to a healthy and productive life in harmony with nature.*[132]

This principle is especially problematic as many of those who are forced to flee from unbearable living conditions do so because of the imposition of forced and unwanted 'development', as local and indigenous communities most often do not desire or consent to corporate activities that will interrupt or even eliminate their chosen 'healthy and productive life in harmony with nature',[133] only to replace it with unsafe water, including leachings from their cyanide pond perhaps, and food scarcity, as well as exposure to the multiple hazardous substances that characterize industrial mining and extractive activities in general.[134]

A number of regional instruments recognize human environmental rights. The World Charter for Nature (1982) was the first instrument 'to adopt an ecocentric approach',[135] although it is not a binding instrument. Other regional and international instruments that make some reference to various aspects of environmental rights are the African Charter,[136] the 1966 ICESCR[137] and the 1961 European Social Charter,[138] among others. These instruments refer to human entitlement to a decent, healthy or viable environment, rather than to enforceable rights.

In addition, the relevant jurisprudence includes little more than a handful of cases, some of which have already been discussed above; these are, for the most part, decisions of the UNHRC and the ECHR;[139] however, no case, to my knowledge, recognizes the rights of communities displaced by so-called 'development' or affected by the results of the activities (and the ecological footprint) of Western industrial countries.

In 1994, the UN Sub-commission on the Prevention of Discrimination of Minorities proposed a Declaration of Principles on Human Rights and the Environment that includes the following:

1 *freedom from pollution, environmental degradation and activities that adversely affect the environment, or threaten life, health, livelihood, well-being or sustainable development;*
2 *protection and preservation of the air, soil, water, sea ice, flora and fauna, and the essential processes and areas necessary to maintain biological diversity and ecosystems;*
3 *the highest attainable standard of health;*
4 *safe and healthy food, water and working environment;*
5 *adequate housing, land tenure and living conditions in a secure, healthy and ecologically sound environment;*
6 *ecologically sound access to nature and the conservation and sustainable use of nature and natural resources;*
7 *preservation of unique sites;*
8 *enjoyment of traditional life and subsistence for indigenous peoples.*[140]

The comprehensive and well-thought-out document, however, is only *lex ferenda*, and nothing even comparable exists in *lex lata* today.[141] If such a document could be entrenched against trade and property agreement, the present refugee crisis might not exist. The necessity for protected environmental conditions is a 'basic condition of life, indispensable to the promotion of human dignity and welfare, and to the fulfilment of other human rights'.[142]

Some will argue that such rights cannot be viewed as inalienable or non-derogable (hence they cannot be seen to fit under the category of *jus cogens* norms) like other natural rights.[143] Yet, those who hesitate, such as Handl[144] to accept the vital importance of environmental human rights have been writing long before the full impact of climate change and industrial exposures were well understood and documented.[145] Hence, borrowing a page from Judge Weeramantry (cited above) and his classic 'dissenting opinion', we can respond that we cannot set the standards for human rights to a much lower earlier level, when much more has been learned since the time when court decisions or treaties were put in place that embraced a totally different understanding of the real situation. Human rights must be respected with full knowledge of *present* scientific research, rather than favouring the economic interests of institutions and organizations that refuse to change their perceptions in order to protect legal, not natural, persons.

Equally flawed is the approach of Kiss and Shelton, who propose that given 'the impossibility of defining an ideal environment in abstract terms', institutions and courts should develop 'their own interpretations'.[146] But neither legislators nor courts are prepared to keep up with the scientific knowledge required to understand such complex issues, unless an institution such as the WHO steps in, as argued above in this chapter.

A simple point is that the protection of birds starts with the protection of the air they need as well as their food; protection of fish begins with unpolluted water of a temperature that is suited to their natural development. Like it or not, most human beings are in the same position, although those who are wealthy enough are, at least for a time, protected from the raw environmental damage that does not spare the poor and vulnerable.

Even from a practical point of view, the adoption of an instrument such as the one cited above would eliminate, for the most part, the hazardous conditions that form the basis of the discrimination towards racial and ethnic minorities that we have discussed, and would reinstitute respect for fragile ecosystems, thus probably restoring many of the areas that no longer support life and health, and hence fostering displacement and migrations.

6. GLOBAL GOVERNANCE FOR ECOLOGICAL INTEGRITY

The Earth Charter – II Ecological Integrity

5 *Protect and restore the integrity of Earth's ecological systems with special concern for biological diversity and the natural processes that sustain life.*[147]

Ecological integrity and its protection have been present in national, bi-national and international law since 1972.[148] Ecological integrity was also discussed as the basis for normative principles in Chapter 4. At this time, ecological integrity either as a scientific notion or as a normative one is not the main issue. Both aspects have been treated at length during the last 20 years or so.[149]

However, in law, which is the main concern at this time, it is primarily used in the preambular sections of treaties, declarations and mission statements.[150] The most thorough and authoritative use can be found in Principle II of the Earth Charter cited above. The Earth Charter is a soft law instrument, and it has been adopted by the World Conservation Union (IUCN) and other bodies, as well as several countries and cities. Yet there is no binding instrument available for the protection of ecological integrity except for some local instruments intended to protect a specific park or area; in international law, ecological integrity is mentioned in water law, starting with the US Clean Water Act (1972).[151] For land areas, there is no specific instrument for its protection. Birnie and Boyle address the topic only from the standpoint of the Convention on Biological Diversity.[152] Ecological integrity and the protection of 'core' areas, as well as the need for buffer zones to surround areas of integrity, is discussed and promoted in scientific research.[153] What is needed, however, is to recognize and cement the connection between integrity and human rights.

In Chapter 2 we noted that the year 2008 marks the 60th anniversary of the UN Declaration of Human Rights. In addition, in the previous chapters, we noted the importance of some aspects of the proliferation of human rights instruments during recent years, as well as the extension of the 'law of war', humanitarian law, to deal with situations well beyond those engendered by military conflicts.[154] The main problem is that almost all of the newly established rights are individual liberal rights, since universal rights must be understood as *either* liberal and individualistic *or* based on collective interests and concerns. Michael Rosenfeld explains these two contrasting conceptions:

> *One [is] the liberal conception of universalism, which is steeped in enlightenment philosophy, individualism and liberalism. The other one, the Marxist conception of universalism ... is shaped on collectivist approach, but is also, we should not forget, a universalistic proposition: that all human beings are the same.*[155]

Although no particular meeting or special journal issue has so far been produced to celebrate 60 years of human rights, 50 years did merit recognition. A whole issue of the *Pace International Law Review* was devoted to that topic, including special sessions/articles on the meaning of human rights in contrast to relativism, and the discussion of human rights and non-state actors, among other issues. These two topics are particularly relevant for this work, and will be discussed in the next section.

6a. Universal human rights: Individuals or collectives? Universalism and relativism

> *One of those problems is the problem of group rights, which is the one that brings out most acutely the issue of where do we draw the line between particularism and universalism.*[156]

Rosenfeld argues that particularism, rather than relativism, poses the most serious problem to the universality of human rights. One of the examples he proposes is the question of female genital mutilation (FGM); another is the problem of a woman's status within an indigenous community. In both cases, some believe that 'the group ought to be given external protection'[157] – the rules that prevail inside separate minority social groups and communities ought to be free from any attempts from outside the group.[158]

Rosenfeld argues that a merely procedural answer, one that leaves the substantive issue unanswered, is insufficient. He notes that:

> *Therefore there has been a return to considering what is the content [of each issue]. We have to have a sort of thicker vision of society and of rights.*[159]

It is too easy to answer a relativist by saying 'you have your community (or religious) position, and we have ours'. In the case of FGM, which is one of the possible accepted CSR grounds of 'persecution', when women use it to ensure refugee status for themselves and their children, this is clearly an insufficient answer. In order to engage the relativist, however, one must have a standard to evaluate competing rights. Rosenfeld concludes by saying that:

> *... one ought to have a pluralist answer, meaning one ought to look at the claims, weigh the claims and take into account the desire, for instance, of individuals within the group to ... generate changes within their own group.*[160]

In the case of FGM and many others, this would be essentially a non-answer. I doubt that long-entrenched practices are often open to change in the groups where they are practised, and even if a 'counting of (dissenting) heads' were possible, I doubt that a majority of entrenched believers in the practice would make FGM morally (or legally) acceptable. Nor do I see any reason to attempt to 'make bridges', as Rosenfeld proposes,[161] with those who hold positions that are universally (or almost) held to be morally repugnant, and with those who support their positions.

It might be better to look elsewhere for answers, rather than seek appeasement and extend tolerance. Whether it is for the consideration of those who seek asylum or any other human rights debate between a universalistic and a relativistic position, a standard may be found in natural law.

As H. Lauterpacht argued as early as 1950:

> *There is nothing inevitably arbitrary about the law of nature. On the contrary, it has been a constant challenge to arbitrariness in the name of what is, in the long run universal, because generally accepted, and commendable to reason and to the nature of man, including his sense of justice.*[162]

> *It is sheer nonsense to reject natural law because of its alleged 'religious' – hence, partisan – point of view. Such a viewpoint ignores clear historical evidence: both Aristotle before Aquinas, and Grotius after him, were supporters of natural law, yet were not committed to the Christian faith. Grotius clearly states that natural law 'would have a degree of validity even if we should concede ... that there is no God'.*[163]

To return to the question of the interface between ecological integrity and human rights, I have argued that the connection between the two is of cardinal importance, and that serious attacks on the ecological integrity of an area or on the biological integrity of its inhabitants ought to be treated as 'eco-crimes' rather than as breaches of environmental regulations.[164] This is a position held by many international non-governmental organizations (INGOs) through their concrete defence of the victims of many such crimes. For instance, Amnesty International and the Goldman Prize Organization played an important role in the fight against Royal Dutch Shell for its treatment of the Ogoni people and, eventually, the incarceration of Ken Saro-Wiwa and others, culminating in their murder, despite the work of these organizations.[165]

Both state and non-state actors, as we saw in the previous chapters, play important roles in the plight of ecological refugees, as they do in all other aspects of globalization,[166] although their 'law-making' capacities remain limited and informal. Nevertheless they maintain a pivotal role, as they often counter the claims and assertions originating from corporate actors. For instance, Human Rights Watch has 'targeted its work' specifically on extractive industries and, especially, on oil extraction.[167] Human rights 'were not drafted to apply to corporations', and a real 'conceptual gap' results in the application of human rights in these cases:

> *Recognizing that corporations have become a potent force in the shaping of human rights worldwide, Human Rights Watch believes that businesses have a duty to avoid complicity in or advantage from, human rights violations... We are most concerned about situations of direct corporate complicity. In these instances, businesses facilitate or collaborate in government human rights violations. So while government forces commit the violations, corporations have acted as accomplices and beneficiaries.*[168]

There is no need to belabour a point that has been made repeatedly in these pages. A final example might be the role that the World Bank plays and some of the positive steps it has taken recently to mitigate (though not to eliminate) its role in the violations of human rights in local communities in developing countries:

> ... the human rights issues presented by Bank-supported projects are often more directly related to the overall human rights environment that exists in the country.[169]

The World Bank supports almost all of the major projects in various continents – hence, its potential impact on the life conditions of many local communities in developing countries. As well, many of the forced migrations originate from the displacements caused by developments that they might support. In its favour, one may consider the excellent *Operational Manual*,[170] but most of the problems arise when the rules are operationalized in a flawed manner. The Bank's 'Investigative Panels,' however, most often take the part of the affected or displaced people, who can request an investigation and intervention.[171] Much more could be said about the role of state and non-state actors in engendering the conditions that cause the very displacements that we have been discussing, with the very projects that are described as 'development' and as improving the living conditions of these communities. But the living conditions of any community cannot be engendered while violating their right to life, health, normal development and their chosen place of residence.

6b. Conclusion

> In the way the International Tribunal for the former Yugoslavia has adjudicated these crimes, they appear to be profound, apolitical offences against the international community – indeed, against humanity. In some regard, this is the criminal law's transformative goal, mediating the universal and the particular through principles emphasizing racial motive.[172]

In the last section, we surveyed some of the ways in which the development of human rights was discussed during the 60 years since the inception of the Universal Declaration. Most of the discussions reported in the special issue of the *Pace International Law Review* are just as timely today. But it seems as though the last ten years have been a period of simply marking time, rather than forging ahead with needed progress in many areas. In fact, the exponential growth of the problem of displaced persons and ecological refugees, together with the increasing hazards engendered by climate change, indicate that, if anything, global justice and human rights protections have receded rather than progressed.

In a 50th anniversary publication, Guy Goodwin-Gill admits that in 2001, the 1951 Convention on Refugee Status was viewed as flawed for many reasons; but, he argues, it is still an important and valid document, although he admits 'its failing focus':

> ... its inability to accommodate the 'new refugees' from ethnic violence and gender-based persecution; in its deafness to national, regional and international security concerns; in its inflexibility when faced with **the changing nature of flight and movement**.[173]

It is worthy of note that only the vague reference to the 'changing nature of flight and movement' *may* be viewed as referring to the grave problems and issues discussed in this work: no mention is made of climate change and the extreme conditions it engenders, to highlight just one major problem.

In contrast, James Hathaway sees clearly the present 'challenges' to refugee rights. However, for him, it is mostly a matter of implementation:

> *To be clear, it is suggested here that the goal should be to re-conceive the* mechanisms *by which international refugee law, including the refugee rights regime are implemented – not to undertake a renegotiation of the Refugee Convention itself.*[174]

Still, like Goodwin-Gill, Hathaway only considers convention refugees. IDPs and ecological refugees are almost totally beyond the radar of these major scholars. Even for convention refugees, domestic legal systems ought to incorporate the international legal regime of the CSR.[175] Yet, enforceability falters, even for convention refugees, and the underfunded and under-supported UNHCR cannot possibly extend its protection to the increasing numbers who need it:

> *The generality of UNHCR's Article 35 authority notwithstanding, supervision of refugee rights by the agency remains very much a matter of standard-setting and private representations to states.*[176]

Equally telling, 'no application has ever been made to the International Court of Justice, as contemplated by Article 38 of the Refugee Convention'.[177]

In that case, if it is generally acknowledged that the CSR, as currently formulated and implemented, is insufficient to protect those that it was designed to protect, then it must be clear that the human rights of IDPs and other victims of displacement today are ignored.

Hathaway proposes using the ICCPR, the ICESCR and other such instruments to force accountability on the part of states, and to question the treatment of asylum seekers.[178] He recognizes that, even aside from the mechanics of implementation, the 'political will' of the international community appears to be faltering as well.

For ecological refugees, this has been an ongoing challenge, as indicated in this book, although a thorough analysis of the issue is beyond the scope of the present work. Nevertheless Hathaway's 'epilogue', with its timely concerns, demonstrates once again the necessity for a thorough evaluation of an under-inclusive instrument that not only does not serve its own avowed constituency, but is also almost impossible to extend to protect the mounting numbers of those who are currently excluded.

Teitel advocates the use of humanitarian law (or the 'law of war') for crimes that are, for the most part, 'apolitical', and which attack humanity. But this is a strategy that could (and should) be employed to punish after the fact. The migrants discussed in these pages are the most vulnerable of humanity – hence our first consideration ought to be an appeal to a health convention, or a new convention echoing the Convention against Torture, as we have argued above, to mitigate the actions and events that lead to the flight of asylum seekers. However, a legal regime that might succeed by using criminal law's 'transformative power' to ensure a new approach, and perhaps a new legal instrument, might help to eliminate the present gap between existing international instruments for the protection of environment, health and human rights and the reality that confronts us.

Such a document has been drafted by Michel Prieur and his collaborators in December 2008 (see Appendix 3). The 'Considerations' proposed to the 'Contracting Parties' are extremely instructive, as they include 'natural and technological hazards', as well as listing the causes of a number of negative and hazardous environmental conditions, thus reaching far beyond the harms caused by single catastrophic environmental events. Equally important are the references to 'the preservation of cultures', 'those who cannot subsist in arid zones and will become ecological refugees' and 'environmental displacement' in relation to indigenous and tribal peoples in independent countries.

The reference to the Convention to Combat Desertification might also be applied to the situation of circumpolar people, who might have been mentioned as well, together with their suit before the ECHR, in relation to CERD. The latter, it can be argued, has an important role to play and could be better utilized for the protection of ecological refugees.

Chapter 3 (Article 11) of the document proposes a World Agency for Environmentally-Displaced Persons (WAEP) as well as a possible World Fund for the Environmentally-Displaced (WFED): the existence of such institutions, combined with the presence of this convention, would aid immeasurably the cause of environmentally displaced persons, or ecological refugees, as does the fact that the document starts by enumerating existing international legal instruments which, if properly understood and enforced, might be able to limit the environmental harms before the need for flight would arise. Perhaps this is the most significant aspect of this important new initiative.

NOTES

1 Westra, R. (2008) 'Green Marxism and institutional structure of a global socialist future', in R. Albritton, R. Jessop and R. Westra (eds) *Political Economy and Global Capitalism*, Anthem Press, London, pp219–236.
2 Wackernagel, M. and Rees, W. E. (1996) *Our Ecological Footprint*, New Society Publishers, Gabriola Island, Canada.
3 Pimentel, D. (2008) 'The ecological and energy integrity of corn ethanol production', in L. Westra, K. Bosselmann and R. Westra (eds) *Reconciling Human Existence and Ecological Integrity*, Earthscan, London, UK, pp245–255; see also McKenna, B. (2008) 'Basic commodities crunch – the new global menace: Food inflation', *The Globe and Mail*, Ontario edition, 29 March, ppA1, A8.
4 Euronews, 21 March 2008.
5 Pogge, T. (2008) 'Aligned: Global justice and ecology', in L. Westra, K. Bosselmann and R. Westra (eds) *Reconciling Human Existence with Ecological Integrity*, Earthscan, London, pp147–158; Pogge, T. (2001) 'Priorities of global justice', in T. Pogge (ed) *Global Justice*, Blackwell Publishers, Oxford, UK, pp6–23; O'Neill, O. (2001) 'Agents of justice', in T. Pogge (ed) *Global Justice*, Blackwell Publishers, Oxford, UK, pp188–203; LaFollette, H. and May, L. (1996) 'Suffer the little children', in W. Aiken and H. LaFollette (eds) *World Hunger and Morality*, Prentice Hall, Upper Saddle River, NJ, pp70–84.

6 See Dellapenna, J. (2008) 'A human right to water: An ethical position or a realizable goal?', in L. Westra, K. Bosselmann and R. Westra (eds) *Reconciling Human Existence with Ecological Integrity*, Earthscan, London, pp183–194.
7 Westra, L. (2004) *Ecoviolence and the Law*, Transnational Publishers Inc., Ardsley, NY.
8 Smith, T. (2008) 'Technological dynamism and the normative justification of global capitalism', in R. Albritton, R. Jessop and R. Westra (eds) *Political Economy and Global Capitalism*, Anthem Press, London, UK, pp25–42.
9 Daily, G. (1997) *Nature's Services: Societal Dependence on Natural Ecosystems*, Island Press, Washington, DC.
10 Westra, L. (2006) *Environmental Justice and the Rights of Unborn and Future Generations*, Earthscan, London.
11 Regulation (EC) No. 1907/2006 of the European Parliament and of the Council on the Registration, Evaluation, Authorization and Restriction of Chemicals (REACH)
12 Westra, L. (1998) *Living in Integrity*, Rowman Littlefield, Lanham, MD.
13 Westra (2006), op cit Note 10.
14 See Robert Bullard's 'Decision making' (pp3–28), Laura Westra's 'The faces of environmental racism: Titusville, Alabama and BFI' (pp113–140) and Daniel Wigley and Kristin Shrader-Frechette's 'Consent, equity and environmental justice: A Louisiana case study' (pp141–166), all three being chapters in L. Westra and B. Lawson (eds) *Faces of Environmental Racism* (second edition), Rowman Littlefield, Lanham, MD; also, regarding Canada, Westra, L. (1997) 'Terrorism at Oka', in A. Wellington, A. Greenbaum and W. Cragg (eds) *Canadian Issues in Environmental Ethics*, Broadview Press, Peterborough, Ontario, Canada; and also see Westra, L. (1998) 'Development and environmental racism: The case of Ken Saro-Wiwa and the Ogoni', in L. Westra (ed) *Living in Integrity*, Rowan Littlefield, Lanham, MD, Chapter 5.
15 Daily, G. (1997), op cit Note 9.
16 McKenna (2008), op cit Note 3.
17 Polya, G. (2008) 'World food price crisis – genocidal UK, EU, US biofuel perversion threatens billions', 31 March, www.countercurrent.org/polya310.htm.
18 See James Lovelock at www.businessandmedia.org/printer/2007/2007102222/13333.aspx.
19 Polya (2008), op cit Note 17, p5.
20 Falstrom, D. Z. (2001) 'Stemming the flow of environmental displacement: Creating a Convention to Protect Persons and Preserve the Environment', *Colorado Journal of International Law and Policy*, vol 1, pp2–3; see also Westra (1998), op cit Note 12, Chapter 5.
21 Cooper, J. B. (1998) 'Environmental refugees: Meeting the requirements of the refugee definition', *New York University Environmental Law Journal*, vol 6, pp480–488.
22 Penn State University, College of Earth and Mineral Sciences, *Environmental Refugees*, www.ems.psu.edu/info/explore/Envirefu.html.
23 Falstrom (2001), op cit Note 20, p5.
24 Ibid.
25 UNHCR (1997) *The State of The World's Refugees 1997: A Humanitarian Agenda*, Oxford University Press, Oxford, UK, available for download from www.unhcr.org/publ/3eef1d896.html. The quotation is from Box 1.2 in Chapter 1, 'Safeguarding human security' (pages unnumbered in the web edition).
26 Falstom (2001), op cit Note 20, p22, note 46.
27 Ibid, pp13–14.
28 Lean, G. (2006) 'Disappearing world: Global warming claims tropical island', *The Independent*, 24 December 2006; referring to research by Jadavpur University's School of Oceanographic Studies.
29 McAdam, J. (2007) *Climate Change 'Refugees' and International Law*, NSW Bar Association, 24 October, 2007, p1.

30 Falstrom (2001), op cit Note 20, p5.
31 *Universal Declaration of Human Rights*, G.A. Res. 217 A(III), UN GAOR, 3rd Sess., at 71, UN Doc. A/210(1948).
32 The International Covenant on Economic, Social and Cultural Rights, G.A. Res. 2200A (XXI), 21 UN GAOR Supp. (No. 16) at 49, UN Doc. A/6316 (1966), 993 U.N.T.S. 3, entered into force 3 Jan 1976; and the International Covenant on Political and Civil Rights, G.A. Res. 2200A (XXI), 21 UN GAOR Supp. (No. 16) at 52, UN Doc. A/6316 (1966), 999 U.N.T.S. 171, entered into force 23 Mar 1976; see also the Rio Declaration on Environment and Development, UN Conference on Environment and Development (UNCED) at Rio de Janeiro, 13 June 1992, UN Doc. A/CONF.151/26 (vol 1)(1992); Declaration of the United Nations Conference on the Human Environment, Stockholm, 16 June 1972, UN Doc. A/CONF.48/14/Rev. 1 (1972); African Charter on Human and Peoples' Rights, adopted 27 June 1981, OAU Doc. CAB/LEG/67/3 rev. 5, 21 I.L.M. 58 (1982), entered into force, 21 Oct 1986; Additional Protocol to the American Convention on Human Rights in the Area of Economic, Social and Cultural Rights (Protocol of San Salvador), OAS Doc. OES/Ser.L.V/II.82 Doc.6 Rev.1, at 67 (1992); Convention on the Elimination of All Forms of Discrimination Against Women, adopted 18 Dec 1979, entered into force 3 Sept 1981, G.A. Res. 34/180, 34 UN GAOR Supp. (No. 46) at 193, UN Doc. A/34/46 (1980); Convention on the Elimination of All Forms of Racial Discrimination, opened for signature 7 Mar 1966, entered into force 4 Jan 1969, 660 U.N.T.S. 195; Convention on the Rights of the Child, opened for signature 20 Nov 1989, entered into force, 2 Sept 1990, GA Res. 44/25; Convention on the Prevention and Punishment of the Crime of Genocide, adopted 9 Dec 1948, entered into force 12 Jan 1951, 78 U.N.T.S. 277; Vienna Convention for the Protection of the Ozone Layer, adopted 22 Mar, 1985, entered into force 22 Sept 1988, UNEP Doc. IG.53/5, 26 I.L.M. 1529 (1987); United Nations Framework Convention on Climate Change, adopted 29 May 1992, entered into force, 21 Mar 1994, 31 I.L.M. 849 (1992); Convention on Biological Diversity, adopted 5 June 1992, entered into force 29 December 1993, 31 I.L.M. 818 (1992); United Nations Convention to the Combat Desertification in Countries Experiencing Serious Drought and/or Desertification Particularly in Africa, adopted 14 Oct, 1994, entered into force 26 Dec 1996, 33 I.L.M. 1328 (1994); Kyoto Protocol to the United Nations Framework Convention on Climate Change, adopted 10 Dec, 1997, 37 I.L.M. 22 (1998).
33 Falstrom (2001), op cit Note 20, p26.
34 Rosencranz, A. and Campbell, R. (1999) 'Foreign environmental and human rights suits against US corporations in US courts', *Stanford Environmental Law Journal*, vol 18, no 2, June, pp145–208.
35 Vienna Convention on the Law of Treaties, 1155 UNTS 331, 23 May 1969, in force 1980.
36 Thorson, E. J. (2008) 'On thin ice: The failure of the United States and the World Heritage Committee to take climate change mitigation pursuant to the World Heritage Convention seriously', *Environmental Law*, vol 38, pp139–162, n.133.
37 *Gabcikovo-Nagymaros Project* (Hungary/Slovakia), 1997, I.C.J. 4 (Judgment of 25 Sept).
38 UNESCO, World Heritage Commission, *Report: Convention Concerning the Protection of the World Cultural and Natural Heritage*, at VIII(A.1), UN Doc.WHC-95/CONF.203/16/Jan31/96.
39 Maheu, R., Director General of UNESCO, address to the drafters of the Convention, World Heritage Ctr., World Heritage List, http://whc.unesco.org/en/list/[WHC].
40 Thorson (2008), op cit Note 36, p139.
41 Scovazzi, T. (2007) *Le Patrimoine Culturel de l'Humanité*, Martinus Nijhoff, Leiden.
42 Ibid, p4.
43 D'Amato, A. (1987) 'Trashing customary international law', *American Journal of International Law*, vol 81, pp101–104.
44 Daily, G. (1997) *Nature's Services: Societal Dependence on Natural Ecosystems*, Island Press, Washington, DC.

45 Thorson (2008), op cit Note 36, p142, n.11; see also Hannah, L. et al (2002) 'Conservation biology in a changing climate', *Conservation Biology*, vol 16, pp264–265.
46 Thorson (2008), op cit Note 36, p143.
47 Dellapenna (2008), op cit Note 6.
48 Westra (2006), op cit Note 10, Chapter 8 and Appendices.
49 McAdam (2007), op cit Note 29, p5; see Ban Ki Moon, 16 June 2007, 'A climate culprit in Darfur', www.washingtonpost.com, pA15.
50 Thorson (2008), op cit Note 36, p160.
51 Ibid, p162; see also *Commonwealth of Australia versus Tasmania*, 158 C.L.R. 1, para 63.
52 Falstrom (2001), op cit Note 20, pp22–23.
53 Ibid, p22.
54 Ibid.
55 Westra (2004), op cit Note 7.
56 Falstrom (2001), op cit Note 20, p27.
57 But see Westra, L. (1994) *An Environmental Proposal for Ethics: The Principle of Integrity*, Rowman Littlefield, Lanham, MD; Westra, L. (1998) *Living in Integrity*, Rowman Littlefield, Lanham, MD, attempting to bridge that gap.
58 Bullard, R. (2001) 'Decision making', in L. Westra and B. Lawson (eds) *Faces of Environmental Racism* (second edition), Rowman Littlefield, Lanham, MD; Rees, W. and Westra, L. (2006) 'Environmental justice in a resource-limited world', in J. Agyeman, R. D. Bullard and R. Evans (eds), *Just Sustainabilities*, Earthscan, London, pp99–124.
59 Westra (2004), op cit Note 7.
60 Gostin, L. O. (2008) 'Meeting basic survival needs of the world's least healthy people: Toward a framework convention on global health', *Georgetown Law Journal*, vol 96, no 2, January, pp331–392; Heinzerling, L. (2008) 'Climate change, human health and the post-cautionary principle', *Georgetown Law Journal*, vol 96, no 2, January, pp445–460.
61 Gostin (2008), ibid.
62 Ibid.
63 Ibid; WHO Commission on Social Determinants of Health, at www.who.int/social_determinants/en; also Hill, K. (2006) 'Making deaths count', in *Bulletin of the WHO*, vol 84, p161; Ruger, J. and Hak-Ju, K. (2006) 'Global health inequalities: An international comparison', *Journal of Epidemiology Community Health*, vol 60, pp928–936; Westra (2006), op cit Note 10, Appendix 5 Developing Countries Reports on CRC Implementation.
64 Gostin (2008), op cit Note 60, p337; see also Global Health Council, *Child Health Fact Sheet*, www.globehealth.org.view_top.php3?id=226; Gawtkin, D. R. and Guillot, M. (2000) *The Burden of Disease among the Global Poor: Current Situation, Future Trends, and Implications for Strategy*, pp19–20.
65 Sachs, W. (2007) *Climate Change and Human Rights*, WDEV Special Report 1, World Economy and Development In Brief, Luxembourg; Westra (2006), op cit Note 10.
66 Gostin (2008), op cit Note 60, p341.
67 Ibid; see also Kunitz, S. J. (2000) 'Globalization, states, and the health of indigenous peoples', *American Journal of Public Health*, vol 90, no 10, p1531; Rojas, R. (2005) *Health Programs of the Indigenous Peoples of the Americas: Action Plan 2005–2007*, www.paho.org/English/AD/THS/OS/Indigne_PLANOS_05_07_eng.pdf.
68 Gostin (2008), op cit Note 60, p348.
69 Ibid.; see also Thomas, S. L. and Thomas, S. D. M. (2004) 'Displacement and health', *British Medical Bulletin*, vol 69, pp115–127.
70 Gostin (2008), op cit Note 60, p348.
71 WHO, *WHO Issues Emergency Travel Advisory* (15 March 2003); see also Fidler, D. P. (2004) 'Germs, governance, and global public health in the wake of SARS', *Journal of Clinical Investigation*, vol 113, p799.

72 Westra, L. (2007) *Environmental Justice and the Rights of Indigenous Peoples*, Earthscan, London, pp264–267.
73 Epstein, S. (1978) *The Politics of Cancer*, Sierra Club Books, San Francisco, CA.
74 Grandjean, P. and Landrigan, P. (2006) 'Developmental neurotoxicity of industrial chemicals', *The Lancet*, November; see also Westra (2007), op cit Note 72.
75 Gostin (2008), op cit Note 60, p375; Burci, G. L. and Vignes, C.-H. (2004) *World Health Organization*, Kluwer, The Hague, The Netherlands; see also WHO Constitution, Preamble.
76 Taylor, A. L. (1992) 'Making the World Health Organization work: A legal framework for universal access to the conditions for health', *American Journal of Law and Medicine*, vol 18, pp301–346.
77 WHA, the legislative organ of WHO, issued the WHA Res. 30.43, 30th World Health Assembly, 14th plenary meeting (19 May 1977), in WHO (1985) *Handbook of Resolutions and Decisions of the World Health Assembly and the Executive Board*, World Health Organization, Geneva.
78 Resolution 2006/2 – Working Group of the Commission on Human Rights to elaborate a draft declaration in accordance with paragraph 5 of the General Assembly resolution 49/214 of 23 December 1994.
79 Report of the Working Group on its 11th Sess., Geneva, 5–16 December 2005, and 30 Jan–3 Feb 2006 (E/CN.4/2006/79).
80 Taylor (1992), op cit Note 76, p302, fn.1.
81 See, for instance, a summary of some of these reports from five developing countries in Westra (2006), op cit Note 10, Chapter 9, and 'Templates' in Appendix 2.
82 WHO (2002) 'Summary', in *World Report on Violence and Health*, WHO, Geneva; Licari, L., Nemer, L. and Tamburlini, G. (eds) (2005) *Children's Health and the Environment*, World Health Organization Regional Office for Europe, Copenhagen, Denmark.
83 WHO Commission – Social Determinants of Health.
84 Grandjean and Landrigan (2006), op cit Note 74.
85 Taylor (1992), op cit Note 76, p306; see also Gelert, G. A. et al (1989) 'The obsolescence of distinct domestic and international health sectors', *Journal of Public Health Policy*, vol 10, p421.
86 UN GAOR, 21st Sess., Supp. No. 16, 49, UN Doc. A/631 (1966).
87 Taylor (1992), op cit Note 76, p310.
88 Westra (2004), op cit Note 7.
89 International Bill of Human Rights, UN Doc. A/565 1948.
90 WHO, Framework Convention on Tobacco Control, WHO Doc. A56/VR/4 (21 May 2003) available at www.who.int/gb/ebwha/pdf_files/WHA56/ea56rl.pdf; see also Taylor, A. and Leviriere, J. (2005) 'Origins of the WHO Framework Convention on Tobacco Control', *American Journal of Public Health*, vol 95, p936.
91 Gostin (2008), op cit Note 60, p378.
92 General Comment No. 1 on Economic, Social and Cultural Rights, 'The Rights to the Highest Attainable Standard of Health', UN Doc. E/C.12/2000/4(2000); UN Commission on Human Rights, *The Right of Everyone to the Enjoyment of the Highest Attainable Standard of Physical and Mental Health*, Commission on Human Rights Resolution 2002/31, UN Doc. E/CN./2005/51 (22 Apr 2002).
93 Gostin (2008), op cit Note 60, p383–384.
94 UN Charter, Article 55.
95 Universal Declaration of Human Rights G.A. Res. 217, Art. 25, UN Doc. A/810, at 71 (1948).
96 ICESCR, GA Res. 2200A (XXI), 21 UN GAOR Supp. No. 16, at 59, UN Doc. A/6316 (1966), 999 U.N.T.S. 302, into force 23 Mar 1976.
97 Cooper (1998), op cit Note 21.
98 Scovazzi (2007), op cit Note 41.

99 Falstrom (2001), op cit Note 20.
100 CSDH (2008) *Closing the Gap in a Generation: Health Equity through Action on the Social Determinants of Health*, Final Report of the Commission on Social Determinants of Health, World Health Organization, Geneva, available at www.who.int/social_determinants/thecommission/finalreport/en/index.html.
101 Ibid, p26.
102 Ibid, p1.
103 Ibid, p2.
104 Ibid, p3. Note that this period is defined as starting from the prenatal time to eight years of age. See also Irwin, L. G., Siddiqi, A. and Hertzman, C. (2007) *Early Child Development: A Powerful Equalizer*, Final Report for the World Health Organization's Commission on the Social Determinants of Health, Early Child Development Knowledge Network, June, available at www.who.int/social_determinants/publications/earlychilddevelopment/en/index.html.
105 CSDH (2008), op cit Note 100, p10, citing Elinder, L. S. (2005) 'Obesity, hunger, and agriculture: The damaging role of subsidies', *BMJ*, vol 331, pp1333–1336.
106 CSDH (2008), op cit Note 100, p11.
107 Ibid, p4.
108 Ibid.
109 Ibid, p8.
110 Ibid, p14.
111 Ibid, p15.
112 Westra (2007), op cit Note 72.
113 CSDH (2008), op cit Note 100, p19.
114 Ibid, p22.
115 Gostin (2008), op cit Note 60, p349; see Millennium Ecosystem Assessment Board; *Living Beyond our Means: Natural Assets and Human Well-Being*, www.millenniumassessment.org/en/BoardStatement.aspx.
116 Shue, H. (1996) *Basic Rights: Subsistence, Affluence and American Foreign Policy*, Princeton University Press, Princeton, NJ.
117 'The Almeria Statement on Desertification and Migration', International Symposium on Desertification and Migration, 9–11 February 1994, Almeria, Spain.
118 Christian Aid (2007) *Human Tide: The Real Migration Crisis*, www.christianaid.org.uk/Images/human-tide.pdf.
119 Friends of the Earth, June 2006, 'Briefing note: Immigration, population and the environment', London, UK; see also Howse, R. (2001) 'The WHO/WTO study on trade and public health: A critical assessment,' *Journal of Risk Assessment*, vol 24, p501.
120 Atapattu, S. (2002–2003) 'The right to a healthy life, or the right to die polluted?: The emergence of a human right to a healthy environment under international law', *Tulane Environmental Law Journal*, vol 16, p65.
121 Howse, R. (2001), op cit Note 119; see also Westra (2006), op cit Note 70.
122 Westra, L. and Lawson, B. (2001) *Faces of Environmental Racism* (second edition), Rowman Littlefield, Lanham, MD; see also Westra (2007), op cit Note 72, Chapters 4 and 5.
123 Atapattu (2002–2003), op cit Note 120, p67.
124 Westra (1994, 1998), op cit Note 57.
125 Taylor, P. (1998) *An Ecological Approach to International Law: Responding to the Challenges of Climate Change*, Routledge, London, UK, p19.
126 Atapattu (2002–2003), op cit Note 120, p73.
127 Kofi Annan, Address by United Nations Secretary-General to the 51st session of the Executive Committee of the High Commissioner for Refugees, Palais des Nations, on 2 October 2000.

128 Birnie, P. and Boyle, A. (2002) *International Law and the Environment*, 2nd edition, Oxford University Press, Oxford, UK, p250.
129 Westra (2004), op cit Note 7, Chapter 4, contains a detailed discussion of corporate responsibility for eco-crimes because of the knowledge and research that inform corporate agency in all cases.
130 Birnie and Boyle (2002), op cit Note 128, p252.
131 Principle 1, Declaration on the Human Environment, *Report of the United Nations Conference on the Human Environment*, U.N.Doc.A/CONF.48/14 Rev.1.
132 Principle 1, Declaration on Environment and Development, *Report of the UN Conference on Environment and Development*, UN Doc.A/CONF.151/26/Rev.1.
133 See for instance Caracol Production (2005) *Sipakapa No Se Vende*, a video produced by Mayan indigenous peoples in Guatemala, describing the advent of Glamis Gold, a US/Canadian corporation, which initiated and continued production, in breach of the international law rule to obtain consent and of the Constitution of Guatemala itself.
134 Grandjean and Landrigan (2006), op cit Note 74.
135 Atapattu (2002–2003), op cit Note 120, p75; World Charter for Nature, G.A. Res. 37/7, UN GAOR, 37th Sess., UN Doc. A./RES/37/7 (1982), 22 I.L.M. 455.
136 African Charter on Human and Peoples' Rights, 21 I.L.M. (1982) 52.
137 UN Covenant on Economic, Social and Cultural Rights (ICESCR) Article 12, 6 ILM (1967) 360.
138 European Social Charter, Article 1, 529 UNTS 89.
139 *Powell and Rayner versus UK* (1990) ECHR Ser.A/172; *Lopez-Ostra versus Spain* (1994) 20 EHRR 277; *Guerra versus Italy* (1998) 26 EHRR 357; *LCV versus UK* (1999) 27 EHRR 277; *LCB versus UK* (1999) 27 EHRR 212; *Gronus versus Poland* (1999) ECHR Case No. 29695/96; *Port Hope Environmental Group versus Canada*, Communication No. 67/1980, 2 Selected Decisions of the Human Rights Committee (1990); *Ominyak and the Lubicon Lake Band versus Canada*, UNHRC No. 167/1984, Rept. Human Rights Committee (1996) GAOR A/45/40, vol II; *Yanomani Indians versus Brazil* (1985), Decision 7615, Inter-American Commission on HR, Interamerican YB on Hum.Rts. (1985), 264.
140 ECOSOC, *Human Rights and the Environment*, Final Report (1994), UN Doc. E/CN.4Sub.2/1994/9, p59.
141 Atapattu (2002), op cit Note 120, p79.
142 Birnie and Boyle (2002), op cit Note 130, p255; see also separate opinion of Judge C. Weeramantry, *Gabcikovo-Nagymaros* case, ICJ Rep. 9(1997) 7.
143 Birnie and Boyle (2002), ibid; see also Handl, G. (1992) 'Human rights and protection of the environment: A mildly "revisionist" view', in C. Trindade (ed) *Human Rights, Sustainable Development and the Environment*, Inter-American Institute of Human Rights, San Jose, Brazil, p117.
144 Ibid.
145 WHO (2002), op cit Note 82; Licari et al (2005), op cit Note 82; Grandjean and Landrigan (2006), op cit Note 74; Gostin (2008), op cit Note 60.
146 Kiss, A. and Shelton, D. (1991) *International Environmental Law*, Transnational Publishers Inc., Ardsley, NY, pp24–25.
147 The Earth Charter Initiative, The Earth Council, info@earthcharter.org.
148 For some of the history of the concept of ecological integrity, see Westra, L. (2008) 'Ecological integrity: Its history, its future and the development of the ecological integrity group', in L. Westra, K. Bosselmann and R. Westra (eds) *Reconciling Ecological Existence with Ecological Integrity*, Earthscan, London, UK, pp5–20; also Manno, J. (2008) 'Preface', in L. Westra, K. Bosselmann and R. Westra (eds) *Reconciling Ecological Existence with Ecological Integrity*, Earthscan, London, UK, pxiii.

149 See 15th anniversary volume: L. Westra, K. Bosselmann and R. Westra (eds) (2008) *Reconciling Ecological Existence with Ecological Integrity*, Earthscan, London, UK.
150 See Westra (1994), op cit Note 57.
151 See discussion in Manno (2008), op cit Note 148.
152 Birnie and Boyle (2002), op cit Note 142, pp571–590; see also UNEP/BIO.Div/17-ING 5/2(1992); see also Bowman, M. and Redgwell, C. (1996) *International Law and the Conservation of Biological Diversity*, Kluwer Publishers, The Hague.
153 Westra (1998), op cit Note 57; Noss, R. (1992) 'The Wildlands Project: Land conservation strategy', *Wild Earth Special Issue*; Noss, R. and Cooperrider, A. (1994) *Saving Nature's Legacy*, Island Press, Washington, DC.
154 Teitel, R. (2002) 'Humanity's law: Rule of law for the new global politics', *Cornell International Law Journal*, vol 35, pp356–387.
155 Rosenfeld, M. (1999) 'What is a human right? Universalism and the challenge of cultural relativism', *Pace International Law Review*, vol 11, pp107–122.
156 Ibid, p124.
157 Kymlicka, W. (1991) *Liberalism, Community and Culture*, Clarendon Paperbacks, Oxford, UK.
158 Rosenfeld (1999), op cit Note 155, pp126–127.
159 Ibid, p124.
160 Ibid, p127.
161 Ibid.
162 Lauterpacht, H. (1950) *International Law and Human Rights*, Steven and Sons, London; see also Bassiouni, C. (1996) 'International crimes: *Jus cogens* and *obligatio erga omnes*,' *Law Contemporary Problems*, vol 59, no 4.
163 Lauterpacht, ibid.
164 Westra, L. (2004), op cit Note 7, pp308–309.
165 Westra, L. (1998), op cit Note 57, see Chapter 5 for the case study of that tragedy.
166 Winston P. Nagan, panellist, on 'Human rights, INGOs and global civil society' in McDonnell, T. M. (moderator) (1999) 'Human rights and non-state actors', panel discussion, *Pace International Law Review*, vol 11, pp205–229.
167 Richard Dicker, panellist, in McDonnell (1999), ibid, p232.
168 Ibid, p233.
169 Ibid, p246.
170 World Bank Group (2004) *The World Bank Operational Manual, Operational Policy 4.10: Indigenous Peoples*, 1 December 2004, Washington, DC.
171 Westra (2007), op cit Note 72, pp71–102.
172 Teitel, R. (2002), op cit Note 154, pp146.
173 Goodwin-Gill, G. S. (2001) 'Asylum 2001 – a convention and a purpose', *International Journal of Refugee Law*, vol 13, p1 (emphasis added).
174 Hathaway, J. (2005) *The Rights of Refugees under International Law*, Cambridge University Press, Cambridge, UK, 'Epilogue', pp991–1002.
175 Countries that have legal systems based on civil law 'provide for the direct incorporation of international law into domestic law', while common law regimes 'insist on domestic transformation of international law as a condition for domestic enforceability'(ibid, p991, no 3).
176 Hathaway (2005), op cit Note 174, p994.
177 Ibid.
178 Ibid, p997.

APPENDIX 1

Convention Relating to the Status of Refugees (1951)

Preamble

The High Contracting parties,

considering that the Charter of the United Nations and the Universal Declaration of Human Rights approved on 10 December 1948 by the General Assembly have affirmed the principle that human beings shall enjoy fundamental rights and freedoms without discrimination,

considering that the United Nations has, on various occasions, manifested its profound concern for refugees and endeavoured to assure refugees the widest possible exercise of these fundamental rights and freedoms,

considering that it is desirable to revise and consolidate previous international agreements relating to the status of refugees and to extend the scope of and protection accorded by such instruments by means of a new agreement,

considering that the grant of asylum may place unduly heavy burdens on certain countries, and that a satisfactory solution of a problem of which the United Nations has recognized the international scope and nature cannot therefore be achieved without international co-operation,

expressing the wish that all States, recognizing the social and humanitarian nature of the problem of refugees, will do everything within their power to prevent this problem from becoming a cause of tension between States,

noting that the United Nations High Commissioner for Refugees is charged with the task of supervising international conventions providing for the protection of refugees, and recognizing that the effective co-ordination of measures taken to deal with this problem will depend upon the co-operation of States with the High Commissioner,

have agreed as follows:

Chapter I: General Provisions

Article 1

Definition of the term 'refugee'

A. For the purposes of the present Convention, the term 'refugee' shall apply to any person who:

(1) Has been considered a refugee under the Arrangements of 12 May 1926 and 30 June 1928 or under the Conventions of 28 October 1933 and 10 February 1938, the Protocol of 14 September 1939 or the Constitution of the International Refugee Organization; Decisions of non-eligibility taken by the International Refugee Organization during the period of its activities shall not prevent the status of refugee being accorded to persons who fulfil the conditions of paragraph 2 of this section;

(2) As a result of events occurring before 1 January 1951 and owing to well-founded fear of being persecuted for reasons of race, religion, nationality, membership of a particular social group or political opinion, is outside the country of his nationality and is unable or, owing to such fear, is unwilling to avail himself of the protection of that country; or who, not having a nationality and being outside the country of his former habitual residence as a result of such events, is unable or, owing to such fear, is unwilling

to return to it. In the case of a person who has more than one nationality, the term 'the country of his nationality' shall mean each of the countries of which he is a national, and a person shall not be deemed to be lacking the protection of the country of his nationality if, without any valid reason based on well-founded fear, he has not availed himself of the protection of one of the countries of which he is a national.

B. (1) For the purposes of this Convention, the words 'events occurring before 1 January 1951' in article 1, section A, shall be understood to mean either

  (a) 'events occurring in Europe before 1 January 1951'; or

  (b) 'events occurring in Europe or elsewhere before 1 January 1951', and each Contracting State shall make a declaration at the time of signature, ratification or accession, specifying which of these meanings it applies for the purpose of its obligations under this Convention.

  (2) Any Contracting State which has adopted alternative (a) may at any time extend its obligations by adopting alternative (b) by means of a notification addressed to the Secretary-General of the United Nations.

C. This Convention shall cease to apply to any person falling under the terms of section A if:

  (1) He has voluntarily re-availed himself of the protection of the country of his nationality; or

  (2) Having lost his nationality, he has voluntarily re-acquired it, or

  (3) He has acquired a new nationality, and enjoys the protection of the country of his new nationality; or

  (4) He has voluntarily re-established himself in the country which he left or outside which he remained owing to fear of persecution; or

  (5) He can no longer, because the circumstances in connexion with which he has been recognized as a refugee have ceased to exist, continue to refuse to avail himself of the protection of the country of his nationality;

  Provided that this paragraph shall not apply to a refugee falling under section A(1) of this article who is able to invoke compelling reasons arising out of previous persecution for refusing to avail himself of the protection of the country of nationality;

  (6) Being a person who has no nationality he is, because of the circumstances in connexion with which he has been recognized as a refugee have ceased to exist, able to return to the country of his former habitual residence;

  Provided that this paragraph shall not apply to a refugee falling under section A (1) of this article who is able to invoke compelling reasons arising out of previous persecution for refusing to return to the country of his former habitual residence.

D. This Convention shall not apply to persons who are at present receiving from organs or agencies of the United Nations other than the United Nations High Commissioner for Refugees protection or assistance.

When such protection or assistance has ceased for any reason, without the position of such persons being definitively settled in accordance with the relevant resolutions adopted by the General Assembly of the United Nations, these persons shall *ipso facto* be entitled to the benefits of this Convention.

E. This Convention shall not apply to a person who is recognized by the competent authorities of the country in which he has taken residence as having the rights and obligations which are attached to the possession of the nationality of that country.

F. The provisions of this Convention shall not apply to any person with respect to whom there are serious reasons for considering that:

  (a) he has committed a crime against peace, a war crime, or a crime against humanity, as defined in the international instruments drawn up to make provision in respect of such crimes;

  (b) he has committed a serious non-political crime outside the country of refuge prior to his admission to that country as a refugee;

  (c) he has been guilty of acts contrary to the purposes and principles of the United Nations.

Article 2

General obligations

Every refugee has duties to the country in which he finds himself, which require in particular that he conform to its laws and regulations as well as to measures taken for the maintenance of public order.

Article 3

Non-discrimination

The Contracting States shall apply the provisions of this Convention to refugees without discrimination as to race, religion or country of origin.

Article 4

Religion

The Contracting States shall accord to refugees within their territories treatment at least as favourable as that accorded to their nationals with respect to freedom to practice their religion and freedom as regards the religious education of their children.

Article 5

Rights granted apart from this convention

Nothing in this Convention shall be deemed to impair any rights and benefits granted by a Contracting State to refugees apart from this Convention.

Article 6

The term 'in the same circumstances'

For the purposes of this Convention, the term 'in the same circumstances' implies that any requirements (including requirements as to length and conditions of sojourn or residence) which the particular individual would have to fulfil for the enjoyment of the right in question, if he were not a refugee, must be fulfilled by him, with the exception of requirements which by their nature a refugee is incapable of fulfilling.

Article 7

Exemption from reciprocity

1. Except where this Convention contains more favourable provisions, a Contracting State shall accord to refugees the same treatment as is accorded to aliens generally.

2. After a period of three years' residence, all refugees shall enjoy exemption from legislative reciprocity in the territory of the Contracting States.

3. Each Contracting State shall continue to accord to refugees the rights and benefits to which they were already entitled, in the absence of reciprocity, at the date of entry into force of this Convention for that State.

4. The Contracting States shall consider favourably the possibility of according to refugees, in the absence of reciprocity, rights and benefits beyond those to which they are entitled according to paragraphs 2 and 3, and to extending exemption from reciprocity to refugees who do not fulfil the conditions provided for in paragraphs 2 and 3.

5. The provisions of paragraphs 2 and 3 apply both to the rights and benefits referred to in articles 13, 18, 19, 21 and 22 of this Convention and to rights and benefits for which this Convention does not provide.

Article 8

Exemption from exceptional measures

With regard to exceptional measures which may be taken against the person, property or interests of nationals of a foreign State, the Contracting States shall not apply such measures to a refugee who is formally a national of the said State solely on account of such nationality. Contracting States which, under their legislation, are prevented from applying the general principle expressed in this article, shall, in appropriate cases, grant exemptions in favour of such refugees.

Article 9

Provisional measures

Nothing in this Convention shall prevent a Contracting State, in time of war or other grave and exceptional circumstances, from taking provisionally measures which it considers to be essential to the national security in the case of a particular person, pending a determination by the Contracting State that that person is in fact a refugee and that the continuance of such measures is necessary in his case in the interests of national security.

Article 10

Continuity of residence

1. Where a refugee has been forcibly displaced during the Second World War and removed to the territory of a Contracting State, and is resident there, the period of such enforced sojourn shall be considered to have been lawful residence within that territory.

2. Where a refugee has been forcibly displaced during the Second World War from the territory of a Contracting State and has, prior to the date of entry into force of this Convention, returned there for the purpose of taking up residence, the period of residence before and after such enforced

displacement shall be regarded as one uninterrupted period for any purposes for which uninterrupted residence is required.

Article 11

Refugee seamen

In the case of refugees regularly serving as crew members on board a ship flying the flag of a Contracting State, that State shall give sympathetic consideration to their establishment on its territory and the issue of travel documents to them or their temporary admission to its territory particularly with a view to facilitating their establishment in another country.

Chapter II: Juridical Status

Article 12

Personal status

1. The personal status of a refugee shall be governed by the law of the country of his domicile or, if he has no domicile, by the law of the country of his residence.

2. Rights previously acquired by a refugee and dependent on personal status, more particularly rights attaching to marriage, shall be respected by a Contracting State, subject to compliance, if this be necessary, with the formalities required by the law of that State, provided that the right in question is one which would have been recognized by the law of that State had he not become a refugee.

Article 13

Movable and immovable property

The Contracting States shall accord to a refugee treatment as favourable as possible and, in any event, not less favourable than that accorded to aliens generally in the same circumstances, as regards the acquisition of movable and immovable property and other rights pertaining thereto, and to leases and other contracts relating to movable and immovable property.

Article 14

Artistic rights and industrial property

In respect of the protection of industrial property, such as inventions, designs or models, trade marks, trade names, and of rights in literary, artistic, and scientific works, a refugee shall be accorded in the country in which he has his habitual residence the same protection as is accorded to nationals of that country. In the territory of any other Contracting State, he shall be accorded the same protection as is accorded in that territory to nationals of the country in which he has his habitual residence.

Article 15

Right of association

As regards non-political and non-profit-making associations and trade unions the Contracting States shall accord to refugees lawfully staying in their territory the most favourable treatment accorded to nationals of a foreign country, in the same circumstances.

Article 16

Access to courts

1. A refugee shall have free access to the courts of law on the territory of all Contracting States.

2. A refugee shall enjoy in the Contracting State in which he has his habitual residence the same treatment as a national in matters pertaining to access to the Courts, including legal assistance and exemption from *cautio judicatum solvi*.

3. A refugee shall be accorded in the matters referred to in paragraph 2 in countries other than that in which he has his habitual residence the treatment granted to a national of the country of his habitual residence.

Chapter III: Gainful Employment

Article 17

Wage-earning employment

1. The Contracting State shall accord to refugees lawfully staying in their territory the most favourable treatment accorded to nationals of a foreign country in the same circumstances, as regards the right to engage in wage-earning employment.

2. In any case, restrictive measures imposed on aliens or the employment of aliens for the protection of the national labour market shall not be applied to a refugee who was already exempt from them at the date of entry into force of this Convention for the Contracting State concerned, or who fulfils one of the following conditions:

(a) He has completed three years' residence in the country;

(b) He has a spouse possessing the nationality of the country of residence. A refugee may not invoke the benefits of this provision if he has abandoned his spouse;

(c) He has one or more children possessing the nationality of the country of residence.

3. The Contracting States shall give sympathetic consideration to assimilating the rights of all refugees with regard to wage-earning employment to those of nationals, and in particular of those refugees who have entered their territory pursuant to programmes of labour recruitment or under immigration schemes.

Article 18

Self-employment

The Contracting States shall accord to a refugee lawfully in their territory treatment as favourable as possible and, in any event, not less favourable than that accorded to aliens generally in the same circumstances, as regards the right to engage on his own account in agriculture, industry, handicrafts and commerce and to establish commercial and industrial companies.

Article 19

Liberal professions

1. Each Contracting State shall accord to refugees lawfully staying in their territory who hold diplomas recognized by the competent authorities of that State, and who are desirous of practicing a liberal profession, treatment as favourable as possible and, in any event, not less favourable than that accorded to aliens generally in the same circumstances.

2. The Contracting States shall use their best endeavours consistently with their laws and constitutions to secure the settlement of such refugees in the territories, other than the metropolitan territory, for whose international relations they are responsible.

Chapter IV: Welfare

Article 20

Rationing

Where a rationing system exists, which applies to the population at large and regulates the general distribution of products in short supply, refugees shall be accorded the same treatment as nationals.

Article 21

Housing

As regards housing, the Contracting States, in so far as the matter is regulated by laws or regulations or is subject to the control of public authorities, shall accord to refugees lawfully staying in their territory treatment as favourable as possible and, in any event, not less favourable than that accorded to aliens generally in the same circumstances.

Article 22

Public education

1. The Contracting States shall accord to refugees the same treatment as is accorded to nationals with respect to elementary education.

2. The Contracting States shall accord to refugees treatment as favourable as possible, and, in any event, not less favourable than that accorded to aliens generally in the same circumstances, with respect to education other than elementary education and, in particular, as regards access to studies, the recognition of foreign school certificates, diplomas and degrees, the remission of fees and charges and the award of scholarships.

Article 23

Public relief

The Contracting States shall accord to refugees lawfully staying in their territory the same treatment with respect to public relief and assistance as is accorded to their nationals.

Article 24

Labour legislation and social security

1. The Contracting States shall accord to refugees lawfully staying in their territory the same treatment as is accorded to nationals in respect of the following matters:

(a) In so far as such matters are governed by laws or regulations or are subject to the control of administrative authorities: remuneration, including family allowances where these form part of remuneration, hours of work, overtime arrangements, holidays with pay, restrictions on home work, minimum age of employment, apprenticeship and training, women's work and the work of young persons, and the enjoyment of the benefits of collective bargaining;

(b) Social security (legal provisions in respect of employment injury, occupational diseases, maternity, sickness, disability, old age, death, unemployment, family responsibilities and any other contingency which, according to national laws or regulations, is covered by a social security scheme), subject to the following limitations:

  (i) There may be appropriate arrangements for the maintenance of acquired rights and rights in course of acquisition;

  (ii) National laws or regulations of the country of residence may prescribe special arrangements concerning benefits or portions of benefits which are payable wholly out of public funds, and concerning allowances paid to persons who do not fulfil the contribution conditions prescribed for the award of a normal pension.

1. The right to compensation for the death of a refugee resulting from employment injury or from occupational disease shall not be affected by the fact that the residence of the beneficiary is outside the territory of the Contracting State.

2. The Contracting States shall extend to refugees the benefits of agreements concluded between them, or which may be concluded between them in the future, concerning the maintenance of acquired rights and rights in the process of acquisition in regard to social security, subject only to the conditions which apply to nationals of the States signatory to the agreements in question.

4. The Contracting States will give sympathetic consideration to extending to refugees so far as possible the benefits of similar agreements which may at any time be in force between such Contracting States and non-contracting States.

Chapter V: Administrative Measures

Article 25

Administrative assistance

1. When the exercise of a right by a refugee would normally require the assistance of authorities of a foreign country to whom he cannot have recourse, the Contracting States in whose territory he is residing shall arrange that such assistance be afforded to him by their own authorities or by an international authority.

2. The authority or authorities mentioned in paragraph 1 shall deliver or cause to be delivered under their supervision to refugees such documents or certifications as would normally be delivered to aliens by or through their national authorities.

3. Documents or certifications so delivered shall stand in the stead of the official instruments delivered to aliens by or through their national authorities, and shall be given credence in the absence of proof to the contrary.

4. Subject to such exceptional treatment as may be granted to indigent persons, fees may be charged for the services mentioned herein, but such fees shall be moderate and commensurate with those charged to nationals for similar services.

5. The provisions of this article shall be without prejudice to articles 27 and 28.

Article 26

Freedom of movement

Each Contracting State shall accord to refugees lawfully in its territory the right to choose their place of residence to move freely within its territory, subject to any regulations applicable to aliens generally in the same circumstances.

Article 27

Identity papers

The Contracting States shall issue identity papers to any refugee in their territory who does not possess a valid travel document.

Article 28

Travel documents

1. The Contracting States shall issue to refugees lawfully staying in their territory travel documents for the purpose of travel outside

their territory, unless compelling reasons of national security or public order otherwise require, and the provisions of the Schedule to this Convention shall apply with respect to such documents. The Contracting States may issue such a travel document to any other refugee in their territory; they shall in particular give sympathetic consideration to the issue of such a travel document to refugees in their territory who are unable to obtain a travel document from the country of their lawful residence.

2. Travel documents issued to refugees under previous international agreements by parties thereto shall be recognized and treated by the Contracting States in the same way as if they had been issued pursuant to this article.

Article 29

Fiscal charges

1. The Contracting States shall not impose upon refugees duties, charges or taxes, of any description whatsoever, other or higher than those which are or may be levied on their nationals in similar situations.

2. Nothing in the above paragraph shall prevent the application to refugees of the laws and regulations concerning charges in respect of the issue to aliens of administrative documents including identity papers.

Article 30

Transfer of assets

1. A Contracting State shall, in conformity with its laws and regulations, permit refugees to transfer assets which they have brought into its territory, to another country where they have been admitted for the purposes of resettlement.

2. A Contracting State shall give sympathetic consideration to the application of refugees for permission to transfer assets wherever they may be and which are necessary for their resettlement in another country to which they have been admitted.

Article 31

Refugees unlawfully in the country of refugee

1. The Contracting States shall not impose penalties, on account of their illegal entry or presence, on refugees who, coming directly from a territory where their life or freedom was threatened in the sense of article 1, enter or are present in their territory without authorization, provided they present themselves without delay to the authorities and show good cause for their illegal entry or presence.

2. The Contracting States shall not apply to the movements of such refugees restrictions other than those which are necessary and such restrictions shall only be applied until their status in the country is regularized or they obtain admission into another country. The Contracting States shall allow such refugees a reasonable period and all the necessary facilities to obtain admission into another country.

Article 32

Expulsion

1. The Contracting States shall not expel a refugee lawfully in their territory save on grounds of national security or public order.

2. The expulsion of such a refugee shall be only in pursuance of a decision reached in accordance with due process of law. Except where compelling reasons of national security otherwise require, the refugee shall be allowed to submit evidence to clear himself, and to appeal to and be represented for the purpose before competent authority or a person or persons specially designated by the competent authority.

3. The Contracting States shall allow such a refugee a reasonable period within which to seek legal admission into another country. The Contracting States reserve the right to apply during that period such internal measures as they may deem necessary.

Article 33

Prohibition of expulsion or return ('*refoulement*')

1. No Contracting State shall expel or return ('*refouler*') a refugee in any manner whatsoever to the frontiers of territories where his life or freedom would be threatened on account of his race, religion, nationality, membership of a particular social group or political opinion.

2. The benefit of the present provision may not, however, be claimed by a refugee whom there are reasonable grounds for regarding as a danger to the security of the country in which he is, or who, having been convicted by a final judgment of a particularly serious crime, constitutes a danger to the community of that country.

Article 34

Naturalization

The Contracting States shall as far as possible facilitate the assimilation and naturalization of refugees. They shall in particular make every effort to expedite naturalization proceedings and to reduce as far as possible the charges and costs of such proceedings.

Chapter VI: Executory and Transitory Provisions

Article 35

Co-operation of the national authorities with the United Nations

1. The Contracting States undertake to co-operate with the Office of the United Nations High Commissioner for Refugees, or any other agency of the United Nations which may succeed it, in the exercise of its functions, and shall in particular facilitate its duty of supervising the application of the provisions of this Convention.

2. In order to enable the Office of the High Commissioner or any other agency of the United Nations which may succeed it, to make reports to the competent organs of the United Nations, the Contracting States undertake to provide them in the appropriate form with information and statistical data requested concerning:

    (a) The condition of refugees,
    (b) The implementation of this Convention, and;
    (c) Laws, regulations and decrees which are, or may hereafter be, in force relating to refugees.

Article 36

Information on national legislation

The Contracting States shall communicate to the Secretary-General of the United Nations the laws and regulations which they may adopt to ensure the application of this Convention.

Article 37

Relation to previous conventions

Without prejudice to article 28, paragraph 2, of this Convention, this Convention replaces, as between parties to it, the Arrangements of 5 July 1922, 31 May 1924, 12 May 1926, 30 June 1928 and 30 July 1935, the Conventions of 28 October 1933 and 10 February 1938, the Protocol of 14 September 1939 and the Agreement of 15 October 1946.

Chapter VII: Final Clauses

Article 38

Settlement of disputes

Any dispute between parties to this Convention relating to its interpretation or application, which cannot be settled by other means, shall be referred to the International Court of Justice at the request of any one of the parties to the dispute.

Article 39

Signature, ratification and accession

1. This Convention shall be opened for signature at Geneva on 28 July 1951 and shall thereafter be deposited with the Secretary-General of the United Nations. It shall be open for signature at the European Office of the United Nations from 28 July to 31 August 1951 and shall be re-opened for signature at the Headquarters of the United Nations from 17 September 1951 to 31 December 1952.

2. This Convention shall be open for signature on behalf of all States Members of the United Nations, and also on behalf of any other State invited to attend the Conference of Plenipotentiaries on the Status of Refugees and Stateless Persons or to which an invitation to sign will have been addressed by the General Assembly. It shall be ratified and the instruments of ratification shall be deposited with the Secretary-General of the United Nations.

3. This Convention shall be open from 28 July 1951 for accession by the States referred to in paragraph 2 of this article. Accession shall be effected by the deposit of an instrument of accession with the Secretary-General of the United Nations.

Article 40

Territorial application clause

1. Any State may, at the time of signature, ratification or accession, declare that this Convention shall extend to all or any of the territories for the international relations of which it is responsible. Such a declaration shall take effect when the Convention enters into force for the State concerned.

2. At any time thereafter any such extension shall be made by notification addressed to the Secretary-General of the United Nations and shall take effect as from the ninetieth day after the day of receipt by the Secretary-General of the United Nations of this notification, or as from the date of entry into force of the Convention for the State concerned, whichever is the later.

3. With respect to those territories to which this Convention is not extended at the time of signature, ratification or accession, each State concerned shall consider the possibility of taking the necessary steps in order to extend the application of this Convention to such territories, subject, where necessary for constitutional reasons, to the consent of the Governments of such territories.

Article 41

Federal clause

In the case of a Federal or non-unitary State, the following provisions shall apply:

(a) With respect to those articles of this Convention that come within the legislative jurisdiction of the federal legislative authority, the obligations of the Federal Government shall to this extent be the same as those of Parties which are not Federal States;

(b) With respect to those articles of this Convention that come within the legislative jurisdiction of constituent States, provinces or cantons which are not, under the constitutional system of the federation, bound to take legislative action, the Federal Government shall bring such articles with a favourable recommendation to the notice of the appropriate authorities of states, provinces or cantons at the earliest possible moment.

(c) A Federal State Party to this Convention shall, at the request of any other Contracting State transmitted through the Secretary-General of the United Nations, supply a statement of the law and practice of the Federation and its constituent units in regard to any particular provision of the Convention showing the extent to which effect has been given to that provision by legislative or other action.

Article 42

Reservations

1. At the time of signature, ratification or accession, any State may make reservations to articles of the Convention other than to articles 1, 3, 4, 16(1), 33, 36-46 inclusive.

2. Any State making a reservation in accordance with paragraph 1 of this article may at any time withdraw the reservation by a communication to that effect addressed to the Secretary-General of the United Nations.

Article 43

Entry into force

1. This Convention shall come into force on the ninetieth day following the day of deposit of the sixth instrument of ratification or accession.

2. For each State ratifying or acceding to the Convention after the deposit of the sixth instrument of ratification or accession, the Convention shall enter into force on the ninetieth day following the date of deposit by such State of its instrument or ratification or accession.

Article 44

Denunciation

1. Any Contracting State may denounce this Convention at any time by a notification addressed to the Secretary-General of the United Nations.

2. Such denunciation shall take effect for the Contracting State concerned one year from the date upon which it is received by the Secretary-General of the United Nations.

3. Any State which has made a declaration or notification under article 40 may, at any time thereafter, by a notification to the Secretary-General of the United Nations, declare that the Convention shall cease to extend to such territory one year after the date of receipt of the notification by the Secretary-General.

Article 45

Revision

1. Any Contracting State may request revision of this Convention at any time by a notification addressed to the Secretary-General of the United Nations.

2. The General Assembly of the United Nations shall recommend the steps, if any, to be taken in respect of such request.

Article 46

Notifications by the Secretary-General of the United Nations

The Secretary-General of the United Nations shall inform all Members of the United Nations and non-member States referred to in article 39:

(a) Of declarations and notifications in accordance with section B of article 1;

(b) Of signatures, ratifications and accessions in accordance with article 39;

(c) Of declarations and notifications in accordance with article 40;

(d) Of reservations and withdrawals in accordance with article 42;

(e) Of the date on which this Convention will come into force in accordance with article 43;

(f) Of denunciations and notifications in accordance with article 44;

(g) Of requests for revision in accordance with article 45.

in faith whereof the undersigned, duly authorized, have signed this Convention on behalf of their respective Governments,

done at Geneva, this twenty-eighth day of July, one thousand nine hundred and fifty-one, in a single copy, of which the English and French texts are equally authentic and which shall remain deposited in the archives of the United Nations, and certified true copies of which shall be delivered to all Members of the United Nations and to the non-member States referred to in article 39.

APPENDIX 2

Other Relevant Instruments

UNIVERSAL DECLARATION OF HUMAN RIGHTS (1948)

Preamble

Whereas recognition of the inherent dignity and of the equal and inalienable rights of all members of the human family is the foundation of freedom, justice and peace in the world,

Whereas disregard and contempt for human rights have resulted in barbarous acts which have outraged the conscience of mankind, and the advent of a world in which human beings shall enjoy freedom of speech and belief and freedom from fear and want has been proclaimed as the highest aspiration of the common people,

Whereas it is essential, if man is not to be compelled to have recourse, as a last resort, to rebellion against tyranny and oppression, that human rights should be protected by the rule of law,

Whereas it is essential to promote the development of friendly relations between nations,

Whereas the peoples of the United Nations have in the Charter reaffirmed their faith in fundamental human rights, in the dignity and worth of the human person and in the equal rights of men and women and have determined to promote social progress and better standards of life in larger freedom,

Whereas Member States have pledged themselves to achieve, in cooperation with the United Nations, the promotion of universal respect for and observance of human rights and fundamental freedoms,

Whereas a common understanding of these rights and freedoms is of the greatest importance for the full realization of this pledge,

Now, Therefore the GENERAL ASSEMBLY proclaims THIS UNIVERSAL DECLARATION OF HUMAN RIGHTS as a common standard of achievement for all peoples and all nations, to the end that every individual and every organ of society, keeping this Declaration constantly in mind, shall strive by teaching and education to promote respect for these rights and freedoms and by progressive measures, national and international, to secure their universal and effective recognition and observance, both among the peoples of Member States themselves and among the peoples of territories under their jurisdiction.

Article 1

All human beings are born free and equal in dignity and rights. They are endowed with reason and conscience and should act towards one another in a spirit of brotherhood.

Article 2

Everyone is entitled to all the rights and freedoms set forth in this Declaration, without distinction of any kind, such as race, colour, sex, language, religion, political or other opinion, national or social origin, property, birth or other status. Furthermore, no distinction shall be made on the basis of the political, jurisdictional or international status of the country or territory to which a person belongs, whether it be independent, trust, non-self-governing or under any other limitation of sovereignty.

Article 3

Everyone has the right to life, liberty and security of person.

Article 4

No one shall be held in slavery or servitude; slavery and the slave trade shall be prohibited in all their forms.

Article 5

No one shall be subjected to torture or to cruel, inhuman or degrading treatment or punishment.

Article 6

Everyone has the right to recognition everywhere as a person before the law.

Article 7

All are equal before the law and are entitled without any discrimination to equal protection of the law. All are entitled to equal protection against any discrimination in violation of this Declaration and against any incitement to such discrimination.

Article 8

Everyone has the right to an effective remedy by the competent national tribunals for acts violating the fundamental rights granted him by the constitution or by law.

Article 9

No one shall be subjected to arbitrary arrest, detention or exile.

Article 10

Everyone is entitled in full equality to a fair and public hearing by an independent and impartial tribunal, in the determination of his rights and obligations and of any criminal charge against him.

Article 11

(1) Everyone charged with a penal offence has the right to be presumed innocent until proved guilty according to law in a public trial at which he has had all the guarantees necessary for his defence.

(2) No one shall be held guilty of any penal offence on account of any act or omission which did not constitute a penal offence, under national or international law, at the time when it was committed. Nor shall a heavier penalty be imposed than the one that was applicable at the time the penal offence was committed.

Article 12

No one shall be subjected to arbitrary interference with his privacy, family, home or correspondence, nor to attacks upon his honour and reputation. Everyone has the right to the protection of the law against such interference or attacks.

Article 13

(1) Everyone has the right to freedom of movement and residence within the borders of each state.

(2) Everyone has the right to leave any country, including his own, and to return to his country.

Article 14

(1) Everyone has the right to seek and to enjoy in other countries asylum from persecution.

(2) This right may not be invoked in the case of prosecutions genuinely arising from non-political crimes or from acts contrary to the purposes and principles of the United Nations.

Article 15

(1) Everyone has the right to a nationality.

(2) No one shall be arbitrarily deprived of his nationality nor denied the right to change his nationality.

Article 16

(1) Men and women of full age, without any limitation due to race, nationality or religion, have the right to marry and to found a family. They are entitled to equal rights as to marriage, during marriage and at its dissolution.

(2) Marriage shall be entered into only with the free and full consent of the intending spouses.

(3) The family is the natural and fundamental group unit of society and is entitled to protection by society and the State.

Article 17

(1) Everyone has the right to own property alone as well as in association with others.

(2) No one shall be arbitrarily deprived of his property.

Article 18

Everyone has the right to freedom of thought, conscience and religion; this right includes freedom to change his religion or belief, and freedom, either alone or in community with others and in public or private, to manifest his religion or belief in teaching, practice, worship and observance.

Article 19

Everyone has the right to freedom of opinion and expression; this right includes freedom to hold opinions without interference and to seek, receive and impart information and ideas through any media and regardless of frontiers.

Article 20

(1) Everyone has the right to freedom of peaceful assembly and association.

(2) No one may be compelled to belong to an association.

Article 21

(1) Everyone has the right to take part in the government of his country, directly or through freely chosen representatives.

(2) Everyone has the right of equal access to public service in his country.

(3) The will of the people shall be the basis of the authority of government; this will be expressed in periodic and genuine elections which shall be by universal and equal suffrage and shall be held by secret vote or by equivalent free voting procedures.

Article 22

Everyone, as a member of society, has the right to social security and is entitled to realization, through national effort and international cooperation and in accordance with the organization and resources of each State, of the economic, social and cultural rights indispensable for his dignity and the free development of his personality.

Article 23

(1) Everyone has the right to work, to free choice of employment, to just and favourable conditions of work and to protection against unemployment.

(2) Everyone, without any discrimination, has the right to equal pay for equal work.

(3) Everyone who works has the right to just and favourable remuneration ensuring for himself and his family an existence worthy of human dignity, and supplemented, if necessary, by other means of social protection.

(4) Everyone has the right to form and to join trade unions for the protection of his interests.

Article 24

Everyone has the right to rest and leisure, including reasonable limitation of working hours and periodic holidays with pay.

Article 25

(1) Everyone has the right to a standard of living adequate for the health and well-being of himself and of his family, including food, clothing, housing and medical care and necessary social services, and the right to security in the event of unemployment, sickness, disability, widowhood, old age or other lack of livelihood in circumstances beyond his control.

(2) Motherhood and childhood are entitled to special care and assistance. All children, whether born in or out of wedlock, shall enjoy the same social protection.

Article 26

(1) Everyone has the right to education. Education shall be free, at least in the elementary and fundamental stages. Elementary education shall be compulsory. Technical and professional education shall be made generally available and higher education shall be equally accessible to all on the basis of merit.

(2) Education shall be directed to the full development of the human personality and to the strengthening of respect for human rights and fundamental freedoms. It shall promote understanding, tolerance and friendship among all nations, racial or religious groups, and shall further the activities of the United Nations for the maintenance of peace.

(3) Parents have a prior right to choose the kind of education that shall be given to their children.

Article 27

(1) Everyone has the right freely to participate in the cultural life of the community, to enjoy the arts and to share in scientific advancement and its benefits.

(2) Everyone has the right to the protection of the moral and material interests resulting from any scientific, literary or artistic production of which he is the author.

Article 28

Everyone is entitled to a social and international order in which the rights and freedoms set forth in this Declaration can be fully realized.

Article 29

(1) Everyone has duties to the community in which alone the free and full development of his personality is possible.

(2) In the exercise of his rights and freedoms, everyone shall be subject only to such limitations as are determined by law solely for the purpose of securing due recognition and respect for the rights and freedoms of others and of meeting the just requirements of morality, public order and the general welfare in a democratic society.

(3) These rights and freedoms may in no case be exercised contrary to the purposes and principles of the United Nations.

Article 30

Nothing in this Declaration may be interpreted as implying for any State, group or person any right to engage in any activity or to perform any act aimed at the destruction of any of the rights and freedoms set forth herein.

PROTOCOL RELATING TO THE STATUS OF REFUGEES (1967)

The States Parties to the present Protocol,

Considering that the Convention relating to the Status of Refugees done at Geneva on 28 July 1951 (hereinafter referred to as the Convention) covers only those persons who have become refugees as a result of events occurring before 1 January 1951,

Considering that new refugee situations have arisen since the Convention was adopted and that the refugees concerned may therefore not fall within the scope of the Convention,

Considering that it is desirable that equal status should be enjoyed by all refugees covered by the definition in the Convention irrespective of the dateline 1 January 1951,

Have agreed as follows:

Article I

General provision

1. The States Parties to the present Protocol undertake to apply articles 2 to 34 inclusive of the Convention to refugees as hereinafter defined.

2. For the purpose of the present Protocol, the term 'refugee' shall, except as regards the application of paragraph 3 of this article, mean any person within the definition of article 1 of the Convention as if the words 'As a result of events occurring before 1 January 1951 and …' and the words '… as a result of such events', in article 1 A (2) were omitted.

3. The present Protocol shall be applied by the States Parties hereto without any geographic limitation, save that existing declarations made by States already Parties to the Convention in accordance with article 1 B(1)(a) of the Convention, shall, unless extended under article 1 B (2) thereof, apply also under the present Protocol.

Article II

Co-operation of the national authorities with the United Nations

1. The States Parties to the present Protocol undertake to co-operate with the Office of the United Nations High Commissioner for Refugees, or any other agency of the United Nations which may succeed it, in the exercise of its functions, and shall in particular facilitate its duty of supervising the application of the provisions of the present Protocol.

2. In order to enable the Office of the High Commissioner, or any other agency of the United Nations which may succeed it, to make reports to the competent organs of the United Nations, the States Parties to the present Protocol undertake to provide them with the information and statistical data requested, in the appropriate form, concerning:

   (a) The condition of refugees;

   (b) The implementation of the present Protocol;

   (c) Laws, regulations and decrees which are, or may hereafter be, in force relating to refugees.

Article III

Information on national legislation

The States Parties to the present Protocol shall communicate to the Secretary-General of the United Nations the laws and regulations which they may adopt to ensure the application of the present Protocol.

Article IV

Settlement of disputes

Any dispute between States Parties to the present Protocol which relates to its interpretation or application and which cannot be settled by other means shall be referred to the International Court of Justice at the request of any one of the parties to the dispute.

Article V

Accession

The present Protocol shall be open for accession on behalf of all States Parties to the Convention and of any other State Member of the United Nations or member of any of the specialized agencies or to which an invitation to accede may have been addressed by the General Assembly of the United Nations. Accession shall be effected by the deposit of an instrument of accession with the Secretary-General of the United Nations.

Article VI

Federal clause

In the case of a Federal or non-unitary State, the following provisions shall apply:

(a) With respect to those articles of the Convention to be applied in accordance with article I, paragraph 1, of the present Protocol that come within the legislative jurisdiction of the federal legislative authority, the obligations of the Federal Government shall to this extent be the same as those of States Parties which are not Federal States;

(b) With respect to those articles of the Convention to be applied in accordance with article I, paragraph 1, of the present Protocol that come within the legislative jurisdiction of constituent States, provinces or cantons which are not, under the constitutional system of the Federation, bound to take legislative action, the Federal Government shall bring such articles with a favourable recommendation to the notice of the appropriate authorities of States, provinces or cantons at the earliest possible moment;

(c) A Federal State Party to the present Protocol shall, at the request of any other State Party hereto transmitted through the Secretary-General of the United Nations, supply a statement of the law and practice of the Federation and its constituent units in regard to any particular provision of the Convention to be applied in accordance with article I, paragraph 1, of the present Protocol, showing the extent to which effect has been given to that provision by legislative or other action.

Article VII

Reservations and declarations

1. At the time of accession, any State may make reservations in respect of article IV of the present Protocol and in respect of the application in accordance with article I of the present Protocol of any provisions of the Convention other than those contained in articles 1, 3, 4, 16(1) and 33 thereof, provided that in the case of a State Party to the Convention reservations made under this article shall not extend to refugees in respect of whom the Convention applies.

2. Reservations made by States Parties to the Convention in accordance with article 42 thereof shall, unless withdrawn, be applicable in relation to their obligations under the present Protocol.

3. Any State making a reservation in accordance with paragraph 1 of this article may at any time withdraw such reservation by a communication to that effect addressed to the Secretary-General of the United Nations.

4. Declarations made under article 40, paragraphs 1 and 2, of the Convention by a State Party thereto which accedes to the present Protocol shall be deemed to apply in respect of the present Protocol, unless upon accession a notification to the contrary is addressed by the State Party concerned to the Secretary-General of the United Nations. The provisions of article 40, paragraphs 2 and 3, and of article 44, paragraph 3, of the Convention shall be deemed to apply *mutatis mutandis* to the present Protocol.

Article VIII

Entry into force

1. The present Protocol shall come into force on the day of deposit of the sixth instrument of accession.

2. For each State acceding to the Protocol after the deposit of the sixth instrument of accession, the Protocol shall come into force on the date of deposit by such State of its instrument of accession.

Article IX

Denunciation

1. Any State Party hereto may denounce this Protocol at any time by a notification addressed to the Secretary-General of the United Nations.

2. Such denunciation shall take effect for the State Party concerned one year from the date on which it is received by the Secretary-General of the United Nations.

Article X

Notifications by the Secretary-General of the United Nations

The Secretary-General of the United Nations shall inform the States referred to in article V above of the date of entry into force, accessions, reservations and withdrawals of reservations to and denunciations of the present Protocol, and of declarations and notifications relating hereto.

Article XI

Deposit in the archives of the Secretariat of the United Nations

A copy of the present Protocol, of which the Chinese, English, French, Russian and Spanish texts are equally authentic, signed by the President of the General Assembly and by the Secretary-General of the United Nations, shall be deposited in the archives of the Secretariat of the United Nations. The Secretary-General will transmit certified copies thereof to all States Members of the United Nations and to the other States referred to in article V above.

UNITED NATIONS DECLARATION ON TERRITORIAL ASYLUM (1967)

The General Assembly,

Noting that the purposes proclaimed in the Charter of the United Nations are to maintain international peace and security, to develop friendly relations among all nations and to achieve international co-operation in solving international problems of an economic, social, cultural or humanitarian character and in promoting and encouraging respect for human rights and for fundamental freedoms for all without distinction as to race, sex, language or religion,

Mindful of the Universal Declaration of Human Rights, which declares in article 14 that:

'1. Everyone has the right to seek and to enjoy in other countries asylum from persecution.

'2. This right may not be invoked in the case of prosecutions genuinely arising from non-political crimes or from acts contrary to the purposes and principles of the United Nations',

Recalling also article 13, paragraph 2, of the Universal Declaration of Human Rights, which states:

'Everyone has the right to leave any country, including his own, and to return to his country',

Recognizing that the grant of asylum by a State to persons entitled to invoke article 14 of the Universal Declaration of Human Rights is a peaceful and humanitarian act and that, as such, it cannot be regarded as unfriendly by any other State,

Recommends that, without prejudice to existing instruments dealing with asylum and the status of refugees and stateless persons, States should base themselves in their practices relating to territorial asylum on the following principles:

Article 1

1. Asylum granted by a State, in the exercise of its sovereignty, to persons entitled to invoke article 14 of the Universal Declaration of Human Rights, including persons struggling against colonialism, shall be respected by all other States.

2. The right to seek and to enjoy asylum may not be invoked by any person with respect to whom there are serious reasons for considering that he has committed a crime against peace, a war crime or a crime against humanity, as defined in the international instruments drawn up to make provision in respect of such crimes.

3. It shall rest with the State granting asylum to evaluate the grounds for the grant of asylum.

Article 2

1. The situation of persons referred to in article 1, paragraph 1, is, without prejudice to the sovereignty of States and the purposes and principles of the United Nations, of concern to the international community.

2. Where a State finds difficulty in granting or continuing to grant asylum, States individually or jointly or through the United Nations shall consider, in a spirit of international solidarity, appropriate measures to lighten the burden on that State.

Article 3

1. No person referred to in article 1, paragraph 1, shall be subjected to measures such as rejection at the frontier or, if he has already entered the territory in which he seeks asylum, expulsion or compulsory return to any State where he may be subjected to persecution.
2. Exception may be made to the foregoing principle only for overriding reasons of national security or in order to safeguard the population, as in the case of a mass influx of persons.
3. Should a State decide in any case that exception to the principle stated in paragraph I of this article would be justified, it shall consider the possibility of granting to the persons concerned, under such conditions as it may deem appropriate, an opportunity, whether by way of provisional asylum or otherwise, of going to another State.

Article 4

States granting asylum shall not permit persons who have received asylum to engage in activities contrary to the purposes and principles of the United Nations.

UNITED NATIONS CONVENTION AGAINST TORTURE AND OTHER CRUEL, INHUMAN OR DEGRADING TREATMENT OR PUNISHMENT (1984)

Adopted and opened for signature, ratification and accession by General Assembly resolution 39/46 of 10 December 1984

entry into force 26 June 1987, in accordance with article 27 (1)

The States Parties to this Convention,

Considering that, in accordance with the principles proclaimed in the Charter of the United Nations, recognition of the equal and inalienable rights of all members of the human family is the foundation of freedom, justice and peace in the world,

Recognizing that those rights derive from the inherent dignity of the human person,

Considering the obligation of States under the Charter, in particular Article 55, to promote universal respect for, and observance of, human rights and fundamental freedoms,

Having regard to article 5 of the Universal Declaration of Human Rights and article 7 of the International Covenant on Civil and Political Rights, both of which provide that no one shall be subjected to torture or to cruel, inhuman or degrading treatment or punishment,

Having regard also to the Declaration on the Protection of All Persons from Being Subjected to Torture and Other Cruel, Inhuman or Degrading Treatment or Punishment, adopted by the General Assembly on 9 December 1975,

Desiring to make more effective the struggle against torture and other cruel, inhuman or degrading treatment or punishment throughout the world,

Have agreed as follows:

Part I

Article 1

1. For the purposes of this Convention, the term 'torture' means any act by which severe pain or suffering, whether physical or mental, is intentionally inflicted on a person for such purposes as obtaining from him or a third person information or a confession, punishing him for an act he or a third person has committed or is suspected of having committed, or intimidating or coercing him or a third person, or for any reason based on discrimination of any kind, when such pain or suffering is inflicted by or at the instigation of or with the consent or acquiescence of a public official or other person acting in an official capacity. It does not include pain or suffering arising only from, inherent in or incidental to lawful sanctions.
2. This article is without prejudice to any international instrument or national legislation which does or may contain provisions of wider application.

Article 2

1. Each State Party shall take effective legislative, administrative, judicial or other measures to prevent acts of torture in any territory under its jurisdiction.
2. No exceptional circumstances whatsoever, whether a state of war or a threat of war, internal political instability or any other public emergency, may be invoked as a justification of torture.

3. An order from a superior officer or a public authority may not be invoked as a justification of torture.

Article 3

1. No State Party shall expel, return ('*refouler*') or extradite a person to another State where there are substantial grounds for believing that he would be in danger of being subjected to torture.

2. For the purpose of determining whether there are such grounds, the competent authorities shall take into account all relevant considerations including, where applicable, the existence in the State concerned of a consistent pattern of gross, flagrant or mass violations of human rights.

Article 4

1. Each State Party shall ensure that all acts of torture are offences under its criminal law. The same shall apply to an attempt to commit torture and to an act by any person which constitutes complicity or participation in torture.

2. Each State Party shall make these offences punishable by appropriate penalties which take into account their grave nature.

Article 5

1. Each State Party shall take such measures as may be necessary to establish its jurisdiction over the offences referred to in article 4 in the following cases:

    (a) When the offences are committed in any territory under its jurisdiction or on board a ship or aircraft registered in that State;

    (b) When the alleged offender is a national of that State;

    (c) When the victim is a national of that State if that State considers it appropriate.

2. Each State Party shall likewise take such measures as may be necessary to establish its jurisdiction over such offences in cases where the alleged offender is present in any territory under its jurisdiction and it does not extradite him pursuant to article 8 to any of the States mentioned in paragraph 1 of this article.

3. This Convention does not exclude any criminal jurisdiction exercised in accordance with internal law.

Article 6

1. Upon being satisfied, after an examination of information available to it, that the circumstances so warrant, any State Party in whose territory a person alleged to have committed any offence referred to in article 4 is present shall take him into custody or take other legal measures to ensure his presence. The custody and other legal measures shall be as provided in the law of that State but may be continued only for such time as is necessary to enable any criminal or extradition proceedings to be instituted.

2. Such State shall immediately make a preliminary inquiry into the facts.

3. Any person in custody pursuant to paragraph 1 of this article shall be assisted in communicating immediately with the nearest appropriate representative of the State of which he is a national, or, if he is a stateless person, with the representative of the State where he usually resides.

4. When a State, pursuant to this article, has taken a person into custody, it shall immediately notify the States referred to in article 5, paragraph 1, of the fact that such person is in custody and of the circumstances which warrant his detention. The State which makes the preliminary inquiry contemplated in paragraph 2 of this article shall promptly report its findings to the said States and shall indicate whether it intends to exercise jurisdiction.

Article 7

1. The State Party in the territory under whose jurisdiction a person alleged to have committed any offence referred to in article 4 is found shall in the cases contemplated in article 5, if it does not extradite him, submit the case to its competent authorities for the purpose of prosecution.

2. These authorities shall take their decision in the same manner as in the case of any ordinary offence of a serious nature under the law of that State. In the cases referred to in article 5, paragraph 2, the standards of evidence required for prosecution and conviction shall in no way be less stringent than those which apply in the cases referred to in article 5, paragraph 1.

3. Any person regarding whom proceedings are brought in connection with any of the offences referred to in article 4 shall be guaranteed fair treatment at all stages of the proceedings.

Article 8

1. The offences referred to in article 4 shall be deemed to be included as extraditable offences in any extradition treaty existing between States Parties. States Parties undertake to include such offences as extraditable offences in every extradition treaty to be concluded between them.

2. If a State Party which makes extradition conditional on the existence of a treaty receives a request for extradition from another State Party with which it has no extradition treaty, it may consider this Convention as the legal basis for extradition in respect of such offences. Extradition shall be subject to the other conditions provided by the law of the requested State.

3. States Parties which do not make extradition conditional on the existence of a treaty shall recognize such offences as extraditable offences between themselves subject to the conditions provided by the law of the requested State.

4. Such offences shall be treated, for the purpose of extradition between States Parties, as if they had been committed not only in the place in which they occurred but also in the territories of the States required to establish their jurisdiction in accordance with article 5, paragraph 1.

Article 9

1. States Parties shall afford one another the greatest measure of assistance in connection with criminal proceedings brought in respect of any of the offences referred to in article 4, including the supply of all evidence at their disposal necessary for the proceedings.

2. States Parties shall carry out their obligations under paragraph I of this article in conformity with any treaties on mutual judicial assistance that may exist between them.

Article 10

1. Each State Party shall ensure that education and information regarding the prohibition against torture are fully included in the training of law enforcement personnel, civil or military, medical personnel, public officials and other persons who may be involved in the custody, interrogation or treatment of any individual subjected to any form of arrest, detention or imprisonment.

2. Each State Party shall include this prohibition in the rules or instructions issued in regard to the duties and functions of any such person.

Article 11

Each State Party shall keep under systematic review interrogation rules, instructions, methods and practices as well as arrangements for the custody and treatment of persons subjected to any form of arrest, detention or imprisonment in any territory under its jurisdiction, with a view to preventing any cases of torture.

Article 12

Each State Party shall ensure that its competent authorities proceed to a prompt and impartial investigation, wherever there is reasonable ground to believe that an act of torture has been committed in any territory under its jurisdiction.

Article 13

Each State Party shall ensure that any individual who alleges he has been subjected to torture in any territory under its jurisdiction has the right to complain to, and to have his case promptly and impartially examined by, its competent authorities. Steps shall be taken to ensure that the complainant and witnesses are protected against all ill-treatment or intimidation as a consequence of his complaint or any evidence given.

Article 14

1. Each State Party shall ensure in its legal system that the victim of an act of torture obtains redress and has an enforceable right to fair and adequate compensation, including the means for as full rehabilitation as possible. In the event of the death of the victim as a result of an act of torture, his dependants shall be entitled to compensation.

2. Nothing in this article shall affect any right of the victim or other persons to compensation which may exist under national law.

Article 15

Each State Party shall ensure that any statement which is established to have been made as a result of torture shall not be invoked as evidence in any proceedings, except against a person accused of torture as evidence that the statement was made.

Article 16

1. Each State Party shall undertake to prevent in any territory under its jurisdiction other acts of cruel, inhuman or degrading treatment or punishment which do not amount to torture as defined in article 1, when such acts are

committed by or at the instigation of or with the consent or acquiescence of a public official or other person acting in an official capacity. In particular, the obligations contained in articles 10, 11, 12 and 13 shall apply with the substitution for references to torture of references to other forms of cruel, inhuman or degrading treatment or punishment.

2. The provisions of this Convention are without prejudice to the provisions of any other international instrument or national law which prohibits cruel, inhuman or degrading treatment or punishment or which relates to extradition or expulsion.

Part II

Article 17

1. There shall be established a Committee against Torture (hereinafter referred to as the Committee) which shall carry out the functions hereinafter provided. The Committee shall consist of ten experts of high moral standing and recognized competence in the field of human rights, who shall serve in their personal capacity. The experts shall be elected by the States Parties, consideration being given to equitable geographical distribution and to the usefulness of the participation of some persons having legal experience.

2. The members of the Committee shall be elected by secret ballot from a list of persons nominated by States Parties. Each State Party may nominate one person from among its own nationals. States Parties shall bear in mind the usefulness of nominating persons who are also members of the Human Rights Committee established under the International Covenant on Civil and Political Rights and who are willing to serve on the Committee against Torture.

3. Elections of the members of the Committee shall be held at biennial meetings of States Parties convened by the Secretary-General of the United Nations. At those meetings, for which two thirds of the States Parties shall constitute a quorum, the persons elected to the Committee shall be those who obtain the largest number of votes and an absolute majority of the votes of the representatives of States Parties present and voting.

4. The initial election shall be held no later than six months after the date of the entry into force of this Convention. At least four months before the date of each election, the Secretary-General of the United Nations shall address a letter to the States Parties inviting them to submit their nominations within three months. The Secretary-General shall prepare a list in alphabetical order of all persons thus nominated, indicating the States Parties which have nominated them, and shall submit it to the States Parties.

5. The members of the Committee shall be elected for a term of four years. They shall be eligible for re-election if re-nominated. However, the term of five of the members elected at the first election shall expire at the end of two years; immediately after the first election the names of these five members shall be chosen by lot by the chairman of the meeting referred to in paragraph 3 of this article.

6. If a member of the Committee dies or resigns or for any other cause can no longer perform his Committee duties, the State Party which nominated him shall appoint another expert from among its nationals to serve for the remainder of his term, subject to the approval of the majority of the States Parties. The approval shall be considered given unless half or more of the States Parties respond negatively within six weeks after having been informed by the Secretary-General of the United Nations of the proposed appointment.

7. States Parties shall be responsible for the expenses of the members of the Committee while they are in performance of Committee duties.

Article 18

1. The Committee shall elect its officers for a term of two years. They may be re-elected.

2. The Committee shall establish its own rules of procedure, but these rules shall provide, *inter alia*, that:

    (a) Six members shall constitute a quorum;

    (b) Decisions of the Committee shall be made by a majority vote of the members present.

3. The Secretary-General of the United Nations shall provide the necessary staff and facilities for the effective performance of the functions of the Committee under this Convention.

4. The Secretary-General of the United Nations shall convene the initial meeting of the Committee. After its initial meeting, the Committee shall

meet at such times as shall be provided in its rules of procedure.

5. The States Parties shall be responsible for expenses incurred in connection with the holding of meetings of the States Parties and of the Committee, including reimbursement to the United Nations for any expenses, such as the cost of staff and facilities, incurred by the United Nations pursuant to paragraph 3 of this article.

Article 19

1. The States Parties shall submit to the Committee, through the Secretary-General of the United Nations, reports on the measures they have taken to give effect to their undertakings under this Convention, within one year after the entry into force of the Convention for the State Party concerned. Thereafter the States Parties shall submit supplementary reports every four years on any new measures taken and such other reports as the Committee may request.

2. The Secretary-General of the United Nations shall transmit the reports to all States Parties.

3. Each report shall be considered by the Committee which may make such general comments on the report as it may consider appropriate and shall forward these to the State Party concerned. That State Party may respond with any observations it chooses to the Committee.

4. The Committee may, at its discretion, decide to include any comments made by it in accordance with paragraph 3 of this article, together with the observations thereon received from the State Party concerned, in its annual report made in accordance with article 24. If so requested by the State Party concerned, the Committee may also include a copy of the report submitted under paragraph I of this article.

Article 20

1. If the Committee receives reliable information which appears to it to contain well-founded indications that torture is being systematically practised in the territory of a State Party, the Committee shall invite that State Party to co-operate in the examination of the information and to this end to submit observations with regard to the information concerned.

2. Taking into account any observations which may have been submitted by the State Party concerned, as well as any other relevant information available to it, the Committee may, if it decides that this is warranted, designate one or more of its members to make a confidential inquiry and to report to the Committee urgently.

3. If an inquiry is made in accordance with paragraph 2 of this article, the Committee shall seek the co-operation of the State Party concerned. In agreement with that State Party, such an inquiry may include a visit to its territory.

4. After examining the findings of its member or members submitted in accordance with paragraph 2 of this article, the Commission shall transmit these findings to the State Party concerned together with any comments or suggestions which seem appropriate in view of the situation.

5. All the proceedings of the Committee referred to in paragraphs I to 4 of this article shall be confidential, and at all stages of the proceedings the co-operation of the State Party shall be sought. After such proceedings have been completed with regard to an inquiry made in accordance with paragraph 2, the Committee may, after consultations with the State Party concerned, decide to include a summary account of the results of the proceedings in its annual report made in accordance with article 24.

Article 21

1. A State Party to this Convention may at any time declare under this article that it recognizes the competence of the Committee to receive and consider communications to the effect that a State Party claims that another State Party is not fulfilling its obligations under this Convention. Such communications may be received and considered according to the procedures laid down in this article only if submitted by a State Party which has made a declaration recognizing in regard to itself the competence of the Committee. No communication shall be dealt with by the Committee under this article if it concerns a State Party which has not made such a declaration. Communications received under this article shall be dealt with in accordance with the following procedure;

   (a) If a State Party considers that another State Party is not giving effect to the provisions of this Convention, it may, by written communication, bring the matter to the attention of that State Party. Within three months after the receipt of the communication the receiving State shall afford the State which sent the communication an explanation or any other statement in writing clarifying the matter, which should include, to the extent possible and pertinent, reference to domestic procedures and remedies taken, pending or available in the matter;

(b) If the matter is not adjusted to the satisfaction of both States Parties concerned within six months after the receipt by the receiving State of the initial communication, either State shall have the right to refer the matter to the Committee, by notice given to the Committee and to the other State;

(c) The Committee shall deal with a matter referred to it under this article only after it has ascertained that all domestic remedies have been invoked and exhausted in the matter, in conformity with the generally recognized principles of international law. This shall not be the rule where the application of the remedies is unreasonably prolonged or is unlikely to bring effective relief to the person who is the victim of the violation of this Convention;

(d) The Committee shall hold closed meetings when examining communications under this article;

(e) Subject to the provisions of subparagraph (c), the Committee shall make available its good offices to the States Parties concerned with a view to a friendly solution of the matter on the basis of respect for the obligations provided for in this Convention. For this purpose, the Committee may, when appropriate, set up an ad hoc conciliation commission;

(f) In any matter referred to it under this article, the Committee may call upon the States Parties concerned, referred to in subparagraph (b), to supply any relevant information;

(g) The States Parties concerned, referred to in subparagraph (b), shall have the right to be represented when the matter is being considered by the Committee and to make submissions orally and/or in writing;

(h) The Committee shall, within twelve months after the date of receipt of notice under subparagraph (b), submit a report:

(i) If a solution within the terms of subparagraph (e) is reached, the Committee shall confine its report to a brief statement of the facts and of the solution reached;

(ii) If a solution within the terms of subparagraph (e) is not reached, the Committee shall confine its report to a brief statement of the facts; the written submissions and record of the oral submissions made by the States Parties concerned shall be attached to the report. In every matter, the report shall be communicated to the States Parties concerned.

2. The provisions of this article shall come into force when five States Parties to this Convention have made declarations under paragraph 1 of this article. Such declarations shall be deposited by the States Parties with the Secretary-General of the United Nations, who shall transmit copies thereof to the other States Parties. A declaration may be withdrawn at any time by notification to the Secretary-General. Such a withdrawal shall not prejudice the consideration of any matter which is the subject of a communication already transmitted under this article; no further communication by any State Party shall be received under this article after the notification of withdrawal of the declaration has been received by the Secretary-General, unless the State Party concerned has made a new declaration.

Article 22

1. A State Party to this Convention may at any time declare under this article that it recognizes the competence of the Committee to receive and consider communications from or on behalf of individuals subject to its jurisdiction who claim to be victims of a violation by a State Party of the provisions of the Convention. No communication shall be received by the Committee if it concerns a State Party which has not made such a declaration.

2. The Committee shall consider inadmissible any communication under this article which is anonymous or which it considers to be an abuse of the right of submission of such communications or to be incompatible with the provisions of this Convention.

3. Subject to the provisions of paragraph 2, the Committee shall bring any communications submitted to it under this article to the attention of the State Party to this Convention which has made a declaration under paragraph I and is alleged to be violating any provisions of the Convention. Within six months, the receiving

State shall submit to the Committee written explanations or statements clarifying the matter and the remedy, if any, that may have been taken by that State.

4. The Committee shall consider communications received under this article in the light of all information made available to it by or on behalf of the individual and by the State Party concerned.

5. The Committee shall not consider any communications from an individual under this article unless it has ascertained that:

   (a) The same matter has not been, and is not being, examined under another procedure of international investigation or settlement;

   (b) The individual has exhausted all available domestic remedies; this shall not be the rule where the application of the remedies is unreasonably prolonged or is unlikely to bring effective relief to the person who is the victim of the violation of this Convention.

6. The Committee shall hold closed meetings when examining communications under this article.

7. The Committee shall forward its views to the State Party concerned and to the individual.

8. The provisions of this article shall come into force when five States Parties to this Convention have made declarations under paragraph 1 of this article. Such declarations shall be deposited by the States Parties with the Secretary-General of the United Nations, who shall transmit copies thereof to the other States Parties. A declaration may be withdrawn at any time by notification to the Secretary-General. Such a withdrawal shall not prejudice the consideration of any matter which is the subject of a communication already transmitted under this article; no further communication by or on behalf of an individual shall be received under this article after the notification of withdrawal of the declaration has been received by the Secretary General, unless the State Party has made a new declaration.

Article 23

The members of the Committee and of the ad hoc conciliation commissions which may be appointed under article 21, paragraph I (e), shall be entitled to the facilities, privileges and immunities of experts on mission for the United Nations as laid down in the relevant sections of the Convention on the Privileges and Immunities of the United Nations.

Article 24

The Committee shall submit an annual report on its activities under this Convention to the States Parties and to the General Assembly of the United Nations.

Part III

Article 25

1. This Convention is open for signature by all States.

2. This Convention is subject to ratification. Instruments of ratification shall be deposited with the Secretary-General of the United Nations.

Article 26

This Convention is open to accession by all States. Accession shall be effected by the deposit of an instrument of accession with the Secretary-General of the United Nations.

Article 27

1. This Convention shall enter into force on the thirtieth day after the date of the deposit with the Secretary-General of the United Nations of the twentieth instrument of ratification or accession.

2. For each State ratifying this Convention or acceding to it after the deposit of the twentieth instrument of ratification or accession, the Convention shall enter into force on the thirtieth day after the date of the deposit of its own instrument of ratification or accession.

Article 28

1. Each State may, at the time of signature or ratification of this Convention or accession thereto, declare that it does not recognize the competence of the Committee provided for in article 20.

2. Any State Party having made a reservation in accordance with paragraph I of this article may, at any time, withdraw this reservation by notification to the Secretary-General of the United Nations.

Article 29

1. Any State Party to this Convention may propose an amendment and file it with the Secretary-General of the United Nations. The Secretary

General shall thereupon communicate the proposed amendment to the States Parties with a request that they notify him whether they favour a conference of States Parties for the purpose of considering and voting upon the proposal. In the event that within four months from the date of such communication at least one third of the States Parties favours such a conference, the Secretary General shall convene the conference under the auspices of the United Nations. Any amendment adopted by a majority of the States Parties present and voting at the conference shall be submitted by the Secretary-General to all the States Parties for acceptance.

2. An amendment adopted in accordance with paragraph I of this article shall enter into force when two thirds of the States Parties to this Convention have notified the Secretary-General of the United Nations that they have accepted it in accordance with their respective constitutional processes.

3. When amendments enter into force, they shall be binding on those States Parties which have accepted them, other States Parties still being bound by the provisions of this Convention and any earlier amendments which they have accepted.

Article 30

1. Any dispute between two or more States Parties concerning the interpretation or application of this Convention which cannot be settled through negotiation shall, at the request of one of them, be submitted to arbitration. If within six months from the date of the request for arbitration the Parties are unable to agree on the organization of the arbitration, any one of those Parties may refer the dispute to the International Court of Justice by request in conformity with the Statute of the Court.

2. Each State may, at the time of signature or ratification of this Convention or accession thereto, declare that it does not consider itself bound by paragraph I of this article. The other States Parties shall not be bound by paragraph I of this article with respect to any State Party having made such a reservation.

3. Any State Party having made a reservation in accordance with paragraph 2 of this article may at any time withdraw this reservation by notification to the Secretary-General of the United Nations.

Article 31

1. A State Party may denounce this Convention by written notification to the Secretary-General of the United Nations. Denunciation becomes effective one year after the date of receipt of the notification by the Secretary-General.

2. Such a denunciation shall not have the effect of releasing the State Party from its obligations under this Convention in regard to any act or omission which occurs prior to the date at which the denunciation becomes effective, nor shall denunciation prejudice in any way the continued consideration of any matter which is already under consideration by the Committee prior to the date at which the denunciation becomes effective.

3. Following the date at which the denunciation of a State Party becomes effective, the Committee shall not commence consideration of any new matter regarding that State.

Article 32

The Secretary-General of the United Nations shall inform all States Members of the United Nations and all States which have signed this Convention or acceded to it of the following:

(a) Signatures, ratifications and accessions under articles 25 and 26;

(b) The date of entry into force of this Convention under article 27 and the date of the entry into force of any amendments under article 29;

(c) Denunciations under article 31.

Article 33

1. This Convention, of which the Arabic, Chinese, English, French, Russian and Spanish texts are equally authentic, shall be deposited with the Secretary-General of the United Nations.

2. The Secretary-General of the United Nations shall transmit certified copies of this Convention to all States.

CONSTITUTION OF THE INTERNATIONAL ORGANIZATION FOR MIGRATION (1987)

Preamble

THE HIGH CONTRACTING PARTIES

RECALLING the Resolution adopted on 5 December 1951 by the Migration Conference in Brussels,

RECOGNIZING that the provision of migration services at an international level is often required to ensure the orderly flow of migration movements throughout the world and to facilitate, under the most favourable conditions, the settlement and integration of the migrants into the economic and social structure of the country of reception,

that similar migration services may also be required for temporary migration, return migration and intra-regional migration,

that international migration also includes that of refugees, displaced persons and other individuals compelled to leave their homelands, and who are in need of international migration services,

that there is a need to promote the co-operation of States and international organizations with a view to facilitating the emigration of persons who desire to migrate to countries where they may achieve self-dependence through their employment and live with their families in dignity and self-respect,

that migration may stimulate the creation of new economic opportunities in receiving countries and that a relationship exists between migration and the economic, social and cultural conditions in developing countries,

that in the co-operation and other international activities for migration the needs of developing countries should be taken into account,

that there is a need to promote the co-operation of States and international organizations, governmental and non-governmental, for research and consultation on migration issues, not only in regard to the migration process but also the specific situation and needs of the migrant as an individual human being, that the movement of migrants should, to the extent possible, be carried out with normal transport services but that, on occasion, there is a need for additional or other facilities,

that there should be close co-operation and co-ordination among States, international organizations, governmental and non-governmental, on migration and refugee matters,

that there is a need for the international financing of activities related to international migration,

DO HEREBY ESTABLISH

the INTERNATIONAL ORGANIZATION FOR MIGRATION, hereinafter called the Organization, and

ACCEPT THIS CONSTITUTION.

Chapter I: Purposes and Functions

Article 1

1. The purposes and functions of the Organization shall be:

    (a) to make arrangements for the organized transfer of migrants, for whom existing facilities are inadequate or who would not otherwise be able to move without special assistance, to countries offering opportunities for orderly migration;

    (b) to concern itself with the organized transfer of refugees, displaced persons and other individuals in need of international migration services for whom arrangements may be made between the Organization and the States concerned, including those States undertaking to receive them;

    (c) to provide, at the request of and in agreement with the States concerned, migration services such as recruitment, selection, processing, language training, orientation activities, medical examination, placement, activities facilitating reception and integration, advisory services on migration questions, and other assistance as is in accord with the aims of the Organization;

    (d) to provide similar services as requested by States, or in co-operation with other interested international organizations, for voluntary return migration, including voluntary repatriation;

    (e) to provide a forum to States as well as international and other organizations for the exchange of views and experiences, and the promotion of co-operation and co-ordination of efforts on international migration issues, including studies on such issues in order to develop practical solutions.

2. In carrying out its functions, the Organization shall co-operate closely with international organizations, governmental and non-governmental, concerned with migration, refugees and human resources in order, *inter alia*, to facilitate the co-ordination of international activities in these fields. Such co-operation shall be carried out in the mutual respect of the competences of the organizations concerned.

3. The Organization shall recognize the fact that control of standards of admission and the number of immigrants to be admitted are matters within the domestic jurisdiction of States, and, in carrying out its functions, shall conform to the laws, regulations and policies of the States concerned.

Chapter II: Membership

Article 2

The Members of the Organization shall be:

(a) the States being Members of the Organization which have accepted this Constitution according to Article 34, or to which the terms of Article 35 apply;

(b) other States with a demonstrated interest in the principle of free movement of persons which undertake to make a financial contribution at least to the administrative requirements of the Organization, the rate of which will be agreed to by the Council and by the State concerned, subject to a two-thirds majority vote of the Council and upon acceptance by the State of this Constitution.

Article 3

Any Member State may give notice of withdrawal from the Organization effective at the end of a financial year. Such notice must be in writing and must reach the Director General of the Organization at least four months before the end of the financial year. The financial obligations to the Organization of a Member State which has given notice of withdrawal shall include the entire financial year in which notice is given.

Article 4

1. If a Member State fails to meet its financial obligations to the Organization for two consecutive financial years, the Council may by a two-thirds majority vote suspend the voting rights and all or part of the services to which this Member State is entitled. The Council shall have the authority to restore such voting rights and services by a simple majority vote.

2. Any Member State may be suspended from membership by a two-thirds majority vote of the Council if it persistently violates the principles of this Constitution. The Council shall have the authority to restore such membership by a simple majority vote.

Chapter III: Organs

Article 5

There are established as the organs of the Organization:

(a) the Council;

(b) the Executive Committee;

(c) the Administration.

Chapter IV: Council

Article 6

The functions of the Council, in addition to those mentioned in other provisions of this Constitution, shall be:

(a) to determine the policies of the Organization;

(b) to review the reports and to approve and direct the activities of the Executive Committee;

(c) to review the reports and to approve and direct the activities of the Director General;

(d) to review and approve the programme, the Budget, the expenditure and the accounts of the Organization;

(e) to take any other appropriate action to further the purposes of the Organization.

Article 7

1. The Council shall be composed of representatives of the Member States.

2 Each Member State shall have one representative and such alternates and advisers as it may deem necessary.

3. Each Member State shall have one vote in the Council.

Article 8

The Council may admit, upon their application, non-member States and international organizations, governmental or non-governmental, concerned with migration, refugees or human resources as observers at its meetings under conditions which may be prescribed in its rules of procedure. No such observers shall have the right to vote.

Article 9

1. The Council shall meet in regular session once a year.

2. The Council shall meet in special session at the request of:

    (a) one third of its members;

    (b) the Executive Committee;

    (c) the Director General or the Chairman of the Council in urgent circumstances.

3. The Council shall elect, at the beginning of each regular session, a Chairman and other officers for a one-year term.

Article 10

The Council may set up such sub-committees as may be required for the proper discharge of its functions.

Article 11

The Council shall adopt its own rules of procedure.

Chapter V: Executive Committee

Article 12

The functions of the Executive Committee shall be:

(a) to examine and review the policies, programmes and activities of the Organization, the annual reports of the Director General and any special reports;

(b) to examine any financial or budgetary questions falling within the competence of the Council;

(c) to consider any matter specifically referred to it by the Council, including the revision of the Budget, and to take such action as may be deemed necessary thereon;

(d) to advise the Director General on any matters which he may refer to it;

(e) to make, between sessions of the Council, any urgent decisions on matters falling within the competence of the Council, which shall be submitted for approval by that body at its next session;

(f) to present advice or proposals to the Council or the Director General on its own initiative;

(g) to transmit reports and/or recommendations to the Council on the matters dealt with.

Article 13

1. The Executive Committee shall be composed of the representatives of nine Member States. This number may be increased by a two-thirds majority vote of the Council, provided it shall not exceed one third of the total membership of the Organization.

2. These Member States shall be elected by the Council for two years and shall be eligible for re-election.

3. Each member of the Executive Committee shall have one representative and such alternates and advisers as it may deem necessary.

4. Each member of the Executive Committee shall have one vote.

Article 14

1. The Executive Committee shall meet at least once a year. It shall meet, as necessary, in order to perform its functions, at the request of:

    (a) its Chairman;

    (b) the Council;

    (c) the Director General after consultation with the Chairman of the Council;

    (d) a majority of its members.

2. The Executive Committee shall elect a Chairman and a Vice-Chairman from among its members for a one-year term.

Article 15

The Executive Committee may, subject to review by the Council, set up such sub-committees as may be required for the proper discharge of its functions.

Article 16

The Executive Committee shall adopt its own rules of procedure.

Chapter VI: Administration

Article 17

The Administration shall comprise a Director General, a Deputy Director General and such staff as the Council may determine.

Article 18

1. The Director General and the Deputy Director General shall be elected by a two-thirds majority vote of the Council and may be re-elected. Their term of office shall normally be five years but may, in exceptional cases, be less if a two-thirds majority of the Council so decides. They shall serve under contracts approved by the Council, which shall be signed on behalf of the Organization by the Chairman of the Council.

2. The Director General shall be responsible to the Council and the Executive Committee. The Director General shall discharge the administrative and executive functions of the Organization in accordance with this Constitution and the policies and decisions of the Council and the Executive Committee and the rules and regulations established by them. The Director General shall formulate proposals for appropriate action by the Council.

Article 19

The Director General shall appoint the staff of the Administration in accordance with the staff regulations adopted by the Council.

Article 20

1. In the performance of their duties, the Director General, the Deputy Director General and the staff shall neither seek nor receive instructions from any State or from any authority external to the Organization. They shall refrain from any action which might reflect adversely on their position as international officials.

2. Each Member State undertakes to respect the exclusively international character of the responsibilities of the Director General, the Deputy Director General and the staff and not to seek to influence them in the discharge of their responsibilities.

3. Efficiency, competence and integrity shall be the necessary considerations in the recruitment and employment of the staff which, except in special circumstances, shall be recruited among the nationals of the Member States of the Organization, taking into account the principle of equitable geographical distribution.

Article 21

The Director General shall be present, or be represented by the Deputy Director General or another designated official, at all sessions of the Council, the Executive Committee and any sub-committees. The Director General or the designated representative may participate in the discussions but shall have no vote.

Article 22

At the regular session of the Council following the end of each financial year, the Director General shall make to the Council, through the Executive Committee, a report on the work of the Organization, giving a full account of its activities during that year.

Chapter VII: Headquarters

Article 23

1. The Organization shall have its Headquarters in Geneva. The Council may, by a two-thirds majority vote, change its location.

2. The meetings of the Council and the Executive Committee shall be held in Geneva, unless two-thirds of the members of the Council or the Executive Committee respectively have agreed to meet elsewhere.

Chapter VIII: Finance

Article 24

The Director General shall submit to the Council, through the Executive Committee, an annual budget covering the administrative and operational requirements and the anticipated resources of the Organization, such supplementary estimates as may be required and the annual or special accounting statements of the Organization.

Article 25

1. The requirements of the Organization shall be financed:

(a) as to the Administrative part of the Budget, by cash contributions from Member States, which shall be due at the beginning of the financial year to which they relate and shall be paid promptly;

(b) as to the Operational part of the Budget, by contributions in cash, in kind or in services from Member States, other States, international organizations, governmental or non-governmental, other legal entities or individuals, which shall be paid as early as possible and in full prior to the expiration of the financial year to which they relate.

2. Member States shall contribute to the Administrative part of the Budget of the Organization at a rate agreed to by the Council and by the Member State concerned.

3. Contributions to the operational expenditure of the Organization shall be voluntary and any contributor to the Operational part of the Budget may stipulate with the Organization terms and conditions, consistent with the purposes and functions of the Organization, under which its contributions may be used.

4. (a) All Headquarters administrative expenditure and all other administrative expenditure except that incurred in pursuance of the functions outlined in paragraph 1 (c) and (d) of Article 1 shall be attributed to the Administrative part of the Budget;

(b) all operational expenditure and such administrative expenditure as is incurred in pursuance of the functions outlined in paragraph 1 (c) and (d) of Article 1 shall be attributed to the Operational part of the Budget.

5. The Council shall ensure that the management is conducted in an efficient and economical manner.

Article 26

The financial regulations shall be established by the Council.

Chapter IX: Legal Status

Article 27

The Organization shall possess full juridical personality. It shall enjoy such legal capacity, as may be necessary for the exercise of its functions and the fulfilment of its purposes, and in particular the capacity, in accordance with the laws of the State:

(a) to contract;

(b) to acquire and dispose of immovable and movable property;

(c) to receive and disburse private and public funds;

(d) to institute legal proceedings.

Article 28

1. The Organization shall enjoy such privileges and immunities as are necessary for the exercise of its functions and the fulfilment of its purposes.

2. Representatives of Member States, the Director General, the Deputy Director General and the staff of the Administration shall likewise enjoy such privileges and immunities as are necessary for the independent exercise of their functions in connection with the Organization.

3. These privileges and immunities shall be defined in agreements between the Organization and the States concerned or through other measures taken by these States.

Chapter X: Miscellaneous Provisions

Article 29

1. Except as otherwise expressly provided in this Constitution or rules made by the Council or the Executive Committee, all decisions of the Council, the Executive Committee and all sub-committees shall be taken by a simple majority vote.

2. Majorities provided for in this Constitution or rules made by the Council or the Executive Committee shall refer to members present and voting.

3. No vote shall be valid unless a majority of the members of the Council, the Executive Committee or the sub-committee concerned are present.

Article 30

1. Texts of proposed amendments to this Constitution shall be communicated by the Director General to Governments of Member States at least three months in advance of their consideration by the Council.

2. Amendments shall come into force when adopted by two-thirds of the members of the Council and accepted by two-thirds of the Member States in accordance with their respective constitutional processes, provided, however, that amendments involving new obligations for Members shall come into force in respect of a particular Member only when that Member accepts such amendments.

Article 31

Any dispute concerning the interpretation or application of this Constitution which is not settled by negotiation or by a two-thirds majority vote of the Council shall be referred to the International Court of Justice in conformity with the Statute of the Court, unless the Member States concerned agree on another mode of settlement within a reasonable period of time.

Article 32

Subject to approval by two-thirds of the members of the Council, the Organization may take over from any other international organization or agency the purposes and activities of which lie within the purposes of the Organization such activities, resources and obligations as may be determined by international agreement or by mutually acceptable arrangements entered into between the competent authorities of the respective organizations.

Article 33

The Council may, by a three-quarters majority vote of its members, decide to dissolve the Organization.

Article 34*

This Constitution shall come into force, for those Governments Members of the Intergovernmental Committee for European Migration which have accepted it in accordance with their respective constitutional processes, on the day of the first meeting of that Committee after:

(a) at least two-thirds of the Members of the Committee,

(b) a number of Members whose contributions represent at least 75 per cent of the Administrative part of the Budget, shall have communicated to the Director their acceptance of this Constitution.

Article 35

Those Governments Members of the Intergovernmental Committee for European Migration which have not by the date of coming into force of this Constitution communicated to the Director their acceptance of this Constitution may remain Members of the Committee for a period of one year from that date if they contribute to the administrative requirements of the Committee in accordance with paragraph 2 of Article 25, and they shall retain during that period the right to accept the Constitution.

Article 36

The English, French and Spanish texts of this Constitution shall be regarded as equally authentic.

Notes: The present text incorporates into the Constitution of 19 October 1953 of the Intergovernmental Committee for European Migration (former designation of the Organization) the amendments adopted on 20 May 1987 and which entered into force on 14 November 1989.

* Articles 34 and 35 were implemented at the time of the entry into force of the Constitution on 30 November 1954.

UNITED NATIONS CONVENTION ON THE RIGHTS OF THE CHILD (1989)

Preamble

The States Parties to the present Convention,

Considering that, in accordance with the principles proclaimed in the Charter of the United Nations, recognition of the inherent dignity and of the equal and inalienable rights of all members of the human family is the foundation of freedom, justice and peace in the world,

Bearing in mind that the peoples of the United Nations have, in the Charter, reaffirmed their faith in fundamental human rights and in the dignity and worth of the human person, and have determined to promote social progress and better standards of life in larger freedom,

Recognizing that the United Nations has, in the Universal Declaration of Human Rights and in the International Covenants on Human Rights, proclaimed and agreed that everyone is entitled to all the rights and freedoms set forth therein, without distinction of any kind, such as race, colour, sex, language, religion, political or other opinion, national or social origin, property, birth or other status,

Recalling that, in the Universal Declaration of Human Rights, the United Nations has proclaimed that childhood is entitled to special care and assistance,

Convinced that the family, as the fundamental group of society and the natural environment for the growth and well-being of all its members and particularly children, should be afforded the necessary protection and assistance so that it can fully assume its responsibilities within the community,

Recognizing that the child, for the full and harmonious development of his or her personality, should grow up in a family environment, in an atmosphere of happiness, love and understanding,

Considering that the child should be fully prepared to live an individual life in society, and brought up in the spirit of the ideals proclaimed in the Charter of the United Nations, and in particular in the spirit of peace, dignity, tolerance, freedom, equality and solidarity,

Bearing in mind that the need to extend particular care to the child has been stated in the Geneva Declaration of the Rights of the Child of 1924 and in the Declaration of the Rights of the Child adopted by the General Assembly on 20 November 1959 and recognized in the Universal Declaration of Human Rights, in the International Covenant on Civil and Political Rights (in particular in articles 23 and 24), in the International Covenant on Economic, Social and Cultural Rights (in particular in article 10) and in the statutes and relevant instruments of specialized agencies and international organizations concerned with the welfare of children, '

Bearing in mind that, as indicated in the Declaration of the Rights of the Child, "the child, by reason of his physical and mental immaturity, needs special safeguards and care, including appropriate legal protection, before as well as after birth",

Recalling the provisions of the Declaration on Social and Legal Principles relating to the Protection and Welfare of Children, with Special Reference to Foster Placement and Adoption Nationally and Internationally; the United Nations Standard Minimum Rules for the Administration of Juvenile Justice (The Beijing Rules) ; and the Declaration on the Protection of Women and Children in Emergency and Armed Conflict,

Recognizing that, in all countries in the world, there are children living in exceptionally difficult conditions, and that such children need special consideration,

Taking due account of the importance of the traditions and cultural values of each people for the protection and harmonious development of the child,

Recognizing the importance of international co-operation for improving the living conditions of children in every country, in particular in the developing countries,

Have agreed as follows:

Part I

Article 1

For the purposes of the present Convention, a child means every human being below the age of eighteen years unless, under the law applicable to the child, majority is attained earlier.

Article 2

1. States Parties shall respect and ensure the rights set forth in the present Convention to each child within their jurisdiction without discrimination of any kind, irrespective of the child's or his or her parent's or legal guardian's race, colour, sex, language, religion, political or other opinion, national, ethnic or social origin, property, disability, birth or other status.

2. States Parties shall take all appropriate measures to ensure that the child is protected against all forms of discrimination or punishment on the basis of the status, activities, expressed opinions, or beliefs of the child's parents, legal guardians, or family members.

Article 3

1. In all actions concerning children, whether undertaken by public or private social welfare institutions, courts of law, administrative authorities or legislative bodies, the best interests of the child shall be a primary consideration.

2. States Parties undertake to ensure the child such protection and care as is necessary for his or her well-being, taking into account the rights and duties of his or her parents, legal guardians, or other individuals legally responsible for him or her, and, to this end, shall take all appropriate legislative and administrative measures.

3. States Parties shall ensure that the institutions, services and facilities responsible for the care or protection of children shall conform with the

standards established by competent authorities, particularly in the areas of safety, health, in the number and suitability of their staff, as well as competent supervision.

Article 4

States Parties shall undertake all appropriate legislative, administrative, and other measures for the implementation of the rights recognized in the present Convention. With regard to economic, social and cultural rights, States Parties shall undertake such measures to the maximum extent of their available resources and, where needed, within the framework of international co-operation.

Article 5

States Parties shall respect the responsibilities, rights and duties of parents or, where applicable, the members of the extended family or community as provided for by local custom, legal guardians or other persons legally responsible for the child, to provide, in a manner consistent with the evolving capacities of the child, appropriate direction and guidance in the exercise by the child of the rights recognized in the present Convention.

Article 6

1. States Parties recognize that every child has the inherent right to life.

2. States Parties shall ensure to the maximum extent possible the survival and development of the child.

Article 7

1. The child shall be registered immediately after birth and shall have the right from birth to a name, the right to acquire a nationality and, as far as possible, the right to know and be cared for by his or her parents.

2. States Parties shall ensure the implementation of these rights in accordance with their national law and their obligations under the relevant international instruments in this field, in particular where the child would otherwise be stateless.

Article 8

1. States Parties undertake to respect the right of the child to preserve his or her identity, including nationality, name and family relations as recognized by law without unlawful interference.

2. Where a child is illegally deprived of some or all of the elements of his or her identity, States Parties shall provide appropriate assistance and protection, with a view to speedily re-establishing his or her identity.

Article 9

1. States Parties shall ensure that a child shall not be separated from his or her parents against their will, except when competent authorities subject to judicial review determine, in accordance with applicable law and procedures, that such separation is necessary for the best interests of the child. Such determination may be necessary in a particular case such as one involving abuse or neglect of the child by the parents, or one where the parents are living separately and a decision must be made as to the child's place of residence.

2. In any proceedings pursuant to paragraph 1 of the present article, all interested parties shall be given an opportunity to participate in the proceedings and make their views known.

3. States Parties shall respect the right of the child who is separated from one or both parents to maintain personal relations and direct contact with both parents on a regular basis, except if it is contrary to the child's best interests.

4. Where such separation results from any action initiated by a State Party, such as the detention, imprisonment, exile, deportation or death (including death arising from any cause while the person is in the custody of the State) of one or both parents or of the child, that State Party shall, upon request, provide the parents, the child or, if appropriate, another member of the family with the essential information concerning the whereabouts of the absent member(s) of the family unless the provision of the information would be detrimental to the well-being of the child. States Parties shall further ensure that the submission of such a request shall of itself entail no adverse consequences for the person(s) concerned.

Article 10

1. In accordance with the obligation of States Parties under article 9, paragraph 1, applications by a child or his or her parents to enter or leave a State Party for the purpose of family reunification shall be dealt with by States Parties in a positive, humane and expeditious manner. States Parties shall further ensure that the submission of such

a request shall entail no adverse consequences for the applicants and for the members of their family.

2. A child whose parents reside in different States shall have the right to maintain on a regular basis, save in exceptional circumstances personal relations and direct contacts with both parents. Towards that end and in accordance with the obligation of States Parties under article 9, paragraph 2, States Parties shall respect the right of the child and his or her parents to leave any country, including their own, and to enter their own country. The right to leave any country shall be subject only to such restrictions as are prescribed by law and which are necessary to protect the national security, public order (*ordre public*), public health or morals or the rights and freedoms of others and are consistent with the other rights recognized in the present Convention.

Article 11

1. States Parties shall take measures to combat the illicit transfer and non-return of children abroad.

2. To this end, States Parties shall promote the conclusion of bilateral or multilateral agreements or accession to existing agreements.

Article 12

1. States Parties shall assure to the child who is capable of forming his or her own views the right to express those views freely in all matters affecting the child, the views of the child being given due weight in accordance with the age and maturity of the child.

2. For this purpose, the child shall in particular be provided the opportunity to be heard in any judicial and administrative proceedings affecting the child, either directly, or through a representative or an appropriate body, in a manner consistent with the procedural rules of national law.

Article 13

1. The child shall have the right to freedom of expression; this right shall include freedom to seek, receive and impart information and ideas of all kinds, regardless of frontiers, either orally, in writing or in print, in the form of art, or through any other media of the child's choice.

2. The exercise of this right may be subject to certain restrictions, but these shall only be such as are provided by law and are necessary:

    (a) For respect of the rights or reputations of others; or

    (b) For the protection of national security or of public order (*ordre public*), or of public health or morals.

Article 14

1. States Parties shall respect the right of the child to freedom of thought, conscience and religion.

2. States Parties shall respect the rights and duties of the parents and, when applicable, legal guardians, to provide direction to the child in the exercise of his or her right in a manner consistent with the evolving capacities of the child.

3. Freedom to manifest one's religion or beliefs may be subject only to such limitations as are prescribed by law and are necessary to protect public safety, order, health or morals, or the fundamental rights and freedoms of others.

Article 15

1. States Parties recognize the rights of the child to freedom of association and to freedom of peaceful assembly.

2. No restrictions may be placed on the exercise of these rights other than those imposed in conformity with the law and which are necessary in a democratic society in the interests of national security or public safety, public order (*ordre public*), the protection of public health or morals or the protection of the rights and freedoms of others.

Article 16

1. No child shall be subjected to arbitrary or unlawful interference with his or her privacy, family, home or correspondence, nor to unlawful attacks on his or her honour and reputation.

2. The child has the right to the protection of the law against such interference or attacks.

Article 17

States Parties recognize the important function performed by the mass media and shall ensure that the child has access to information and material from a diversity of national and international sources, especially those aimed at the promotion of his or her social, spiritual and moral well-being and physical and mental health. To this end, States Parties shall:

(a) Encourage the mass media to disseminate information and material of social and cultural benefit to the child and in accordance with the spirit of article 29;

(b) Encourage international co-operation in the production, exchange and dissemination of such information and material from a diversity of cultural, national and international sources;

(c) Encourage the production and dissemination of children's books;

(d) Encourage the mass media to have particular regard to the linguistic needs of the child who belongs to a minority group or who is indigenous;

(e) Encourage the development of appropriate guidelines for the protection of the child from information and material injurious to his or her well-being, bearing in mind the provisions of articles 13 and 18.

Article 18

1. States Parties shall use their best efforts to ensure recognition of the principle that both parents have common responsibilities for the upbringing and development of the child. Parents or, as the case may be, legal guardians, have the primary responsibility for the upbringing and development of the child. The best interests of the child will be their basic concern.

2. For the purpose of guaranteeing and promoting the rights set forth in the present Convention, States Parties shall render appropriate assistance to parents and legal guardians in the performance of their child-rearing responsibilities and shall ensure the development of institutions, facilities and services for the care of children.

3. States Parties shall take all appropriate measures to ensure that children of working parents have the right to benefit from child-care services and facilities for which they are eligible.

Article 19

1. States Parties shall take all appropriate legislative, administrative, social and educational measures to protect the child from all forms of physical or mental violence, injury or abuse, neglect or negligent treatment, maltreatment or exploitation, including sexual abuse, while in the care of parent(s), legal guardian(s) or any other person who has the care of the child.

2. Such protective measures should, as appropriate, include effective procedures for the establishment of social programmes to provide necessary support for the child and for those who have the care of the child, as well as for other forms of prevention and for identification, reporting, referral, investigation, treatment and follow-up of instances of child maltreatment described heretofore, and, as appropriate, for judicial involvement.

Article 20

1. A child temporarily or permanently deprived of his or her family environment, or in whose own best interests cannot be allowed to remain in that environment, shall be entitled to special protection and assistance provided by the State.

2. States Parties shall in accordance with their national laws ensure alternative care for such a child.

3. Such care could include, *inter alia*, foster placement, kafalah of Islamic law, adoption or if necessary placement in suitable institutions for the care of children. When considering solutions, due regard shall be paid to the desirability of continuity in a child's upbringing and to the child's ethnic, religious, cultural and linguistic background.

Article 21

States Parties that recognize and/or permit the system of adoption shall ensure that the best interests of the child shall be the paramount consideration and they shall:

(a) Ensure that the adoption of a child is authorized only by competent authorities who determine, in accordance with applicable law and procedures and on the basis of all pertinent and reliable information, that the adoption is permissible in view of the child's status concerning parents, relatives and legal guardians and that, if required, the persons concerned have given their informed consent to the adoption on the basis of such counselling as may be necessary;

(b) Recognize that inter-country adoption may be considered as an alternative means of child's care, if the child cannot be placed in a foster or an adoptive family or cannot in any suitable manner be cared for in the child's country of origin;

(c) Ensure that the child concerned by inter-country adoption enjoys safeguards and standards equivalent to those existing in the case of national adoption;

(d) Take all appropriate measures to ensure that, in inter-country adoption, the placement does not result in improper financial gain for those involved in it;

(e) Promote, where appropriate, the objectives of the present article by concluding bilateral or multilateral arrangements or agreements, and endeavour, within this framework, to ensure that the placement of the child in another country is carried out by competent authorities or organs.

Article 22

1. States Parties shall take appropriate measures to ensure that a child who is seeking refugee status or who is considered a refugee in accordance with applicable international or domestic law and procedures shall, whether unaccompanied or accompanied by his or her parents or by any other person, receive appropriate protection and humanitarian assistance in the enjoyment of applicable rights set forth in the present Convention and in other international human rights or humanitarian instruments to which the said States are Parties.

2. For this purpose, States Parties shall provide, as they consider appropriate, co-operation in any efforts by the United Nations and other competent intergovernmental organizations or non-governmental organizations co-operating with the United Nations to protect and assist such a child and to trace the parents or other members of the family of any refugee child in order to obtain information necessary for reunification with his or her family. In cases where no parents or other members of the family can be found, the child shall be accorded the same protection as any other child permanently or temporarily deprived of his or her family environment for any reason, as set forth in the present Convention.

Article 23

1. States Parties recognize that a mentally or physically disabled child should enjoy a full and decent life, in conditions which ensure dignity, promote self-reliance and facilitate the child's active participation in the community.

2. States Parties recognize the right of the disabled child to special care and shall encourage and ensure the extension, subject to available resources, to the eligible child and those responsible for his or her care, of assistance for which application is made and which is appropriate to the child's condition and to the circumstances of the parents or others caring for the child.

3. Recognizing the special needs of a disabled child, assistance extended in accordance with paragraph 2 of the present article shall be provided free of charge, whenever possible, taking into account the financial resources of the parents or others caring for the child, and shall be designed to ensure that the disabled child has effective access to and receives education, training, health care services, rehabilitation services, preparation for employment and recreation opportunities in a manner conducive to the child's achieving the fullest possible social integration and individual development, including his or her cultural and spiritual development.

4. States Parties shall promote, in the spirit of international cooperation, the exchange of appropriate information in the field of preventive health care and of medical, psychological and functional treatment of disabled children, including dissemination of and access to information concerning methods of rehabilitation, education and vocational services, with the aim of enabling States Parties to improve their capabilities and skills and to widen their experience in these areas. In this regard, particular account shall be taken of the needs of developing countries.

Article 24

1. States Parties recognize the right of the child to the enjoyment of the highest attainable standard of health and to facilities for the treatment of illness and rehabilitation of health. States Parties shall strive to ensure that no child is deprived of his or her right of access to such health care services.

2. States Parties shall pursue full implementation of this right and, in particular, shall take appropriate measures:

    (a) To diminish infant and child mortality;

    (b) To ensure the provision of necessary medical assistance and health care to all children with emphasis on the development of primary health care;

(c) To combat disease and malnutrition, including within the framework of primary health care, through, *inter alia*, the application of readily available technology and through the provision of adequate nutritious foods and clean drinking-water, taking into consideration the dangers and risks of environmental pollution;

(d) To ensure appropriate pre-natal and post-natal health care for mothers;

(e) To ensure that all segments of society, in particular parents and children, are informed, have access to education and are supported in the use of basic knowledge of child health and nutrition, the advantages of breast-feeding, hygiene and environmental sanitation and the prevention of accidents;

(f) To develop preventive health care, guidance for parents and family planning education and services.

3. States Parties shall take all effective and appropriate measures with a view to abolishing traditional practices prejudicial to the health of children.

4. States Parties undertake to promote and encourage international co-operation with a view to achieving progressively the full realization of the right recognized in the present article. In this regard, particular account shall be taken of the needs of developing countries.

Article 25

States Parties recognize the right of a child who has been placed by the competent authorities for the purposes of care, protection or treatment of his or her physical or mental health, to a periodic review of the treatment provided to the child and all other circumstances relevant to his or her placement.

Article 26

1. States Parties shall recognize for every child the right to benefit from social security, including social insurance, and shall take the necessary measures to achieve the full realization of this right in accordance with their national law.

2. The benefits should, where appropriate, be granted, taking into account the resources and the circumstances of the child and persons having responsibility for the maintenance of the child, as well as any other consideration relevant to an application for benefits made by or on behalf of the child.

Article 27

1. States Parties recognize the right of every child to a standard of living adequate for the child's physical, mental, spiritual, moral and social development.

2. The parent(s) or others responsible for the child have the primary responsibility to secure, within their abilities and financial capacities, the conditions of living necessary for the child's development.

3. States Parties, in accordance with national conditions and within their means, shall take appropriate measures to assist parents and others responsible for the child to implement this right and shall in case of need provide material assistance and support programmes, particularly with regard to nutrition, clothing and housing.

4. States Parties shall take all appropriate measures to secure the recovery of maintenance for the child from the parents or other persons having financial responsibility for the child, both within the State Party and from abroad. In particular, where the person having financial responsibility for the child lives in a State different from that of the child, States Parties shall promote the accession to international agreements or the conclusion of such agreements, as well as the making of other appropriate arrangements.

Article 28

1. States Parties recognize the right of the child to education, and with a view to achieving this right progressively and on the basis of equal opportunity, they shall, in particular:

(a) Make primary education compulsory and available free to all;

(b) Encourage the development of different forms of secondary education, including general and vocational education, make them available and accessible to every child, and take appropriate measures such as the introduction of free education and offering financial assistance in case of need;

(c) Make higher education accessible to all on the basis of capacity by every appropriate means;

(d) Make educational and vocational information and guidance available and accessible to all children;

(e) Take measures to encourage regular attendance at schools and the reduction of drop-out rates.

2. States Parties shall take all appropriate measures to ensure that school discipline is administered in a manner consistent with the child's human dignity and in conformity with the present Convention.

3. States Parties shall promote and encourage international cooperation in matters relating to education, in particular with a view to contributing to the elimination of ignorance and illiteracy throughout the world and facilitating access to scientific and technical knowledge and modern teaching methods. In this regard, particular account shall be taken of the needs of developing countries.

Article 29

1. States Parties agree that the education of the child shall be directed to:

    (a) The development of the child's personality, talents and mental and physical abilities to their fullest potential;

    (b) The development of respect for human rights and fundamental freedoms, and for the principles enshrined in the Charter of the United Nations;

    (c) The development of respect for the child's parents, his or her own cultural identity, language and values, for the national values of the country in which the child is living; the country from which he or she may originate, and for civilizations different from his or her own;

    (d) The preparation of the child for responsible life in a free society, in the spirit of understanding, peace, tolerance, equality of sexes, and friendship among all peoples, ethnic, national and religious groups and persons of indigenous origin;

    (e) The development of respect for the natural environment.

2. No part of the present article or article 28 shall be construed so as to interfere with the liberty of individuals and bodies to establish and direct educational institutions, subject always to the observance of the principles set forth in paragraph 1 of the present article and to the requirements that the education given in such institutions shall conform to such minimum standards as may be laid down by the State.

Article 30

In those States in which ethnic, religious or linguistic minorities or persons of indigenous origin exist, a child belonging to such a minority or who is indigenous shall not be denied the right, in community with other members of his or her group, to enjoy his or her own culture, to profess and practise his or her own religion, or to use his or her own language.

Article 31

1. States Parties recognize the right of the child to rest and leisure, to engage in play and recreational activities appropriate to the age of the child and to participate freely in cultural life and the arts.

2. States Parties shall respect and promote the right of the child to participate fully in cultural and artistic life and shall encourage the provision of appropriate and equal opportunities for cultural, artistic, recreational and leisure activity.

Article 32

1. States Parties recognize the right of the child to be protected from economic exploitation and from performing any work that is likely to be hazardous or to interfere with the child's education, or to be harmful to the child's health or physical, mental, spiritual, moral or social development.

2. States Parties shall take legislative, administrative, social and educational measures to ensure the implementation of the present article. To this end, and having regard to the relevant provisions of other international instruments, States Parties shall in particular:

    (a) Provide for a minimum age or minimum ages for admission to employment;

    (b) Provide for appropriate regulation of the hours and conditions of employment;

    (c) Provide for appropriate penalties or other sanctions to ensure the effective enforcement of the present article.

Article 33

States Parties shall take all appropriate measures, including legislative, administrative, social and educational measures, to protect children from the illicit use of narcotic drugs and psychotropic substances as defined in the relevant international treaties, and to prevent the use of children in the illicit production and trafficking of such substances.

Article 34

States Parties undertake to protect the child from all forms of sexual exploitation and sexual abuse. For these purposes, States Parties shall in particular take all appropriate national, bilateral and multilateral measures to prevent:

(a) The inducement or coercion of a child to engage in any unlawful sexual activity;

(b) The exploitative use of children in prostitution or other unlawful sexual practices;

(c) The exploitative use of children in pornographic performances and materials.

Article 35

States Parties shall take all appropriate national, bilateral and multilateral measures to prevent the abduction of, the sale of or traffic in children for any purpose or in any form.

Article 36

States Parties shall protect the child against all other forms of exploitation prejudicial to any aspects of the child's welfare.

Article 37

States Parties shall ensure that:

(a) No child shall be subjected to torture or other cruel, inhuman or degrading treatment or punishment. Neither capital punishment nor life imprisonment without possibility of release shall be imposed for offences committed by persons below eighteen years of age;

(b) No child shall be deprived of his or her liberty unlawfully or arbitrarily. The arrest, detention or imprisonment of a child shall be in conformity with the law and shall be used only as a measure of last resort and for the shortest appropriate period of time;

(c) Every child deprived of liberty shall be treated with humanity and respect for the inherent dignity of the human person, and in a manner which takes into account the needs of persons of his or her age. In particular, every child deprived of liberty shall be separated from adults unless it is considered in the child's best interest not to do so and shall have the right to maintain contact with his or her family through correspondence and visits, save in exceptional circumstances;

(d) Every child deprived of his or her liberty shall have the right to prompt access to legal and other appropriate assistance, as well as the right to challenge the legality of the deprivation of his or her liberty before a court or other competent, independent and impartial authority, and to a prompt decision on any such action.

Article 38

1. States Parties undertake to respect and to ensure respect for rules of international humanitarian law applicable to them in armed conflicts which are relevant to the child.

2. States Parties shall take all feasible measures to ensure that persons who have not attained the age of fifteen years do not take a direct part in hostilities.

3. States Parties shall refrain from recruiting any person who has not attained the age of fifteen years into their armed forces. In recruiting among those persons who have attained the age of fifteen years but who have not attained the age of eighteen years, States Parties shall endeavour to give priority to those who are oldest.

4. In accordance with their obligations under international humanitarian law to protect the civilian population in armed conflicts, States Parties shall take all feasible measures to ensure protection and care of children who are affected by an armed conflict.

Article 39

States Parties shall take all appropriate measures to promote physical and psychological recovery and social reintegration of a child victim of: any form of neglect, exploitation, or abuse; torture or any other form of cruel, inhuman or degrading treatment or punishment; or armed conflicts. Such recovery and reintegration shall take place in an environment which fosters the health, self-respect and dignity of the child.

Article 40

1. States Parties recognize the right of every child alleged as, accused of, or recognized as having infringed the penal law to be treated in a manner consistent with the promotion of the child's sense of dignity and worth, which reinforces the child's respect for the human rights and fundamental freedoms of others and which takes into account the child's age and the desirability of promoting the child's reintegration and the child's assuming a constructive role in society.

2. To this end, and having regard to the relevant provisions of international instruments, States Parties shall, in particular, ensure that:

   (a) No child shall be alleged as, be accused of, or recognized as having infringed the penal law by reason of acts or omissions that were not prohibited by national or international law at the time they were committed;

   (b) Every child alleged as or accused of having infringed the penal law has at least the following guarantees:

      (i) To be presumed innocent until proven guilty according to law;

      (ii) To be informed promptly and directly of the charges against him or her, and, if appropriate, through his or her parents or legal guardians, and to have legal or other appropriate assistance in the preparation and presentation of his or her defence;

      (iii) To have the matter determined without delay by a competent, independent and impartial authority or judicial body in a fair hearing according to law, in the presence of legal or other appropriate assistance and, unless it is considered not to be in the best interest of the child, in particular, taking into account his or her age or situation, his or her parents or legal guardians;

      (iv) Not to be compelled to give testimony or to confess guilt; to examine or have examined adverse witnesses and to obtain the participation and examination of witnesses on his or her behalf under conditions of equality;

      (v) If considered to have infringed the penal law, to have this decision and any measures imposed in consequence thereof reviewed by a higher competent, independent and impartial authority or judicial body according to law;

      (vi) To have the free assistance of an interpreter if the child cannot understand or speak the language used;

      (vii) To have his or her privacy fully respected at all stages of the proceedings.

3. States Parties shall seek to promote the establishment of laws, procedures, authorities and institutions specifically applicable to children alleged as, accused of, or recognized as having infringed the penal law, and, in particular:

   (a) The establishment of a minimum age below which children shall be presumed not to have the capacity to infringe the penal law;

   (b) Whenever appropriate and desirable, measures for dealing with such children without resorting to judicial proceedings, providing that human rights and legal safeguards are fully respected.

4. A variety of dispositions, such as care, guidance and supervision orders; counselling; probation; foster care; education and vocational training programmes and other alternatives to institutional care shall be available to ensure that children are dealt with in a manner appropriate to their well-being and proportionate both to their circumstances and the offence.

Article 41

Nothing in the present Convention shall affect any provisions which are more conducive to the realization of the rights of the child and which may be contained in:

(a) The law of a State Party; or

(b) International law in force for that State.

Part II

Article 42

States Parties undertake to make the principles and provisions of the Convention widely known, by appropriate and active means, to adults and children alike.

Article 43

1. For the purpose of examining the progress made by States Parties in achieving the realization of the obligations undertaken in the present Convention, there shall be established a Committee on the Rights of the Child, which shall carry out the functions hereinafter provided.

2. The Committee shall consist of ten experts of high moral standing and recognized competent in the field covered by this Convention. The members of the Committee shall be elected

by States Parties from among their nationals and shall serve in their personal capacity, consideration being given to equitable geographical distribution, as well as to the principal legal systems.

3. The members of the Committee shall be elected by secret ballot from a list of persons nominated by States Parties. Each State Party may nominate one person from among its own nationals.

4. The initial election to the Committee shall be held no later than six months after the date of the entry into force of the present Convention and thereafter every second year. At least four months before the date of each election, the Secretary-General of the United Nations shall address a letter to States Parties inviting them to submit their nominations within two months. The Secretary-General shall subsequently prepare a list in alphabetical order of all persons thus nominated, indicating States Parties which have nominated them, and shall submit it to the States Parties to the present Convention.

5. The elections shall be held at meetings of States Parties convened by the Secretary-General at United Nations Headquarters. At those meetings, for which two thirds of States Parties shall constitute a quorum, the persons elected to the Committee shall be those who obtain the largest number of votes and an absolute majority of the votes of the representatives of States Parties present and voting.

6. The members of the Committee shall be elected for a term of four years They shall be eligible for re-election if renominated. The term of five of the members elected at the first election shall expire at the end of two years; immediately after the first election, the names of these five members shall be chosen by lot by the Chairman of the meeting.

7. If a member of the Committee dies or resigns or declares that for any other cause he or she can no longer perform the duties of the Committee, the State Party which nominated the member shall appoint another expert from among its nationals to serve for the remainder of the term, subject to the approval of the Committee.

8. The Committee shall establish its own rules of procedure.

9. The Committee shall elect its officers for a period of two years.

10. The meetings of the Committee shall normally be held at United Nations Headquarters or at any other convenient place as determined by the Committee The Committee shall normally meet annually. The duration of the meetings of the Committee shall be determined, and reviewed, it necessary, by a meeting of the States Parties to the present Convention, subject to the approval of the General Assembly.

11. The Secretary-General of the United Nations shall provide the necessary staff and facilities for the effective performance of the functions of the Committee under the present Convention.

12. With the approval of the General Assembly, the members of the Committee established under the present Convention shall receive emoluments from United Nations resources on such terms and conditions as the Assembly may decide.

Article 44

1. States Parties undertake to submit to the Committee, through the Secretary-General of the United Nations, reports on the measures they have adopted which give effect to the rights recognized herein and on the progress made on the enjoyment of those rights:

    (a) Within two years of the entry into force of the Convention for the State Party concerned;

    (b) Thereafter every five years.

2. Reports made under the present article shall indicate factors and difficulties, if any, affecting the degree of fulfilment of the obligations under the present Convention. Reports shall also contain sufficient information to provide the Committee with a comprehensive understanding of the implementation of the Convention in the country concerned.

3. A State Party which has submitted a comprehensive initial report to the Committee need not, in its subsequent reports submitted in accordance with paragraph 1 (b) of the present article, repeat basic information previously provided.

4. The Committee may request from States Parties further information relevant to the implementation of the Convention.

5. The Committee shall submit to the General Assembly, through the Economic and Social Council, every two years, reports on its activities.

6. States Parties shall make their reports widely available to the public in their own countries.

Article 45

In order to foster the effective implementation of the Convention and to encourage international co-operation in the field covered by the Convention:

(a) The specialized agencies, the United Nations Children's Fund, and other United Nations organs shall be entitled to be represented at the consideration of the implementation of such provisions of the present Convention as fall within the scope of their mandate. The Committee may invite the specialized agencies, the United Nations Children's Fund and other competent bodies as it may consider appropriate to provide expert advice on the implementation of the Convention in areas falling within the scope of their respective mandates. The Committee may invite the specialized agencies, the United Nations Children's Fund, and other United Nations organs to submit reports on the implementation of the Convention in areas falling within the scope of their activities;

(b) The Committee shall transmit, as it may consider appropriate, to the specialized agencies, the United Nations Children's Fund and other competent bodies, any reports from States Parties that contain a request, or indicate a need, for technical advice or assistance, along with the Committee's observations and suggestions, if any, on these requests or indications;

(c) The Committee may recommend to the General Assembly to request the Secretary-General to undertake on its behalf studies on specific issues relating to the rights of the child;

(d) The Committee may make suggestions and general recommendations based on information received pursuant to articles 44 and 45 of the present Convention. Such suggestions and general recommendations shall be transmitted to any State Party concerned and reported to the General Assembly, together with comments, if any, from States Parties.

Part III

Article 46

The present Convention shall be open for signature by all States.

Article 47

The present Convention is subject to ratification. Instruments of ratification shall be deposited with the Secretary-General of the United Nations.

Article 48

The present Convention shall remain open for accession by any State. The instruments of accession shall be deposited with the Secretary-General of the United Nations.

Article 49

1. The present Convention shall enter into force on the thirtieth day following the date of deposit with the Secretary-General of the United Nations of the twentieth instrument of ratification or accession.

2. For each State ratifying or acceding to the Convention after the deposit of the twentieth instrument of ratification or accession, the Convention shall enter into force on the thirtieth day after the deposit by such State of its instrument of ratification or accession.

Article 50

1. Any State Party may propose an amendment and file it with the Secretary-General of the United Nations. The Secretary-General shall thereupon communicate the proposed amendment to States Parties, with a request that they indicate whether they favour a conference of States Parties for the purpose of considering and voting upon the proposals. In the event that, within four months from the date of such communication, at least one third of the States Parties favour such a conference, the Secretary-General shall convene the conference under the auspices of the United Nations. Any amendment adopted by a majority of States Parties present and voting at the conference shall be submitted to the General Assembly for approval.

2. An amendment adopted in accordance with paragraph 1 of the present article shall enter into force when it has been approved by the General Assembly of the United Nations and accepted by a two-thirds majority of States Parties.

3. When an amendment enters into force, it shall be binding on those States Parties which have accepted it, other States Parties still being bound by the provisions of the present Convention and any earlier amendments which they have accepted.

Article 51

1. The Secretary-General of the United Nations shall receive and circulate to all States the text of reservations made by States at the time of ratification or accession.

2. A reservation incompatible with the object and purpose of the present Convention shall not be permitted.

3. Reservations may be withdrawn at any time by notification to that effect addressed to the Secretary-General of the United Nations, who shall then inform all States. Such notification shall take effect on the date on which it is received by the Secretary-General.

Article 52

A State Party may denounce the present Convention by written notification to the Secretary-General of the United Nations. Denunciation becomes effective one year after the date of receipt of the notification by the Secretary-General.

Article 53

The Secretary-General of the United Nations is designated as the depositary of the present Convention.

Article 54

The original of the present Convention, of which the Arabic, Chinese, English, French, Russian and Spanish texts are equally authentic, shall be deposited with the Secretary-General of the United Nations.

IN WITNESS THEREOF the undersigned plenipotentiaries, being duly authorized thereto by their respective Governments, have signed the present Convention.

DECLARATION OF STATES PARTIES TO THE 1951 CONVENTION AND/OR ITS 1967 PROTOCOL RELATING TO THE STATUS OF REFUGEES (2001)

Preamble

We, representatives of States Parties to the 1951 Convention relating to the Status of Refugees and/or its 1967 Protocol, assembled in the first meeting of States Parties in Geneva on 12 and 13 December 2001 at the invitation of the Government of Switzerland and the United Nations High Commissioner for Refugees (UNHCR),

1. Cognizant of the fact that the year 2001 marks the 50th anniversary of the 1951 Geneva Convention relating to the Status of Refugees,

2. Recognizing the enduring importance of the 1951 Convention, as the primary refugee protection instrument which, as amended by its 1967 Protocol, sets out rights, including human rights, and minimum standards of treatment that apply to persons falling within its scope,

3. Recognizing the importance of other human rights and regional refugee protection instruments, including the 1969 Organization of African Unity (OAU) Convention governing the Specific Aspects of the Refugee Problem in Africa and the 1984 Cartagena Declaration, and recognizing also the importance of the common European asylum system developed since the 1999 Tampere European Council Conclusions, as well as the Programme of Action of the 1996 Regional Conference to Address the Problems of Refugees, Displaced Persons, Other Forms of Involuntary Displacement and Returnees in the Countries of the Commonwealth of Independent States and Relevant Neighbouring States,

4. Acknowledging the continuing relevance and resilience of this international regime of rights and principles, including at its core the principle of *non-refoulement*, whose applicability is embedded in customary international law,

5. Commending the positive and constructive role played by refugee-hosting countries and recognizing at the same time the heavy burden borne by some, particularly developing countries and countries with economies in transition, as well as the protracted nature of many refugee situations and the absence of timely and safe solutions,

6. Taking note of complex features of the evolving environment in which refugee protection has to be provided, including the nature of armed conflict, ongoing violations of human rights and international humanitarian law, current patterns of displacement, mixed population flows, the high costs of hosting large numbers of refugees and asylum-seekers and of maintaining asylum systems, the growth of associated trafficking and smuggling of persons, the problems of safeguarding asylum systems against abuse and of excluding and returning those not entitled to

or in need of international protection, as well as the lack of resolution of long-standing refugee situations,

7 Reaffirming that the 1951 Convention, as amended by the 1967 Protocol, has a central place in the international refugee protection regime, and believing also that this regime should be developed further, as appropriate, in a way that complements and strengthens the 1951 Convention and its Protocol,

8 Stressing that respect by States for their protection responsibilities towards refugees is strengthened by international solidarity involving all members of the international community and that the refugee protection regime is enhanced through committed international cooperation in a spirit of solidarity and effective responsibility and burden-sharing among all States,

Operative paragraphs

1 Solemnly reaffirm our commitment to implement our obligations under the 1951 Convention and/or its 1967 Protocol fully and effectively in accordance with the object and purpose of these instruments;

2 Reaffirm our continued commitment, in recognition of the social and humanitarian nature of the problem of refugees, to upholding the values and principles embodied in these instruments, which are consistent with Article 14 of the Universal Declaration of Human Rights, and which require respect for the rights and freedoms of refugees, international cooperation to resolve their plight, and action to address the causes of refugee movements, as well as to prevent them, *inter alia*, through the promotion of peace, stability and dialogue, from becoming a source of tension between States;

3 Recognize the importance of promoting universal adherence to the 1951 Convention and/or its 1967 Protocol, while acknowledging that there are countries of asylum which have not yet acceded to these instruments and which do continue generously to host large numbers of refugees;

4 Encourage all States that have not yet done so to accede to the 1951 Convention and/or its 1967 Protocol, as far as possible without reservation;

5 Also encourage States Parties maintaining the geographical limitation or other reservations to consider withdrawing them;

6 Call upon all States, consistent with applicable international standards, to take or continue to take measures to strengthen asylum and render protection more effective including through the adoption and implementation of national refugee legislation and procedures for the determination of refugee status and for the treatment of asylum-seekers and refugees, giving special attention to vulnerable groups and individuals with special needs, including women, children and the elderly;

7 Call upon States to continue their efforts aimed at ensuring the integrity of the asylum institution, *inter alia*, by means of carefully applying Articles 1F and 33(2) of the 1951 Convention, in particular in light of new threats and challenges;

8 Reaffirm the fundamental importance of UNHCR as the multilateral institution with the mandate to provide international protection to refugees and to promote durable solutions, and recall our obligations as State Parties to cooperate with UNHCR in the exercise of its functions;

9 Urge all States to consider ways that may be required to strengthen the implementation of the 1951 Convention and/or its 1967 Protocol and to ensure closer cooperation between States parties and UNHCR to facilitate UNHCR's duty of supervising the application of the provisions of these instruments;

10 Urge all States to respond promptly, predictably and adequately to funding appeals issued by UNHCR so as to ensure that the needs of persons under the mandate of the Office of the High Commissioner are fully met;

11 Recognize the valuable contributions made by many non-governmental organizations to the well-being of asylum-seekers and refugees in their reception, counselling and care, in finding durable solutions based on full respect of refugees, and in assisting States and UNHCR to maintain the integrity of the international refugee protection regime, notably through advocacy, as well as public awareness and information activities aimed at combating racism, racial discrimination, xenophobia and related intolerance, and gaining public support for refugees;

12 Commit ourselves to providing, within the framework of international solidarity and burden-sharing, better refugee protection through comprehensive strategies, notably

regionally and internationally, in order to build capacity, in particular in developing countries and countries with economies in transition, especially those which are hosting large-scale influxes or protracted refugee situations, and to strengthening response mechanisms, so as to ensure that refugees have access to safer and better conditions of stay and timely solutions to their problems;

13 Recognize that prevention is the best way to avoid refugee situations and emphasize that the ultimate goal of international protection is to achieve a durable solution for refugees, consistent with the principle of *non-refoulement*, and commend States that continue to facilitate these solutions, notably voluntary repatriation and, where appropriate and feasible, local integration and resettlement, while recognizing that voluntary repatriation in conditions of safety and dignity remains the preferred solution for refugees;

14 Extend our gratitude to the Government and people of Switzerland for generously hosting the Ministerial Meeting of States Parties to the 1951 Convention and/or its 1967 Protocol relating to the Status of Refugees.

APPENDIX 3

Draft Convention on the International Status of Environmentally-Displaced Persons[1]

PREAMBLE

The Contracting Parties:

Considering the alarming condition of the global environment and the increasing rate of its deterioration,

Considering the causes of this degradation, in particular climate change and/or the loss of biological diversity, drought, desertification, deforestation, soil erosion, epidemics, armed conflict and more generally, natural and technological hazards,

Considering that these negative environmental phenomena produce victims who encounter injury to their health and their dignity, and even impairment of the essence their fundamental right to life,

Considering that the gravity of environmental harm necessitates the displacement of individuals, families and populations,

Considering that the exponential growth and clear foreseeability of such movements constitute a threat to the stability of human societies, the preservation of cultures, and world peace,

Considering the many appeals from non-governmental organizations to recognize a status for environmentally-displaced persons, and insisting on the urgent necessity of responding to their plight,

Considering that several international declarations underline the existence of this category of displaced persons (Principle 18 of the Rio Declaration on Environment and Development, concerning ecological assistance; Agenda 21, Chapter 12, 12.47 ; and the Directive principles relating to internally-displaced persons),

Considering the numerous international conferences that also refer to such situations, including the Kyoto Conference (1997) and that of The Hague (2000) which set forth the risks of large migrations linked to climate change, and the World Conference on the Prevention of Natural Disasters (Hyogo, January 2005) which insisted on prevention linked in particular to ecological refugees,

Considering that certain organs of the United Nations have spoken of this matter:

- The General Assembly of the United Nations in resolutions 2956 (1972) and 3455 (1975) on displaced persons, resolution 36/255 of 17 December 1981 on strengthening the capacity of the United Nations system in the face of natural disasters and other catastrophes, resolution 43/131 of 8 December 1988 on humanitarian assistance to victims of natural disasters and emergency situations of the same type, resolutions 45/100 of 14 December relative to humanitarian assistance to victims of natural disasters and emergency situations of the same type, resolution 49/22 of 13 December 1994 concerning the international decade for the prevention of natural disasters,

- The Security Council (5663rd session of 17 April 2007) making the link between the impact of climate change and international security, in particular in respect to persons who risk displacement by 2050;

- The Secretary General of the United Nations in his message of 5 June 2006 exhorted governments and societies through the world to think of those who cannot subsist in arid zones and will become ecological refugees,

Considering that the specialized institutions of the United Nations such as the World Health Organization, UNESCO, the World Bank, and other institutions in the United Nations system, such as the High Commissioner for Refugees, the United Nations Environment Programme, and the United Nations Development Programme, regional organizations such as the Council of Europe, the European Union, and the African Union have drawn attention to the challenges of environmental migrations,

Considering the international agreements that already take into consideration environmental displacements, including International Labour Organization Convention No. 169 concerning Indigenous and Tribal Peoples in Independent Countries of 27 June 1989 and the Convention to Combat Desertification of 12 September 1994,

Recognizing the duty of the international community to assist a State that suffers ecological disaster,

Considering that, despite numerous international agreements aimed at protecting the environment, international refugee law lacks an instrument specifically foreseeing the situation of environmentally-displaced persons which can be invoked in their favor,

Reaffirming the principle of common but different responsibilities of States as recognized in article 3 of the Framework Convention on Climate Change,

Considering that in these circumstances it is the duty of the international community of States to organize their solidarity and that of other actors by elaborating an agreement on the international status of environmentally-displaced persons

Considering that this status should encompass individuals, families and populations forced to move either within or away from their State of residence,

Considering that the status of environmentally-displaced persons should be based on respect for the international legal instruments and protective principles relating to human rights and the environment,

Have agreed to the following:

CHAPTER 1: OBJECTIVE, DEFINITIONS, SCOPE OF APPLICATION, PRINCIPLES

Article 1 – Objective

The objective of this Convention is to contribute to guaranteeing the rights of environmentally-displaced persons and to organize their reception as well as their eventual return, in application of the principle of solidarity.

Each Contracting Party undertakes to accept environmentally-displaced persons with strict respect for the human rights guaranteed by international conventions to which the State is a party and to confer additionally those rights specifically set forth by the present text.

Article 2 – Definitions

1. The term 'State Party' refers, unless otherwise indicated, to a Contracting Party to the present Convention.

2. 'Environmentally-displaced persons' are individuals, families and populations confronted with a sudden or gradual environmental disaster that inexorably impacts their living conditions and results in their forced displacement, at the outset or throughout, from their habitual residence and requires their relocation and resettlement.

   2.1 The terms 'persons' and 'families' refers to the individual dimension of displacement necessitated by environmental disaster and the term 'populations' refers to the collective dimension of phenomena which can affect rural or urban communities, cities, countries, or continents...

   2.2 'Sudden environmental disaster' is a rapidly-occurring catastrophe of natural and/or human origin.

   2.3 'Gradual environmental disaster' is a degradation of natural and/or human origin that is slow, progressive or planned.

   2.4 'Habitual residence' means that area which defines the identity of individuals, families and populations.

3. 'Forced displacement' is any temporary or permanent displacement made inevitable by

environmental disaster, either within a State or from the State of residence to one or more receiving States, of individuals, families or populations.

    3.1 'Temporary displacement' is any displacement made necessary by an environmental disaster leaving open the possibility of return in a short or medium term.

    3.2 'Permanent displacement' is any displacement made necessary by an environmental disaster eliminating any perspective of return in a long or very long term.

4. 'Relocation' means that environmentally-displaced persons obtain, within a State Party, temporary places to live in conditions equivalent to those which prevailed before their displacement.

5. 'Resettlement' means the integration of environmentally-displaced persons in healthy conditions that permit them a life of dignity where they can enjoy their rights and exercise their obligations without discrimination.

Article 3 – Scope of Application

The present Convention has a universal aim. It applies to inter-State environmental displacements as well as to internal displacements.

Article 4 – Principles

1. **Principle of common but differentiated responsibilities**

    In the interests of present and future generations and on the basis of equity, the obligations set forth in the present Convention shall be implemented with respect to the principle of common but differentiated responsibilities.

    The States Parties, within one year of its opening for signature, undertake to adopt an additional protocol, on the liability of public and private actors with the aim of prevention and reparation.

    Such liability derives from breach of positive or negative obligations of a nature to make inevitable, directly or indirectly, environmental displacements.

2. **Principle of proximity**

    The present Convention shall be implemented, as much as possible and respecting the principle of common but differentiated responsibilities, in the framework of the principle of proximity, which requires the least separation of persons from their cultural area.

3. **Principle of proportionality**

    The present Convention shall be implemented according to the principle of proportionality in the framework of an international system of financial aid.

4. **Principle of effectiveness**

    In order to render concrete and effective the rights conferred by the present Convention, the World Agency for Environmentally-Displaced Persons (WAEP) and the States Parties shall, as soon as environmentally-displaced persons are welcomed in temporary residences, develop and implement policies permitting environmentally-displaced persons to leave these temporary residences in order to establish normal conditions of life. Such policies shall be elaborated with the participation of the environmentally-displaced persons, organizations which represent them, and the concerned States.

CHAPTER 2: RIGHTS GUARANTEED BY THE CONVENTION

Article 5 – Rights guaranteed to all environmentally-displaced persons

1. **Rights to information and participation**

    Each person, each family and each population has the right of access, as early as possible, to information relating to environmental threats and critical situations implied by these threats.

    Each person, each family and each population has the right to participate in the determination of policies to prevent environmental disasters and to take charge, at the outset or throughout, of the consequences.

    The States Parties undertake to implement the rights to information and participation in a manner that will enable their exercise to have a real influence on decisions relating to environmental threats.

2. **Right to assistance**

   Each person, each family and each population victim of an environmental disaster has the right to assistance in all locations. This right exists from the moment when the situation becomes critical, during and after the environmental disaster.

   The States Parties undertake to place no obstacle in the way of concrete and effective implementation of this right. They undertake also to elaborate and implement a permanent and regularly updated program of assistance to environmentally-displaced persons.

3. **Right to water and to food aid**

   Each environmentally-displaced person has the right to water and the right to receive a subsistence food supply.

4. **Right to housing**

   Each environmentally-displaced person has the right to salubrious and secure housing.

5. **Right to health care**

   Each environmentally-displaced person has the right to receive necessary health care.

6. **Right to juridical personality**

   Each environmentally-displaced person has the right everywhere to recognition of his or her juridical personality.

   Each environmentally-displaced person has the right to replacement of the documentation necessary to fully enjoy the rights derived from having legal personality.

7. Each person environmentally-displaced to a State that is not his or her own retains the civil and political rights in his or her State of origin.

8. **Right to respect for the family**

   Each environmentally-displaced person has the right:

   (a) not to be separated from family members,

   (b) to the reunification of the family when the members are dispersed by an environmental disaster.

9. **Right to education and training**

   Each environmentally-displaced person has the right to receive education and training with respect to his or her cultural identity.

10. **Right to work**

    Each environmentally-displaced person has the right to gain his living by work.

Article 6 – Rights of Temporarily Displaced Persons

1. **Right to safe shelter**

   Each temporarily displaced person has the right to be sheltered, if necessary, in provisional housing that the States Parties undertake to establish and maintain with full respect for human dignity.

   Each temporarily displaced person housed in a temporary shelter has the right to circulate freely and to choose freely to establish a residence elsewhere.

2. **Right to reintegration**

   Each temporarily displaced person sheltered in his or her own State of residence has the right to resettlement. It imply positive obligation for States Parties to ensure the reinstallation of its residents in their normal place of residence.

3. **Right to return**

   Each temporarily displace person sheltered in a receiving State has the right to return to his or her normal residence when that become habitable. It imply positive obligation for State of origin to ensure the return of its nationals to their normal place of residence.

4. **Right to prolonged shelter**

   Each temporarily displaced person has the right to prolong his or her stay when his or her normal place of residence becomes habitable. In such instance, the person loses the status of a temporarily displaced person but, if the person is not a national of the receiving State, may have the rights conferred on a lawful alien.

Article 7 – Rights of Permanently Displaced Persons

1. **Right to resettlement**

   After a temporary shelter, as brief as possible, each permanently displaced person has the right to resettlement.

2. Right to nationality

   Each permanently displaced person has the right to conserve the nationality of his or her State of origin affected by the environmental disaster and to acquire the nationality of the receiving State.

Article 8 – Rights of families and of populations

1. Families displaced by environmental disasters have the right to preserve their unity.

2. Displaced populations benefit, in the receiving State, of rights equivalent to those recognized for minorities by international agreements, notably the right to constitute themselves collectively and maintain their collective identity.

Article 9 – Grant of the status of environmentally-displaced person

The States Parties shall elaborate within two years from the entry into force of the Convention transparent and open legal procedures for the demand and grant or refusal of the status of environmentally-displace person based on the rights set forth in the present chapter.

The elaboration of the procedures shall be accomplished in cooperation with the High Authority, which shall propose guidelines following signature of the Convention.

Article 10 – Principle of non-discrimination

The enjoyment of the rights recognized in the present Convention shall be ensured without distinction based, inter alia, on sex, sexual orientation, race, color, language, religion, political or other opinions, national or social origin, ethnicity, wealth, birth, disability or age.

CHAPTER 3: INSTITUTIONS

Article 11 – World Agency for Environmentally-Displaced Persons (WAEP)

Due to the foreseeable growth and permanence of environmental displacements, a World Agency for Environmentally-Displaced Persons (WAEP) shall oversee the application of the present Convention. A High Authority, a World Fund for the Environmentally-Displaced (WFED), a Scientific Council and a Secretariat assist WAEP. These institutions shall exercise their functions in accordance with the requirements of the Aarhus Convention on Rights of Information, Public Participation and Access to Justice.

WAEP is constituted a specialized agency of the United Nations.

1. **Functions of WAEP**

   WAEP has as functions:

   - conduct prospective studies on the evolution of environmental displacements;
   - evaluate policies susceptible of creating environmental displacements;
   - mobilize the means that can reduce vulnerabilities which are at the origin of environmental displacements;
   - contribute to the general organization of assistance aiming at preventing and limiting displacements and promoting the most rapid possible return of environmentally-displaced persons;
   - evaluate programs to prevent environmental displacements and to aid the displaced;
   - support actively the organization of receipt and return, when it is possible, of the environmentally-displaced.

2. **Organization of the WAEP**

   The organization of the administrative council, bureau, scientific council, secretariat, and the High Authority shall be set forth in an additional protocol, elaborated within one year following the opening for signature of the present Convention.

3. **The High Authority**

   a) The High Authority is composed of 21 persons recognized in the fields of human rights, environmental protection and peace. The selection shall be based on equitable geographic distribution.

   The members are elected by a majority vote of those present and voting, by secret ballot of the Conference of the Parties. Each State Party can present two candidates. NGOs can present a total of 5 candidates.

   The members of the High Authority serve in their personal capacity.

   b) The High Authority has the power to:

   - define the criteria and the procedures for acquiring the status of environmentally-displaced person;

   - provide an appeal from decisions to grant or refuse the status of environmentally displace person, at the request of individuals, families, populations, or interested non-governmental organizations;

   - decide directly and definitively requests for status from nationals of States not Party to the Convention or in case of failure by a State Party;

   - reply to questions concerning the interpretation and application of the Convention at the request of national commissions or any interested physical or moral person;

   - assess the compliance of national provisions with the Convention at the request of any interested physical or moral person and make a synthesis of national implementation reports. This synthesis shall indicate deficiencies as well as good practices;

   - propose recommendations to the Conference of the Parties;

   - propose amendments to the present Convention.

   c) The decisions of the High Authority are definitive. The Contracting Parties undertake to comply with the decisions of the High Authority that concern them. The High Authority can request the Conference of the Parties to suspend the right to vote of States Parties which manifest consistent non-compliance with these decisions.

4. **World Fund for the Environmentally-Displaced (WFED)**

   a) Functions

   The WFED shall ensure the functioning of the WAEP and provide financial and material assistance for the receipt and return of the environmentally-displaced. This assistance shall be granted to the States of residence and to the receiving States. It can also be given to non-governmental organizations, international and regional organizations, and to local governments.

   b) Resources

   The WFED is notably supported by:

   - voluntary contributions from States and private actors;

   - mandatory contributions funded by a tax based principally on the causes of sudden or gradual environmental disasters susceptible of creating environmental displacements.

An additional protocol to the present Convention is adopted in the year following the opening for signature of the Convention in order to set for the base, the taking and the allocation of the tax.

Article 12 – National Commissions on Environmental Displacements

Each State Party, following entry into force of the Convention, shall create a national Commission to attribute the status of environmentally-displaced person. Each Commission shall consist of 9 independent members, experts in the fields of human rights, environmental law, and peace. 'The members shall be named by the highest judicial authorities of the country.

CHAPTER 4: MEASURES OF IMPLEMENTATION

Article 13 – Cooperation

The implementation of the present Convention rests in the first place on the institutions which it creates with the active cooperation of international and regional organizations as well as the secretariats of international agreements for the protection of the environment and protection of human rights.

Article 14 – Conference of the Parties

The first meeting of the Conference of the Parties shall take place one year at the latest after the date of the entry into force of the present Convention. The Convention depository will convoke the meeting. Thereafter, the Parties shall meet regularly at least one time each two years. The proceedings shall be open to the public.

An extraordinary meeting can be called at the request of at least one-quarter of the States Parties.

The Conference of the Parties designates the members of the Executive Council of the WFED and the High Authority.

Article 15 – National implementation reports

1. The Parties shall permanently review the application of the present Convention on the basis of reports communicated by the States Parties, and having this aim in spirit shall:

    a) Associate civil society through the process of elaborating reports. The methodology of the report shall be fixed by a tripartite committee made up of the State Party, universities and representatives of the present Convention;

    b) Draw lessons from the conclusion and application of bilateral and multilateral agreements or other arrangements relevant to the object of the present Convention, to which one or several among them are Parties.

2. The meeting of the Parties examine and evaluate the policies that the Parties apply, notably the programs aimed at article 5.2 of the present Convention and the legal measures and methodologies that they follow to assure aid, assistance and receipt of the environmentally-displaced in order to improve again the situation in this regard;

CHAPTER 5: FINAL DISPOSITIONS

Article 16 – Relations with non-Parties

1. The Parties may invite, if appropriate, States that are not a party to the present Convention to cooperate to the implementation of the present Convention.

2. The Parties shall take appropriate measures, in accordance with international law, to ensure that no one undertakes any activities that are contrary to the purpose, the object and the principles of the present Convention.

Article 17 – Dispute Settlement

In case of a dispute between two or more Parties about the interpretation or the application of the Convention, the concerned Parties shall attempt to settle it through negotiation or other peaceful means of their choice.

If the concerned Parties cannot settle the dispute through the ways mentioned in the paragraph above, the dispute is submitted to the High Authority.

Article 18 – Amendments to the Convention and Protocols

Each Party can propose an amendment to the present Convention. Each Party to a Protocol can propose an amendment to this Protocol.

The text of each proposed amendment is communicated by the Secretariat to the Parties at least six month before the meeting to which the amendment is proposed for adoption. If all efforts to adopt an amendment through consensus are unsuccessful, the amendment may be adopted through a two-thirds majority vote of the Parties present and voting at the meeting.

Article 19 – Protocols

The Protocols foreseen by articles 4 (Responsibility), 11.3.b (WFED), and 11.4 (General management of the WAEP) shall negotiated within one year following the opening for signature of the Convention. They shall be adopted by a two-thirds majority of the Parties present and voting at the meeting.

The meeting of the Parties can adopt any new Protocols by the same majority.

Article 20 – Reservations

No reservations may be made to the present Convention and the Protocols.

Article 21 – Signature, ratification, acceptance or approval

The present Convention and the Protocols are open for signature by every State and every Regional Economic Integration Organization. The Convention and the Protocols shall be submitted for ratification, acceptance or approval. The instruments of ratification, acceptance or approval shall be deposited with the Secretary General of the United Nations who shall act as depository.

Article 22 – Entry into force

The present Convention will entry into force the thirtieth (30) day following the date of deposit of the tenth (10) instrument of ratification, acceptance or approval.

Article 23 – Authentic texts

The present Convention whose authentic languages are Arabic, Chinese, English, French, Russian and Spanish, shall be deposited with the depository.

In witness of which, the undersigned, duly authorized, have signed the present Convention.

Done at .... on .... two thousand ....

Limoges (FRANCE), the 2nd December 2008.

Had written this draft convention:

Michel Prieur, Professor of Law at University of Limoges, Chairman of the CIDCE, International Centre of Comparative Environmental Law;

Jean-Pierre Marguénaud, Professor of private Law at the Faculty of Law and Economic Science, Limoges, Director of the CRDP (Centre of Research on Persons Rights);

Gérard Monédiaire, Professor of public Law, Director of the CRIDEAU (Interdisciplinary Centre of Research on Environmental, Planning and Urban Law);

Julien Bétaille, PhD candidate and Lecturer at University of Limoges;

Bernard Drobenko, Professor of Law, University of littoral Côte d'Opale;

Jean-Jacques Gouguet, Professor of Economy at University of Limoges;

Jean-Marc Lavieille, Professor of public Law at University of Limoges;

Séverine Nadaud, Professor of Private Law at University of Limoges;

Damien Roets, Professor of Private Law at University of Limoges.

Had contributed to the draft convention:

Frédéric Bouin, Professor of Public Law at University of Perpignan;

Florence Burgat, Research Director, INRA, University of Paris I;

Christel Cournil, Professor of Public Law at University of Paris XIII;

Van Dinh, PhD candidate at University of Limoges;

José Juste, Professor of Law at University of Valence, Spain;

Yves Lador, Earth Justice Permanent Representative to the UN in Geneva;

Pierre Mazzega, Geophysician, Research Director, CNRS, Toulouse;

Agnès Michelot, Professor of Public Law at University of La Rochelle;

Dinah Shelton, Professor of Law at the George Washington University Law School.

English translation:

Dinah Shelton, Professor of Law at the George Washington University Law School.

NOTE

1 This draft convention has been published as 'Projet de convention relative au statut international des déplacés environnementaux' in the *Revue Européenne de Droit de l'Environnement*, no 4, 2008, p381. For further information, see www.cidce.org.

List of Acronyms and Abbreviations

AF	after flight
ATCA	Alien Torts Claims Act
BAU	business as usual
BF	before flight
BIOT Agreement	British Indian Ocean Territory Agreement
BSE	bovine spongiform encephalopathy
EU	European Union
CERD	Committee on the Elimination of Racial Discrimination
CIEL	Centre for International Environmental Law
CIL	customary international law
CRC	Convention on the Rights of the Child
CSR	Convention on the Status of Refugees
CTY	Criminal Tribunal for Yugoslavia
ECD	early child development
ECHR	European Court of Human Rights
ENMOD	Convention on the Prohibition of Environmental Modification Techniques
FCGH	Framework Convention for Global Health
FGM	female genital mutilation
GHG	greenhouse gas
GPS	global positioning system
IACHR	Inter-American Court of Human Rights
ICC	International Criminal Court
ICCPR	International Covenant on Civil and Political Rights
ICESCR	International Covenant on Economic, Social and Cultural Rights
ICJ	International Court of Justice
ICTR	International Criminal Tribunal for Rwanda
ICTY	International Criminal Tribunal for the Former Yugoslavia
IDP	internally displaced person
ILC	International Law Commission
ILO	International Labour Organization
INGO	international non-governmental organization
IUCN	World Conservation Union
MNC	multinational corporation
NAFTA	North American Free Trade Agreement
NGO	non-governmental organization
OLC	Office of Legal Counsel
PGC	Principle of Generic Consistency
RAD	Refugee Appeal Division
SARS	severe acute respiratory syndrome

TexPet	Texaco Petroleum Company
UDHR	United Nations Universal Declaration of Human Rights
UK	United Kingdom
UNDP	United Nations Development Programme
UNEP	United Nations Environment Programme
UNESCO	United Nations Educational, Scientific and Cultural Organization
UNFCCC	United Nations Framework Convention on Climate Change
UNHCR	United Nations High Commissioner for Refugees
UNHRC	United Nations Human Rights Committee
UNICEF	United Nations Children's Fund
UNRWA	United Nations Relief and Works Agency
US	United States
WHA	World Health Assembly
WHO	World Health Organization
WTO	World Trade Organization

List of Cases

AUSTRALIA

Commonwealth of Australia v. Tasmania, 158 C.L.R. 1, para. 63
Gunaleela v. Minister for Immigration and Ethnic Affairs, (1978) 74, ALR 263
Simmathamby v. Minister for Immigration and Ethnic Affairs (1986) 66 ALR 502 506

CANADA

Al-Kateb v. Goodwin [2004] HCA 37, 6 Aug 2004
Baker v. Canada (M.C.I.) [1999] 2 S.C.R. 817(S.C.C.)
Boleslaw Dylow, Immigration Appeal Board Decision V87-6040X, 7 July 1987
Canada Attorney General v. Ward [1993] 2 S.C.R. 689, @ para. 17
Chan v. Minister for Immigration and Ethnic Affairs (1989) 169 CLR 379, H.C.A.
Dashowa, Inc. v. Friends of the Lubicon (1998), 158 DLR(4) 699 (Ont. Gen. Div.)
Ganganee Janet Permanand, Immigration Appeal Board Decision T87-10167, 10 August 1967
Musial v. Minister of Employment and Immigration [1982], I.F.C 290, p. 550
Pappajohn v. the Queen, (1980) 2 S.C.R. 120
Pierre Katanku Tshiabut Tshibola, Immigration Appeal Board Decision M84-1074, 30 May 1985
Port Hope Environmental Group v. Canada, Communication No. 67/1980, 2 Selected Decisions of the Human Rights Committee (1990)
Rasaratnam v. Canada (Minister of Employment and Immigration) (1992) IFC 706
Sahin v. Canada [1995] 1F.C. 214
Sahin v. Canada (Minister of Citizenship and Immigration) [1995] 1 F.C.214
Trail Smelter Arbitration, U.S. v. Canada, 1931–1941 3 R.I.A.A. 1905

EUROPE

(2008) UKHL 61: an appeal from: [2007] EWCA Civ. 498
Gronus v. Poland (1999) ECHR Case No. 29695/96
Guerra v. Italy (1998) 26 EHRR 357; (1994) ECHR 16798/90
Hopu and Besent v. France, UN GAOR, 52 Sess., Supp., No. 4, UN Doc. A/52/40 (1997)
LCB v. UK (1999) 27 EHRR 212
LCV v. UK (1999) 27 EHRR 277
Lopez-Ostra v. Spain (1994) 20 EHRR 277

Oneryildiz v. Turkey (App. no. 48939/99), [2004] ECHR 48939/99
Oseri v. Oseri (1953) 8 PM 76; 17 ILR III (1950)

INTERNATIONAL

Barcelona Traction, Light and Power Co. Ltd., Second Phase, ICJ Reports, 1970
Bernard Ominayak, Chief of the Lubicon Cree Band v. Canada, Communication No. 167/1984, Report of the Human Rights Committee, UN GAOR, 45th Sess., Supp. no 40, vol 2, @10, UN Doc. A/45/40, Annex IX (A) (1990), view adopted on 26 Mar 1990 at the 38th Sess.
Gabcikovo-Nagymaros Project. (Hungary/Slovakia), 1997, I.C.J. 4 (Judgment of 25 Sept)
Kumamoto Minimata Disease case, 696 Hanjil 5 Kumamoto District Court, 20 Mar 1973 (reprinted in J. Gresser, K. Fugikura and A. Morishima, *Environmental Law in Japan*, 1981)
Kupreskic et al, IT-95-16-T, Judgment, 14 Jan 2000, para. 636
Niigata Minimata case, 642 Hanji (Miigata District Court, 29 Sept 1971)
Nuclear Test Case, Australia v. France; New Zealand v. France (1974) I.C.J. Rep. 253
Ominyak and the Lubicon Lake Band v. Canada, UNHRC No. 167/1984, Rept. Human Rights Committee (1996) GAOR A/45/40, vol II
Omynayak v. Canada, UN GAOR, 45 Sess., Supp. No. 40, Annex 9 at 27, UN Doc.A/45/40 (1990)
Prosecutor v. Akayesu, Case No. ICTR-96-4-T, paras 510–516 (2 Sept 1998)
Prosecutor v. Duko Tadic, Case No. IT-94-I-A, Judgment, para. 271, 15 July 1999
Prosecutor v. Jelisic, Case No. IT-95-10-T paras 69-72 (14 Dec 1999)
Prosecutor v. Kupresic, Case No. IT-95-16-A, Judgment (23 Oct 2001)
Toyama Itai-tai case, 635 Hanji 17 (Toyama District Court, 30 June 1991)
Yanomani Indians v. Brazil (1985), Decision 7615, Inter-American Commission on HR, Interamerican YB on Hum.Rts. (1985), 264
Yokkaichi Asthma case, 672 Hanji 30 (Tsu District Court, Yokkaichi Branch, 24 July 1972)

UK

Chagos Islanders v. Attorney General (2003) EWCH 2222 (QB), (2003) All ER (D) 166
Powell and Rayner v. UK (1990) ECHR Ser.A/172
R (Bancoult) v. Secretary of State for Foreign and Commonwealth Affairs [2007] QB 1067 (Bancoult 1)
R. v. Secretary of State for the Home Department ex parte Bugdaycay, [1987] AC 514 (UK HL, Feb.19, 1987) per Lord Bridge of Harwich @525
Reg. v. Secretary of State for the Home Department ex parte Adan [1998] H.L.J. No. 15 (H.L.); per Lord Loyd of Berwick, at para. 34

US

Aguinda v. Texaco, Inc., 142 F. Supp. 2d 534 (S.D.N.Y. 2001)
Aguinda v. Texaco, Inc., 1945 F. Supp. 625 (5 D.N.Y. 1996)
Alvarez-Machain v. United States, 331 F.3d 604, 620 (9th Cir.2003)
Bancoult v. McNamara, 217 FRD 280, 2003

Coriolan v. INS, 559 F 2d 993 (5th Cir.1977)
Doe/Roe v. Unocal Corp., 110 F. Supp. 2d 1294, 1306 (C.D. Cal. 2000)
Filartiga v. Pena Irala, 630 F.2d 876(2d Cir.1980)
Foster v. Florida, 537 U.S. 990(2002)
Immigration and Naturalization Service v. Stevic, 467 U.S. 407, p453 and fn.24; Jefferson County Circuit Court House No. CV-93-6975; Supreme Court case 1931248; Alabama Court of Civil Appeals, AV 93000104
Jota v. Texaco Inc. 157 F 3d 153 (2d Cir 1998)
Kadic v. Karadzic (1996) 74 F.3d 153 (2d Cir. 1998)
Maria Aguinda and others including the Federation of the Yagua People of the Lower Amazon and Lower Napo v. Texaco, Inc., 303 F 3d 470; 2002 U.S. App. LEXIScl6540; 157 Oil and Gas Rep. 333, 16 Aug 2002, Decided
Rhodes v. Chapman 452 U.S. 337 (1981)
Salerno, 481 U.S. @755-56
Shafiq Rasul et al Petitioners v. George W. Bush, President of the United States, et al, Fawzi Khalid Abdullah Fahad Al Odah, et al, Petitioners v. United States et al (No. 03-334),(No. 03-343) 542 U.S. 466; 124 S. Ct. 2686, 28 June 2004, Decided
Sosa v. Alvarez-Machain, 124 S. Ct. 2739, pp2764-2765
Sosa, 542 U.S. at 725
United States v. Salerno, 481 U.S. 739 (1987)
United States v. Smith, 18 U.S. 153, 160-161, 5 L. Ed. 57 (1920)
Wilson v. Seiler (89-7376) 501 U.S. 294 (1991)
WmF. Horn et al v. City of Birmingham et al, Jefferson Circuit Court CV-93-50132-14 October, 1994
Zadvydas v. Davis, 121 S. Ct. 2491 (2001)

List of Documents

1967 Protocol Relating to the Status of Refugees, UN Doc. HCR/IP/4/Eng. Rev.1 (1979) re-edited January 1992
1990 US Asylum Regulations, 8CFR§ 208.13 (b)(2)(1); §208.16 (3)(i)(ii)
1993 Declaration of Principles of Interim Self-Government Arrangements in the West Bank and Gaza; 32 ILM 1520 (1993)
1996 Illegal Immigration Reform and Immigrant Responsibility Act, INA §241(a)(6), 8 U.S.C. §1231(a)(6) (2000)
Additional Protocol to the American Convention on Human Rights in the Area of Economic, Social and Cultural Rights (Protocol of San Salvador), OAS Doc. OES/Ser.L.V/II.82 Doc.6 Rev.1, at 67 (1992)
African Charter on Human and Peoples' Rights, 21 I.L.M. (1982) 52
African Charter on Human and Peoples' Rights, adopted 27 June 1981, OAU Doc. CAB/LEG/67/3 rev. 5, 21 I.L.M. 58 (1982), entered into force, 21 Oct 1986
Alien Torts Claims Act, 28 USC 1350, 1798
Alien Torts Claims Act 28 U.S.C.S. 1350 (2002)
Almeria Statement on Desertification and Migration, International Symposium on Desertification and Migration 9–11 February 1994, Almeria, Spain
British Indian Ocean Territories Order 1865 SI No. 1920
Capotorti, F. (1979) *Study on the Rights of Persons Belonging to Ethnic Religions and Linguistic Minorities*, UN Doc. E/CN.4 Sub.2/384/Rev/I,1979, pp353–354
Cartagena Declaration, UNGA, 30 Nov 1973; res 3068 (XXVIII), into force 18 July 1976
Charter of the United Nations, Article 1(3), 13(1), (b), 55(c), 56, 59 and 76(c)
Committee on the Elimination of Racial Discrimination (CERD), adopted 18 Aug 1997, UN Doc. CERD/C/51/misc.13/Rev.4 (1997)
Constitutional Law and Minorities, Minority Rights Group, Report No. 36
Continued Detention of Aliens Subject to Final Orders of Removal, 66 Fed.Reg. 56, 967, 56, 967-82 (15 Nov 2001)
Convention Governing the Specific Aspects of Refugee Problems in Africa, Organization of African Unity (OAU) (1969) 10 September, Addis Ababa
Convention on Biological Diversity, adopted 5 June 1992, entered into force 29 December 1993, 31 I.L.M. 818 (1992)
Convention on Biological Diversity, 2003, Briefing note from the Executive Secretary for the Ad Hoc, Open-Ended Intersessional Working Group on Article 8(j) and Related Provisions of the CBD
Convention on the Elimination of All Forms of Discrimination against Women, adopted 18 Dec 1979, entered into force 3 Sept 1981, G.A. Res. 34/180, 34 UN GAOR Supp. (No. 46) at 193, UN Doc. A/34/46 (1980)
Convention on the Elimination of All Forms of Racial Discrimination, opened for signature 7 Mar 1966, entered into force 4 Jan 1969, 660 UNTS 195

Convention on the Prevention and Punishment of the Crime of Genocide, adopted 9 Dec 1948, entered into force 12 Jan 1951, 78 UNTS 277

Convention on the Prohibition of Military or any other Hostile Use of Environmental Modification Techniques, 18 May 1977, 31 U.S.T. 333, T.I.A.S. No. 9614

Convention on the Rights of the Child, opened for signature 20 Nov 20, 1989, entered into force, 2 Sept 1990, GA Res. 44/25

Convention on the Status of Refugees (CSR) (1951), 189 UNTS 150; into force 22 April 1954

Declaration of the European Parliament, DC/523 175 FR.doc., PE342.103 Or.Fr. February 2004

Declaration of the United Nations Conference on the Human Environment, Stockholm, 16 June 1972, UN Doc. A/CONF.48/14/Rev. 1 (1972)

The Earth Charter Initiative, The Earth Council, info@earthcharter.org

ECOSOC Resolution 1655 (LII), June 1972; eventually the UNGA Resolution 3271 (XXIX), 18 Dec 1974; 3454 (XXX) 9 Dec 1975

ECOSOC, *Human Rights and the Environment*, Final Report (1994), UN Doc. E/CN.4Sub.2/1994/9, p59

European Council Directive of 2001, Schengen Directive (28 June 2001) (28 June Council Directive 2001/51/EC Supplementing the Provision of Article 26 of the Convention Implementing the Schengen Directive (of 2001 L 187/46)

European Social Charter, Article 1, 529 UNTS 89

Federal Employees Liability Reform and Tort compensation Act of 1988, Fub.L. No. 100-694, 102 Stat.4563 (1988) (codified at 28 U.S.C. & 2671-2680)

Framework Convention on Tobacco Control, WHO Doc. A56/VR/4 (21 May 2003), available at www.who.int/gb/ebwha/pdf_files/WHA56/ea56rl.pdf

General Comment No. 1 on Economic, Social and Cultural Rights, 'The rights to the highest attainable standard of health', UN Doc. E/C.12/2000/4(2000)

Geneva Convention Act R.S.C. 1985, c.G-3

Human Rights Committee, General Comments adopted under Article 40, para.4, of the CP Covenant, UN Doc. CCPR/C/21/Rev.1 (19 May 1989) at 51-52

Human Rights Situation in Palestine and Other Occupied Arab Territories: Report of the Special Rapporteur on the Situation of Human Rights in the Palestinian Territories Occupied since 1967, John Dugard, UN Doc. A/HRC/7/17, 21 January 2008

IASC (2006) *Operational Guidelines on Human Rights and Natural Disasters, Protecting Persons Affected by Natural Disasters*

ILO Convention No. 169, of 1989, 28 ILM 138

Immigration Act, R.S.C., 1985 (4th Suppl.) s.103

International Bill of Human Rights, UN Doc. A/565 1948

International Convention on the Elimination of all Forms of Racial Discrimination (1965) Art.14(1), 660 UNTS 195, 230 5 ILM 350

International Covenant on Economic, Social, and Cultural Rights, G.A. Res.2200A (XXI), 21 UNGAOR Supp. No. 16, at 59, UN Doc. A/6316 (1966), 999 UNT.S. 302, into force 23 Mar 1976

International Covenant on Economic, Social and Cultural Rights, UN Doc.E/C.12/2002/11, 26 November 2002

International Covenant on Civil and Political Rights, G.A. res. 2200A (XXI), 21 UN GAOR Supp. (No. 16) at 52, UN Doc. A/6316 (1966), 999 UNTS 171, entered into force 23 Mar 1976

International Tribunal in the Former Yugoslavia (ICTY) IT-97-24-Trial Chamber Judgment, 31 July 2003, para. 516

Israel–Jordan Treaty of Peace, 34 I.L.M. 43(1995), 26 Oct 1994

Kyoto Protocol to the United Nations Framework Convention on Climate Change, adopted 10 Dec 1997, 37 I.L.M. 22 (1998)

LIST OF DOCUMENTS   277

Madison Declaration on Mercury Pollution, www.unbc.ca/assets/media/2007/03_chan.html
Maresca's intervention, UNC.L.T.Off.Rec., First Sess., Vienna, 26 Mar–24 May 1968, 'Summary records of the plenary meetings and of the committee of the whole', p311, para. 42
Medjelle Code, 1870
Nunavut Act, 1993, c.28 [assented to 10 June 1993]
Nunavut Land Claims Agreement Act, 1993, c.29 [assented to 10 June 1993]
Nuremberg Trial Proceedings Vol. 1: Charter of the International Military Tribunal (1945), Article 6
Pope John-Paul II and Patriarch Bartholomew I of Constantinople, 10 June 2000, Rome-Venice, text issued by the Vatican Press Office
Principle 1, Declaration on the Human Environment, *Report of the United Nations Conference on the Human Environment*, UN Doc. A/CONF.48/14 Rev.1
Progress Report of the United Nations Mediator, GA Res. 194 (III), UN GAOR, 3d Sess. at §11, UN Doc. A/RES/194(III) (1948)
Protocol Additional to the Geneva Conventions Relating to the Protection of the Victims of International Armed Conflicts, 8 June 1977, 16 I.L.M. 1391, UN Doc. A/32/144(1977), Article 55
Protocol Relating to the Status of Refugees, 606 UNTS 267, in force 4 Oct 1967
Question of the Violation of Human Rights in the Occupied Arab Territories, including Palestine, Report of the Special Rapporteur of the Commission on Human Rights, John Dugard, on the Situation of Human Rights in the Palestinian Territories Occupied by Israel since 1967; E/CN.4/2005/29, 7 Dec 2004; and E/CN.4/2005/29/Add.1, 3 Mar 2005
Regulation (EC) No. 1907/2006 of the European Parliament and of the Council on the Registration, Evaluation, Authorization and Restriction of Chemicals (REACH)
Report of the UN Conference on Environment and Development, UN Doc. A/CONF.151/26/Rev.1
Rio Declaration on Environment and Development, UN Conference on Environment and Development (UNCED) at Rio de Janeiro, 13 June 1992, UN Doc. A/CONF.151/26 (vol 1) (1992)
Rome Statute of the International Criminal Court, 17 July 1998, 2187 UNTS 90
Sogli, S. (2001) *The Elaboration of a Declaration on Human Rights and Extreme Poverty*, UNHCR, Geneva, 7–9 Feb 2001, UN, Doc HR/GVA/Poverty/SEM/2001/BP:1
Standards of Conduct for Interrogation under 18 U.S.C. §§2340-2340A, Aug 2002
Statute of the International Criminal Tribunal for Rwanda, 8 Nov 1994, Art. 4, S.C., Res. 955, UNSCOR 3453 mtg., Art. 4, UN Doc. S/Res/955, 33 I.L.M. 15981, 1600
Statute of the International Tribunal Criminal for the Former Yugoslavia, 25 May 1993, Art. 4, UN Doc. S/25704 (1993), Approved by UNSCOR Res. 827, 32 I.L.M. 1192 (1993)
Statute of the Iraqi Special Tribunal (10 Dec 2003)
Stockholm Declaration of the United Nations Conference for the Human Environment, 16 June 1972, ILM 11 141
UN Climate Change Conference in Bali, COP 13, CMP3, SB 27, AWG 4, December 2007
UN Commission on Human Rights, *The Right of Everyone to the Enjoyment of the Highest Attainable Standard of Physical and Mental Health*, Commission on Human Rights Resolution 2002/31, UN Doc. E/CN./2005/51 (22 April 2002)
UN Convention on the Rights of the Child (UNCROC) 20 Nov 1989, GA 44/25
UN Convention on Torture and Other Cruel, Inhuman or Degrading Treatment or Punishment, Art.2, S. Treaty Doc. No. 100-20, @20, 1465 UNTS 85, 114 (entered into force 26 June 1987)
UN Convention to Combat Desertification in Countries Experiencing Serious Drought and/or Desertification Particularly in Africa, adopted 14 Oct 1994, entered into force 26 Dec 1996, 33 I.L.M. 1328 (1994)
UN Declaration of Human Rights, GA Res. 217A (III), UNGA a/810, 10 Dec 1948
UN Declaration on the Rights of Indigenous Peoples, GA Res. 61/295 on 13 September 2007
UN Doc. S/RES/237 (1937)

UN Doc. E/CN.41/1995/50

UNDP (UN Development Programme) (1999) *Facts and Figures on Poverty*, www.undp.org/teams/english/facts.htm

UNESCO (UN Educational, Scientific and Cultural Organization) World Heritage Commission, *Report: Convention Concerning the Protection of the World Cultural and Natural Heritage* at VIII(A.1), UN Doc. WHC-95/CONF.203/16/Jan31/96

UNFCCC (UN Framework Convention on Climate Change), adopted 29 May 1992, entered into force, 21 Mar 1994, 31 I.L.M. 849 (1992)

UNFCCC Executive Secretary press release (6 April 2007), http://unfccc.int/files/press/news_room/press_releases_and_advisories/application/pdf/070406_pressrel_english.pdf

UNGA (UN General Assembly) Resolution 3454 (XXX), 9 Dec 1975; UNGA Resolution 43/116, 8 Dec 1988

UNHCR (UN High Commissioner for Refugees) (2001) *Refugee Protection and Migration Control: Perspectives from the UNHCR and IOM*, UN Doc. EC/GC/01/11 (31 May 2001), p14

UNHCR (2005) *Report of Special Rapporteur on the Right to Food*, Jean Zigler, 25 Jan 2005, E/CN.4/2005 47

UNHCR Executive Committee, Conclusion No. 97 (LIV) 2003

UNHCR, *Guidelines on International Protection: Internal Flight or Relocation Alternative within the Context of Articles 1A(2) of the 1951 Convention and/or 1967 Protocol relating to the status of Refugees*, HCR/GIP/03/04; 23 July 2003, no. 4

UNHCR (1979, re-edited 1992) *Handbook on Procedures and Criteria for Determining Refugee Status*

UNHCR, 13 October 1986, No. 44 (XXXVII)

UNHCR Comm. No. 68/1980, decided 31 Mar 1981

UN Human Rights Committee (1986) 'General Comment No. 15: The position of aliens under the Covenant', UN Doc. HRI/GEN/IRev.7, 12 May 2004 at 140, para. 2

UN Human Rights Committee (1989) 'General Comment No. 18: Non-discrimination', UN Doc. HRI/GEN/1/Rev.7, 12 May 2004@146, para.12

UN Relief and Works Administration (UNRWA) *Who is a Palestinian Refugee?*, available at www.un.org/unrwa/refugeeswhois.html

UN Security Council Resolution S.C. Res. 237, 1, UNSCOR, 22nd Sess., 1361

Universal Declaration of Human Rights, G.A. Res. 217 A(III), UNGAOR, 3rd Sess., at 71, UN Doc. A/210(1948)

US Patriot Act of 2001 Pub.L.No. 107-56, 115 Stat.272

Vienna Convention for the Protection of the Ozone Layer, adopted 22 Mar 1985, entered into force 22 Sept 1988, UNEP Doc. IG.53/5, 26 I.L.M. 1529 (1987)

Vienna Convention on the Law of Treaties (1969) 1155 UNTS 331, in force 1980

Weissbrodt, D. (2003) *The Rights of Non-Citizens: Final Report of the Special Rapporteur*, UN Doc. E/CN.4/Sub.2/2003/23, 26 May 2003

WHO (2002) *World Report on Violence and Health: Summary*, WHO, Geneva

World Bank Group (2004) *The World Bank Operational Manual, Operational Policy 4.10: Indigenous Peoples*, 1 Dec 2004, Washington, DC

World Charter for Nature, G.A. Res. 37/7, UN GAOR, 37th Sess., UN Doc. A./RES/37/7 (1982), 22 I.L.M. 455

World Conference against Racism, Racial Discrimination, Xenophobia, and Related Intolerance, Declaration and Programme for Action, A/Conf. 189/12 (8 Sept 2001)

World Refugee Report 2 (1969) at 3

Bibliography

Abouali, J. (1998) 'Natural resources under occupation: The status of Palestinian water under international law', *PACE International Law Review*, vol 10, pp411–428

Ahmad, A. (2001) *Cosmopolitan Orientation of the Process of International Environmental Law: An Islamic Law Genre*, University Press of America, Lanham, MD, pp89–91

Akram, S. M. and Rempel, T. (2004) 'Temporary protection as an instrument for implementing the right of return for Palestinian refugees', *Boston University International Law Journal*, vol 22, no 1, pp1–43

Akram, S. and Rempel, T. (2005) 'Temporary protection as an instrument for implementing the right of return for Palestinian refugees', *Boston University International Law Journal*, vol 22, pp1–112

Aleinikoff, A. T. (2002) 'Detaining plenary power: The meaning and impact of Zadvydas v. Davis', *Georgetown Immigration Law Journal*, vol 16, pp365–389

Allen, J. A. (1998) 'Water in the Middle East and in Israel and Palestine: Some local and global issues', in E. Feitelson and M. Haddad (eds) *Identification of Joint Management Structures for Shared Aquifers*, World Bank, Washington, DC

Aminzadeh, S. C. (2007) 'A moral imperative: The human rights implications of climate change', *Hastings International and Comparative Law Review*, vol 30

Amnesty International (2007) 'Canada and the international protection of human rights: An erosion of leadership? An update to Amnesty International's human rights agenda for Canada', Amnesty International, Canada, p17, available at www.fafia-afai.org/files/HumanRightsAgenda2007.pdf

Amnesty International UK, CARE International UK, CAFOD, Christian Aid, Médecins du Monde UK, OXFAM, Save The Children and Trocaire (2008) *The Gaza Strip: A Humanitarian Implosion*, report issued jointly on 6 March, available for download at www.amnesty.org.uk/news_details.asp?NewsID=17689

Anaya, S. J. (2004) *Indigenous Peoples in International Law*, 2nd edition, Oxford University Press, Oxford, UK

Anghie, T. (2006) *Imperialism, Sovereignty and International Law*, Cambridge University Press, Cambridge, UK

Atapattu, S. (2002–2003) 'The right to a healthy life, or the right to die polluted?: The emergence of a human right to a healthy environment under international law', *Tulane Environmental Law Journal*, vol 16, p65

Austin, R. and Schill, M. (1991) 'Black, brown, poor, and poisoned: Minority grassroot environmentalism and the quest for eco-justice', *Kansas Journal of Law and Public Policy*, vol 1, pp69–82

Barlow, M. and Clarke, T. (2002) *Global Showdown*, Stoddard Publishing Co. Ltd, Toronto, Canada

Bassiouni, C. (1996) *Crimes Against Humanity in International Criminal Law*, Dordrecht, The Netherlands, Martinus Nijhoff Publishers

Bassiouni, C. (1996) 'International crimes: *Jus cogens* and *obligatio erga omnes*,' *Law Contemporary Problems*, vol 59, no 4

Bassiouni, C. (1998) 'The normative framework of international humanitarian law: Overlaps, gaps, and ambiguities', *Transnational Law and Contemporary Problems*, vol 8, pp201–202

Baxi, U. (2002) 'Geographies of injustice: Human rights at the altar of convenience', in C. Scott, *Torture as Tort*, Hart Publishing, Oxford, UK, Chapter 7

BBC (2009) 'New Israel phosphorus accusation', *BBC News* website, 20 January, available at http://news.bbc.co.uk/1/hi/world/middle_east/7838598.stm (accessed 1 April 2009)

BBC (2009) 'Gaza "looks like earthquake zone"', *BBC News* website, 20 January, available at http://news.bbc.co.uk/1/hi/world/middle_east/7838618.stm (accessed 1 April 2009)

Bell, D. (1980) 'Brown v. Board of Education and interest convergence dilemma', *Harvard Law Review*, vol 93, p518

Berat, L (1993) 'Defending the right to a healthy environment: Toward a crime of genocide in international law', *Boston University International Law Journal*, vol 11

Beyani, C. (1995) 'State responsibility for the prevention and resolution of forced population displacement in international law', *International Journal of Refugee Law*, Special Issue, Oxford University Press, pp130–147

Beyleveld, D. and Brownsword, R. (2001) *Human Dignity in Bioethics and Biolaw*, Oxford University Press, Oxford, UK

Biermann, F. and Boas I. (2007) 'Preparing for a warmer world towards a global governance system to protect climate refugees', Global Governance Working Paper no 33, November, www.glogov.org

Birnie, P. and Boyle, A. (2002) *International Law and the Environment*, 2nd edition, Oxford University Press, Oxford, UK, p250

Blackmun, H. A. (1994) 'The Supreme Court and the law of nations', *Yale Law Journal*, vol 104, p39

Blackstone, W. (1765–1769) *Commentaries on the Laws of England*, vol 1, Clarendon Press, Oxford

Bluemel, E. (2004) 'Human right to water', *Ecology Law Quarterly*, vol 31, pp959–970

Boano, C., Zetter, R. and Morris, T. (2008) *Environmentally Displaced People: Understanding the Linkages between Environmental Change, Livelihoods and Forced Migration*, Forced Migration Policy Briefing 1, Refugee Studies Centre, Oxford, available at www.rsc.ox.ac.uk

Borrows, J. (1997/1998) 'Frozen rights in Canada: Constitutional interpretation and the trickster', *American Indian Law Review*, vol 22, pp37–64

Bowman, M. and Redgwell, C. (1996) *International Law and the Conservation of Biological Diversity*, Kluwer Publishers, The Hague

Bridgeford, T. A. (2003) 'Imputing human rights violations on multinational corporations: The Ninth Circuit strikes again in judicial activism', *American University International Law Review*, vol 18, no 4, pp1009–1054

Brouwer, A. and Kumin, J. (2003) ' Interception and asylum: When migration control and human rights collide', *Refuge*, vol 21, no 4, December, pp6–24

Brown, P. (2003) 'Refugee warning to global polluters: Up to 20 million likely to flee environmental damage, report predicts', *The Guardian*, 30 September

Bullard, R. (1990) *Dumping in Dixie: Race, Class and Environmental Quality*, Westview Press, Boulder, CO

Bullard, R. D. (2001) 'Decision making', in L. Westra and B. Lawson (eds) *Faces of Environmental Racism* (second edition), Rowman Littlefield, Lanham, MD, pp3–28

Burci, G. L. and Vignes, C.-H. (2004) *World Health Organization*, Kluwer, The Hague, The Netherlands

Caponera, D. A. (1992) *Principles of Water Law and Administration: National and International*, A. A. Balkema Publishers, Rotterdam

Capotorti, F. (1979) 'Study on the rights of persons belonging to ethnic religions and linguistic minorities', UN Doc. E/CN.4 Sub.2/384/Rev/I,1979,353–354

Caracol Production, Guatemala (2005) 'Sipakapa no se vende', www.sipakapanosevende.org

Cassese, A. (2001) 'Terrorism is also disrupting some legal categories of international law', European Journal of International Law, vol 12, p993

Chabot, M. (2003) 'Economic changes, household strategies, and social relations in contemporary Nunavik Inuit', *Polar Record*, vol 39, pp19–34

Charlesbois, C. T. (1977) 'An overview of the Canadian mercury problem,' *Science*, vol 10, pp17–20

Chemillier Gendreau, M. (1995) *Humanité et Souveraineté – Essai sur la Function du Droit International*, Editions de la Decouverte, Paris

Christian Aid (2007) *Human Tide: The Real Migration Crisis*, www.christianaid.org.uk/Images/human-tide.pdf.

Christian Aid (2007) *Human Tide: The Real Migration Crisis*, report, May, available at www.christianaid.org.uk/resources/policy/climate_change.aspx

Clark, T. and Niessen J. (1996) 'Equality rights and non-citizens in Europe and America: The promise, the practice and some remaining issues', *Netherlands Quarterly of Human Rights*, vol 14, no 3, p245

Colborn, T., Myers, D. and Patterson, J. (1996) *Our Stolen Future*, Dutton (Penguin Books), New York

Cole, D. (2006) 'The idea of humanity: Human rights and immigrants' rights', *Columbia Human Rights Law Review*, vol 37

Cooper, J. (1998) 'Environmental refugees: Meeting the requirements of the refugee definition', *New York University Environmental Law Journal*, vol 6, pp480–488

Couldrey, M. and Herson, M. (eds) (2008) *Forced Migration Review*, University of Oxford, Issue 31, October

Cournil, C. and Mazzega, P. (2006) 'Catastrophes écologiques et flux migratoires: comment protéger les "réfugiés écologiques"?', *Revue Européenne de Droit de l'Environnement*, no 4, December, p417

Crawford, J. (2002) *The International Law Commission's Articles on State Responsibility*, Cambridge University Press, Cambridge, UK

Crawford, J. and Hyndman, P. (1989) 'Three heresies in the application of the refugee convention', *International Journal of Refugee Law*, vol 1, no 2, pp155–160

Crisp, J. (2002) *No Solution in Sight: The Problem of Protracted Refugee Situation in Africa*, Center for Comparative Immigration Studies, p1, available at www.ccis-ucsd.org/publications/wrkg68.pdf

CSDH (2008) *Closing the Gap in a Generation: Health Equity through Action on the Social Determinants of Health*, Final Report of the Commission on Social Determinants of Health, World Health Organization, Geneva, available at www.who.int/social_determinants/thecommission/finalreport/en/index.html

Dacyl, J. (1996) 'Sovereignty versus human rights: From past discourses to contemporary dilemmas', *Journal of Refugee Studies*, vol 9

Daily, G. (1997) *Nature's Services: Societal Dependence on Natural Ecosystems*, Island Press, Washington, DC

Damas, D. (1972) 'Central Eskimo systems of food sharing', *Ethnology*, vol 11, pp220–240

Damas, D. (2002) *Arctic Migrants/Arctic Villagers: The Transformation of Inuit Settlement in the Central Arctic*, McGill-Queens University Press, Montreal, Canada

D'Amato, A. (1987) 'Trashing customary international law', *American Journal of International Law*, vol 81, pp101–104

Danner, M. (2004) *Torture and Truth: America, Abu Ghraib, and the War on Terror*, New York Review Books, New York

Davidsson, E. (2005) 'Economic oppression as an international wrong or as a crime against humanity', *Netherlands Quarterly of Human Rights*, vol 23, no 2, pp173–212

Dellapenna, J. (2008) 'A human right to water: An ethical position or a realizable goal?', in L. Westra, K. Bosselmann and R. Westra (eds) *Reconciling Human Existence with Ecological Integrity*, Earthscan, London, pp183–194

Drumbl, M. A. (2005) 'Collective violence and individual punishment: The criminality of mass atrocity', *Northwestern University Law Review*, vol 99

Dudley, N., Higgins-Zogib, L. and Mansourian, S. (2005) *Beyond Belief: Linking Faiths and Protected Areas to Support Biodiversity Conservation*, a research report by World Wide Fund for Nature (WWF), Gland, Switzerland, with Alliance of Religions and Conservation (ARC), Manchester, UK, available for download from www.forestrynepal.org/publications/reports/267

Dupuy, P-M. (1989) 'The Institutionalization of International Crimes of state', in J. H. Weiler, A Cassese and, M. Spinedi (eds) *International Crimes of State*, Walter de Gruuyter, Berlin, pp170–188

Dyson, R. (2000) *Mind Abuse in an Information Age*, Black Rose Press, Montreal, Canada

Edgerton, H. W. (1927) 'Negligence, inadvertence and indifference', *Harvard Law Review*, vol 39

Eichstaedt, P. H. (1994) *If You Poison Us: Uranium and Native Americans*, Red Crane Books, Santa Fe

El Hinnawi, E. (1985) *Environmental Refugees*, United Nations Environment Programme (UNEP), Nairobi, Kenya

Elinder, L. S. (2005) 'Obesity, hunger, and agriculture: The damaging role of subsidies', *BMJ*, vol 331, pp1333–1336

Ellis, D. (1974) 'Aliens and activities of the United Nations in the field of human rights', *Human Rights Journal*, vol 7, no 291, pp314–315

Epstein, S. (1978) *The Politics of Cancer*, Sierra Club Books, San Francisco, CA

Falah, G. (1999) 'Arabs versus Jews in Galilee: Competition for regional resources', *Georgetown Journal of International Law*, vol 21, pp325–330

Falk, R. (1973) 'Environmental warfare and ecocide: Facts, appraisal and proposals', *Belgian Review of International Law*, vol 9

Falk, R. (1981) *Human Rights and State Sovereignty*, Holmes and Meier Publishers, Teaneck, NJ

Falstrom, D. (2001) 'Stemming the flow of environmental displacement: Creating a convention to protect persons and preserve the environment', *Colorado Journal of International Environmental Law and Policy*, vol 1, pp2–32

Fidler, D. P. (2004) 'Germs, governance, and global public health in the wake of SARS', *Journal of Clinical Investigation*, vol 113, p799

Fitzmaurice, G. G. (1950) 'The law and procedure of the International Court of Justice: General principles and substantive law,' *The British Yearbook of International Law*, vol 27

Ford, J. (2005) 'Living with change in the Arctic', *WorldWatch*, September/October, pp15–21

Ford, J., Smit, B. and Wandel, J. (2006) 'Vulnerability to climate change in the Arctic: A case study from Arctic Bay, Canada', *Global Environmental Change*, vol 16

Forst, R. (2001) 'Towards a critical theory of transnational justice', in T. W. Pogge (ed) *Global Justice*, Blackwell Publishers, Oxford, UK, pp169–179

Foucault, M. (1975) *Discipline and Punish: The Birth of the Prison*, Pantheon, New York (translation by Alan Sheridan from the French *Surveiller et Punir: Naissance de la Prison*, Gallimard, Paris, 1975)

Fragomen, A. T. Jr. (1970/1971) 'The refugee: A problem of definition', *Case Western Journal of International Law*, vol 3, pp45–56

Friends of the Earth (2007) *A Citizen's Guide to Climate Refugees*, Friends of the Earth, Australia, available at www.foe.org.au/resources/publications/climate-justice/CitizensGuide.pdf/view

Gagliardi, D. P. (1987/1988) 'The inadequacy of cognizable grounds of persecution as a criterion for awarding refugee status', *Stanford Journal of International Law*, vol 24, pp259–273

Garcia-Amador, F. V. et al (1974) *Recent Codification of the Law of State Responsibility for Injuries to Aliens*

Gardner, J. (2008) 'Simply in virtue of being human: The whos and whys of human rights', *Journal of Ethics and Social Philosophy*, vol 2, no 2, February

Gawtkin, D. R. and Guillot, M. (2000) *The Burden of Disease among the Global Poor: Current Situation, Future Trends, and Implications for Strategy*, pp19–20

Gaylord, C. E. and Bell, E. (2001) 'Environmental justice: A national priority', in L. Westra and B. Lawson (eds) *Faces of Environmental Racism*, Rowman Littlefield, Lanham, MD

Gehring, T. and Jachtenfuchs, M. (1993) 'Liability for transboundary environmental damage towards a general liability regime?', *European Journal of International Law*, vol 4, no 1

Gelert, G. A. et al (1989) 'The obsolescence of distinct domestic and international health sectors', *Journal of Public Health Policy*, vol 10, p421

Gewirth, A. (1982) *Starvation and Human Rights: Essays in Justification and Application*, University of Chicago Press, Chicago, IL

Ghannam, J. (2000) 'Where will they go?', *ABA Journal*, Cover Story/Human Rights Law, December, p40

Gillespie, A. (2004) 'Small island states in the face of climate change: The end of the line in international environmental responsibility', *University of California at Los Angeles, Journal of Environmental Law and Policy*, vol 22, pp107–129

Gleick, P. (1996) 'Minimum water requirements for human activities: Meeting basic needs', *Water International*, vol 21, pp83–92

Goddard, J. (1991) *Last Stand of the Lubicon Cree*, Douglas and McMillan, Vancouver, BC

Goodland, R. (2008) 'The World Bank's financing of climate change damages integrity', in L. Westra, K. Bosselmann and R. Westra (eds) *Reconciling Human Existence with Ecological Integrity*, Earthscan, London, UK, pp219–244

Goodland, R. and Counsell, S. (2008) 'How the World Bank could lead the world in alleviating climate change', in L. Westra, K. Bosselman and R. Westra (eds) *Reconciling Human Existence with Ecological Integrity*, Earthscan, London, Chapter 13.

Goodwin-Gill, G. (1983) *The Refugee in International Law*, Oxford University Press, Oxford, UK.

Goodwin-Gill, G. S. (1986) 'Non-refoulement and the new asylum seekers', *Virginia Journal of International Law*, vol 26, pp897–918

Goodwin-Gill, G. S. (1996) *The Refugee in International Law* (second edition), Clarendon Press, Oxford, UK

Goodwin-Gill, G. S. (2001) 'Asylum 2001 – a convention and a purpose', *International Journal of Refugee Law*, vol 13, p1

Goodwin-Gill, G. S. and McAdam, J. (2007) *The Refugee in International Law* (third edition), Oxford University Press, Oxford, UK

Gostin, L. O. (2004) 'Law and ethics in population health', *Australian and New Zealand Journal of Public Health*, vol 28, no 1, pp7–12

Gostin, L. O. (2008) 'Meeting basic survival needs of the world's least healthy people: Toward a framework convention on global health', *Georgetown Law Journal*, vol 96, no 2, January, pp331–392

Gouget, J-J. (2006) 'Réfugiés écologiques: Un débat controversé', *Revue Européenne de Droit de l'Environnement*, CRIDEAU, Pulim, Limoges

Grahl-Madsen, A. (1966) *The Status of Refugees in International Law: Volume 1*, A. W. Sijthoff, Leyden

Grandjean, P. and Landrigan, P. (2006) 'Developmental neurotoxicity of industrial chemicals', *The Lancet*, November

Gresser, J., Fugikura, K. and Morishima, A. (1981) *Environmental Law in Japan*, MIT Press, Cambridge, MA

Hamilton, B. F. (2006) 'Human rights, refugees and the fate of minorities', in A. Bayefsky (ed) *Human Rights and Refugees, Internally Displaced Persons and Migrant Workers*, Martinus Nihoff, The Hague, pp235–247

Handl, G. (1992) 'Human rights and protection of the environment: A mildly "revisionist" view', in C. Trindade (ed) *Human Rights, Sustainable Development and the Environment*, Inter-American Institute of Human Rights, San Jose, Brazil

Hannah, L. et al (2002) 'Conservation biology in a changing climate', *Conservation Biology*, vol 16, pp264–265

Harrington, C. (2002) 'Doe v. Unocal Corp. (2002 WL 31063976(9th Cir.2002))', *Tulane Environmental Law Journal*, vol 16, pp247–249

Hart, H. L. A. and Honoré, T. (1985) *Causation in the Law* (second edition), Clarendon Press, Oxford, UK

Hathaway, J. (1991) *The Law of Refugee Status*, Butterworth's, Toronto

Hathaway, J. (1996) 'Can international refugee law be made relevant again?' US Committee for Refugees, *World Refugee Survey*, vol 14

Hathaway, J. (2005) *The Rights of Refugees under International Law*, Cambridge University Press, Cambridge, UK

Hathaway, J. and Neve, A. (1997) 'Making refugee law relevant again: A proposal for collectivized and situation-oriented protection', *Harvard Human Rights Journal*, vol 10, no 115, spring

Heinzerling, L. (2008) 'Climate change, human health and the post-cautionary principle', *Georgetown Law Journal*, vol 96, no 2, January, pp445–460

Held, D., McGrew, A., Goldblatt, D. and Perraton, J. (1999) *Global Transformations: Politics, Economics and Culture*, Polity Press, Oxford, UK

Helton, A. C. and Jacoby, E. (2006) 'What is forced migration?', in Anne F. Bayefsky (ed.) *Human Rights and Refugees, Internally Displaced Persons*, Martinus Nijhoff Publishers, Leiden, The Netherlands, pp3–13

Higgins, R. (1994) *Problems and Process: International Law and How We Use It*, Clarendon Press, Oxford

Hill, K. (2006) 'Making deaths count', in *Bulletin of the WHO*, vol 84, p161

Hirsch, A. (1957) *International Rivers in the Middle East*, PhD thesis, Columbia University, NY

Hirsch, A. (2009) 'Israeli war crimes allegations: What the law says', *The Guardian*, 24 March, available at www.guardian.co.uk/world/2009/mar/24/israel-war-crime-allegations-law (accessed 1 April 2009)

Howse, R. (2001) 'The WHO/WTO study on trade and public health: A critical assessment,' *Journal of Risk Assessment*, vol 24, p501

Huff, A. I. (1999) 'Resource development and human rights: A look at the case of the Lubicon Cree Indian Nation of Canada', *Colorado Journal of International Environmental Law Policy*, vol 1, no 120, pp161–174

Imai, S. (2001) 'Treaty rights and Crown obligations: In search of accountability', *Queen's Law Journal*, vol 27, no 1, p49

International Law Commission (1998) *Yearbook of the International Law Commission*, volume 1, International Law Commission, New York, available for download at http://untreaty.un.org/ilc/publications/yearbooks/1998.htm

Irwin, L. G., Siddiqi, A. and Hertzman, C. (2007) *Early Child Development: A Powerful Equalizer*, Final Report for the World Health Organization's Commission on the Social Determinants of Health, Early Child Development Knowledge Network, June, available at www.who.int/social_determinants/publications/earlychilddevelopment/en/index.html

Jabaily, A. (2004) 'Water rites: A comparative study of the dispossession of American Indians and Palestinians from natural resources', *Georgetown Journal of Environmental Law*, vol 16, p225

Jennings, R. (1938) 'Some international law aspects of the refugee question', *Year Book of International Law*, vol 20

Karin-Frank, S. (2000) 'The water conflict in the Middle East: A test case for international intervention', in P. Crabbe, A. Holland, L. Ryszkowsi, and L. Westra (eds) *Implementing Ecological Integrity*, NATO Science Series, vol 1, Kluwer, Dordrecht, The Netherlands

Kattsov, V. M. and Källén, E. (2005) 'Future climate change: Modeling and scenarios for the Arctic', in ACIA (ed.) *Arctic Climate Impact Assessment: Scientific Report*, Cambridge University Press, Cambridge, UK, pp99–150, available for download at www.acia.uaf.edu/pages/scientific.html

Keinon, H. (2008) 'UNHRC rapporteur denied entry to Israel', *Jerusalem Post*, 15 December, available at www.jpost.com/servlet/Satellite?cid=1228728204503&pagename=JPost%2FJPArticle%2FShowFull (accessed 1 April 2009)

Kendall, C. (2006) 'Life at the edge of a warming world', *The Ecologist*, vol 36, no 5, July/August

Kiss, A. and Shelton, D. (1991) *International Environmental Law*, Transnational Publishers Inc., Ardsley, NY, pp24–25

Kissell, J. L. (1999) 'Causation: The challenge for complicity', paper presented at the Eastern Meeting of the American Philosophical Association

Koh, H. H. (1991) 'Transnational public law litigation', *Yale Law Journal*, vol 100

Koh, H. H. (2004) 'Agora: The United States Constitution and international law: International law as part of our law', *American Journal of International Law*, vol 98, no 1, pp43–56.

Kral, M. (2003) *Unikkaartui Meaning of Well-being, Sadness, Suicide, and Change in Two Inuit Communities*, Final Report to the National Health Research and Development Programs, Health Canada

Ku, J. (2005) 'The third wave: The Alien Tort Statute and the war on terrorism', *Emory International Law Review*, vol 19, p105

Kunitz, S. J. (2000) 'Globalization, states, and the health of indigenous peoples', *American Journal of Public Health*, vol 90, no 10, p1531

Kymlicka, W (1991) *Liberalism, Community and Culture*, Clarendon Paperbacks, Oxford, UK

Kymlicka, W. (1995) *Multicultural Citizenship*, Oxford University Press, Oxford, UK

LaFollette, H. and May, L. (1996) 'Suffer the little children', in W. Aiken and H. LaFollette (eds) *World Hunger and Morality*, Prentice Hall, Upper Saddle River, NJ, pp70–84

Lamm, R. and Imhoff, G. (1985) *The Immigration Time Bomb: The Fragmenting of America*, E. P. Dutton, New York

Lanktree, G. (2008) 'Oilsands whistleblower MD cleared', *National Review of Medicine*, vol 5, no 1, 15 January

Lantis, M. (1938) 'The Alaskan whale hunt and its affinities', *American Anthropologist*, vol 40, pp438–464

Lauterpacht, E. and Bethlehem, D. (2003) 'The scope and content of the principle of *non-refoulement*', in E. Feller, V. Türk and F. Nicholson (eds) *Refugee Protection in International Law*, Cambridge University Press, Cambridge, UK

Lauterpacht, H. (1933) *The Function of Law in the International Community*, Clarendon Press, Oxford, UK

Lauterpacht, H. (1950) *International Law and Human Rights*, Steven and Sons, London

Lavelle, M., Coyle, M. and MacLachlan, C. (1992) 'Unequal protection', *National Law Journal*, 21 September, pp1–2

Leader, S. (2004) 'Collateralism', in R. Brownsword (ed) *Global Governance and the Quest for Justice* (Volume IV), Hart Publishing, Oxford, UK

Lean, G. (2006) 'Disappearing world: Global warming claims tropical island', *The Independent*, 24 December 2006

Lee (1986) 'The right to compensation: Refugees and the countries of asylum', *American Journal of International Law*, vol 80, pp532–567

Lee, L. (1993) 'The Cairo Declaration of Principles of International Law on Compensation to Refugees', *American Journal of International Law*, vol 87, pp157–159

Leighton Schwartz, M. (1993) 'International legal protection for victims of environmental abuse', *Yale Journal of International Law*, vol 18

Lein, Y. (2000) *Thirsty for a Solution: The Water Crisis in the Occupied Territories and its Resolution in the Final-Status Agreement*, B'Tselem, Jerusalem, July

Leinwand, A. J. (2001) 'The Palestinian poverty problem in the era of globalization', *Indiana Journal of Global Legal Studies*, vol 9, pp325–330

Lemkin, R. (1944) *Axis Rule in Occupied Europe*, Carnegie Endowment for International Peace, Washington, DC

Lemkin, R. (1947) 'Genocide as a crime in international law', *American Journal of International Law*, vol 41, no 1, p145

Leopold, A. (1949) *A Sand County Almanac and Sketches Here and There*, Oxford University Press, NY

Licari, L., Nemer, L. and Tamburlini, G. (eds) (2005) *Children's Health and the Environment*, World Health Organization Regional Office for Europe, Copenhagen, Denmark

Lillich, R. and Hannum, H. (1995) *International Human Rights: Problems of Law, Policy and Practice*, Little Brown, Boston, MA

Loescher, G., Betts, A. and Milner, J. (2008) *The United Nations High Commissioner for Refugees (UNHCR): The Politics and Practice of Refugee Protection into the Twenty-First Century*, Routledge, London, p50

Lonergan, S. (1998) 'The role of environmental degradation in population displacement', Environmental Change and Security Project Report 5, Spring, available at www.wilsoncenter.org/topics/pubs/ACF26C.pdf

Lopez, A. (2007) 'The protection of environmentally-displaced persons in international law', *Environmental Law*, vol 37, Spring, pp365–380

Lowi, M. (1993) *Water and Power*, Cambridge University Press, Cambridge, UK

Luban, D. (2004) 'A theory of crimes against humanity', *Yale International Law Journal*, vol 29, pp85–90

Luban, D. (2006) 'Liberalism, torture, and the ticking bomb', in K. J. Greenberg (ed) *The Torture Debate in America*, Cambridge University Press, Cambridge, UK, pp55–68

Luban, D. (2006) 'Calling genocide by its rightful name: Lemkin's word, Darfur, and the UN report', *Chicago Journal of International Law*, vol 7

Luban, D. (2007) 'The torture lawyers of Washington', in *Legal Ethics and Human Dignity*, Cambridge University Press, Cambridge, UK

Manno, J. (2008) 'Preface', in L. Westra, K. Bosselmann and R. Westra (eds) *Reconciling Ecological Existence with Ecological Integrity*, Earthscan, London, UK, pxiii

Mappes, T. and Zembaty, J. (eds) (1991) *Biomedical Ethics*, McGraw-Hill, New York

Marrus, M. R. (2002) *The Unwanted: European Refugees from the First World War Through the Cold War* (second edition), Temple University Press, Philadelphia, PA

Martin, S., Warner, J. G. and Fagen, P. (2004) 'Palestinian refugees in Gaza', *Fordham International Law Journal*, vol 28, 1457–1458

Martone, G. (2006) 'Life with dignity: What is the minimum standard?', in A. Bayefski (ed) *Human Rights and Refugees, Internally Displaced Persons and Migrant Workers*, Martinus Nihoff Publishers, The Hague, pp129–144

May, L. (2005) *Crimes Against Humanity: A Normative Account*, Cambridge University Press, Cambridge, UK, pp80–90

McAdam, J. (2007) *Climate Change 'Refugees' and International Law*, NSW Bar Association, 24 October, 2007

McCaffrey, S. (1997) 'Middle East water problems: The Jordan River', in E. H. P. Brans, E. J. de Haa, A. Nollkaemper and J. Rinzema (eds) *The Scarcity of Water – Emerging Legal and Policy Responses*, Kluwer Law International, The Netherlands, pp158–161

McCaffrey, S. C. (2005) 'The human right to water', in E. Brown-Weiss, L. Boisson de Chazourness and N. Bernasconi-Osterwalder (eds) *Fresh Water and International Economic Law*, Oxford University Press, Oxford, pp93–116

McCarthy, J., Canziani, O. F., Leary, N. A., Dokken, D. J. and White, K. S. (2001) 'Climate change 2001: Impacts, adaptation, vulnerability', contribution of Working Group II to the *Third Assessment Report of The Intergovernmental Panel on Climate Change*, Cambridge University Press, Cambridge, UK

McCue, G. S. (1993) 'Environmental refugees: Applying international environmental law to involuntary migration', Georgetown International Environmental Law Review, vol 6

McDonnell, T. M. (moderator) (1999) 'Human rights and non-state actors', panel discussion, *Pace International Law Review*, vol 11, pp205–257.

McKenna, B. (2008) 'Basic commodities crunch – the new global menace: Food inflation', *The Globe and Mail*, Ontario edition, 29 March, ppA1, A8

McMichael, A. et al (2003) 'Climate change and human health-risks and responses', WHO/UNEP/WMO, Geneva

Meehan, P. (1997), 'Combating restrictions on immigrant access to public benefits: A human rights perspective', *Georgetown Immigration Law Journal*, vol 11, p389

Meron, T. (1989) *Human Rights and Humanitarian Norms as Customary Law*, Oxford University Press, Oxford, UK

Michelot, A. (2006) 'Enjeux de la reconnaissance du statut de réfugié écologique pour la construction d'une nouvelle responsibilite internationale', *Revue Francaise de Droit de l'Environnement*, 4 December

Millennium Ecosystem Assessment Board; *Living Beyond our Means: Natural Assets and Human Well-Being*, www.millenniumassessment.org/en/BoardStatement.aspx.

Miller, P. and Westra, L. (eds) (2002) *Just Ecological Integrity: The Ethics of Maintaining Planetary Life*, Rowman and Littlefield, Lanham, MD

Minchin, L. and Murdoch, L. (2006) 'Aboriginal cancer doubles near uranium mine', www.theage.com.au/news/national/aboriginal-cancer-doubles-near-uranium-mine/2006/11/22/116387182163.html, 23 November

Morton, A., Bancour, P. and Laczko, F. (2008) 'Human security police challenge', in Couldrey and Herson (eds) *Forced Migration Review*, University of Oxford, issue 31, October

Myers, N. (1993) 'Environmental refugees in a globally warmed world', *Bioscience*, vol 43

Myers, N. (1993) *Ultimate Security: The Environmental Basis of Political Stability*, W. W. Norton, New York

Myers, N. (1995) *Environmental Exodus: An Emergent Crisis in the Global Arena*, Climate Institute, Washington, DC

Myers, N. (2005) 'Environmental refugees: An emergent security issue', 13th Economic Forum, Prague, 23–27 May

Naff, T. and Matson, R. (eds) (1984) *Water in The Middle East: Conflict or Cooperation*, Westview Press, Boulder, CO

Nickel, J. W. (1996) 'A human rights approach to world hunger', in W. Aiken and H. LaFollette (eds) *World Hunger and Morality* (second edition), Prentice Hall, Upper Saddle River, NJ, pp171–185

Nilsen, E. S. (2007) 'Decency, dignity and desert: Restoring ideals of humane punishment to constitutional discourse,' *University of California, Davis Law Review*, vol 41, p111

Noss, R. (1992) 'The Wildlands Project: Land conservation strategy', *Wild Earth Special Issue*

Noss, R. and Cooperrider, A, (1994) *Saving Nature's Legacy*, Island Press, Washington, DC

OCHA (2007) 'The closure of the Gaza Strip: The economic and humanitarian consequences', *OCHA Special Focus*, United Nations Office for the Coordination of Humanitarian Affairs, December

O'Neill, O. (1996) *Towards Justice and Virtue*, Cambridge University Press, Cambridge, UK

O'Neill, O. (2001) 'Agents of justice', in T. Pogge (ed) *Global Justice*, Blackwell Publishers, Oxford, UK, pp188–203

Palley, C. (1978) *Constitutional Law and Minorities*, Report no 36, Minority Rights Group, London

Parry, M. L. C., Rosenzweig, A., Igelsias, M., Livermore, G. and Fischer, J. (2004) 'Effects of climate change on global food production under SRES emission and social economic scenarios', *Global Environmental Change*, vol 14, no 1, April

Passel, J. S. and Fix, M. (1994) 'US immigration in a global context: Past, present and future', *Indiana Journal of Global Legal Studies*, vol 22

Patz, J. A., Campbell-Lendrum, D., Holloway, T. and Foley, J. A. (2005) 'Impact of regional climate change on human health', *Nature*, vol 438, pp310–317

Pellet, A. (1997) 'Vive le crime! Remarques sur les degrés de l'illicite en droit international', in *International Law on the Eve of the 21st Century*, United Nations, NY

Pentassuglia, G. (2002) *Minorities in International Law*, Council of Europe Publishing, Koelblin-Fortuna, Druck, Germany

Perry, M. (2005) 'Rising seas, disappearing islands to cause environmental refugees in a warming world', Reuters (Sydney), 24 November, available at http://news.mongabay.com/2005/1124-reuters.html (accessed 27 March 2009)

Petersen, K. (2003) 'Mass murder by complicity', in *Africa Forgotten*, 11 April, www.dissidentvoice.org

Phuong, C. (2004) *The International Protection of Internally Displaced Persons*, Cambridge University Press, Cambridge, UK

Pimentel, D. (2008) 'The ecological and energy integrity of corn ethanol production', in L. Westra, K. Bosselmann and R. Westra (eds) *Reconciling Human Existence and Ecological Integrity*, Earthscan, London, UK, pp245–255

Pimentel, D., Westra, L. and Noss, R. F. (2000) *Ecological Integrity: Integrating Environment, Conservation and Health*, Island Press, Washington, DC

Pogge, T. (2001) 'Priorities of global justice', *Metaphilosophy*, vol 32

Pogge, T. (2001) 'Priorities of global justice', in T. Pogge (ed) *Global Justice*, Blackwell Publishers, Oxford, UK, pp6–23

Pogge, T. (2008) 'Aligned: Global justice and ecology', in L. Westra, K. Bosselmann and R. Westra (eds) *Reconciling Human Existence with Ecological Integrity*, Earthscan, London, pp147–158

Polya, G. (2008) 'World food price crisis – genocidal UK, EU, US biofuel perversion threatens billions', 31 March, www.countercurrent.org/polya310.htm

Purrington, R. and Wynne, M. (1998) 'Environmental racism: Is a nascent social science concept a sound basis for legal relief?', *Houston Law Journal*, vol 35, March/April

Ragazzi, M. (1997) *The Concept of Obligations* Erga Omnes, Clarendon Press, Oxford, UK, pp43–59

Ragazzi, M. (1999) 'International obligations *erga omnes*: Their moral foundations and criteria of identification in light of two Japanese contributions', in G. S. Goodwin-Gill and S. Talmon (eds) *The Reality of International Law: Essays in Honour of Ian Brownlie*, Clarendon Press, Oxford, UK, pp455–477

Ramasastry, A. (2002) 'Corporate complicity from Nuremberg to Rangoon: An examination of forced labor cases and their impact on the liability of multinational corporations', *Berkeley Journal of International Law*, vol 20, no 1, pp91–159

Ramcharan, B. G. (1985) 'The concept and dimension of the right to life', in B. G. Ramcharan (ed) *The Right to Life in International Law*, Martinus Nijhoff, The Hague

Ratner, S. R. (2007) 'Can we compare evils? The enduring debate on genocide and crimes against humanity', *Washington University Global Studies Law Review*, vol 6

Raz, J. (1984) 'On the nature of rights', *Mind*, vol 93, no 194, pp208–209

Raz, J. (1992) 'Rights and individual well-being', *Ratio Juris*, vol 5

Rees, W. E. (2006) 'Ecological footprints and bio-capacity: Essential elements in sustainability assessment', Chapter 9 in J. Dewulf and H. Van Langenhove (eds) *Renewables-Based Technology: Sustainability Assessment*, John Wiley and Sons, Chichester, UK, pp143–158

Rees, W. and Westra, L. (2006) 'Environmental justice in a resource-limited world', in J. Agyeman, R. D. Bullard and R. Evans (eds), *Just Sustainabilities*, Earthscan, London, pp99–124

Ridenour, A. (2001) 'Apples and oranges: Why courts should use international standards to determine liability for violations of the law of nations under the Alien Tort Claims Act', *Tulane Journal of International and Comparative Law*, vol 9, Spring, pp581–603

Risse, M. (2005) 'What we owe to the global poor', *Ethics*, vol 9, p81

Rodriguez-Rivera, L. (2001) 'Is the human right to environment recognized under international law? It depends on the source', *Colorado Journal of International Environmental Law and Policy*, vol 12, pp1–19

Rosencranz, A. and Campbell, R. (1999) 'Foreign environmental and human rights suits against US corporations in US courts', *Stanford Environmental Law Journal*, vol 18, no 2, June, pp145–208

Rosenfeld, M. (1999) 'What is a human right? Universalism and the challenge of cultural relativism', *Pace International Law Review*, vol 11, pp107–122

Ross, M. A. (1992) 'Environmental warfare and the Persian Gulf War: Possible remedies to combat intentional destruction of the environment', *Dickinson Journal of International Law*, vol 10, no 3, pp515–539

Roth, K. (2000) 'The charade of US ratification of international human rights treaties', *Chicago Journal of International Law*, vol 1, no 2, Fall, pp347–354

Rousseau, C., Crepeau, F., Faxen, P. and Houle, F. (2002) 'The complexity of determining refugeehood: A multidisciplinary analysis of the decision-making process of the Canadian Immigration and Refugee Board', *Journal of Refugee Studies*, vol 15, no 1, pp1–28

Ruger, J. and Hak-Ju, K. (2006) 'Global health inequalities: An international comparison', *Journal of Epidemiology Community Health*, vol 60, pp928–936

Sachs, W. (2007) *Climate Change and Human Rights*, WDEV Special Report 1, World Economy and Development In Brief, Luxembourg, posted at www.wdev.eu, 2 January; the report has been published also (2006) in 'Scripta Varia' 106 of the Pontifical Academy of Sciences, Vatican City

Salomon, M. (2007) *Global Responsibility for Human Rights*, Oxford University Press, Oxford, UK

Schabas, W. A. (2000) *Genocide in International Law: The Crime of Crimes*, Kluwer Publishing, The Hague

Schabas, W. (2006) *The UN Criminal International Tribunals*, Cambridge University Press, Cambridge, UK

Schwelb, E. (1949) 'Crimes against humanity', *British Yearbook of International Law*, vol 23, no 8, p181

Scott, C. (2002) *Torture as Tort*, Hart publishing, Oxford, UK

Scovazzi, T. (2007) *Le Patrimoine Culturel de l'Humanité*, Martinus Nijhoff, Leiden

Semple, K. (2007) 'US falters in terror case against 7 in Miami', *The New York Times*, 14 December

Shiva, V. (2002) *Water Wars: Privatization, Pollution and Profit*, Pluto Press, London

Shue, H. (1996) *Basic Rights: Subsistence, Affluence and American Foreign Policy*, Princeton University Press, Princeton, NJ

Simon, J. (1989) *The Economic Consequences of Immigration*, Blackwell, Oxford

Singer, J. (2001) 'No Palestinian return to Israel', *ABA Journal*, January, p14.

Singer, P. (1996) 'Famine, affluence and morality', in *World Hunger and Morality* (second edition), Prentice Hall, Upper Saddle River, NJ, pp26–38

Smith, T. (2008) 'Technological dynamism and the normative justification of global capitalism', in R. Albritton, R. Jessop and R. Westra (eds) *Political Economy and Global Capitalism*, Anthem Press, London, UK, pp25–42

Sogli, S. (2001) 'The elaboration of a declaration on human rights and extreme poverty', UNHCR, Geneva, 7–9 February 2001, UN Doc. HR/GVA/Poverty/SEM/2001/BP

Sohn, L. B. (1982) 'The new international law: Protection of the rights of individuals rather than states', *American University Law Review*, vol 32, no 1

Soskolne, C. (2004) 'On the even greater need for precaution under global change', *International Journal of Occupational Medicine and Environmental Health*, vol 17, no 1, pp69–76

Soskolne, C. L. (ed) (2007) *Sustaining Life on Earth*, Lexington Books, Lanham, MD

Soskolne, C. L. (2008) 'Eco-epidemiology: On the need to measure health effects from global change', in L. Westra, K. Bosselmann and R. Westra (eds) *Reconciling Ecological Existence with Ecological Integrity*, Earthscan, London, UK, pp109–123

Soskolne, C. and Bertollini, R. (1999) *Global Ecological Integrity and 'Sustainable Development': Cornerstones of Public Health*, discussion document based on an international workshop at the World Health Organization European Centre for Environment and Health, Rome Division, Rome, Italy, 3–4 December 1998, www.euro.who.int/document/gch/ecorep5.pdf

Stavropoulos, M. (1994) 'The right not to be displaced', *American University Journal of International Law and Policy*, vol 9

Steiner, H. J., and Alston, P. (2000) *International Human Rights in Context* (second edition), Oxford University Press, Oxford, UK

Stern, Sir Nicholas (2007) *The Economics of Climate Change: The Stern Review*, Cambridge University Press, Cambridge, UK

Takkenberg, L. (1998) *The Status of Palestinian Refugees in International Law*, Clarendon Press, Oxford

Taylor, A. L. (1992) 'Making the World Health Organization work: A legal framework for universal access to the conditions for health', *American Journal of Law and Medicine*, vol 18, pp301–346

Taylor, A. (2005) 'Trade, human rights and the WHO Framework Convention on Tobacco Control: Just what the doctor ordered?', in T, Cottier, J. Puwelyn and E. Burgi Bonanomi (eds) *Human Rights and International Trade*, Oxford University Press, New York, pp322–333

Taylor, A. and Leviriere, J. (2005) 'Origins of the WHO Framework Convention on Tobacco Control', *American Journal of Public Health*, vol 95, p936

Taylor, P. (1998) *An Ecological Approach to International Law: Responding to the Challenges of Climate Change*, Routledge, London, UK, p19

Teitel, R. (2002) 'Humanity's law: Rule of law for the new global politics', *Cornell International Law Journal*, vol 35, pp356–387

Terry, J. (2002) 'Taking Filartiga on the road', in C. Scott, *Torture as Tort*, Hart Publishing, Oxford, UK

Thomas, S. L. and Thomas, S. D. M. (2004) 'Displacement and health', *British Medical Bulletin*, vol 69, pp115–127

Thorson, E. J. (2008) 'On thin ice: The failure of the United States and the World Heritage Committee to take climate change mitigation pursuant to the World Heritage Convention seriously', *Environmental Law*, vol 38, pp139–162, n.133

Todd, R. (2000/2001) 'Between the land and the city: Aboriginal agency, culture and governance in urban areas', *London Journal of Canadian Studies*, vol 16, pp48–66

Tomuschat, C. and Thouvenin, J-M. (eds) (2006) *The Fundamental Rules of International Legal Order: Jus Cogens and Obligations Erga Omnes*, Martinus Nijhoff, Leiden, The Netherlands

Troyer, W. (1977) *No Safe Place*, Clark Irwin, Toronto

UNDP (1994) *Human Development Report*, United Nations Development Programme, Oxford University Press, New York

UNDP (1999) 'Facts and figures on poverty', www.undp.org/teams/english/facts.htm

UNDP (2004) *Reducing Disaster Risk: A Challenge for Development*, United Nations Development Programme, New York

UNHCR (1966) *International Legal Standards Applicable to the Protection of Internally Displaced Persons: A Reference Manual for UNHCR Staff*, United Nations High Commissioner for Refugees, Geneva
UNHCR (1979) *Handbook on Procedures and Criteria for Determining Refugee Status*, UNHCR, Geneva
UNHCR (1992) *Handbook on Procedures and Criteria for Determining Refugee Status Under the 1951 Convention and the 1967 Protocol Relating to the Status of Refugees*, document HCR/IP/4/Eng/REV.1, United Nations High Commissioner for Refugees, Geneva, re-edited January 1992, available at www.unhcr.org/publ/PUBL/3d58e13b4.pdf
UNHCR (1997) *The State of The World's Refugees 1997: A Humanitarian Agenda*, Oxford University Press, Oxford, UK, available for download from www.unhcr.org/publ/3eef1d896.html
UNHCR (2001) 'Refugee protection and migration control: Perspectives from the UNHCR and IOM', UN Doc. EC/GC/01/11, United Nations High Commissioner for Refugees, 31 May
UNHCR (2003) 'Guidelines on international protection: Internal flight or relocation alternative within the context of Articles 1A(2) of the 1951 Convention and/or 1967 Protocol relating to the status of refugees', HCR/GIP/03/04, 23 July
UNHCR (2005) *Report of Special Rapporteur Jean Ziegler on the Right to Food*, 25 January, E/CN.4/2005 47
UNHCR (2006) *The State of the World's Refugees 2006: Human Displacement in the New Millennium*, Oxford University Press, Oxford, UK
United Church of Christ Commission for Racial Justice (1987) 'Toxic wastes and race in the United States: A national study of the racial and socioeconomic characteristics of communities with hazardous waste sites', United Church of Christ, New York
USCR (2002) *World Refugee Survey 2002*, US Committee for Refugees, Washington, DC
Van Boven, T. (1982) 'Distinguishing criteria of human rights', in K. Vasak and P. Alston (eds) *The International Dimensions of Human Rights* (Volume I), Greenwood Press, Westport, CT
von Verdross, A. (1937) 'Forbidden treaties in international law', *American Journal of International Law*, vol 31, pp571–577
von Verdross, A. (1966) '*Jus dispositivum* and *jus cogens* in international law', *American Journal of International Law*, vol 60, pp55–63
Wackernagel, M. and Rees, W. E. (1996) *Our Ecological Footprint*, New Society Publishers, Gabriola Island, Canada
Wald, P. M. (2007) 'Genocide and Crimes against Humanity', *Washington University Global Studies Law Review*, vol 6, no 3, pp621–633
Warren, M. A. (1973) 'On the moral and legal status of abortion', *The Monist*, vol 57, no 1, 27 March, pp43–61
Wasserstrom, R. (1985) 'War, nuclear war and nuclear deterrence: Some conceptual and moral issues', in R. Hardin, J. Mersheimer, G. Dworkin and R. Goodin (eds) *Nuclear Deterrence, Ethics and Strategy*, University of Chicago Press, Chicago, IL, pp15-31
Weber, T. (1988) *Hugging the Trees: The Story of the Chipko Movement*, Viking, London
Weinstein, T. (2005) 'Prosecuting attacks that destroy the environment: Environmental crimes or humanitarian atrocities?', *Georgetown Immigration Law Journal*, vol 17, pp697–722
Weissbrodt, D. (2003) *The Rights of Non-Citizens: Final Report of the Special Rapporteur*, UN Doc. E/CN.4/Sub.2/2003/23, 26 May
West, L. (1987) 'Mediated settlement of environmental disputes: Grassy Narrows and White Dog revisited', *Environmental Law*, vol 18, pp131–150
Westing, A. H. (1992) 'Environmental refugees: A growing category of displaced persons', *Environmental Conservation*, vol 19, no 3, pp201–207.
Westra, L. (1994) *An Environmental Proposal for Ethics: The Principle of Integrity*, Rowman Littlefield, Lanham, MD
Westra, L. (1997) 'Terrorism at Oka', in A. Wellington, A. Greenbaum and W. Cragg (eds) *Canadian Issues in Environmental Ethics*, Broadview Press, Peterborough, Ontario, Canada

Westra, L. (1998) *Living in Integrity*, Rowman Littlefield, Lanham, MD
Westra, L. (1998) 'Development and environmental racism: The case of Ken Saro-Wiwa and the Ogoni', in L. Westra (ed) *Living in Integrity*, Rowman Littlefield, Lanham, MD, Chapter 5
Westra, L. (2001) 'The faces of environmental racism: Titusville, Alabama and BFI', in L. Westra and B. Lawson (eds) *Faces of Environmental Racism* (second edition), Rowman Littlefield, Lanham, MD, pp113–140
Westra, L. (2004) *Ecoviolence and the Law*, Transnational Publishers Inc., Ardsley, NY
Westra, L. (2004) 'Environmental rights and human rights: The final enclosure movement', in Roger Brownsword (ed) *Global Governance and the Quest for Justice, Volume 4: Human Rights*, Hart Publishing, Oxford, UK
Westra, L. (2006) *Environmental Justice and the Rights of Unborn and Future Generations*, Earthscan, London
Westra, L. (2007) *Environmental Justice and the Rights of Indigenous Peoples*, Earthscan, London
Westra, L. (2008) 'Ecological integrity: Its history, its future and the development of the ecological integrity group', in L. Westra, K. Bosselmann and R. Westra (eds) *Reconciling Ecological Existence with Ecological Integrity*, Earthscan, London, UK, pp5–20
Westra, L. and Lawson, B. (2001) *Faces of Environmental Racism* (second edition), Rowman Littlefield, Lanham, MD
Westra, L. and Lawson, B. (2001) 'Introduction', in *Faces of Environmental Racism* (second edition), Rowman Littlefield, Lanham, MD
Westra, L., Miller, P., Karr, J. R., Rees, W. and Ulanowitz, R. E. (2000) 'Ecological integrity and the aims of the Global Integrity Project', in D. Pimentel, L. Westra and R. F. Noss (eds) *Ecological Integrity: Integrating Environment, Conservation and Health*, Island Press, Washington, DC
Westra, L., Bosselmann, K. and Westra, R. (eds) (2008) *Reconciling Ecological Existence with Ecological Integrity*, Earthscan, London.
Westra, R. (2008) 'Socio-material communication in eco-sustainable societies', in L. Westra, K. Bosselmann and R. Westra (eds) *Reconciling Ecological Existence with Ecological Integrity*, Earthscan, London, UK, pp303–318
Westra, R. (2008) 'Green Marxism and institutional structure of a global socialist future', in R. Albritton, R. Jessop and R. Westra (eds) *Political Economy and Global Capitalism*, Anthem Press, London, pp219–236
WHO (1985) *Handbook of Resolutions and Decisions of the World Health Assembly and the Executive Board*, World Health Organization, Geneva
WHO (2009) 'Health situation in Gaza – 4 February 2009', available at www.who.int/hac/crises/international/wbgs/sitreps/gaza_4feb2009/en (accessed 1 April 2009).
WHO (2002) 'Summary', in *World Report on Violence and Health*, WHO, Geneva
Wigley, D. and Shrader-Frechette, K. (2001) 'Consent, equity and environmental justice: A Louisiana case study', in L. Westra and B. Lawson (eds) *Faces of Environmental Racism* (second edition), Rowman Littlefield, Lanham, MD, pp141–166
World Bank (2006) *West Bank and Gaza Update*, World Bank, September.
World Bank (2007) *Investing in Palestinian Economic Reform and Development*, 17 December, World Bank, Paris
World Bank Group (2004) *The World Bank Operational Manual, Operational Policy 4.10: Indigenous Peoples*, 1 December 2004, Washington, DC
World Food Programme (2007) *Food Security and Market Monitoring Report: Report 9*, June World Food Programme, Rome, Italy
Zartner Falstrom, D. (2000) 'Stemming the flow of environmental displacement: Creating a convention to protect persons and preserve the environment', *Colorado Journal of International Environmental Law and Policy*, vol 2

Index

aboriginal peoples
  cultural integrity 37
  health 191
  heritage 184, 185
  land relationships 38
  radiation exposure 121–122
  sacred places 92, 93
  see also indigenous peoples
accomplices 113
accountability 205
active intervention 49–50
adaptation 81
administrative aspects 62, 190–191
AF *see* after flight conditions
African Americans 19–20, 36
African Sahel region 84
after flight (AF) conditions 175, 179–180
agency 150–152
aggression 6, 29, 153, 154, 163
aid 5
air pollution 146–147, 148
Alien Torts Claims Act (ATCA)
  environment and health 150
  forced relocation 65–69
  powerlessness 182
  state responsibility 55, 56, 57, 58, 120
  torture 63
Alien Tort Stature, US 55, 56–57
American Indians 18
anthropocentric focus 79, 197
Appeal of Limoges 41–42
Arctic region 83, 118–119, 141–145
  see also circumpolar peoples
arsenic 122
assimilation 49, 179–180
Atapattu, S. 197
ATCA *see* Alien Torts Claims Act
atrocity 139, 140
Australia 50, 52, 121–122, 179

Bancoult versus McNamara 60–65
Barcelona Traction and Light case 57, 82, 85
basic rights 112, 114–115, 196–197
basic services 166
basic survival needs 188
BAU *see* business as usual practices
before flight (BF) conditions 175, 178–179
Beyani, Chaloka 94
Beyleveld, D. 151
BF *see* before flight conditions
BFI *see* Browning Ferris Industries
Biermann, F. 119
biodiversity 185, 186
biofuels 176, 178
biological genocide 33
BIOT *see* British Indian Ocean Territory
Boas, I 119
British Indian Ocean Territory (BIOT) 60, 64
Browning Ferris Industries (BFI) 19–20
Brownsword, Roger 151
Bullard, Robert 18
bullying 30–31
burial sites 37
business as usual (BAU) 60, 107, 176

camps 105–106, 140, 160, 161, 162
  see also detention
Canada
  Arctic and global warming 141–145
  detention 51–52
  family reunification 111
  human rights 68
  nationality 34–35
  oil extraction 122–125
  organization crime 61
  Rights of Indians 7
  state complicity 13–14
  visas 50
  wilful blindness 109

cancer 121–122, 122–123, 177
capitalism 6, 38, 176, 177
Caponera, Dante 157–158
Cartagena Declaration 29
causality 95, 96, 113, 114
CERD *see* Committee on the Elimination of Racial Discrimination
Chagos Archipelago 60–63
chemical exposure
    health 146, 151, 191
    indigenous peoples 119–127
    persecution 31
    precautionary principle 107
child mortality 188
children 30–31, 67, 105, 191
Christianity 92
CIL *see* customary international law
circumpolar peoples 32–33, 83, 141–145, 206
citizenship 155
civil conflict 13
Civil and Political Covenant 110, 111, 159
climate change
    adaptation 81
    crimes against humanity 175, 176
    cultural genocide 137
    health 141–148, 194
    heritage 185–186
    human rights and environment 149–150
    indigenous communities 118–119
    migration 9, 108
    precautionary principle 106–107
    racial background 33
    see also global warming
coercive immigration restrictions 86
cognizable grounds 15, 16
collateralism 38, 60
collective aspects 31–32, 140, 143, 202–204
comity 59
Committee on the Elimination of Racial Discrimination (CERD) 33, 109, 206
communal rights 31
compassionate grounds 27–28
compassion payments 121
complacency 114, 115
complicity 89–90, 94–100, 113, 114
conspiracy 113
constitutional sensitivity 70
control of water 156, 157–158
Convention Against Genocide 7, 89
    see also genocide

Convention against Torture 21, 68, 186–195, 205
convention for environmentally displaced persons 180–186, 192–195, 205–206
Convention on the Prohibition of Environmental Modification Techniques (ENMOD) 154
Convention on Public Health 187
    see also health
Convention on Refugees (CSR)
    definitions 11–12, 37
    formulation 28
    IDPs 3
    indigenous peoples 34
    institutional rights 150
    insufficiencies 100, 106, 108, 110, 180–181, 204–205
    Palestinian refugees 155
    persecution 14–20, 86, 152
    rights 8, 11, 39
    state responsibility 47
Convention on the Rights of the Child 67
Convention to Combat Desertification 206
Convention to Protect Environmentally Displaced Persons 149
Corfu Channel case 99
corporate activities
    crime 95
    persecution 29–30, 38
    responsibility 56–57, 176–180, 189
    rights 198–199, 203
    state protection 55
Crawford, James 27, 95, 96
crime 7, 95, 97–99, 109, 135, 140, 176
crimes against humanity 88, 89, 112–117, 135–139, 140, 175–176
Criminal Tribunal for Yugoslavia (CTY) 154
CSR *see* Convention on Refugees
CTY *see* Criminal Tribunal for Yugoslavia
cultural aspects
    genocide 12, 119, 137
    heritage 183–186
    integrity 33, 37, 91, 119, 143, 180
    preservation 206
    traditional knowledge 142–144
customary international law (CIL) 66

Darfur 186
death by environment 145
definitions
    crimes against humanity 135–136

INDEX   **295**

environmental disruption 3
environmentally displaced persons 186
genocide 136–137
lack of clarity 28
persecution 152–153
refugees 4–5, 11–12, 37, 108, 181
denationalization 155
depraved indifference 135–136
desertification 84, 206
detention
  genocide 89
  human rights 179, 180
  integration 82
  state protection and responsibility 47, 51–53, 66–67, 68–69, 70–71, 108
  see also camps
developed countries 189
developing countries 20, 28, 29
development 8–11, 120, 123, 178, 199, 204
dignity 105, 106, 150–152
disasters
  classification 83
  impacts 80
  migration 9, 54, 79
  persecution 28, 29
  poverty 5
discrimination 82–86, 88–90, 109, 111
diseases 35, 58, 107–108, 189–190
  see also cancer; health
disenfranchisement 21–22, 32
displacement 84, 178–179, 204
  see also internally displaced persons
documentation 50, 51
Doe versus Unocal Corporation 56–57
dolus specialis 14, 89, 136, 153
  see also intent
domestic laws 29, 67, 68–71
domination 29, 39–40
Drumbl, M. A. 139, 140
dual economies 143
due diligence 96
Dugard, John 160, 161, 163, 164

early child development (ECD) 193
Earth Charter 201
East Jerusalem 163, 164
ECD *see* early child development
ecocide 21, 137
eco-crimes 58, 61, 185, 203
ecological aspects
  footprints 85, 108, 177

  harms 106–108
  integrity 3, 90–91, 177, 185, 195–206
  oppression 112–117
  rights 198–201
economic level
  aggression 6
  crimes against humanity 175
  damages 98–99
  dual 143
  environmental human rights 200
  Gaza Strip 166
  health 190, 194
  immigration 81–82
  migration 94
  oppression 112–117, 114, 135, 153
  persecution 27, 29
eco-violence 114
Ecuador 57–60
El Hinnawi, Essam 3, 5, 180
the end of the line 5, 180
ENMOD *see* Convention on the Prohibition of Environmental Modification Techniques
environmental level
  aggression 153, 154
  degradation 9, 79, 84–85
  displaced persons convention 180–186
  disruption 3
  harms 21, 35, 57–60, 141, 187, 197–198
  health 6, 21, 107, 149–152, 196, 197–198
  human rights 192, 198–200
  indigenous relationships 7, 12, 20, 33–34, 35
  migration 79–82, 83–86
  pollution 99
  racism 18–20, 110, 178, 179, 187
  restraining deterioration 176–177
environmentally displaced persons 149, 186
equality 32, 35–36, 110–111
equitable global governance 193–194
erga omnes obligations *see* obligations
ethnic background 32–34, 82–86
ethnic cleansing 28, 159
European Convention on Human Rights 147, 148
executive detention 66
expression, freedom of 146–147
extermination 136, 137
external protection 32
extractive industries 6, 55, 57–60, 120–122, 122–124, 137, 203
  see also industrial activities

factual grounds 15–16, 17, 65
factual harm 97
Falk, Richard 149, 164
Falstrom, Dana 182, 186, 187
family reunification 111
farmed animals 35
FCGH *see* Framework Convention for Global Health
fear, well-founded
  persecution 15, 16, 17, 27–28, 33, 37
  refugee definition 4–5, 11
female genital mutilation (FGM) 202–203
FGM *see* female genital mutilation
Filartiga versus Pena Irala case 63
First Nations (FNs) 34–35, 92, 126, 144
five grounds for well-founded persecution 27–45, 79–104, 108
flight to safety 11–12
FNs *see* First Nations
food 35, 115, 176, 178
forced displacements 9, 40, 60–63, 65–69, 126, 152, 153, 154
forced stay 126
foreign domination 29
Forst, R. 39–40
forum non conveniens 58, 60
Foucault, Michel 140
Framework Convention for Global Health (FCGH) 188–193, 196
freedom of expression 146–147
free healthcare 194
free trade 54, 84, 94
fundamental marginalization 21–22
funds 206

Gagliardi, D. P. 16
garbage operations 19–20
Gardner, John 150–151
gatekeepers 48–49
Gaza Strip 160, 161–162, 165, 166
Gehring, T. 96–97
generalized oppression 15, 16
genocide
  biological 33
  crimes against humanity contrast 135–139
  cultural 12, 119, 137
  forced relocation 60–63
  intent 37, 89, 109, 116, 135, 136, 137
  persecution 14–15
  racial discrimination 88–90
  state crime 95

Gewirth, Alan 151
Ghannam, J. 159
Glamis Gold 35–36, 120
globalization 6, 10–11, 35, 54, 108, 176
global level
  food crisis 178
  governance 193–194, 195–206
  health 188–193, 196
  new politics 39–42
global warming 81, 83–84, 141–145
  see also climate change
gold mining 35–36, 120
Goodwin-Gill, Guy 12, 51–52, 204
Gostin, Lawrence 188, 191, 192, 196
governance
  global 193–194, 195–206
  self-governance 22, 34, 36, 37, 38, 144–145
government level 17, 21–22, 29–30, 178
  see also national level; state level
Grassy Narrows, Canada 125–126
grave harm 39, 96
greenhouse gases 179
Guantanamo Bay 66
Guatemala 35–36, 120
Guerra versus Italy 146–148

Hamilton, B. F. 109–110
Handbook on Procedures and Criteria for Determining Refugee Status 110
Handl, G. 200
harms 96, 100, 106–108, 124–125
  see also environmental harms
Hathaway, James 15–16, 21–22, 34, 49, 53, 111, 205
hazards 206
health
  chemical exposure 146, 151, 191
  climate change 141–148, 194
  environment 6, 21, 107, 149–152, 196, 197–198
  extractive industries 57–60
  framework global convention 188–193, 196
  Gaza Strip 166
  industrial activities 5
  market responsibility 194
  right to 105–108
  social determinants 193–195
Helton, A. C. 152–153
heritage 183–186
Higgins, N 95
Hinduism 93

Hitler 113
  see also Nazism
HIV/AIDS 114
holy sites 90–93, 94
humanitarian grounds 27–28
humanitarian law
  environmental degradation 79
  expansion of 139, 201
  IDPs 41
  insufficiencies 10, 110, 205
  Palestinian refugees 162–166
human rights
  atrocities 140
  crimes against humanity 114–115, 116
  critical assessment 7–8, 10
  development of law 82
  dignity 150–152
  environment 59, 149–150, 182–183, 187, 192, 198–200
  foundations of 86–90
  globalization 54
  health 194, 197
  integrity 201–202
  Palestinian refugees 160–161, 162–166
  precautionary principle 106–108
  state protection 56
  universal 40, 202–204
  US 67
  victimizing the victims 179–180
  see also rights; Universal Declaration of Human Rights
hunting 7, 92, 118–119, 124, 142–143
Hurricane Katrina 36, 81
Hyndman, Patricia 27

ICCPR *see* International Covenant on Civil and Political Rights
ICESCR *see* International Covenant of Economic, Social and Cultural Rights
ICTR *see* International Criminal Tribunal for Rwanda
ICTY *see* International Criminal Tribunal for the former Yugoslavia
IDPs *see* internally displaced persons
ILC *see* International Law Commission
immediate killing 137
immigration 80, 81–82, 86
indefinite detention 70–71
indifference 135–136
indigenous peoples
  assimilation 49

  ecological refugees contrast 117–127
  environmental refugees 13, 14, 20–22
  health 190
  heritage 184–185
  IDPs 106, 118
  land relationships 7, 12, 20, 33–34, 35
  law interface 6–7
  living conditions 56–57
  oil explorations 57–60
  persecution 38
  racial backgrounds 32, 33–34
  religious beliefs 90–93
  vulnerability 28
  see also aboriginal peoples
individualization 27
individual rights 31–32, 201, 202–204
industrial activities 5, 31, 107, 119–127, 145–148
  see also extractive industries
INGOs *see* international non-governmental organizations
institutional aspects 40, 114, 115, 120–121, 140, 150
integration 82
integrity
  cultural 33, 37, 91, 119, 143, 180
  ecological 3, 90–91, 177, 185, 195–206
  physical 147
  principle of 197
  territorial 185
intent
  crimes against humanity 138
  genocide 37, 89, 109, 116, 135, 136, 137
  persecution 14–20, 181
  state responsibility 95–96
interception 49–51, 179
interdiction 50
internally displaced persons (IDPs)
  emerging crisis 197
  guiding principles 8–11
  humanitarianism 41
  indigenous peoples 106, 118
  lack of CSR recognition 3, 100
  legal status 12–14
  Palestinian refugees 159, 161–162
  persecution 28
  racial background 32–34
  refugee exclusion 181
  regional and international law 198–201
  rights 7–8, 108
  state protection 30, 31

International Covenant on Civil and Political
    Rights (ICCPR) 31, 85, 109, 116
International Covenant of Economic, Social
    and Cultural Rights (ICESCR) 116, 158,
    192
international crimes 7, 97, 98, 135, 140
International Criminal Tribunal for the
    former Yugoslavia (ICTY) 89, 136, 138,
    204
International Criminal Tribunal for Rwanda
    (ICTR) 136, 139, 154
international law
    beyond CSR 135–174
    domestic law 68–71
    human rights 87–88
    instruments 182–183, 198–201
    non-discrimination 110–111
    omissions in 108–109
    US 67
International Law Commission (ILC) 94–95,
    96, 97–98, 99
international level
    assistance 27–45
    development and migration 8–11
    heritage 184
    obligations 183, 185
    responsibility 176–180
    state protection 54, 55
international non-governmental organizations
    (INGOs) 203
International Organization for Migration
    (IOM) 8–9
Inuit peoples 32–33, 83–84, 92, 141–145
IOM *see* International Organization for
    Migration
Iraq 154
Islam 92
Israel 155–166
Italy 146–148

Jacoby, E. 152–153
Jainism 92
Jota versus Texaco 57–60
judicial expertise 62
jus cogens norms
    corporate responsibility 57
    environmentally displaced persons 183,
        187–188
    human rights 86, 87, 88, 112
    state responsibility 97, 99–100
    torture 63

killing, intentional 137
Kiss, A. 200
Kissell, Judith Lee 113
knowledge 6, 116, 117, 142–144, 189, 200
Kupreskic et al 88–90

large-scale migration 4, 48–49, 49–50, 79,
    83–86, 89–90
    see also mass migration
Lauterpacht, H. 203
law of nature 203
law of treaties 87, 97, 183
law of war 41, 139, 201, 205
leather industries 148
Lemkin, Raphael 7, 109, 119
Leopold, Aldo 90
liberal rights 201–202
life expectancy 188
life, right to 116, 145–148, 150, 151
living conditions 53, 56–57, 112, 127, 199
living in integrity 177–178
local communities 56–57, 90–93
loopholes 68–69
Lopez, Aurelie 19
Lopez-Ostra versus Spain 148
Lorca, Spain 148
Luban, David 136
Lubicon Cree Nation 123–125

McCaffrey, C. 158
Manfredonia, Italy 146–148
mass migration 20, 53, 108, 139
Mayan communities 35–36
means of subsistence 85
mens rea 14, 15, 16, 88–89
mental states 14, 20, 37, 61
mercury pollution 125–126
Middle East 155–166
migration
    before flight conditions 175, 178–179
    crimes against humanity 115–116
    development 8–11
    economic activities 94
    emerging crisis 197
    environment 79–82, 83–86
    estimations of 4
    health 189
    large-scale 4, 48–50, 79, 83–86, 89–90
    mass 20, 53, 108, 139
    state responsibility 99–100
    urban 5

military bases 60–63
minority group protection 109
mixed economies 143
Montana Exploradora 120
moral obligations 112
Myers, Norman 4, 149
Myanmar 56–57

nationalist jurisprudence 69
nationality 34–36
national level 9–10, 109, 190, 198–199
  see also government level; state level
Native Americans 120–121
natural disasters 28, 29, 54, 80
  see also disasters
natural heritage 183–186
natural law/ rights 88, 203
natural services 91
Navajo peoples 120–121
Nazism 5, 16, 28, 32, 137
negligence 84–85
New Orleans 81
non-discrimination 110–111
non-indigenous people 20–22
non-intervention 9–10
non-refoulement 48–53, 158–161, 180, 187
normal function, right to 105–108
norms 71, 87, 97
  see also jus cogens norms
nuclear tests 59
Nunavut 141–145
Nuremburg 116–117

obligations
  health 196, 198
  human rights 40, 88, 116, 185
  international 183, 185
  moral 112
  respect for human dignity 105, 106
  serious breaches of 98
  state 100, 108, 186
  see also responsibility
Occupied Palestinian Territories 155–166
O'Connor, Dr John 122–123, 124
oil extraction 57–60, 122–125, 137
Ojibway communities 125–126
omission 61, 94, 113, 115, 116
omnicide 137
oppression 15, 16, 112–117, 135, 153
organization crime 61–62
Ottoman Civil Code 157

Pace International Law Review 202, 204
Palestinian refugees 155–166
particularism 202
Pellet, Alain 99
perceptions
  genocide 136
  migrants as threats 47, 54, 55, 79, 84
  minority groups 81–82
perpetrators 113, 115
persecution
  crimes against humanity 138
  disenfranchisement 21–22
  five grounds of 27–45, 79–104, 108
  government protection 178
  intent 14–20, 181
  lack of universal definition 152–153
  state complicity 13–14
  women 202
personhood 6, 150
PGC *see* Principle of Generic Consistency
physical integrity 147
place-based aspects 36–37
plain moral rights 150
policy 193–194, 195
political economy of punishment 140
political issues 1–76
pollution 18, 99, 125–126, 146–147, 148, 157
post-cautionary principle 107
poverty
  crimes against humanity 112, 114, 115
  disasters 5
  environmental exposures 35
  Gaza Strip 166
  health 188–189
  pollution 18
  vulnerability 20, 105, 177, 178
power 39–40
powerlessness 181–182
pre-birth development 151
precautionary principle 106–108
pre-flight conditions *see* before flight
    conditions
Prieur, Michel 206
Principle of Generic Consistency (PGC) 151
proactive intervention 9
processed foods 35
protected areas 90, 91, 92–93
protection
  comprehensive approaches to 175–214
  ecological refugees 110–112
  lack of 29–32

rights 7–8, 147, 148
  state 30, 47–76, 94–100, 105–108
public level
  health 141–148, 187
  perceptions 47, 54, 55, 81–82, 84, 136
pulp and paper mills 125–127
punishment, political economy of 140

racial aspects 32–34, 82–86, 88–90, 109
racism, environmental 18–20, 110, 178, 179, 187
radiation 59, 120–122
Ramallah 163
Ramcharan, B. G. 145
Rao, Srenivasa 96
Rasul versus Bush 66–67
Ratner, R. 136–137
recklessness 115, 116, 135, 178
refugee camps 140, 160, 161, 162
  see also detention
refugee definitions 4–5, 11–12
regional law 198–201
regulations 41, 157, 177, 190, 192, 198–201
relativism 202–204
religious beliefs 36–38, 90–93, 119, 202, 203
rendition 69
responsibility
  corporate activities 56–57, 176–180, 189
  environmental degradation 182, 187
  freedoms 146–147
  health 194
  state 13, 14, 47–76, 94–100, 108, 120, 187
  see also obligations
restitution 185
Ridenour, Andrew 56–57
rights
  to chosen home 94
  collective 31–32
  crimes against humanity 114–115
  denial of 51–53
  environmental–human interface 182–183
  to food 115
  to health 105–108, 145–148, 190, 191, 197
  indefinite detention 70
  individual 31–32, 201, 202–204
  liberal 201–202
  to life 116, 145–148, 150, 151
  protection of 7–8
  regional and international law 198–201
  to return 65, 158–161, 180, 187
  territorial 123–124
  to be heard 49
  traditional 145
  to water 156, 158, 186
  see also human rights
Rome Statute of the International Court 138, 154
Rosenfeld, Michael 201–202, 203
rule of law 39–42, 139–140
Rwanda 54, 136, 139, 154
Rwandan refugees 54

Sachs, Wolfgang 114, 135
sacred places 6, 36–37, 90–93, 94
Sahin versus Canada 51–52
Schabas, William 136
scientific knowledge 200
Scovazzi, Tullio 184–185
sea level rise 84, 145
self-governance 22, 34, 36, 37, 38, 144–145
Serbia 90
severe harm 96
Shelton, Dinah 200
Singer, Joel 159
slavery 56
social aspects 36–38, 124–125, 143, 193–195
sovereignty 9–10, 51, 139
Spain 148
stakeholder engagement 196
standards of care 61
statehood 155–156
state protection/responsibility
  before and after the fact 176–180
  chemical exposure 120
  complicity 94–100
  ecological refugees 47–76
  environmentally displaced persons convention 181, 186, 187
  health and normal function rights 105–108
  IDPs 9–10, 13–14
  persecution 17, 29–31
  see also government level; national level
substantive claims 58
Summers, Lawrence 18

Talmudic Law 157
Tampa case 50, 54, 179
tar sands operations 122–123
Taylor, Prudence 191, 197
temperature 118
territorial level
  dependency 83–84

indigenous communities 36, 118
integrity 185
rights 123–124
rule of law 139
states 9–10
terrorism 69, 139–140
Texaco 57–60
Titusville, Alabama 19–20
tobacco 191
torture 63, 68–69, 186–195
toxic pollution 18
trade 35, 54, 84, 94, 192, 193
traditional aspects 6, 118–119, 123–124, 142–144, 145, 202–203
transnational jurisprudence 69
treaties
  health 192
  insufficiency of 82, 87
  law of 87, 97, 183
  territorial rights 123, 124
  torture 63
  US 67
  water 157–158

UN *see* United Nations
under-inclusions 152–154
UNESCO *see* United Nations Educational, Scientific and Cultural Organization
UNFCCC *see* United Nations Framework Convention on Climate Change
UNHCR *see* United Nations High Commissioner for Refugees
United Kingdom 60, 64–65
United Nations Educational, Scientific and Cultural Organization (UNESCO) 186
United Nations Framework Convention on Climate Change (UNFCCC) 119
United Nations High Commissioner for Refugees (UNHCR)
  assistance 86
  definitions 181
  detention 47, 51
  indigenous peoples 34
  insufficiencies 205
  refugee protection 110
  state responsibility 13
United Nations (UN) 82, 86, 108, 199–200
United States of America (US)
  environmental racism 18, 19–20
  human rights 54, 55, 56–57, 60–65, 66–67, 141

immigration 80
indefinite detention 70–71
interception 50
racial discrimination 32–33
state protection 59
torture 68–69
uranium mining 120–121
Universal Declaration of Human Rights
  dignity 105
  foundations of 86
  health 192
  internal displacement 10
  law of war 41
  obligations 40
  refugee protection 182–183
  right to chosen home 94
  see also human rights
universalism 202–204
Unocal Corporation 56–57
uranium mining 120–121
urban migration 5
US *see* United States of America
us–them dichotomy 54, 83

victimization 30–31, 179–180
Vienna Convention on the Law of Treaties 87, 97, 183
Vietnam War 154
violence 105–106, 120–121, 140
visa requirements 50
vulnerability
  Arctic region 141–145
  children 105
  developing countries 28
  environmental refugees 20–21
  health 188, 189
  persecution 79–104
  poverty 177, 178
  protection 31

WAEP *see* World Agency for Environmentally Displaced Persons
Wald, Patricia 138
Wall, Israeli built 162–163, 164
war 41, 60–63, 139, 153, 154, 166, 201, 205
Wasserstrom, Richard 113–114
wastewater 148
water 155–166, 176, 186
weather predictions 142–143
Weeramantry, Judge Christian 183, 200
Weinstein, T. 153, 154

well-founded fear *see* fear
well-founded persecution 27–45, 79–104, 108
West Bank 162, 163
WFED *see* World Fund for the Environmentally Displaced
WHA *see* World Health Administration
White Dog Reserves, Canada 125–126
WHO *see* World Health Organization
wilful blindness 13, 14, 38, 84–85, 109, 178
women 202
World Agency for Environmentally Displaced Persons (WAEP) 206
World Bank 18, 55, 204

World Charter for Nature 199
World Fund for the Environmentally Displaced (WFED) 206
World Health Administration (WHA) 190–191
World Health Organization (WHO) 21, 188, 189–190, 191, 193–195, 196
World Heritage Convention 183–186

former Yugoslavia 89, 113, 136, 138, 154, 204

Zadvydas versus Davis 70–71
Zaire 54